MODERN
BATCH
COOKERY

MBc

MODERN
BATCH
COOKERY

VICTOR GIELISSE CMC *and* RON DeSANTIS CMC
THE CULINARY INSTITUTE OF AMERICA

WILEY

John Wiley & Sons, Inc.

Published by John Wiley & Sons, Inc., Hoboken, New Jersey

Published simultaneously in Canada

The Culinary Institute of America

President	Dr. Tim Ryan '77
Vice President, Continuing Education	Mark Erickson '77
Senior Director, Continuing Education	Susan Cussen
Director of Publishing	Nathalie Fischer
Editorial Project Manager	Mary Donovan '83
Editorial Assistants	Shelly Malgee '08
	Erin Jeanne McDowell '08

Design by Vertigo Design NYC

Library of Congress Cataloging-in-Publication Data:
Gielisse, Victor.
  Modern batch cookery / Victor Gielisse and Ron De Santis.
    p. cm.
  Includes index.
  ISBN 978-0-470-29048-4 (cloth)
  1. Quantity cookery. I. De Santis, Ron. II. Title.
  TX820.G515 2011
  641.5'7--dc22
                          2009035902

Printed in China

10 9 8 7 6 5 4 3 2 1

ACKNOWLEDGMENTS

THE WRITING OF ANY BOOK IS A NEVER-ENDING WORK IN PROGRESS AND REQUIRES CONSTANT REFINEMENT AND REVIEW, PARTICULARLY IN THE EVER-CHANGING WORLD OF FOOD AND FLAVOR.

Our journey began as a simple idea that surfaced during one of the many culinary projects involving our work with organizations established as a quantity food production setting. We nurtured the premise of writing a culinary text that could speak to the need for an additional resource for many of these quality high-volume food-service operators in our industry. During the process we approached many culinary experts and our colleagues in the field for their insight and perspective. These colleagues are known for their wealth of experience and knowledge and are respected practitioners of the culinary craft. Their expertise as either a chef or industry professional benefited our opus.

While certain individuals always stand out, we feel that it was truly a collective effort among all of those who contributed. The thing that impressed us the most was the level of enthusiasm and drive for getting the job done right. It truly was an inspiration. To all those of you who assisted us in meaningful ways, we offer our appreciation and most sincere thanks. We also want to express our gratitude to The Culinary Institute of America's leadership, Dr. Tim Ryan, President, and Mark Erickson, Vice President, for their strong support of our project.

Our photographer, Ron Manville, made the creation of the extension art program throughout the book a pleasure to create as well as a pleasure to see on the pages of the book.

Also, a sincere thank you to Ms. Pam Chirls and the entire team at our publishing partner, John Wiley & Sons, Inc., for believing in the purpose of this book and supporting the entire process.

Last but not least, we thank our families for supporting us in all that we do on a day-to-day basis.

INDUSTRY INSIGHTS, CULINARY PERSPECTIVES, AND CONTRIBUTORS

Chef Chris Northmore, CMCP

Chef John Maltby, CEC

Chef John Benson, CEC

Chef Rudy Speckamp, CMC

Chef Greg Fatigati, CEC

Contents

LIST OF RECIPES

Introduction to Modern Batch Cookery

THIS BOOK COMES AT A PIVOTAL TIME FOR AMERICAN FOOD SERVICE. A GROWING PERCENTAGE OF CULINARY SCHOOL GRADUATES ARE TAKING UP A CAREER IN VOLUME COOKING, WHETHER IN HOTELS, LARGE RESTAURANTS, OR ANY OF A VARIETY OF GROUP DINING SITUATIONS. WE ARE ALL TOUCHED BY THIS SEGMENT OF THE INDUSTRY AS CONSUMERS, WHETHER AT HOTELS AND CATERING FACILITIES OR IN CAFETERIAS, HOSPITALS, OR SCHOOLS.

Chefs and operators have never had a wider array of options to meet their guests' expectations in a volume setting. American menus are being fundamentally reshaped by an accelerating interest in world culinary traditions, as Americans are increasingly drawn to bolder, more assertive flavors from a broad range of cultures including Latin America, Asia, and the Mediterranean. At the same time, chefs are discovering that these vibrant ethnic foods and flavors also meet their guests' demands for healthier, more nutritious options. Controlling calories by controlling portion sizes, controlling sodium by increasing other flavoring options, and controlling fat by emphasizing vegetables and whole grains are just some of the strategies today's chefs employ to create vital, appealing menus.

New equipment and technology are enabling volume kitchens to prepare and serve foods that have the same great taste and look as foods produced in an à la carte kitchen. New products and prepared foods, meanwhile, offer solutions to some of the perennial problems in volume food service.

As the members of the Baby Boom generation come into retirement, they are swelling the ranks of assisted living operations. Unlike their parents, this generation isn't going to be content with "plain" food like meatloaf and mashed potatoes. Boomers take their flavors seriously—hot and spicy and exotic. For this generation, great food means great flavors. Chefs are heeding the call and expanding their menus to introduce ingredients, flavors, and techniques from around the globe.

But it is not just people over the age of fifty who are pressing for better service, greater value, and more options from the food-service industry. Consumers, no matter what their age, are demanding flavorful foods, and are increasingly comfortable with ordering ethnic and regional specialties or patronizing restaurants that specialize in a specific cuisine. Indian, Thai, Korean, and Spanish cuisines, for example, may be widely appreciated and understood by today's customers.

Convenience has also been an important factor driving changes in the food-service industry, as restaurants respond to a new demand for quick, easy meal solutions. When people are pressed for time, they may look to restaurants for a solution. Even so-called white-tablecloth restaurants are turning to take-out foods as a way to expand their operations while at the same time offering their guests a service that has value.

Customers today take their health and wellness seriously, too. Some because they have long embraced an active, fit lifestyle including exercise, organic foods, and healthier choices; others because they expect that the foods they eat will help them prevent or cope with a variety of health issues, from diabetes to heart disease and cancer. The nation faces an epidemic of obesity and a number of attendant health complications. Increasing numbers of Americans are being diagnosed with conditions like celiac disease (gluten intolerance) or are afflicted with severe allergies. Chefs must be able to offer appropriate menu choices for all of their guests, which makes it imperative that they understand the ingredients they choose and the techniques they employ in the kitchen.

For their part, chefs and operators of chain restaurants, hotels, supermarkets, and volume food-service operations often feel discouraged about trying to address what they perceive as customers' mixed messages about healthy meal choices, and what they sense is still "shifting ground" under ongoing nutrition research outcomes. And few in the food-service industry have the appetite to repeat failed healthy menu initiatives from the '80s and '90s, when identifying a dish as nutritious or including nutrition information often had the reverse of the desired effect. Rather than choosing the whole-grain, meatless option, consumers typically shunned dishes marked as "healthy."

Today, there is a profoundly different reality facing you as a chef. Consumers are looking for more information and do not need to be convinced of the importance of nutrition and healthy food choices. The challenge has become offering the right information about foods. Your clientele may be interested in knowing the counts for calories, fats, sodium, or refined sugars in a specific menu item. They may need to know about the presence of allergens like peanuts and eggs. They may respond to the fact that your foods are grown locally or organically. The origin of your foods may matter just as much as the way the foods taste after you prepare them, for a whole host of reasons. Some products (like Parmigiano-Reggiano or prosciutto di Parma) are associated with particular areas as a guarantee of quality. As the chef, it is your responsibility to know as much as you can about the foods you cook, the way you prepare them, the benefits they offer your guests, and the improvements they offer to your operation's bottom line.

More chefs are making their careers in the volume food-service sector than ever before. This book is meant as a handbook for those who want to offer their guests something fresh and new, all the while keeping the twin goals of nutrition and flavor in mind.

The first chapter in *Modern Batch Cookery* provides an overview of the volume food service industry. The next chapter is devoted to menu and recipe development. In it, we explore how menus and recipes are used and how to get the most out of them in the kitchen. We have developed a set of menu guidelines to encourage everyone to choose and prepare foods that are better for our guests, better for the environment, and better for the bottom line.

Chapter 3 is all about flavor. Each culinary region has its own flavor profile and in this chapter we examine some of those profiles. Flavor dynamics, or the way combining flavors can create a unique flavor impression, is another tool for the chef. Chapter 4 covers important techniques for the volume kitchen including HACCP, safe food handling, and basic cooking methods. The recipes in this book are built from this foundation of good technique, great ingredients, and undeniable flavors.

chapter one

THE CULINARY PROFESSIONAL

The culinary profession encompasses
artistic endeavors, managerial and
administrative work, practical skills, and
leadership. The goal of any professional,
no matter what the profession, is to
uphold the standards of excellence,
to provide the best possible service
to the public, and to foster a sense
of camaraderie and inclusion for
all members of the profession.

A CONSTANT FOCUS ON HIGH CULINARY STANDARDS AND EXECUTION OF THOSE STANDARDS IS THE HALLMARK OF A CULINARY PROFESSIONAL. AS YOU WILL SEE, THERE ARE OTHER ATTRIBUTES SUCH AS COMMITMENT, RESPONSIBILITY, AND JUDGMENT THAT ARE CHARACTERISTIC OF ALL PROFESSIONALS, BUT FOR THE CULINARY PROFESSIONAL IT ALL BEGINS WITH THE CULINARY CRAFT.

THE CULINARY PROFESSIONAL

The cardinal virtues of the culinary professional are an open and inquiring mind, an appreciation of and dedication to quality wherever it is found, and a sense of responsibility. Success also depends on several character traits; although some of these may be inherent in certain individuals, usually these traits must be diligently cultivated throughout a career. These traits include

Commitment to the profession. No matter what his or her current job description, a true professional is driven to provide the best possible experience to the guest. The degree to which a food-service professional can offer a high-quality product, as well as complete customer satisfaction, is the degree to which he or she will succeed in providing excellent service.

A sense of fairness and responsibility. Chefs have a specific responsibility to provide the customer with well-prepared and wholesome food, excellent service, and a fair value. This includes the knowledge of where foods have come from, an awareness of and willingness to accommodate special needs, the ability to work with producers and purveyors to maintain quality at all levels, and the drive to develop a strong team approach to the operation.

Sound judgment. Good judgment is a prerequisite for becoming and remaining a professional. The ability to judge what is right and appropriate in each work situation is developed throughout a lifetime of experience. Taking others' needs into consideration is more than just polite—it also creates a working atmosphere in which a problem can be understood and resolved fairly.

THE CHEF AS A BUSINESSPERSON

Leadership, perhaps the single most important trait that a chef can develop, is an elusive concept. A leader's role is to inspire employees so that they want to come to work. A leader creates an environment where everyone feels a part of the team. The effort of each team member contributes to the success of the organization.

For some, leadership comes naturally. That doesn't mean that others can't become leaders. A leader is confident in his or her role and has developed a personal philosophy that guides him or her through daily challenges. A leader with a strong philosophy and the ability to articulate that philosophy possesses the foundation necessary to create an organizational vision.

A leader's vision for the business will help all team members understand where they are going. It may not describe how to get there, but it certainly will point everyone in the right direction. The chef starts with a clear vision for the culinary team and follows up with strong leadership to achieve the vision and goals.

Once an overall goal or plan has been laid down, the next tasks are to implement and track that plan. These tasks are primarily administrative in nature. Some administrative duties may not sound at all glamorous—preparing schedules, tracking deliveries, computing costs, and so forth. The best administrators are those who can create a feeling throughout the entire staff that each person has a stake in getting things done correctly. When you give people the opportunity to help make decisions and provide them with the tools they need to perform optimally, it is easier to achieve the goals you have established on an executive level.

Learn to use the important tools of an administrator; budgets, accounting systems, and inventory control systems all play a role. Many organizations, from the largest chains to the smallest one-person catering company, rely upon software systems that allow them to efficiently administer a number of areas: inventory, purchases, losses, sales, profits, food costs, customer complaints, reservations, payroll, schedules, and budgets. If you are not using a system capable of tracking all this information and more, you cannot be as effective as you need to be.

Managing Physical Assets

Physical assets are the equipment and supplies needed to do business. In the case of a restaurant, these might include food and beverage inventory, tables, chairs, linens, china, flatware, glassware, computers and point-of-sale systems, cash registers, kitchen equipment, cleaning supplies, and ware-washing machines. When we talk about managing physical assets, we are considering how anything that you must purchase or pay for affects your ability to do business well.

Managing Time

It may seem that no matter how hard you work or how much planning you do, the days aren't long enough. Learning time-management skills and regularly evaluating your operation to make the best possible use of time are essential to your career development. Some of the most common causes of wasted time are a lack of clear priorities, a lack of essential tools, poor staff training, poor communication, and poor organization.

Reviewing daily operations regularly can help you resolve these problems. Consider the way you, your coworkers, and your staff spend the day. Does everyone have a basic understanding of which tasks are most important? Do they know when to begin a particular task in order to complete it on time?

Managing People (or Managing Communications)

By training your staff properly, you will create an organization that is a model of efficiency. Give your staff members the yardsticks they need to evaluate each job and determine whether they have done exactly what was requested in the appropriate fashion and amount of time.

Whether you are training a new employee, introducing a new menu item, or ordering a piece of equipment, clear communication is also important in maintaining efficiency. Be specific and use the most concise language you can without leaving out any necessary information; this can help ensure that all staff members understand what is being communicated. If tasks are handled by a number of people, be sure to write each task out, from the first step to the last. Encourage people to ask questions if they don't understand you.

CAREER OPPORTUNITIES FOR CULINARY PROFESSIONALS

Culinary professionals are needed not just in hotel dining facilities and traditional restaurants but in a variety of other settings as well—public and private, consumer-oriented, and institutional. An increased emphasis on nutrition, sophistication, and financial and quality control means that all settings, from the white-tablecloth restaurant to the fast-food outlet, offer interesting challenges. An increasing number of culinary professionals find meaningful work in the catering sector. The advantages are significant and the opportunities are more exciting than ever before.

On-site and off-premise catering (used in institutions such as schools, hospitals, colleges, airlines, and business and industry) used to have a specific and not very flattering profile. Meals were prepared in bulk, portioned onto trays, and delivered to the guests. Today, as clients become increasingly sophisticated in their food choices, this scenario is being replaced by an approach more similar to that found in à la carte restaurants. While the menu selections are based on the needs of the guests, there is a growing acceptance of foods that are ethnic or regional in nature. Health concerns are another factor.

Caterers provide a particular service, often tailored to a special client for a particular event, whether it be a wedding, a cocktail reception, or a gallery opening. Caterers may provide on-site services (the client comes to the caterer's premises), off-site services (the caterer comes to the client's premises), or both. (For more about special events, see Chapter 2.)

THE KITCHEN BRIGADE SYSTEM

The brigade system was instituted by Georges-Auguste Escoffier to streamline work in hotel kitchens and eliminate the chaos that could result when workers did not have clear-cut responsibilities. Each position's responsibilities are clearly defined under this system. In smaller operations or in situations where skilled personnel are not readily available, the classic system may be condensed so as to make the best use of workspace and talents. The introduction of new equipment for the professional kitchen has helped to alleviate some of the problems associated with smaller staffs.

In any professional kitchen, the chef is responsible for all kitchen operations, including ordering, supervision of all stations, and development of menu items. He or she may also be known as the chef de cuisine or executive chef. The sous chef is second in command, answers to the chef, and fills in for the chef when needed. He or she may be responsible for scheduling, and assists the station chefs (or line cooks) as necessary. Small operations may not have a sous chef. The positions in a classic brigade also include the following:

The sauté chef (saucier) is responsible for all sautéed items and their sauces. This position is often considered the most demanding, responsible, and glamorous on the line.

The fish chef (poissonier) is responsible for fish items, often including fish butchering, and their sauces. This position is sometimes combined with the saucier position.

The roast chef (rôtisseur) is responsible for all roasted foods and related jus or other sauces.

The grill chef (grillardin) is responsible for all grilled foods. This position may be combined with the rôtisseur position.

The fry chef (friturier) is responsible for all fried foods. This position may be combined with the rôtisseur position.

The vegetable chef (entremetier) is responsible for hot appetizers and frequently has responsibility for soups, vegetables, and pastas and other starches. (In a full, traditional brigade system, soups are prepared by the soup chef or potager, vegetables by the legumier.) The person in this position may also be responsible for egg dishes.

The roundsman (tournant), or swing cook, works as needed throughout the kitchen.

The cold-foods chef (garde manger), also known as the pantry chef, is responsible for the preparation of cold foods, including salads, cold appetizers, pâtés, and the like. This is considered a separate category of kitchen work.

The butcher (boucher) is responsible for butchering meats, poultry, and, occasionally, fish. The butcher may also be responsible for breading meat and fish items.

The pastry chef (pâtissier) is responsible for baked items, pastries, and desserts. The pastry chef frequently supervises a separate kitchen area or a separate shop in larger operations. This position may be further broken down into the following areas of specialization: confiseur (candies and petits fours), boulanger (unsweetened doughs, as for breads and rolls), glacier (frozen and cold desserts), and décorateur (showpieces and special cakes).

The expediter or announcer (aboyeur) accepts orders from the dining room and relays them to the various station chefs. This individual is the last person to see the plate before it leaves the kitchen. In some operations, this may be either the chef or sous chef.

The communard prepares the meal served to the staff (sometimes called the family meal) at some point during the shift.

The apprentice (commis) works under a station chef to learn about the operations and responsibilities of the station.

chapter two

MENUS, RECIPES, AND SPECIAL EVENTS

Menus are used in the dining room to give both waitstaff and guests important information about what the establishment offers. Recipes give detailed instructions to aid kitchen staff in producing menu items. But, more than that, carefully designed menus and comprehensive recipes can help the professional chef streamline kitchen operations and control costs.

MENUS

Menus tell guests what items are available and how much they cost. Even if a written menu is not provided to the guest, some form of recorded list is essential to the smooth operation of a professional kitchen.

Menus give the kitchen staff additional vital information, such as whose responsibility it is to prepare the dish's components or to plate and garnish it. Certain items are typically assigned to a specific station. As the menu changes—daily, weekly, seasonally, or on a specific cycle—the tasks for that station also change. The preparation of certain garnishes, side dishes, sauces, or marinades may be organized so that the work is done by each individual chef or cook, or it may be the specific duty of a single prep cook. A la carte menus call for certain types of advance work and mise en place to help the chef adjust to the unpredictable work flow. Banquet menus and those presented cafeteria- or family-style call for different advance-work strategies. Consult the menu, determine which items you or your staff are responsible for, and then read the recipes for those items carefully so that you understand all the tasks that must be performed in advance of service as well as at the time of plating and serving the food.

People are becoming increasingly sophisticated about food. Americans eat away from home at an ever-increasing rate, but there is also stiff competition for the restaurant dollar. It is therefore essential that the restaurant has an appealing menu. One of the great challenges in developing a menu is putting together a list of offerings that will not only please first-time guests, but also encourage them to return over and over again to try new dishes or to enjoy old favorites.

In addition to their familiarity with an array of cuisines and ethnic flavors, your guests may also be increasingly aware of the importance of nutrition as part of a healthy lifestyle. The American people are focusing more and more on the role good nutrition plays in maintaining physical health and overall well-being. Consequently, culinary professionals must be aware of the nutritional content of their dishes. They must also understand the chemical and physical changes that occur when food is cooked.

The Importance of Nutrition in Menu Development

People choose to eat certain foods for a number of different reasons. One of the most important reasons is, of course, taste. But in addition to flavor, every food contains calories as well as a variety of substances known as nutrients, which are essential to our bodies for energy, growth, repair, and maintenance.

Every five years the USDA revises its dietary guidelines for Americans based on the latest medical and scientific findings. Although these guidelines speak to people on a personal level and cover lifestyle choices as well as dietary ones, it is helpful for chefs and other culinary professionals to be aware of them. Of the four main integrated findings used in developing the 2010 Dietary Guidelines for Americans, three are of particular relevance to the professional chef.

1. Reduce the incidence and prevalence of overweight and obesity of the US population by reducing overall calorie intake and increasing physical activity.

Offer a variety of vegetables, fruits, and fiber-rich whole grains throughout the menu.

Serve smaller portions, especially of high-calorie foods.

Offer lower-calorie options throughout the menu.

Provide improved, easy-to-understand information about restaurant meals, including calorie content and portion size.

2. Shift food intake patterns to a more plant-based diet.

Emphasize vegetables, cooked dry beans and peas, fruits, whole or minimally processed grains, nuts, and seeds.

Increase menu options that feature seafood.

Use fat-free and low-fat milk and milk products

Serve only moderate amounts of lean meats, poultry, and eggs.

3. Significantly reduce intake of foods containing added sugars, solid fats, sodium, and refined grains.

Choose foods that are naturally low in sodium (i.e., fresh foods that have not been highly processed)

Choose foods that are naturally low in calories.

Avoid foods that are high in refined grains, especially refined grains or foods made from refined grains that are coupled with added sugar, solid fat, and sodium.

Menu Guidelines

The following guidelines should be considered as basic principles for developing any menu.

Base menu selections on high-quality ingredients. This is perhaps the most basic tenet of all. The chef must know the best available product, and should select preparations or special dishes to highlight the superior items he or she has purchased. This does not by any means imply that only expensive or difficult-to-find foods are the best. In all probability, the best product is locally produced and in season, whether the food is a fruit, a vegetable, game, or fish. A key factor in ingredient selection is the cost of goods. Your business plan plays a significant role in deciding which foods to purchase.

Keep menus grounded in the season as much as possible. This concept follows naturally from the preceding idea. There are certain times of the year when many foods—a vegetable such as sweet corn, for example—will be at their best. This is the natural time to use them. The menu should be designed so that each item can be handled in imaginative, creative, and, above all, flavorful ways.

There will also be seasonal preferences that may have to do with a change of weather. For example, there is an increased demand for hearty, slowly cooked, savory dishes as the weather cools in the more northern parts of the country. Seasonal preferences exist throughout all of the nation's regions, reflecting the traditional availability of special foods at defined times of the year. Some foods are traditionally associated with holidays, although the holiday itself may not be significant to every single patron. For example, many people, both Irish and non-Irish, look for corned beef and cabbage on St. Patrick's Day.

Use locally produced products, when possible. Restaurants are part of the business community. It is important to try to work together with other businesses as much as possible. Buying locally makes good community sense.

Select items that will offer the guest a reasonable range of options within a price range while still maintaining a good check average. Just as it is a good idea to have wines

Strategies for Developing Healthier Menu Options

Think strategically about flavor, with an emphasis on leveraging long-term flavor trends, the public's growing interest in world cuisines, and its discovery of "culinary adventure," in order to broaden options and provide new approaches to healthier menu development.

Focus on fruits and vegetables first—in a full range of colors and types, and in applications across all meals of the day and all menu parts—knowing that your customers on average need to double their consumption of produce to promote good health.

Highlight the increased use of healthy plant-based oils, eliminate trans fats, and substantially reduce saturated fats.

Increase options for healthy protein choices, adding fish, nuts, and legumes if they are underrepresented on the menu.

Emphasize healthy carbohydrates by increasing the menu presence of whole grains—especially "intact" whole grains—and add food and beverage options with little or no added sugars and other empty-calorie sweeteners.

Look for opportunities to reduce salt and sodium in food preparation. Instead of adding salt, use fresh herbs, citrus juices, vinegars, and wines to add a "bright" flavor to dishes, or use brined ingredients like capers or olives to replace added salt.

Provide a wider range of calorie/portion options, and consider menu concepts that change the value proposition for customers from a focus on quantity to a focus on quality and culinary differentiation.

Leverage small measures of indulgence for maximum creative impact. Instead of adding cream as an ingredient, for example, consider lightly whipping the cream before using it as a garnish. The increased volume from whipping allows the chef to add less and still add a satisfying taste to the dish.

Create new categories or options for healthy menu choices. Consider offering choices such as half-size portions, meatless options, and a wider range of small dishes served as either appetizers or main dishes.

Share nutrition information with customers as appropriate, but emphasize strategies for selling healthier menu options that rely more on the language of flavor and culinary adventure.

Engage colleagues and industry partners in a long-term process of discovery to better understand the art and science of healthy menu research and development, and re-imagine the operational designs, technologies, human resource strategies, and marketing innovation necessary to successfully sell and deliver these flavors to customers.

at a number of different price levels, it is also good to have a range of entrée prices. There will certainly be a general price range appropriate for each particular restaurant—varying according to restaurant type and location—that will determine the upper and lower price limits. Within those boundaries, however, it is usually possible to offer a number of different options. Whatever the menu pricing strategy, it is essential that guests feel they have received top value for their dollar and that the restaurant is able to turn a profit.

Apart from customer appeal, menu development has other important effects on the establishment's overall operation. Careful menu development ensures that the workload is balanced between the stations. An establishment's reputation is damaged if customers feel that they consistently wait too long to get their meals. This can happen all too easily if one particular station is bogged down with too much work. Spreading the responsibilities throughout the kitchen by properly selecting the menu items can often minimize this problem.

Create menus in such a way that the available equipment is properly used. If your kitchen is short on burners but does have a large grill, your menu should reflect that fact. If there is little oven space, limit roasted or braised foods or keep them to a minimum.

Design menus with an eye to your staff's capabilities in preparing the foods properly and consistently. Guests will come to expect a certain performance level from a kitchen, and although they will be delighted to receive food that is of a better caliber than might have been the norm, they will never forgive food that is not up to the level of their previous experiences.

PLATING TECHNIQUES

Once the guest has made a selection from the menu, the kitchen staff's duty is to be sure that the food that ultimately arrives at the table meets—or, better, exceeds—the expectations. The following principles are ways to make sure that food is correctly plated and presented.

Basic Principles

Serve hot food hot; serve cold food cold. Foods must be served at the correct temperature. Nothing is less appealing than tepid soup, salads that are not well chilled, sautéed items that are room temperature. Not only can the wrong temperature be disappointing in terms of taste, but it may actually pose a health hazard if the foods are in the danger zone.

Food should look neat and attractive; plates should be very clean. The appearance of the food should always be appropriate. Sautéed or pan-fried foods should have a golden brown crust; poached foods should look moist. Sauces should be the correct consistency so that they won't run on the plate; any skin or lumps should be strained out and the butter should be properly emulsified. There should be no ragged edges or torn or misshapen pieces that give an impression of carelessly handled food.

Any drops of sauce or smudges should be wiped clean before the plate leaves the kitchen. Food that is simply slapped onto a plate gives the impression that the kitchen staff cares little about what it is doing.

The food must be properly cooked. If a steak is ordered rare, it should be sent out that way. If a sauce was requested on the side, it should be there, in a properly heated sauceboat or ramekin. Foods should be cooked in such a way that their flavors and textures are enhanced, not hidden.

The plate should be attractive. This does not mean that you should elaborately garnish it simply for the sake of decoration, or give the impression that the food was "played" with in the kitchen.

The food should appear to its best advantage on the plate. A certain amount of space between items is desirable to prevent the overall effect from being busy or crowded. On the other hand, the food should not look lost on the plate, as this creates the unfortunate impression of small portions and gives guests the feeling that they are not receiving full value. Some foods may be mounded or piled up a little higher than other items to give the plate a pleasing appearance. This may take a little more care than simply dropping a spoonful of peas or ratatouille on the plate.

The plate's border can act in the same manner as the frame of a painting. The food should not spill out into the border, nor should it look as if it is in danger of falling off the edge of the plate if a knife and fork are used to cut on it.

Beyond these commonsense instructions, there are additional refinements that can mean the difference between an acceptable plate and an exceptional one.

Special Techniques

There are several effective ways to enhance the overall appearance of a dish. A sauce is a good vehicle for giving a plate some drama.

Pool sauce on the plate and then evenly spread the sauce to create a field of color. Then place the entrée on the sauce for the most dramatic appearance. Drizzle, "splash," or drop sauces or condiments of contrasting colors onto a background sauce. To further increase the visual appeal, drag a thin blade through the second sauce to create a marbleized look.

It is important to "feed the eye" and create the correct impression. Slicing pieces of meat on the diagonal and placing them strategically on the plate will give an impression of greater bounty. Shingled slices of a veal loin look larger and more generous than a single medallion, even though the entrée's actual weight may be exactly the same.

Contrast

The plated dish should have a variety of colors, cooking methods, shapes, textures, heights, and seasonings. All-white foods or all-puréed foods on a single plate can be boring to the eye or the palate. If you use garlic in one or two elements on a plate, you should not use it in the others. Too much repetition, be it foods of the same size and shape or flavors that are duplicated, is simply not appealing. A simple entrée may be served with more complicated accompaniments—for example, a grilled chicken breast might be served with a pan-fried vegetable that has its own sauce. But an elaborately sauced and garnished entrée should be paired with very simple, perfectly prepared and seasoned side dishes.

Select foods for their ability to contribute to the overall success of the plate in terms of appearance and flavor. Instead of using a garnish that is not meant to be eaten, add a vegetable to introduce an additional color, as well as flavor and nutrition. For example, use a green vegetable such as broccoli or snow peas rather than the "traditional" bunch of watercress or sprig of parsley.

Harmony

The tastes and colors of the elements of a dish should harmonize to create a pleasing total effect. While an element of surprise may give some excitement to a dish, a flavor or texture that shocks and startles the palate is disturbing. There are no rules carved in stone dictating that you can only combine this sauce with that food; there is room for experimentation and personal expression in preparing a dish. First, however, it is important to develop a sense of balance and to educate both the palate and the eye.

Simplicity

The final rule for plating is to keep the ideal of simplicity firmly in mind. If a food is properly cooked, it should not require fussing in order to look appealing. While elaborately garnished foods, sauces "painted" onto the plate, or architectural constructions can create an impressive effect, if the basic techniques haven't been properly applied or the foods were not at their peak of freshness or quality, the effect will be lost. Worse, the guest will feel cheated. The natural colors, textures, and shapes of foods are very often their own best garnish.

CATERING AND IN-HOUSE SPECIAL FUNCTIONS

To gain an edge over their competitors, organizations often look to special functions and catered events as a point of distinction. To excel in this aspect of food service, your operation must be prepared to distinguish its events not only through the high-quality foods that are served, but also through the successful execution of a unified concept, both delivered with top-notch service. The chef is an integral part of the overall catering operation, working hand in hand with event planners, banquet managers, and clients.

Today catered events can take shape in many forms, such as

Conventions, conferences, and business meetings

Corporate events (holiday parties, luncheon meetings, dinners)

Special occasions (weddings, engagements, reunions)

Outdoor and off-premise events (picnics and barbecues, events in special locations such as yachts, public parks, private homes)

Promotional events (social, corporate, and community)

Political or charitable fund-raising events (dinners, receptions, and galas)

Themed parties (Gatsby, Treasure Island, Halloween, Indonesian, Polynesian, Star Trek, cuisines of the world, bountiful harvest, '50s bebop, casino)

Catered special events that are perfectly executed down to the last detail are a top priority for your customers. Successful banquets and special events depend on careful and detailed planning to account for every phase of the event, from menu development through a final postmortem. Clear communication is a critical factor at every stage of an event, and must include all the members of the team, from the catering manager or event planner and chefs to the kitchen and dining room staff.

Whether it is a meal for ten guests or two thousand, every catered special event should be a celebration on its own, with distinctive ingredients passionately prepared and served in style and elegance. As the chef, you will be responsible for developing a menu that not only delights your client with creative and high-quality dishes, but also delivers the best possible product at the lowest possible cost. The menu itself may be driven by the client's requests, a special theme, or other considerations.

1. Chefs help plan the plating and presentation of each course.

2. Passed hors d'oeuvre serve as a simple plating option for both kitchen and service staff.

The menu can offer many opportunities for you to fulfill your responsibilities to the client and your operation. Once it is approved and finalized, you will use it to determine food and labor costs (and to explore various ways to manage those costs without affecting quality), staffing needs and schedules, equipment needs, and a host of other details.

Menu Criteria and Planning

The chef is responsible for developing the menu, ordering and preparing the foods, and orchestrating the plating and presentation of the food throughout the event.

Operations that offer in-house catering are increasingly challenged to meet new demands from clients asking for top-quality foods and service, great value-added points of differentiation, convenience, and a reasonable price. The job of the food-service professional is to manage these new challenges effectively and productively. The chef can create unexpected and interesting items with a fresh, contemporary approach that is completely new to the guest (especially important for repeat customers) and still be culturally sensitive to the guest's desire for traditional offerings and familiar and comforting foods. The menu may be the genesis of the theme or it may serve to support the theme. (For more about themed parties, see page 20.)

Throughout menu development, there are a number of issues to consider.

How does this menu item affect the total budget for the event? You will consider not only the cost of the raw ingredients, but also the amount of labor required to prepare and serve the menu item, and any equipment you may need to rent or purchase for the event.

How many and how varied are the offerings? Depending upon the type of event, the number of options that should be provided may grow or shrink. It is the chef's job to strike a balance between enough variety to offer interesting choices and so many choices that there is an undue burden on the kitchen and service staff.

How appropriate are the food choices? The dishes you choose should match the event on as many levels as possible. Some events are inherently formal while others are casual. Some events have a specific theme or purpose while others are more "generic." Some are closely tied to a season or holiday; others are not. In all cases, offer a variety of choices appropriate to the theme or occasion.

If the menu includes a sequence of courses, is there a progression from one course to the next or a relationship between the courses? There are a number of ways to orchestrate a menu. Some build gradually from simple to more complex flavors. In all cases, you should avoid repeating flavors and textures.

What does the menu offer that the guest did not expect? Introduce offerings that provide excitement by using unique ingredients or intriguing preparation or presentation options.

Have you done your best to meet your client's specific needs? You may need to accommodate various age groups, an array of personal likes and dislikes, food aversions and avoidances, allergies, and other special dietary requirements of the attendees.

Do the menu items lend themselves to the event's style of service? The way that foods are prepared can vary dramatically depending upon whether they are to be served buffet-style, butler-style, plated (sit-down), or family-style. Some service styles are more labor intensive (and formal) than others.

Do the cooking methods called for adapt easily to the equipment you have on hand? Understand the method completely, from the equipment and ingredients to cooking and holding times. Consider what finishing techniques you require and how complex that stage may be, as well as all of the options available for plating and serving foods to your guests so the food will be at its best.

Do the menu items require special service or preparation equipment? Plan for the rental or purchase of any special equipment necessary for preparation and service, especially if you are planning to include carving stations or other interactive options as part of the overall service.

How difficult will it be to plate and serve the foods on the day of the event? Foods that are easily affected by the surrounding temperature (frozen desserts, hot soufflés)

Chefs must consider both the kitchen and dining space available when beginning to plan an event.

keep the best quality on their trip from the kitchen to the table when they are plated in a temperature-controlled area, but not every facility has enough room in the right spot.

As you develop and evaluate your menu items, try to determine who should be doing the plating and where that should happen. For some dishes, plating may be best accomplished through a group effort of both the kitchen and dining room staff on an assembly line in the kitchen. For other dishes, plating may need to be handled strictly by the dining room staff directly in or just adjacent to the dining area, especially if there are space issues in the kitchen. Still other dishes may call for specific culinary skills, which means that the kitchen staff would need to handle the plating. Items that are served hot directly from the oven require additional labor and skill for service and plating. Items that are served chilled or frozen may require less labor for service.

Food Ordering and Delivery

Once the menu is finalized, you should create precise recipe files for all menu items. These recipes should be scaled to the correct production levels and yields for the specific event to encourage accurate ordering and reduce the loss or waste of food. (For more information about working with recipes, see pages 19–23.)

Just as there are important factors to take into account when developing a menu, there are also several factors to consider when planning your food order.

Will you be able to get full value out of the ingredients and products you order? You should strive toward 100 percent utilization. The ability to take advantage of any wholesome trim or partially used product from the event elsewhere in the operation is an important consideration as you decide exactly which products to order and when to have them delivered.

What type of product is required? Some foods are perishable and cannot be ordered more than a day or two in advance, while others can be ordered and stored for several weeks. As you determine what type of product you need, you may also need to evaluate your storage capacity to be sure that foods do not lose quality while they are waiting for you to prepare them.

Members of the kitchen staff must make the most of available kitchen space. An assembly line can be one of the most efficient uses of time, space, and available staff.

When planning dessert courses, consider all of the components and take temperature into account. Hot and cold components should be plated and served quickly.

What can you do to better manage food costs? You may be able to substitute a more seasonally appropriate food to great advantage on a menu, since foods that are in season are typically of higher quality and lower cost than those that are out of season and have to be shipped to you from greater distances. You may be able to find a high-quality prepared product that virtually eliminates any trim or prep loss, offsetting the difference in price between the "raw" and the prepared ingredient.

What is the optimal time for foods to be delivered? You will need to evaluate your delivery schedule carefully to be sure that you have what you need for advance work delivered in a timely manner. High-cost perishable goods should be ordered once you have a confirmed head count (ideally five days before the event).

Scheduling Advance Work and Preparation

The costs of preparing the food for an event can be better managed if you are diligent throughout the process. Your menu items may include components that can be made ahead and stored until the day of the event. Some dishes can be made ahead completely, while others are constructed in phases that spread the work out over a longer time frame. Still others are partially cooked and then finished at the last moment (vegetables that are blanched or cooked al dente, pastas and risottos that are parcooked, and meats, poultry, and fish that are "marked" or seared in advance, for example).

The complexity of a dish and the number of components that go into the final presentation affect the quantity and quality of workers required to prepare the food—and the labor costs associated with them—as well as the food cost. As you review recipes, look for ways to eliminate steps throughout the process as long as doing so does not spoil the quality of the finished dish. You may be able to find savings of time or money that do not compromise quality during the purchasing phase, advance-work phase, or makeup and production phases.

Purchase prepared or semiprepared components when doing so reduces labor costs, increases efficiency and consistency, and improves quality. Examples include frozen fruit and vegetable purées, IQF (Individually Quick Frozen) fruits, puff pastry, phyllo, or brioche doughs.

Opt for premade versions of garnishes or other components that might require significant effort, time, or specialized equipment to produce consistently in-house, such as chocolate cups and cigarettes or tartlet shells. Purchasing these items rather than making them in-house may actually represent a savings, especially if they call for specialized skills or tools.

Components that freeze well can be produced in advance of the event to manage work flow and timing and to better control labor and food costs. Some examples include compound butters, baked items including cookies and cakes, and hors d'ouevre that are wrapped in pastries.

The timely setup of furniture and equipment in the dining room is crucial to the success of the overall event. The culinary team cannot complete their work if chafing dishes and display areas are not ready on time. Ideally, the scheduling for the setup of the room should take into account any special equipment or decorations and allow enough time for mishaps like missing extension cords or stained linens to be corrected before the guests arrive.

Choosing Cooking Strategies and Techniques for Special Events

With the appropriate amount of time, staff, and equipment, virtually any cooking technique is suitable for special events. Consider your limitations in terms of time, staff, and equipment when you select a dish or technique for a special event, and when possible, opt for techniques that make effective use of do-ahead strategies. Techniques such as braising and stewing, for instance, can often be fully or partially completed a day or two in advance; doing so may even improve the quality of some dishes.

Casseroles, gratins, and similar composed dishes can be assembled ahead of time. Some can be baked in advance while others are best when served directly from the oven.

Sauces help maintain the quality and appearance of a dish throughout the service period.

Carving stations or other interactive action stations that serve stir fries, pasta, omelets, sandwiches, and other foods minimize the need for precooking, since foods are essentially made to order for one person at a time.

Equipment Options

Your recipes should reflect their suitability for large-quantity production. Base them upon the standard operating procedures for cooking in greater quantities in your kitchen, including appropriate equipment selection and use, ingredient-handling standards, and food safety limits (CCPs or Critical Control Points). For more about the recipe conversions and calculations you will need to make, see pages 22–23.

Take full advantage of the equipment already in your facility before you decide to purchase additional equipment. You may be able to manage even a very large event with what you have in-house as long as you plan carefully and assemble a full and complete mise en place in the days leading up to the event.

Large-batch cooking techniques are based on the equipment used for makeup. Rack ovens, steam kettles, tilting kettles, combi steamers, and large-capacity mixers can produce large single batches during both the advance-work phase as well as during the production and plating phases.

Each time you handle, cut, and store production pieces, the labor costs go up. Use specialized tools such as molds or baking forms to produce foods that are uniform in size and shape and that are properly portioned in one step rather than two.

Tools that eliminate steps or reduce the time required to complete a task may have an up-front cost, but if that investment consistently helps to reduce labor costs at the same time that it improves quality, it will be recouped in a relatively short time. Large freestanding equipment like tilting kettles or vertical chopping machines, for example, makes it possible to process large quantities in a single batch, resulting in a more consistent product with less preparation time.

Not all such tools represent a big investment of money, though you may be required to invest some of your own time in evaluating how work is accomplished and how it can be improved. Simple tools that are widely available such as pastry bags, ladles, or scoops can be used to simplify and speed up both preproduction and service.

In a large-quantity food production setting, strong consideration should be given to the appropriate use of freezing techniques and blast freezer equipment. These units do

1. Consider ingredients and dishes that are cost-effective but will still provide the best quality to customers.

2. Many components of menu items can be prepared in advance, allowing preparation and plating time during the event to run more smoothly.

more than just streamline production and makeup. They also may make it easier to offer more creative and higher-quality items to your clients. Layers and forms of flavor components and texture components can be easily combined into a cake, sheet, or individual dessert form when handled frozen. Unlike conventional freezers, blast chiller/freezers allow for the food products to cool down and freeze quickly, therefore preserving the quality and integrity of the product. This use of quick-freezing/blast-chilling techniques can speed the production process in comparison to standard freezing, as two-day production processes can be completed in just one day in many cases.

Renting or Owning

In all major cities of the United States we are fortunate to have rental companies and themed party-planning services that, for a fee, offer extra buffet setup items, china, silver, and other equipment that can be rented and added to the price of the catered event. These companies may also be able to work with your operation and your client to develop a theme idea and then locate the props, costumes, and service pieces necessary for a one-of-a-kind event, leaving it to you, the chef, to produce a menu that complements the overall theme.

An operation that does a great deal of banquet business may find it effective and profitable to develop one or more themes unique to that individual operation, complete with the corresponding props for the tables, backdrops or scenes for decoration, costumes for the servers, and entertainment options. An important consideration before embarking on such a plan is the operation's ability to store and secure the theme equipment.

The ultimate goal, and the payoff from any expenses your operation incurs, is attracting new business. The marketing team or catering coordinator can develop a photo album to use in booking other events, or even to promote your operation to the local media when you plan a community-sponsored event. As each event is booked and each additional client pays a rental fee for the use of your operation's equipment, the initial outlay will eventually be recovered, and ideally the cost of maintaining, repairing, or replacing the equipment will be less than the costs you might face if required to rent the items for each event.

RECIPES

A recipe is a written record of the ingredients and preparation steps needed to make a particular dish, and is meant to provide instructions for a cook. However, in the professional kitchen, a recipe can be much more than that. It can be used as a powerful tool to improve

Creating Unique Themed Events

Themed events are always popular, particularly with convention and social event planners. An operation can become known for its wonderful themed events if they are well conceived, professionally executed down to the last detail, and properly promoted.

Typically, the theme is linked to the event in some way—perhaps to the location (luaus in Hawaii, barbecues in Texas, seafood bakes in New England), the season (harvest banquets in the fall, strawberry feasts in the spring, mushroom extravaganzas in the winter), or the client (a sock hop for a soda and ice cream manufacturer, a glittering winter arcade for a client who produces ski wear, or a pirate ship for a travel agency that specializes in cruises). But what if you want to offer something that isn't typical?

First, gather the key players in your organization and brainstorm for theme ideas. Select the best ideas, the ones that are most likely to sell and attract new business. Then determine the start-up costs to produce this party for a specific event. As you calculate the costs, remember that the planning and effort that goes into this event will help reduce the costs (and the labor) involved in subsequent similar events. If you've developed a fantasy theme, for instance, you could easily tweak the menu to make it work for a sweet sixteen party, a retirement gala, a fund-raising event, or a high school prom.

efficiency and organization, and to increase profits. Learning to read recipes carefully and to use them to be more productive is an important step in developing your professional skills.

Before starting to cook from any recipe, the first step is always to read through the recipe in its entirety to gain an understanding of exactly what is required. This step will alert you to any surprises that the recipe might contain, such as requiring an unusual piece of equipment or an overnight cooling period.

This is also the point at which you must decide if any modifications to the recipe are in order. Perhaps the recipe makes only ten portions and you want to make fifty, or vice versa. You will have to convert the recipe (see page 22). In increasing or decreasing the yield, you may discover that you also need to make equipment modifications to accommodate the new volume of food. Or you might decide that you want to omit, add, or substitute an ingredient. All of these decisions should be made before any ingredient preparation or cooking begins.

Once you have read through and evaluated or modified the recipe, it is time to get your mise en place (the ingredients and equipment) together. In many recipes, the ingredient list will indicate how the ingredient should be prepared (for example, if it should be parboiled or cut into pieces of a certain size) before the actual cooking or assembling begins.

Measuring Ingredients Accurately

Accurate measurements are crucial to following recipes. In order to keep costs in line and ensure consistency of quality and quantity, ingredients and portion sizes must be measured correctly each time a recipe is made.

Ingredients are purchased and used according to one of three measuring conventions: count, volume, or weight. They may be purchased according to one system and measured for use in a recipe according to another.

Count is a measurement of whole items as one would purchase them. The terms *each*, *bunch*, and *dozen* all indicate units of count measure. If the individual item has been processed, graded, or packaged according to established standards, count can be a useful, accurate way to measure ingredients. It is less accurate for ingredients requiring some advance preparation or without any established standards for purchasing. Garlic cloves illustrate the point well. If a recipe calls for two garlic cloves, the intensity of garlic in the dish will change depending upon whether the cloves you use are large or small.

Volume is a measurement of the space occupied by a solid, liquid, or gas. The terms *teaspoon (tsp)*, *tablespoon (tbsp)*, *fluid ounce (fl oz)*, *cup (c)*, *pint (pt)*, *quart (qt)*, *gallon (gal)*, *milliliter (ml)*, and *liter (l)* all indicate units of volume measure. Graduated containers (measuring cups) and utensils for which the volume is known (such as a 2-ounce ladle or a teaspoon) are used to measure volume.

Volume measurements are best suited to liquids, though they are also used for solids, especially spices, in small amounts. Tools used for measuring volume are not always as precise as necessary, especially if you must often increase or decrease a recipe. Volume measuring tools need not conform to any regulated standards. Therefore, the amount of an ingredient measured with one set of spoons, cups, or pitchers could be quite different from the amount measured with another set.

Weight is a measurement of the mass or heaviness of a solid, liquid, or gas. The terms *ounce (oz)*, *pound (lb)*, *gram (g)*, and *kilogram (kg)* all indicate units of weight measure. Scales are used to measure weight, and they must meet specific standards for accuracy. In professional kitchens, weight is usually the preferred type of measurement because it is easier to attain accuracy with weight than it is with volume.

Standardized Recipes

The recipes used in a professional kitchen are known as standardized recipes. Unlike published recipes, standardized recipes are tailored to suit the needs of an individual kitchen. Preparing well-written and accurate standardized recipes is a big part of the professional chef's work in all food-service settings, as they include much more than just ingredient names and preparation steps.

Standardized recipes establish total yields, portion sizes, holding and serving practices, and plating information, and they set standards for cooking temperatures and times. These standards help to ensure consistent quality and quantity, and permit chefs to monitor the efficiency of their work and reduce costs by eliminating waste.

Standardized recipes can be recorded by hand or electronically, using a recipe-management program or other computerized database. They should be recorded in a consistent, clear, easy-to-follow form and should be readily accessible to all staff members. Instruct kitchen staff to follow standardized recipes to the letter unless instructed otherwise, and encourage service staff to refer to standardized recipes when a question arises about ingredients or preparation methods.

As you prepare a standardized recipe, be as precise and consistent as you can. Include as many of the following elements as necessary:

Name/title of the food item or dish

Yield information for the recipe, expressed as one or more of the following: total weight, total volume, total number of portions

Portion information for each serving, expressed as one or more of the following: a specific number of items (count), volume, weight

Ingredient names expressed in appropriate detail, specifying variety or brand as necessary

Ingredient measures expressed as one or more of the following: count, volume, weight

Ingredient preparation instructions, sometimes included in the ingredient name, sometimes expressed in the method itself as a step

Equipment information for preparing, cooking, storing, holding, and serving an item

Preparation steps detailing mise en place, cooking methods, and temperatures for safe food handling (see Hazard Analysis Critical Control Point [HACCP] System, page 42)

Service information describing how to finish and plate a dish and add side dishes, sauces, and garnishes, if any, and listing proper service temperatures

Holding and reheating information describing procedures, equipment, times, and temperatures for safe storage

Critical control points (CCPs) at appropriate stages in the recipe to indicate temperatures and times for safe food-handling procedures during storage, preparation, holding, and reheating

Recipe Calculations

Often you will need to modify a recipe. Sometimes a recipe must be increased or decreased. You may be adapting a recipe from another source into a standardized format, or you may be adjusting a standardized recipe for a special event, such as a banquet or a reception. You may need to convert from volume measures to weight or from metric measurements to the U.S. system. You will also need to be able to translate between purchase units and recipe measurements. In some circumstances you may be called upon to increase or decrease the suggested portion size for a recipe. Or you may want to determine how much the food in a particular recipe costs.

USING A RECIPE CONVERSION FACTOR (RCF) TO CONVERT RECIPE YIELDS

To adjust the yield of a recipe to make either more or less, you need to determine the recipe conversion factor.

Desired yield / Original yield = Recipe conversion factor (RCF)

Note that the desired yield and the original yield must be expressed the same way before you can use the formula. To convert measurements to a common unit (by weight or volume), use Table 2-1: Converting to a Common Unit of Measure (see opposite page). If your original recipe says that it makes five portions, for example, and does not list the amount of each portion, you may need to test the recipe to determine what size portion it actually makes. Similarly, if your recipe lists the yield in ounces and you want to make 3 quarts of the soup, you need to convert quarts into fluid ounces before you can determine the recipe conversion factor.

Once you know the recipe conversion factor, you first multiply all the ingredient amounts by it. Then you convert the new measurements into appropriate recipe units for your kitchen. This may require converting items listed originally as a count into a weight or a volume, or rounding measurements into reasonable quantities. In some cases you will have to make a judgment call about those ingredients that do not scale up or down exactly, such as spices, salt, and thickeners.

The new ingredient amounts usually need some additional fine-tuning. You may need to round the result or convert it to the most logical unit of measure. For some ingredients, a straightforward increase or decrease is all that is needed. For example, to increase a recipe for chicken breasts from 5 servings to 50, you would simply multiply 5 chicken breasts by 10; no further adjustments are necessary.

However, other ingredients, such as thickeners, aromatics, seasonings, and leavenings, may not multiply as simply. If a soup to serve 4 requires 2 tablespoons of flour to make a roux, it is not necessarily true that you will need 20 tablespoons (or 1¼ cups) of flour to thicken the same soup when you prepare it for 40. The only way to be sure is to test the new recipe and adjust it until you are satisfied with the result.

Other considerations when converting recipe yields include the equipment you have to work with, the production issues you face, and the skill level of your staff. Rewrite the steps to suit your establishment at this point. It is important to do this now, so you can uncover any further changes to the ingredients or methods that the new yield might force. For instance, a soup to serve four would be made in a small pot, but a soup for forty requires a larger cooking vessel. However, using a larger vessel might result in a higher rate of evaporation, so you may find that you need to cover the soup as it cooks or increase the liquid to offset the evaporation.

CONVERTING PORTION SIZES

Sometimes you will also need to modify the portion size of a recipe. For instance, say you have a soup recipe that makes four 8-ounce portions, but you need to make enough to have forty 6-ounce portions. To make the conversion:

1. Determine the total original yield and the total desired yield of the recipe.

    Number of portions × Portion size = Total yield

    Example: 4 × 8 fl oz = 32 fl oz (total original yield)

    40 × 6 fl oz = 240 fl oz (total desired yield)

2. Determine the recipe conversion factor and modify the recipe as described above.

    240 fl oz (total desired yield) / 32 fl oz (total original yield) = 7.5 (recipe conversion factor)

Table 2-1	CONVERTING TO A COMMON UNIT OF MEASURE		
	RECIPE MEASURE	COMMON CONVERSION	COMMON UNIT (U.S.)
	1 lb	N/A	16 oz
	1 gal	4 qt	128 fl oz
	1 qt	2 pt	32 fl oz
	1 pt	2 cups	16 fl oz
	1 cup	16 tbsp	8 fl oz
	1 tbsp	3 tsp	½ fl oz

THE IMPORTANCE OF FLAVOR

Good cooking is the art of capturing the
most appropriate flavors in a dish. The
first step in mastering this art form lies in
understanding exactly what constitutes
flavor. Learning how to develop flavors,
as well as when to bring them into
balance and when to allow one flavor
to dominate in a dish, is a matter of
practice, experimentation, and tasting.

THE TERM *FLAVOR DYNAMICS* INDICATES THAT TWO OR MORE FLAVORS HAVE BEEN BLENDED IN SOME WAY TO PRODUCE A NEW FLAVOR EXPERIENCE. SOMETIMES THE DYNAMICS ARE THE RESULT OF MIXING THINGS TOGETHER SO THAT YOU CAN'T EASILY RECOGNIZE SPECIFIC FLAVORS. THE TERM ALSO APPLIES WHEN TWO OR MORE FLAVORS ARE PUT INTO AN UNEXPECTED JUXTAPOSITION SO THAT ONE FLAVOR ACTS TO IMPROVE THE WAY ANOTHER FLAVOR IS EXPERIENCED.

Flavor profile is a culinary shorthand term used for describing the specific preferences you might find within a cuisine. An Asian flavor profile includes ginger, garlic, soy sauce, cilantro, and lemongrass, for instance; a Mexican flavor profile includes chiles, pumpkin seeds, cilantro, and cumin.

SENSING FLAVOR

All five of our senses provide us with perceptions that, when taken collectively, become "flavor." How we perceive a dish depends on its appearance and texture as much as it does on its aroma and taste.

Flavor is nothing if not subjective. What one person thinks is delicious another thinks is anything but, and what one person perceives as much too salty or spicy may be "just right" to someone else.

Preferences for flavors can develop over time or through repeated exposure. Although humans are not born with an affinity for salty or spicy foods, we often develop a taste for them. Too much exposure to some flavors can result in "flavor fatigue." Over time, people can develop a tolerance for some flavors and may become desensitized to them. Chefs themselves need to be especially careful to guard against this, as they may end up adding far more seasoning to a dish than customers prefer.

The human tongue recognizes five basic tastes: sweet, sour, salty, bitter, and *umami*, a Japanese word meaning "deliciousness" that can be described as savory, brothy, or meaty. Additionally, we are capable of discerning incredibly subtle variations on an almost infinite number of combinations of those tastes, in large part due to the aromas of food. Lemon juice and distilled vinegar are both sour, and white sugar and maple syrup are both sweet, but no one would ever confuse one for the other.

Most foods have extremely complicated combinations of flavors. The chemical composition of foods is what gives them their flavors—cruciferous vegetables like cabbage and Brussels sprouts contain sulfur compounds that give them a bitter, pungent taste; the acids in citrus fruits provide a tartness that their sugars tame somewhat. Umami appears to be related to glutamate, an amino acid in foods like beef and mushrooms.

Preparation affects the flavor of foods as well. Foods like garlic and onions get their flavor from volatile oils, which are released when the food is cut. Finely minced or crushed garlic has more exposed surfaces to release these oils than sliced garlic, so crushing will impart a stronger garlic taste than slicing. Heat changes the chemical makeup of foods, too. Raw garlic is harsh and pungent. Sauté it quickly and it becomes palatable yet retains a strong, distinctive flavor; roast it slowly and it becomes sweet and mellow. Another example is white sugar, which has a purely sweet taste. Heat the sugar until it melts and caramelizes, though, and you have a complex array of sweetness, bitterness, and sourness.

Layers of flavor can be developed using dried and ground spices, fresh and dried herbs, and ingredients such as garlic and ginger.

Understanding Flavor

Individual foods and ingredients can often have complicated flavors on their own. Combining ingredients and then cooking them, whether in a dish or a meal, can heighten or intensify a specific flavor, or may blend several flavors to make them even more intricate.

To better understand the flavor of a dish, first consider what attributes each ingredient contributes to the overall flavor profile of the dish. Take one of your favorite recipes and ask yourself why each ingredient is there. For many ingredients, the answer is obvious, but for others, the function may not be immediately clear.

Imagine how the dish would taste if you replaced the main ingredient. Could you substitute a chicken breast for a pork chop? Brown rice and quinoa for couscous? Similar foods can often be substituted for one another, but look to less obvious substitutions. Duck breast, for example, has a rich, savory flavor and succulent texture that stands up well to robust seasonings, making it an appropriate option in a dish that typically features beef.

Next, explore the other ingredients. Does one provide most of the flavor, such as dill in a sauce to accompany salmon? Or do the other ingredients combine to become something completely different from their individual flavors, such as chili powder, cumin, garlic, and onion in chili? How would the flavor of a dressing change if you used sherry vinegar instead of red wine vinegar or lemon juice as the acid? Could you use tapenade or fish sauce in a marinade in place of salt?

If you are cooking grains, how flavorful are they? Simmering them in water allows their flavor to dominate, but not all grains are interesting enough to withstand such exposure. Bland grains may benefit from a more flavorful cooking liquid that enhances their taste, or you may wish to use a different, more flavorful grain. Even pastas and noodles present an opportunity to change the flavor of a dish, whether the pasta itself contributes a different flavor or the choice of pasta encourages you to rethink a dish's flavor profile.

Take a look at how the technique affects the dish's flavor. Dry-heat cooking methods allow browning to occur. How do the resulting browning and crust development affect the food?

Imagine how the dish might taste if you used a different technique, or a combination of techniques. Steamed broccoli has a much simpler, purer taste than roasted broccoli,

Steaming is just one of many potential methods of preparing broccoli, and will have a different resulting flavor than roasting, sautéing, or boiling.

for example, and a stew that is made without first browning the meat or sautéing aromatic vegetables will taste quite different from one that uses these techniques.

Timing affects flavor as well. Look at when the ingredients are added to the pot, and how long they cook. Adding different ingredients at certain times helps to maximize flavor and ensures that each ingredient is cooked just enough. Onions, garlic, and some spices are normally added at the beginning of the cooking process and cooked with a touch of oil or fat to develop their sweetness and allow their flavors to permeate everything else that is added to the pot. Fresh herbs, on the other hand, are often added to foods shortly before serving so their delicate flavors aren't muted and their aromas and colors really stand out.

By adding ingredients in a certain sequence, you create a layering of flavors. A fairly simple example is when you add freshly minced chives to an onion soup just before serving. The chives, members of the onion family, deliver another dimension of onion flavor, and their sharp, pungent note contrasts dramatically with the sweet, mellow caramelized onions.

A more intricate layering occurs when you add several different ingredients. Consider what happens when you cook meat and then make a mushroom sauce. You might sauté beef medallions or filets. After you remove them from the pan, you deglaze the pan by adding a bit of wine to release the bits of meat that are left in the pan into the sauce. The wine adds a bright acidic flavor of its own; as it simmers, the wine loses some harsh flavors and mellows to become a background flavor. The mushrooms are added next so that they can release their essence into the sauce. Aromatic components—a dash of Madeira, fresh herbs, and a little pepper—are added just before serving so that their volatile compounds are not lost to prolonged cooking.

When we eat this dish, we perceive each of these flavors in nearly the opposite order. First, the bright aromatic quality of the herbs and the spiciness of the pepper become apparent, quickly followed by the darker earth tones of wine, mushrooms, and fond de veau lié. At the base of all this is rich, meaty beef. This inverse linear quality of flavor perception is one of the key elements in composing successful recipes.

Describing Flavor

The terms used to discuss flavor are defined below. Any discussion of flavors has some inherent difficulties. First, we all experience flavor in a subjective manner. And second, the words used to stand in for our sensory experiences are often poorly defined and vague. Chefs must be able to discuss flavor effectively, however. Like wine professionals, culinary professionals also need a list of clearly defined terms they can use to evaluate the dishes they develop and prepare for their clients, as well as some appropriate descriptive terms. Two practical applications for this type of sensory evaluation are writing effective menu copy and scoring new menu items that meet your high-quality standards. (A sample evaluation form can be found on page 428.)

FLAVOR. Foods that are at their peak of quality, raw or cooked, have distinctive smells. The combination of smells gives a food its particular aroma. The descriptors for flavor can include balanced, salty, sour, sweet, bitter, and umami (or savory).

AROMA. Aromas are experienced before the food is eaten. They impart fragrance and flavor to the dish. The aroma should give a preview of the dish and create a desire to eat the food. Descriptors for aroma might include floral, citrus, woodsy, earthy, berry, roasted, perfumed, complex, musky, musty, heady, layered.

APPEARANCE AND EYE APPEAL. Bright colors indicate fresh products. Foods with an attractive appearance look appetizing and high quality. Just looking at the food should make the guest anticipate eating the food. The flavor descriptors for appearance can include neat, ragged, colors (orange, red, brown, gold, etc.), shiny, dull, or height (tall, flat, wide).

TEXTURE. Texture is a critical indicator that the food is properly cooked or that it has the characteristics associated with fresh, raw, or cold food. The descriptors for texture include smooth, melting, dense, frothy, coarse, soft, hard, crispy.

FINISH AND MOUTHFEEL. Finish and mouthfeel are the sensations you experience in your mouth after the food is tasted, chewed, and swallowed. Mouthfeel has to do with the way the food feels when you eat it. Finish is associated with the way flavors linger on the palate. Both experiences should be pleasant and entice you to eat more. The flavor descriptors for finish and mouthfeel can include long-lasting or lingering, clean, unctuous, fizzy, biting, silky, slippery, or astringent.

BITE. Bite is directly a result of proper cooking, or in the case of salads or raw vegetables, the crisp resistance experienced when biting into the food. The flavor descriptors for bite can include snap, yielding, chewy, rubbery, crumble, dissolve.

MOISTURE. The correct amount of juiciness hints at succulence in a food product and contributes to crispness in raw foods like celery or apple, giving them a snap or crunch. The descriptors for moisture include moist, dry, soggy, crisp, juicy, powdery.

SPECIAL DESCRIPTOR: SMOKINESS. Some popular cooking techniques, including grilling, roasting, and barbecuing, are meant to introduce a smoky flavor in foods. The level of smokiness should complement the final product and not detract from the overall flavor profile and characteristics. The descriptors for smokiness include smoky, meaty, acrid, burnt.

Flavor Profiles

Each ingredient and dish has a flavor profile—a "fingerprint," so to speak—that makes it unique. But the term can also be used to describe the distinctive combination of ingredients and techniques that make each cuisine unique. Cultural, economic, political, religious, and geographic factors play influential roles in the development of flavor profiles.

Climate often makes geographically disparate cuisines somewhat similar. Even though they may share common flavors and ingredients, the cuisines differ in important ways. Thai and Mexican cooking both use lime and chiles as flavorings, for example, but Mexican cuisine uses different chiles and herbs, as well as tomatoes, and Mexico's most common grain is corn while Thai cuisine is based upon rice. Indian and Moroccan cooking both use "hot" spices like cinnamon, cloves, and ginger. But Moroccan cooking is associated with tagines and couscous and mint tea, whereas Indian cooking is associated with curries and breads and poultry from the tandoor oven. In India, flavor profiles vary considerably from one region to another, but also from cook to cook. Each makes his or her own blend of curry powder and garam masala, and thus each cook puts his or her own stamp on dishes that contain these spice blends.

Northern European cooking is significantly different from the cooking of Mediterranean countries. Scandinavian and German foods tend to be heavier in texture, and they rely on fruits and vegetables that thrive in colder climates and that keep well through long winters: cabbages and kale, potatoes, and apples are far more common than tomatoes and citrus fruit. Throughout the Mediterranean, olives and olive oil, pastas, and breads are the backdrop for dishes that feature a host of wild and bitter greens, chickpeas, and garlic.

Even within countries, this geographic influence can be seen. Compare the cooking of Brittany and Paris to that of the Côte d'Azur: northern France has more in common with many northern European countries than it does with southern France. This is also seen in Italy. Landlocked and mountainous regions in the north such as Lombardy and Parma have culinary traditions that are dramatically different from those of the southern regions of Sicily and Puglia.

Even in the United States, these regional differences can be seen. Agriculture and climate play a part in each region's preference, but immigration does as well. Northern Europeans settled in the upper Midwest, so menus in the Dakotas, Minnesota, and Wisconsin may well feature Swedish meatballs, pickled red cabbage, and a number of wursts and sausages. Portuguese fishermen in Rhode Island and Massachusetts added tomatoes to New England's cream-based chowder. Louisiana's famous Creole cooking shows the influence of Choctaw Indians, French and Spanish settlers, African and Caribbean blacks, and Canadians (or Cajuns).

In addition to the crops that grow in a particular climate, livestock also plays a role in flavor profiles—sometimes in unexpected ways. Greece's rocky terrain is more suited to raising sheep than cattle, for example. As a result, Greek dairy foods are typically made with sheep's milk instead of cow's milk, and have a tangier, deeper flavor.

Flavor profiles evolve over time. At first, they are based primarily on the foods indigenous to a region or area. However, colonization and exploration can influence flavor profiles; as foreign powers invade and settle in an area, they bring with them their culinary traditions, including ingredients, equipment, and techniques. Lemongrass, cilantro, mint, chiles, and fish, for example, are common in both Thai and Vietnamese cooking. But Vietnam was for decades a French colony, and its cuisine bears a distinctively French stamp that Thai cooking does not. It is difficult to imagine the cuisines of Mediterranean Europe without tomatoes, but this ingredient did not appear in Europe until the sixteenth century, when Spanish

The flavor profile of Mexican cuisine includes the ingredients shown here. Clockwise from top center: cilantro, corn, tomatoes, dried epazote, cornmeal, Mexican chocolate, jalapeños, poblanos, Anaheim chiles, potatoes, and kidney beans.

explorers brought it home. Tomatoes were considered poisonous for a few more centuries and did not become widely used until the 1800s. Each country, however, has combined tomatoes with other ingredients that reflect its profile: Italy with basil and mozzarella; Spain with garlic, olive oil, and peppers; Greece with oregano, mint, basil, and dill.

Travel has allowed people to encounter authentic cooking that they seek to enjoy at home. Before World War II, pizza was found only in Italian neighborhoods. But as GIs returned home, they sought out this and other Italian foods. As air travel became affordable in the '60s, people went to Europe, Africa, and Asia and discovered how different authentic foods could be from the versions served in U.S. restaurants. People came home from their travels and wished to recreate or experience the flavors and textures they discovered on their journeys. Chefs often returned home from traveling to experiment with new ingredients and techniques, coming up with different combinations.

When playing with flavor profiles, it is wise to stay within flavor families when substituting one ingredient for another. Say, for example, you wish to introduce an Italian flavor to a Thai dish. If the recipe contains fish sauce, you might first try replacing it with anchovies. If the change isn't quite what you were looking for, experiment with other salty foods: capers or olives might be acceptable alternatives.

DEVELOPING FLAVOR

At every step, a chef controls the flavor of a dish. At the same time, every chef is limited by his or her customers' expectations and what they are willing to pay. A chef at a three-star restaurant is expected to use pristinely fresh produce, properly aged meats, well-made cheeses, and high-quality dry goods to produce elegant plates that look like works of art. The prices on the menu are generally high, and the food budget is correspondingly generous. The director of food service for a school will most likely be working with a significantly less lavish budget, but is by no means exempt from the customers' expectation of delicious, flavorful foods. Regardless of what type of budget or kitchen is at the chef's command, any cook worth his or her salt knows that a mediocre chef can ruin high-quality, expensive ingredients in any number of ways, but a talented chef can turn ordinary or inexpensive ingredients into something fabulous.

This control begins with selecting the best ingredients the budget allows, from reliable purveyors. Chefs who are concerned with providing healthy, nutritious options would do well to select foods based on those positive attributes. Rather than focusing on what should be avoided, chefs should choose healthy ingredients for their flavors, then consider how those ingredients can be integrated into a menu for widest appeal. Say you want to use kale as an accompaniment to pork medallions. A side dish of steamed kale is rich in several nutrients, but its fairly pronounced flavor might be too intense for many diners. Preparing it with an Italian-style agrodolce sauce or dressing, however, gives it another dimension without detracting from its rich flavors and nutritional benefits, and will complement the richness of the pork better than the unadorned steamed version.

Once the best ingredients have been selected, the chef must make sure they are stored properly. Dairy foods, for example, can absorb odors from pungent foods and should be kept away from citrus and onions. Improperly stored produce may lose nutrients and texture as well as flavor. Flaccid carrots, limp greens, and mushy apples will only detract from a dish. Proper storage does more than preserve flavor and texture; it helps to ensure that foods will not be exposed to contaminants.

Braised and stewed dishes develop flavor during their lengthy cooking time. Resting them an additional day allows their flavors to continue to develop.

Food safety and flavor extend to how food is handled as it is prepared for cooking. Some foods may need to come to room temperature before use to attain the proper texture or flavor when cooked—eggs to be beaten, some cuts of meat before cooking—but the chef should ensure that they are not left out for extended periods.

Foods that are seasoned before cooking taste different from foods that are not. Salt and other spices and marinades can penetrate the food, so even when mixtures are wiped off, as with gravlax, their essence remains. Whether the chef grinds spices fresh every day or relies on containers of ground spices matters, as does whether the spices are toasted before use and when they are added during the cooking process.

One of the biggest areas where chefs influence flavor is in choosing the cooking technique. Heat alters the chemical structure of food, breaking down cell walls, releasing flavor compounds and nutrients, and making the food more tender. Dry-heat cooking techniques attain temperatures higher than moist-heat methods. These higher temperatures allow foods to brown and develop a crust. Moist-heat cooking methods are typically gentler. Because foods do not brown, their flavors tend to be simpler and purer. Compare the difference between grilled or roasted salmon and poached salmon.

Balancing Flavor

Balance is something that we often assume to be the ultimate goal in the creation of pleasing flavor combinations. This is not always the case, however. Colors, sounds, textures, tastes, aromas, and temperatures can either complement or contrast with each other. Sometimes perfectly complementary flavors are desirable, as in the case of a slowly cooked lentil stew. Here, balance is the goal because the desired result is the melding of several ingredients into a singular taste experience that is completely different from the individual ingredients. If the stew isn't cooked long enough, the ingredients may still retain their distinct flavors.

Other times, though, the chef may wish to highlight a particular flavor. In this case, contrasting flavors can be used to let one or more elements come to the forefront of the flavor profile. Pesto, for instance, showcases the flavor of fresh basil or other herbs and uses the contrasting flavors of garlic, pine nuts, Parmesan, and olive oil to round out the flavor profile. The amount of time that a flavor lingers on the palate after we have swallowed also influences our perception of the dish's overall flavor. We refer to this as the flavor "finish." Consider, for example, a clear soup versus a puréed soup. The clear soup has a lighter and cleaner finish than the thick and creamy puréed soup.

Presenting Flavor

Finally, the chef controls how flavors are perceived through the texture of foods and in how the food is presented. A silky smooth bisque and a chunky potage may have the same ingredients, but the puréed soup's flavor may be subtler than the flavor of the potage, where each ingredient remains distinct. Imagine, too, the difference in flavor between a crab cake with large, meaty chunks of crab and one with small shreds. Because all of our senses are involved in tasting (see "Sensing Flavor," page 26), food that looks attractive on the plate is more appealing than a carelessly arranged dish.

How long a food stands between the initial preparation and when it is actually eaten also affects flavor. Some foods, such as delicate vegetables, fish, and sautéed meats, are best immediately after they are cooked because the quality of their flavor, texture, and nutrient content begins to degrade quite quickly. Other foods, like soups and braised dishes, benefit from being prepared a day or so before they are to be eaten. The extra time allows their flavors to fully mature.

Finally, temperature can be used to add an unexpected element to a dish. Very hot and very cold foods tend to have less discernable flavors. Foods like ice cream, cheeses, and fruits have more developed flavors if they have been allowed to sit at room temperature for a while. Piping hot foods and beverages can deaden the palate.

We generally tend to separate hot foods from cold foods to keep the two temperatures from canceling each other out, but by serving hot and cold foods together, an interesting contrast can be created. In cuisines where food is often spicy, this is a time-honored tradition. For example, in Indian cuisine, a mango lassi (mangos, yogurt, spices) might be served as a beverage with a fiery pork vindaloo and spicy mango chutney. Some of the ingredients are similar, and several are the same (mangos, spices), but the temperature and creamy quality of the chilled drink provide a cooling counterpoint to the hot and spicy pork dish. Dairy is traditionally served with very spicy foods because proteins in milk interfere with pain receptors in the mouth and lessen the burning sensations caused by capsaicin (the active component in chile peppers).

Developing Flavor in Meats, Fish, and Poultry Dishes with Dry Rubs and Marinades

When a spice blend is used as a dry rub (also called a dry marinade) to coat food, the food is refrigerated after application to allow it to absorb the flavors. Very often these rubs contain some salt to help intensify all the flavors in the dish. Dry rubs may be left on the food during cooking or they may be scraped away first. Spice blends may also be added to aromatic vegetables as they cook during the initial stages of preparing a braise or stew.

To use a marinade, combine the marinade and meat in a resealable plastic bag or shallow container. Turn the meat to coat it evenly, cover, and marinate it in the refrigerator for thirty minutes to overnight, depending on the size of the pieces and the level of acidity in the marinade. During longer marinating times, turn the meat once or twice. The marinade is often used to brush or mop foods as they grill or broil. If a recipe calls for using part of the marinade in an accompanying sauce, reserve some of it before adding the meat.

1. Dry rubs penetrate the meat's surface with flavor that will turn into an even more flavorful crust upon cooking.

2. Marinating food allows flavors to develop prior to cooking. .

SEASONING AND FLAVORING FOODS

Various seasoning and flavoring ingredients, ranging from single items like salt or pepper to more complicated mixtures, are used in many different preparations. Classic seasoning combinations include mirepoix, matignon, marinades, oignon piqué, and oignon brûlé. These combinations of aromatic vegetables, herbs, and spices are meant to enhance and support, not dominate, a dish's flavors.

Salting Foods

Salt is a seasoning that is almost taken for granted. Nearly everyone notices when you leave it out of a dish, because without it foods taste a little dull and flat. As we continue to learn more about the potential health risks of a diet high in sodium, chefs and nutritionists alike are looking at salt more closely once again. Adding a little salt before you cook foods can have the effect of bringing out the best flavor in the cooked foods. If you wait until the very end of cooking to add salt, you may be inclined to add too much, which adds a salty taste. Humans do crave salt, but our craving appears to be out of proportion with both our need for it and our ability to process it once we eat it.

Use kosher salt, as we have done in our recipes, wherever salt is called for. The same volume of kosher salt has about half the sodium of table salt. Use your fingertips to apply salt in a more even coat.

Salt isn't the only source of sodium in foods. Processed and prepared foods are often high in sodium, even when they don't actually taste salty. Look for low- or reduced-sodium versions of ingredients like soy sauce, prepared broths or stocks, and condiments. We do not advocate simply eliminating salt, unless there is a specific reason to do so, but we do encourage all cooks and chefs to use salt wisely.

Making a Pan Sauce

A pan sauce gives you the chance to incorporate the flavorful drippings released by foods as they cook. Those drippings reduce and collect in the pan. Adding a flavorful liquid, such as a broth, wine, prepared sauce, or coulis, helps to dilute and dissolve those drippings. Classic pan sauces were often thickened with flour, roux, butter, or cream. Chefs today prefer to let natural reduction develop the flavor and leave the sauces with a somewhat lighter body.

BASIC AROMATIC AND FLAVORING COMBINATIONS

Certain basic techniques and ingredient proportions should be observed when flavoring foods, as outlined in the following descriptions for some classic flavoring combinations.

Mirepoix

A combination of chopped aromatic vegetables, customarily onions, carrots, and celery, a mirepoix is used to flavor stocks, soups, braises, and stews.

The basic ratio of ingredients is two parts onion, one part carrot, and one part celery, by weight. Because mirepoix usually is not eaten, the vegetables, except for the onions, do not have to be peeled. The size of the cut will depend on how the mirepoix is to be used.

1. Adding salt prior to cooking both seasons the food and brings out flavor during the cooking process.

2. Pan sauces capture all of the flavors from the cooking of the main component.

For preparations with short cooking times, such as fish fumet, the mirepoix should be sliced or chopped small. For preparations with more than an hour of cooking time, such as brown stock, the vegetables may be cut into larger pieces or even left whole.

Other ingredients may be added to the mirepoix, depending on the needs of a specific recipe. Leeks are often used in place of all or part of the onion. Other root vegetables, such as parsnips, may be used in addition to, or in place of, the carrots.

Two mirepoix variations are white mirepoix and matignon. White mirepoix replaces carrots with parsnips, additional onions, and leeks, and occasionally includes chopped mushrooms or mushroom trimmings. It is used for pale or white sauces and stocks, such as fish fumet.

Matignon is an edible mirepoix, intended to be served as part of the finished dish. Consequently, the vegetables are peeled and cut in a uniform dice. Diced ham is often also included to enhance the flavor. Matignons are commonly used in poêléed dishes, such as poêléed capon. The ratio of ingredients in a matignon is generally two parts carrot, one part celery, one part leek, one part onion, one part mushroom (optional), and one part pork product (ham or bacon). Various herbs and spices may be included as desired.

Bouquet Garni

Another combination of herbs and vegetables used to flavor stocks and other savory preparations is the *bouquet garni,* the French term for "bouquet of herbs." A bouquet garni is a combination of fresh vegetables and herbs that typically contains fresh thyme, parsley stems, a celery stalk, and a bay leaf, tied into a bundle. When a bouquet garni has contributed adequate flavor (determined by tasting), it should be removed from the preparation and discarded.

Sachet d'Epices

A standard *sachet d'épices,* French for "bag of spices," contains parsley stems, dried thyme, a bay leaf, and cracked peppercorns in a cheesecloth bag. As with the bouquet garni, it should be removed and discarded after enough flavor has been extracted.

1. Mirepoix is one of the most basic flavor developers, utilizing aromatic vegetables such as carrots, onions, leeks, parsnips, and celery.

2. A bouquet garni uses fresh herbs to add flavor during the preparation of dishes.

3. A sachet d'épices is a combination of fresh herbs used to flavor dishes during cooking.

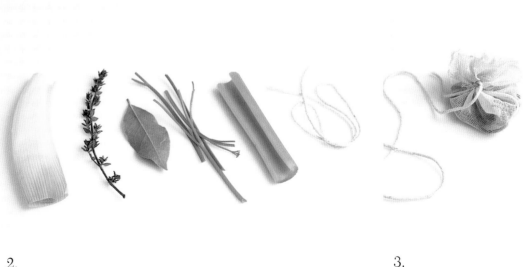

1.

2.

3.

THICKENERS

The consistency of liquid preparations, such as soups, sauces, and braising liquids, often needs to be adjusted to achieve a desired texture. The following techniques and preparations provide ways to thicken liquids.

Reduction

Reduction, a process that removes some or all of the water in a liquid, not only thickens but also concentrates the liquid's flavor. Liquids can be reduced to varying degrees, typically defined by how much water is cooked off. For example, reducing by half means half of the liquid is cooked off. To reduce by three fourths means to cook off three fourths of the liquid, leaving one fourth of the original volume. To reduce *au sec* (to dry) means to reduce until nearly all of the liquid has evaporated.

Heavy pots are recommended, especially for reductions au sec, because as more water evaporates, the reduction is more likely to scorch. When reducing large amounts, it is advisable to transfer the liquid to a succession of smaller pots as it reduces, thereby minimizing the risk of scorching by keeping the liquid from spreading over a large surface area. It is often advisable to strain the liquid as it is transferred.

METHOD FOR REDUCTION

1.   Place the liquid in a heavy pot.

2.   Bring it to a simmer and cook until the desired amount has evaporated.

3.   When reducing au sec, keep the heat very low near the end of cooking and watch the reduction carefully to prevent scorching.

Slurries

A slurry is simply a starch (flour, arrowroot, cornstarch, or rice flour) dissolved in cold liquid. The mixture should have the consistency of heavy cream.

METHOD FOR SLURRY

1.   Blend the starch thoroughly with one to two times its volume of cold liquid. If the slurry has stood for a while, be sure to stir it well before mixing it into the hot liquid, as the starch tends to settle.

2.   Bring the hot liquid to a simmer or a low boil.

3.   Gradually add the slurry, stirring or whisking constantly to prevent lumping and scorching.

4.   Bring the mixture to a boil and cook just until the sauce reaches the desired thickness and clarity.

Roux

Roux is prepared by cooking a fat and a flour together. This mixture is often prepared in advance in large quantities for use as needed. Butter is the most common fat, but chicken fat, vegetable oils, or fats rendered from roasts may also be used. Different fats will have a subtle influence on the finished dish's flavor. The standard proportion of flour to fat is

Gently simmering a brown sauce while it reduces clarifies the sauce and deepens its flavor.

The color of the roux affects the color and flavor of the finished dish. From left to right, roux at various stages of doneness: white, blond, brown, and dark.

three to two by weight, but depending on the types of fat and flour used, this proportion may need to be adjusted slightly. Cooked roux should be moist but not greasy. A common description is "like sand at low tide." There are three basic types of roux, differing according to the length of time they are cooked: white roux, pale or blond roux, and brown roux.

METHOD FOR ROUX

1. Melt the butter or other fat in a pan over medium to low heat.

2. Add the flour and stir until smooth.

3. If necessary, add a small amount of additional flour to achieve the proper consistency.

4. Cook, stirring constantly, to the desired color. Roux should be glossy in appearance. White roux should be barely colored, or chalky. Pale or blond roux should be a golden straw color, with a slightly nutty aroma. Brown roux should be deep brown, with a strong nutty aroma.

5. If the roux will not be used right away, cool it and hold, tightly wrapped, under refrigeration.

Notes. Larger quantities of roux may be made in the oven in a rondeau or brazier. Melt the fat and add the flour on the stovetop, as in the preceding method. Then place the pan in a moderate oven (350° to 375°F/175° to 190°C) and cook to the desired color. Stir occasionally during the cooking time.

METHOD FOR COMBINING ROUX WITH LIQUID

1. Be sure that the roux and liquid temperatures are different—hot liquid and cold roux or cold liquid and hot roux—to help prevent lumping. Add one to the other gradually and whip constantly to work out lumps.

2. Gradually return the soup or sauce to a boil, whisking occasionally.

3. Reduce the heat and simmer, stirring occasionally, to cook out the taste of the flour, at least 20 minutes. To test for the presence of starch, press a small amount of the sauce to the roof of your mouth with your tongue. It should not feel gritty or gluey. If it does, continue cooking until the starch is completely cooked out.

Table 3-1		

THICKENER TO LIQUID RATIOS FOR VARIOUS THICKNESSES

Quantities of Roux to Thicken 1 Gallon of Liquid

Description	Uses	Quantity of Roux per Gallon of Liquid
Light	Soups	10 to 12 oz/285 to 340 g
Medium	Sauces	12 to 14 oz/340 to 400 g
Heavy	Binder, stuffing, baked pasta dishes	16 to 18 oz /450 to 510 g

chapter four

GENERAL COOKING TECHNIQUES

Properly cooked foods should be full of flavor and texture. They should also look appealing. You can easily achieve these goals by pairing ingredients and cooking methods to maximize flavor, texture, and appearance. If healthy cooking is a goal, you should also plan to minimize nutrient loss.

OODS SHOULD BE COOKED WITH THE GOAL OF RETAINING FLAVOR, MOISTURE, AND SUCCULENCE AS WELL AS NUTRIENTS. FOODS THAT ARE COOKED OR HELD FOR LONG PERIODS START TO LOSE QUALITY; THEY MAY BECOME DRY WHEN THEY SHOULD BE MOIST, OR SOGGY WHEN THEY SHOULD BE CRISP.

Colors can change as well, resulting in dishes that lack eye appeal. Nutrient levels may drop when foods are exposed to light or air, subjected to excessively high levels of heat, cooked in too much liquid, cooked for too long, or cooked under alkaline or very acidic conditions.

Preparation techniques should therefore limit exposure to these elements. Preparing foods as close to cooking time as possible is also one of the best ways to maintain overall quality and minimize nutrient loss. Dishes prepared à la minute are cooked "at the moment" of service to ensure high quality. Batch cooking is the equivalent of à la minute cooking when you are faced with preparing multiple servings at a single time.

Sauces should be chosen to enhance flavor without sacrificing nutritional benefit. Although ingredients such as butter and cream can be used in small amounts for enrichment, sauces should be based primarily on vegetables, fruits, and low-fat reductions and essences. Coulis, salsas, chutneys, relishes, and fonds de veau lié are all good choices.

Dry-heat cooking methods and moist-heat methods that rely on steam retain more water-soluble nutrients than simmering or boiling, which causes nutrients to leach into the cooking liquid and get discarded.

Stewing and braising are also nutrient-conserving methods because the cooking liquid, which is normally served as a sauce, captures those vitamins and minerals that are not destroyed by heat.

Using a bit of fat in preparations helps to make fat-soluble vitamins more available to the body. Although cooking decreases the level of some nutrients, others become more available when foods are cooked. Heat breaks down cell walls in ways that digestion cannot, and it concentrates nutrients.

Overcooking should be avoided at all costs. Foods remain juicy and moist if cooked until just done. Overcooked foods, on the other hand, can become dry and tough or soggy and insipid.

KEEPING FOODS SAFE

Food safety is a vital component of effective batch cookery. Keeping foods safe from delivery through service is the chef's responsibility. Every operation may have its own standards for specific procedures, including storage and handling. These standards should meet those included in the 2005 Food Code published by the U.S. Food and Drug Administration (FDA), which is available at http://www.cfsan.fda.gov/~dms/foodcode.html. This code is updated between revisions and should be consulted frequently to maintain appropriate standards for food handling.

Thawing Frozen Foods Safely

Frozen foods may be safely thawed in several ways. The best—though slowest—method is to allow the food to thaw under refrigeration. Place the food, still wrapped, in a shallow container on a bottom shelf to prevent possible contamination. If there is not time to thaw foods in the refrigerator, place covered or wrapped food in a container under running water of approximately 70°F/21°C or below. Use a stream of water strong enough to wash loose particles off the food. Never thaw food at room temperature.

Individual portions that are to be cooked immediately may be thawed in a microwave oven. Liquids, small items, or individual portions may also be cooked without thawing, but larger pieces that are cooked while still frozen can become overcooked on the outside before they are completely done throughout.

Cooling Foods Safely

One of the leading causes of food-borne illness is improperly cooled food. Cooked foods that are to be stored need to be cooled to below 41°F/5°C as quickly as possible. If you are cooling foods in a single-step process, the food must be cooled within four hours.

A two-stage method is also acceptable. In this approach, foods must be cooled to 70°F/21°C within two hours. In the second stage, foods must reach 41°F/5°C or below within an additional four hours, for a total cooling time of six hours.

To cool liquid foods, you may place them in a metal container in an ice water bath that reaches the same level as the liquid inside the container. The wider and shallower the container, the more quickly the food will cool. Depending upon the type of equipment you have, this process may be automated (see Cook and Chill Equipment, below).

Stir the liquid in the container frequently so that the warmer liquid at the center mixes with the cooler liquid at the outside edges of the container, bringing the overall temperature down more rapidly.

Semisolid and solid foods should be refrigerated in single layers in shallow containers to allow greater surface exposure to the cold air. For the same reason, large cuts of meat or other foods should be cut into smaller portions, cooled to room temperature, and wrapped before refrigerating.

Once the food is properly chilled, it can be transferred into a large container for storage with a label that indicates the contents and the date that they were prepared.

Reheating Foods Safely

When you prepare foods ahead and then reheat them, you should move them through the danger zone as rapidly as possible and reheat them to at least 165°F/74°C for a minimum of fifteen seconds. As long as you follow all proper cooling and reheating procedures each time, you may cool and reheat foods more than once.

Cook and Chill Equipment

Advances in equipment technology have made cooking and chilling large quantities of stocks, soups, and sauces time—and labor—efficient. Manufacturers are selling steam-jacketed kettles that cook soups and have agitator attachments that gently stir soups in the kettle during cooking. The same kettle is equipped with technology that chills the stock, soup, or sauce at the end of the cooking process. This permits you to focus on other tasks while the equipment cooks and chills the product. Once the soup is chilled, it can be emptied from the kettle and properly stored.

Bring foods to the proper temperature over direct heat (burner, flattop, grill, or conventional oven) or in a microwave oven. A steam table will adequately hold reheated foods above 135°F/57°C, but it will not bring foods out of the danger zone quickly enough. Always use a thermometer to check temperatures accurately.

Hold Cooked or Ready-to-Serve Foods Safely

Keep hot foods hot and cold foods cold. Use hot-holding equipment (steam tables, double boilers, bain-maries, heated cabinets or drawers, chafing dishes, etc.) to keep foods at or above 135°F/57°C. Do not use hot-holding equipment for cooking or reheating. Use cold-holding equipment (ice or refrigeration) to keep cold foods at or below a temperature of 41°F/5°C.

Hazard Analysis Critical Control Point (HACCP) System

Hazard Analysis Critical Control Point (HACCP) has become a common term in food service and food safety. HACCP is a scientific state-of-the-art food-safety program originally developed for astronauts. It takes a systematic and preventive approach to the conditions that are responsible for most food-borne illnesses. The HACCP system attempts to anticipate how and when food-safety problems are likely to occur, and then it takes steps to prevent them from occurring.

The HACCP system has been adopted by both food processors and restaurants, as well as by the FDA and USDA. At this time, there are no particular mandates that all food-service establishments must use HACCP. However, many food-service operations have found it useful to institute HACCP as part of their operating procedures. An initial investment of time and human resources is necessary, but this system can ultimately save money and time, as well as improve the quality of food provided to customers.

The essence of HACCP is reflected in the following seven principles:

1. Conduct a hazard analysis. Follow the food from the moment you receive it until you serve it. Think about the points in the process where foods might be exposed to pathogens or other contaminants or where conditions are most likely to encourage the growth of pathogens in a food.

- Design a flowchart that covers the entire process "from dock to dish."
- Have all persons involved in the flow of the food present when setting up an HACCP program.

2. Determine critical control points. A critical control point is the point in the process of food handling where you can prevent, eliminate, or reduce a hazard. To quote the 1999 FDA Food Code, a critical control point is "a point or procedure in a specific food system where loss of control may result in an unacceptable health risk."

   The cooking step, as a rule, is a critical control point. Meeting safe temperatures for storing, holding, cooking, and serving foods is the way that you control the hazard. Other critical control points involve the length of time that a food is kept at a given temperature. There are time-temperature relationships for thawing, hot-holding, cold-holding, cooling, and reheating foods.

- Consider whether a food can be contaminated during a step.
- Determine if the hazard can be prevented through some kind of intervention (referred to as corrective action).
- Determine if hazards can be prevented, eliminated, or reduced by steps taken earlier or later in the work flow.

DRY-HEAT COOKING

Dry-heat methods are so called because the food is cooked either by a direct application of radiant heat or by indirect heat contained in a closed environment. No liquid, including stock, is added to either the food or the cooking vessel during the actual cooking time. The result is a highly flavored exterior and a moist interior. The dry-heat techniques are

Grilling and broiling

Roasting

Poêléing

3. Establish critical limits. Critical limits are established by local health departments. As a chef, you need to know the critical limits for a food when you cook it, serve it, or store it. These limits require you to measure both the temperature of the food and the length of time it is kept at that temperature.

- Make sure equipment is working well and is properly prepared (e.g., preheat the oven before roasting).
- Make sure thermometers are accurately calibrated.
- Know how to take internal temperatures of foods.

4. Establish monitoring procedures. Entering accurate measurements of time and temperature into a logbook gives you a record of how foods were handled. It also alerts you to any corrective steps you may need to take.

- Determine who will take and record measurements.
- Determine what measurements should be taken and how often.

5. Identify corrective actions. Whenever a measurement indicates that a food is not at the right temperature or has been held in the danger zone for too long, you need to do something about it.

- For food held at an incorrect temperature for too long in a steam table (such as 120°F/49°C for more than two hours), the corrective action is to discard it.
- For frozen foods delivered with a buildup of ice, indicating that the food has been defrosted and refrozen again, reject the shipment.

6. Establish procedures for record keeping and documentation. Documentation for HACCP typically consists of time-temperature logs, checklists, and forms. Document enough information to be sure that standards are being met, but not so much that you or your cooks find the work complicated or cumbersome to record.

- Develop forms that are easy to fill out.
- Keep forms readily accessible.
- Have reliable and accurately calibrated thermometers on hand.

7. Develop a verification system. The purpose of this step is to establish procedures to ensure that the HACCP plan is working correctly.

- Have a supervisor, executive chef, or outside party verify that the plan is working.
- If procedures are not being followed, try to find out what modifications you can make so the plan works better.

Grilling is essentially a quick technique that is used with portion-size or smaller pieces of meat, poultry, or fish; this is a direct-heat method. Roasting and poêléing (also called butter-roasting) require longer cooking times because these techniques are most frequently used with large cuts of meat or whole birds or fish; they use indirect heat to cook foods.

Grilling, roasting, and poêléing are used to produce foods that are tender and have a deep flavor. The crust that forms as a result of grilling and roasting contributes to the development of a deep flavor and helps to protect the food. Although dry-heat techniques are notorious for their propensity to dry out foods, this tendency toward dryness will be kept to a minimum if the methods are followed carefully.

Match Foods with Dry-Heat Cooking Techniques

One of the most important factors in successfully using dry-heat techniques without fat is selecting the proper cuts of meat, poultry, and fish. Because dry heat does not have a tenderizing effect, any food prepared by one of these techniques must be naturally tender or should be prepared in a way that will introduce additional moisture.

For grilling or broiling, foods should be of a relatively even thickness and cut thinly enough to allow them to cook properly without excessive exterior charring. Cut all items into the appropriate size and trim away any fat, silverskin, and gristle.

Roasts are usually larger cuts. They should also be naturally tender, although there are some techniques you can use to counteract the drying effect of roasting. Roasts are typically tied before they are cooked to give them a compact and fairly regular shape.

Improving Texture and Enhancing Flavor

Texture and flavor can be enhanced using methods such as marinating or barding. These techniques are typically paired with meats, firm-fleshed fish, poultry, and seafood, as well as some vegetables and fruits.

Because the food should already be tender, marination is useful primarily for introducing additional flavor. The marinade may be a simple bath of olive oil or a more complex, aromatic mixture.

Barding involves stuffing the main item, wrapping it in caul fat, and threading it on skewers. If wooden skewers are used, they must be thoroughly soaked in water to prevent the wood from burning.

Another method for enhancing texture is to brush the item lightly with oil. Although not essential, brushing foods with a neutral or appropriately flavored oil will help to protect them during cooking.

Determining Doneness and Evaluating Quality

Doneness tests include

Internal temperature

Skewers

Touch

Appearance

INTERNAL TEMPERATURE. The most reliable method for determining doneness is to use an instant-read thermometer. Insert the stem into the item's thickest part, away from any bones. Insert the thermometer at an angle to avoid forcing juices to jet from the meat, which could burn your hands or face.

SKEWERS. Some chefs rely on a doneness test that involves using a metal skewer inserted into the food (also at an angle, away from bones, and in the item's thickest portion). The skewer is then held just below the chef's lower lip. The hotter the skewer feels to the lip, the more well-done the item is.

TOUCH. Press the meat with the tip of a finger and gauge its resistance. The less well-done a piece of meat is, the softer and more yielding it will feel. This test also applies to sautéed meats (see page 51). To practice recognizing the feel of meat cooked to various stages of doneness, hold one hand open, palm up, with the fingers slightly curled. Touch the flesh at the base of the thumb. It will feel soft and yielding. As the fingers are gradually spread open and flat, the flesh will feel increasingly less yielding.

APPEARANCE. As the meat cooks, the exterior should develop a deep brown color. If the meat appears pale or even gray, it has not been adequately cooked. The juices that run from the meat, although minimal, should be the correct color; the rarer the meat, the "bloodier" the juices should appear.

Appearance is also an important factor in knowing when to turn a piece of meat. When the meat's upper surface begins to appear very moist (there may even be moisture beads), the meat should be turned. Thin pieces may start to change color at the edges when they are ready for turning. The meat's interior color gives the most certain determination of doneness. Beef cooked "blue" has a very deep maroon color. Beef cooked rare has a very pronounced red interior, but it is no longer maroon. When beef is cooked medium, it has a rosy pink interior and is not quite as juicy. Well-done beef shows no traces of red or pink. Although still somewhat moist in appearance, it is no longer juicy.

It is impossible to give exact times for cooking meats, poultry, and fish, because there are so many variables. The following guidelines apply for all the dry-heat techniques.

RED MEATS. Beef, lamb, and some game meats may be cooked to a range of donenesses. The chef must be able to accurately determine when a piece of meat has reached the doneness requested by the guest. Doneness tests other than a reading from a thermometer are often used by chefs, especially when the main ingredient is very thin; it is difficult to get an accurate reading from a thermometer in this case. The ability to assess doneness based upon touch and appearance alone, without a thermometer, can be acquired only through experience.

WHITE MEATS. Veal, pork, poultry, and some game should be cooked through (à point), but not overcooked. There should be a slight amount of "give" when the meat is pressed with a fingertip. Any juices that run from the meat should show either a "thread of pink" or be nearly colorless. It is best to err on the side of undercooking. Even thin meat pieces will retain some heat, allowing them to continue to cook after they have been removed from the heat and are being held for completion of the sauce. If the meat is not left slightly underdone, it can end up overcooked by the time it is served.

FISH AND SHELLFISH. These are extremely easy to overcook because of their delicacy. Their connective tissues and proteins cook at lower temperatures, so the heat is able to travel rapidly throughout the fish. The fish should offer only the least bit of resistance when pressed

Grilled and broiled foods have a deep, smoky flavor amplified by the flavors reducing directly on the surface of the food under the radiant heat.

with the fingertip. It bears repeating that it is best to err on the side of undercooking. The traditional wisdom that fish is properly cooked when it flakes easily should be disregarded. Some fish, notably lean white fish such as flounder or cod, and freshwater fish such as salmon or trout, will be overcooked if the flesh flakes easily. Other types, such as swordfish, tuna, or shellfish, do not readily flake, so the dictum does not apply at all.

Grilling and Broiling

Grilled foods are cooked by radiant heat from a source located below the food. The drippings that might have collected or reduced in a sauté pan are actually reduced directly on the food's surface. The sauce that accompanies a grilled item is prepared separately. Broiled foods are cooked by radiant heat from a source located above the food.

Typically, grilled or broiled foods should have a distinctly smoky flavor, which is enhanced by a certain amount of charring and by the addition of hardwood or sprigs or stalks of some herbs to the grill. This smoky flavor and aroma should not overpower the food's natural flavor, and the charring should not be so extensive that it gives the food a bitter or carbonized taste. (An exception is a food broiled à l'anglaise, which is a technique used for tender and more delicate foods. See opposite page for more information.)

Grilled foods should have a well-developed crust with a moist and tender interior. Broiled foods, especially those that are prepared à l'anglaise, should have a golden-brown color.

METHOD FOR GRILLING AND BROILING

1.   Thoroughly clean and properly heat the grill or broiler. The racks must be perfectly clean to prevent foods from sticking or charring.

2.   Identify appropriate zones on a grill. You should identify which areas tend to be hotter than others, so that items can be moved to hotter or cooler spots as necessary. Broilers may be adjustable, so that you can better control cooking speed.

3.   Place the main item on the grill or in the broiler only after the grill is properly heated. When the food comes in contact with the heated rack, the rack chars a mark on the food's surface. After the item has been on the grill for a brief time, rotate it so that the top is pointing toward 5 o'clock. This will create the crosshatch marks associated with grilling. Crosshatch marks are made on only one side of the item; the unmarked side rests on the surface of the plate. Delicate foods, such as trout and other fish, should be placed on a lightly oiled hand rack for grilling.

4.   Turn the item once and finish cooking to desired doneness. If necessary, thicker items may be finished in an oven. At this point, some foods should be moved to a cooler area on the grill.

5.   Adjust seasoning if necessary and serve on heated plates with an appropriate sauce.

Roasting

Roasting is a technique in which foods are cooked by surrounding them with dry air in a closed environment. The rendered juices are the foundation for sauces prepared while the roast rests. The flavor and aroma of a roasted food should contribute to an overall sensation of fullness, richness, and depth. This is due in part to the nature of the food and in part to the browning process. Roasted foods should have a golden-brown exterior. The color

Broiling à l'Anglaise

Broiling à l'anglaise is a technique well suited to delicate fish, such as sole or flounder. Adding a topping protects the food and also adds additional levels of interest to the dish.

METHOD FOR BROILING À L'ANGLAISE

1. Butter or oil a sizzler platter generously.

2. Place the main ingredient on the dish, brush it with butter, and top with a coating of fresh bread crumbs.

3. Adjust the broiler rack if necessary to move the food farther away from the heat and avoid scorching the crust. Place the sizzler platter on the rack and broil to the appropriate doneness. (Because the heat from the sizzler platter helps to cook the item, it does not have to be turned.)

has a direct bearing on the flavor. Items that are too pale lack eye appeal and the depth of flavor associated with properly roasted foods.

A roasted food's texture depends upon the nature of the main item. In general, however, roasted foods should be tender and moist. If left on the food, the skin should be crisp, creating a contrast with the meat's texture.

The following are terms related to roasting.

SPIT-ROASTING. This technique involves placing the food on a rod that is turned either manually or with a motor. The constant turning assures that the food cooks evenly and develops a good crust. Spit-roasting may also be done in a specially constructed oven. The tradition of serving roasted and grilled foods on toasted bread or a crouton began when pieces of bread were placed below the cooking food to trap escaping juices. In contemporary kitchens, drip pans are placed under the spit.

BARDING. In this technique, meats are wrapped in thin sheets of fatback or in caul fat before roasting. When barding has been used, the meat will not have a well-developed or flavorful crust, but the interior will be moister.

SMOKE-ROASTING. This technique is an adaptation of roasting that allows foods to take on the rich, smoky flavor of hardwood chips without undergoing lengthy brining and smoking processes. Basically, the food is placed on a rack over smoldering hardwood chips. The pan is tightly covered and the main item is roasted in a hot oven (425° to 450°F/220° to 230°C) to the desired doneness.

JUS OR JUS LIÉ/PAN GRAVY. The sauce made from the accumulated drippings is frequently referred to as a jus. When the jus made from drippings is thickened with arrowroot or cornstarch, it is known as jus lié. If a sauce is made with a roux incorporating the fat rendered from a roast, it is usually called pan gravy.

CARRYOVER COOKING. This is a term used to describe what happens to a piece of meat or fish after it has been removed from the oven. The roasted item holds a certain amount of heat that will continue to cook the food. The larger the item, the greater the amount of heat it will retain. For example, quail or Cornish hen may show an increase in internal temperature of 5° to 10°F/3° to 6°C. A top round of beef's temperature may increase by as much as 15°F/8°C, and the temperature of a steamship round of beef by up to 20°F/11°C.

Roasted foods are cooked in a dry, closed environment to capture their flavors. The rendered juices are used as a foundation for pan sauces.

In order to achieve the correct doneness, the main item should be removed from the oven when the internal temperature is lower than it should be when served.

METHOD FOR ROASTING

1.   Roast the main item, uncovered, in a hot oven (425° to 450°F/220° to 230°C) to the desired doneness. Some foods will require basting during roasting, some may need to be turned to assure even roasting, and some may be placed on a rack so that air can come in contact with the food on all surfaces. In any event, the food must cook uncovered if it is to roast, rather than steam or stew. Covering the pan will trap the steam that escapes from the meat. In a closed environment, the food is cooked by steam rather than the hot air's convection.

2.   Remove the item when it has reached an internal temperature that will allow carryover cooking to bring it to the correct final temperature.

3.   Allow the main item to rest before carving it. As foods roast, their juices become concentrated in the item's center. A resting period allows the juices to redistribute evenly throughout the item.

4.   Prepare the jus or pan gravy after transferring the roast to a carving board or platter to rest. Strain the gravy and finish or garnish the main item according to the recipe.

5.   Carve the food, if appropriate, and serve it on heated serving platters or on individual heated plates, accompanied by the jus or pan gravy.

CARVING

Once the food is properly roasted, the chef's task is not complete. The food must be carved correctly to make the most of the item. The carving techniques for three roasted items follow.

METHOD FOR CARVING STANDING RIB ROAST

This carving method could also be used for a rack of veal or similar bone-in roasts.

1.   Lay the rib roast on its side. Using a sharp meat slicer, make parallel cuts from the outer edge toward the bones.

2.   Use the knife tip to cut the slice of meat away from the bone and serve it.

METHOD FOR CARVING LEG OF LAMB

1.   To steady the leg, hold the shank bone firmly in one hand with a clean side towel. Make parallel cuts from the shank end down to the bone.

2.   Continue cutting slices of meat from the leg, cutting away from the bone to make even slices.

3.   When the slices become very large, begin to cut the meat at a slight angle, first from the left side, then from the right side, alternating until the leg is entirely sliced.

METHOD FOR CARVING BIRDS

These carving techniques could be applied to any bird.

1.   Use a knife tip to cut through the skin at the point where the leg meets the breast. Use the tines of a kitchen fork to gently press the leg away from the body. A properly roasted bird's leg will come away easily.

2.   Use one kitchen fork to hold the breast steady. Insert another kitchen fork at the joint between the drumstick and the thigh. Pull the leg away from the body. Repeat for the other leg.

3.   Cut the leg into two pieces through the joint between the thigh and the drumstick.

4.   Cut through the skin on the breast on either side of the breastbone to begin to remove the breast meat.

5.   Use the tines of a kitchen fork to gently pull the breast meat away from the rib cage. Make short, smooth strokes with the knife tip to cut the meat cleanly and completely away.

Poêléing

Poêléing, a technique most often associated with white meats and game birds, is sometimes known as butter-roasting. Veal, capon, and small game are often prepared by this method. Meats are allowed to cook in their own juices in a covered vessel on a bed of aromatic vegetables known as a matignon. The matignon then becomes a garnish served as part of the sauce. Jus is often used to prepare a sauce from the pan drippings.

DRY-HEAT COOKING WITH FATS AND OILS

All of the cooking techniques presented in this section rely on a fat or oil to act as the cooking medium. As the amount of oil is altered in relation to the quantity of food being cooked, different effects are achieved. The techniques for dry-heat cooking using a fat or oil are

>   Sautéing
>
>   Stir frying
>
>   Pan frying
>
>   Deep frying

Sautéing and stir frying require only a small amount of oil, resulting in a well-developed flavor. Pan frying and deep frying require a proportionately larger amount of oil and require that the item being fried be coated; the result is an interesting combination of flavors and textures. They are all relatively quick cooking methods that rely upon high heat and utilize tender pieces of meat, poultry, or fish that are portion-size or smaller. They are considered dry-heat methods because no liquid (stock or water) is added during the cooking time. The cooking medium must be able to reach relatively high temperatures without breaking down or smoking; options include clarified butter, neutral-flavored oil, olive oil, or rendered fats such as bacon, goose fat, or lard.

In dry-heat cooking with fats and oils, it is extremely important to select the proper cuts, shapes, and sizes of meats and to be adept at determining doneness—a skill acquired through experience. You should also thoroughly understand the role of the cooking medium. In sautéing, for example, the medium contributes flavor as well as pan lubrication, whereas in pan frying and deep frying, the flavor of the cooking oil is less important than its cooking properties. When you understand how these techniques work and how they actually cook the food, it becomes clear that the desired end result should dictate the cooking technique chosen for a particular food.

Selecting Ingredients

Because sautéing is a rapid technique and does not have the tenderizing effect of some of the moist-heat methods, the food to be sautéed must be naturally tender—fish fillets, poultry breasts, and cuts from the rib, loin, or tenderloin, for instance. In this technique food is cooked rapidly in a small amount of fat over relatively high heat. The juices released during cooking form the base for a sauce made in the same pan and served with the sautéed item. The sauce serves three purposes: it captures the food's flavor that is lost during cooking, it introduces additional flavor (an important factor because tender foods have a delicate flavor), and it adds moisture, which counteracts the dryness that results from the sautéing process.

Determining Doneness and Evaluating Quality

To determine doneness in sautéed, stir-fried, pan-fried, and deep-fried foods, chefs rely upon the same guidelines used for grilling, broiling, and roasting. Cooking times for various meats, poultry, and fish are hard to specify, however. While it would be helpful to indicate that a strip loin steak, for example, will be cooked to medium rare in six to seven minutes, such an instruction ignores some crucial factors: the intensity of the heat beneath the pan, the pan's material, the number of meat pieces in the pan, how well aged the meat is, the conditions under which the meat was raised or harvested, and so on. In general, the thinner and more delicate the piece of meat, the more quickly it will cook.

All pan-fried, deep-fried, sautéed, and stir-fried foods should be cooked through (à point).

The following evaluations are for the quality of the sautéed item, not the sauce that accompanies it. The three criteria to use as a gauge of quality for sautéed and stir-fried foods are flavor, color, and texture. The object of sautéing is to produce a flavorful exterior, resulting from proper browning, which serves to intensify the food's flavor. Weak flavor indicates that the food was sautéed at an overly low temperature or that the pan was too crowded. The proper color depends upon the item. Red meats and game should have a deep brown exterior. White meats, such as veal, pork, and poultry, should have a golden or amber exterior. Lean white fish will be pale gold when sautéed as skinless fillets, whereas steaks of firm fish, such as tuna, will take on a darker color. In all cases, the item should not be extremely pale or gray. Improper color is an indication that incorrect pan sizes or improper heat levels were used. Only naturally tender foods should be sautéed, and after sautéing the item should remain tender and moist. Excessive dryness is a signal that the food was allowed to overcook, that it was cooked too far in advance and held too long, or that it was sautéed at a temperature higher than necessary.

The object of pan frying and deep frying is to produce a flavorful exterior with a crisp, brown crust, which acts as a barrier to retain juices and flavor. Because the item itself is not browned, the flavor will be different from that of a sautéed item. The proper color depends upon the type of item, the breading that is used, and, to a certain extent, the item's thickness. The color of relatively thin and delicate items (fish, shellfish, and poultry) should be golden to amber. Thicker pieces may take on a deeper color resulting from the longer cooking time. In all cases, the item should not be extremely pale. As with sautéing, an improper color indicates that improper heat levels or incorrect pan sizes were used. Only naturally tender foods should be pan fried and, after cooking, the item should still be tender and moist. As with sautéing, excessive dryness means the food was allowed to overcook, was cooked too far in advance and held too long, or was cooked at a temperature higher than required.

As with the other methods in this chapter, the important characteristics for deep-fried foods are flavor, color, and texture. Deep-fried foods should taste like the food item being prepared, not like the oil used (or like other foods previously fried in the oil). If the food tastes heavy, oily, or strongly of another food, the oil was not hot enough, the oil was too old, or a strongly flavored food such as fish was fried in the same oil. Most deep-fried foods are done when the items have risen to the oil's surface and their exteriors are evenly brown. In some cases, it may be necessary to finish fried foods, uncovered, in a hot oven (425° to 450°F/220° to 230°C). This is not ideal, because the food's natural juices begin to leak out, resulting in a soggy coating. Foods served very hot, directly from the frying kettle, have a better, less greasy flavor.

With the exception of tempura, which will be light gold in color, most deep-fried foods should have a strong golden color. Overly pale items have been undercooked, cooked in oil that was not hot enough, coated too thickly, or cooked in a crowded fryer. A properly deep-fried food's texture is moist and tender on the interior, with a crisp, delicate crust. If the crust has become soggy, the food may have been held too long after cooking or, again, the oil may not have been at the correct temperature. Another possibility is that the coating was applied too heavily.

Sautéing

METHOD FOR SAUTÉING

1.   Heat a small amount of the cooking medium in an appropriate-size sauté pan over high heat. The cooking medium lubricates the pan and prevents the food from sticking. It also assists in even heat transfer from the pan to the item. Red meats and very thin meat pieces will require the fat to be at, or nearly at, the smoking point. Less intense heat is required for white meats, fish, and shellfish. The pan and the cooking medium must reach the correct temperature before the main item is added, so that a good crust will form on the food's exterior.

2.   Season the main item as desired.

3.   Add the main item to the pan in a single layer, making sure that the pieces do not touch one another. The pan must be large enough to avoid overcrowding. If the pan is crowded, the oil's temperature will drop quickly and a good seal will not form. Without this seal, juices are rapidly released and the result is more a stew than a sauté. Equally important, the pan must not be too large. This can cause the drippings to scorch, rendering them unsuitable for the sauce.

4.   Place the skin side of the main item in the pan first. The side that sautés first will generally have the best appearance. Let the main item sauté undisturbed on the first side

1. Sautéed foods are cooked in a small amount of fat to develop good color and flavor.

2. Heat the pan or wok for stir frying before adding the cooking medium. When the pan is hot, add the vegetables in sequence and stir so that they are in constant motion.

until the proper color develops on the bottom before turning it. Very thin pieces of meat are generally cooked completely on top of the stove, over high heat. Larger cuts or meats that must be cooked through (e.g., veal, chicken, and pork) may need to have the heat beneath them lowered slightly or may need to be finished in an oven, either in the sauté pan or in a second pan.

MAKING A PAN SAUCE FOR A SAUTÉED DISH

1.   Remove the main item and add aromatics and garnish items that require some cooking time, such as shallots, garlic, mushrooms, or tomato concassé. This step must not be overlooked, because juices released into the sauce by these ingredients could cause it to taste bitter or to be overly thin. Shallots and garlic, especially, will impart a harsh flavor if they are not first cooked in butter.

2.   Deglaze the pan by adding a small amount of an appropriate liquid, according to the recipe. Stir the mixture to loosen all the drippings (fond) and allow them to reduce until they are syrupy.

3.   Add jus of the proper flavor or any other base liquid for the sauce. Allow the sauce to simmer until the proper flavor and consistency are reached.

4.   Add prereduced heavy cream, if indicated, as well as ingredients that need only to be heated in the sauce, such as fresh herbs, mustard, peppercorns, and capers. Final adjustments to the sauce's flavor are made at this point. Ingredients such as fortified wines, citrus juices, zest, and salt and pepper are frequently used. Any garnish indicated by the recipe is also added. The sautéed item may need to be returned to the sauce at this point to be reheated briefly and coated thoroughly with the sauce.

5.   Finish the sauce with butter, if indicated. If the item was returned to the sauce for reheating, remove it again and place it on a heated plate or serving dish before adding the butter.

6.   Season the food if necessary and serve it immediately on heated plates.

Stir Frying

Stir frying, generally associated with Asian styles of cooking and successfully borrowed by innovative Western chefs, shares many similarities with sautéing. Foods to be stir fried are customarily cut into small pieces and cooked rapidly in a small amount of oil. Because items to be stir fried are cut into small pieces, which acts as a means of tenderizing the food, the food does not need to be as naturally tender as for sautés, where it is left in portion-size pieces. The foods should be relatively tender, however, and all bits of fat, gristle, or silverskin must be removed for the best results.

A variety of foods may be combined in this technique (meat and vegetables, poultry and fish, and so on), but whatever the main item is, it should be carefully trimmed and cut into evenly shaped pieces.

METHOD FOR STIR FRYING

1.   Cut the main item into an appropriate size and shape, generally thin strips. Marinate it briefly, if required by the recipe, and pat dry before adding it to the cooking oil.

2.   Heat the peanut oil or other cooking oil in a wok or large sauté pan.

3.   Add the main item to the hot oil. The temperature must be very high and the main item must be as dry as possible. This will help lessen splattering that can occur when water comes in contact with hot oil. It will also allow a crust to form on the main item, which intensifies the food's flavor and gives it a good color.

4.   Cook for a short amount of time over high heat, long enough to develop the desired color. Keep the food in constant motion by stirring, lifting, and tossing.

5.   Add any aromatics required by the recipe at the appropriate point (longest-cooking in first, shortest-cooking in last). Continue to stir fry until all of the components are properly cooked and very hot.

6.   Add the liquid for the sauce and any necessary thickener. Cook until the liquid comes to a simmer so that the correct flavor is achieved and the sauce is properly thickened.

7.   Serve the food immediately on heated plates.

Pan Frying

Although pan frying shares similarities with sautéing, it has some important differences. Whereas a sautéed item is often lightly dusted with flour and quickly cooked over high heat in a small amount of oil, a pan-fried food is usually coated with batter or breaded and cooked in a larger amount of oil over less intense heat. The item is cooked more by the oil's heat than by direct contact with the pan.

In pan frying, the hot oil seals the food's coated surface and thereby locks the natural juices inside instead of releasing them. Because no juices are released and a larger amount of oil is involved, any accompanying sauce is made separately.

METHOD FOR PAN FRYING

1.   Add the filling, if required by the recipe. Some items are butterflied and then stuffed. Others may have a pocket cut into them. Do not add too much stuffing because most stuffings will expand during cooking.

2.   Complete the standard breading procedure (see page 54) 1 hour in advance of cooking, and chill the breaded item to allow the coating to firm and dry. Do not stack the breaded items or let them touch each other, or they will become sticky and mat together.

3.   Heat the cooking medium in an appropriate-size sauté pan over medium-high heat. In general, the cooking medium should come one quarter to one half the way up the sides of the food; the thinner the main item, the less oil is required. The pan and the cooking

Add pan-fried foods carefully to hot fat to develop good color and a good crust.

Standard Breading Procedure

1. Dry the main item well.

2. Hold the main item in your left hand (for a right-handed person) and dip it in flour. Shake off any excess.

3. Still using the left hand, transfer the main item to the egg wash. With the right hand, turn the item to coat it evenly.

4. Again using the right hand, transfer the egg-washed item to the bread crumbs. With the left hand, press the crumbs evenly over the surface and transfer the item to a holding tray. (If left-handed, use opposite hands.)

medium must reach the correct temperature before the item is added, so that a good crust will form on the food's exterior. When a faint haze or slight shimmer is noticeable, the cooking medium is hot enough.

4. Add the main item to the pan in a single layer, making sure that the pieces do not touch one another. The pan must be large enough to avoid overcrowding. If the pan is crowded, the oil's temperature will drop quickly and a good seal will not form. If this happens, the food may absorb the oil and the breading can become soggy or even fall away in places.

5. Allow the main item to pan fry on the first side until the breading is well browned. Keep the pieces in motion, either by gently swirling the pan or by moving the pieces with tongs. (Forks are not used for this purpose—or in any other dry-heat method—because they can pierce the food and cause the release of valuable juices.) A layer of cooking fat should lie between the item and the pan. Then turn the food once and cook to the appropriate degree of doneness. Thin pieces of meat are generally cooked completely on top of the stove, over medium heat. Larger cuts or meats that must be cooked through (e.g., veal, chicken, and pork) may need additional cooking over low heat once they have browned or may need to be finished in an oven, uncovered, in the sauté pan or in a second pan.

6. Briefly drain the food on racks or paper towels, season it if necessary, and serve it on heated plates with the appropriate sauce.

Deep Frying

In deep frying, foods are cooked by being completely submerged in hot fat. (Significantly greater amounts of fat are used than for either sautéing or pan frying.) The food is almost always given a coating—a standard breading, a batter such as a tempura or beer batter, or, in some instances, a simple flour coating. The coating acts as a barrier between the fat and the item and also contributes a contrasting flavor and texture. As with the other dry-heat methods that use cooking fats and oils, the foods must be naturally tender and of a shape and size that allow them to cook quickly without becoming tough or dry. Poultry and fish are the most commonly selected foods for deep frying. In some cases, cooked meats are made into croquettes and then deep fried. There are several specific terms related to deep frying.

SWIMMING METHOD. Foods are gently dropped in hot oil; they fall to the bottom of the fryer and are then allowed to "swim" to the surface. They may be gently turned once they reach the surface, to allow them to brown evenly. They are then removed with a skimmer. This method is most often used for batter-coated foods.

BASKET METHOD. The foods are placed in a basket that is lowered into the hot oil, and then they are lifted out in the basket once properly cooked. This method is generally used for breaded items.

DOUBLE-BASKET METHOD. Certain types of food, in order to develop a good crust, need to be fully submerged in hot oil for a fairly long time. Foods that would tend to rise to the surface too rapidly are placed in a basket that is lowered into the hot oil, and then held under the oil's surface by the bottom of a second basket.

RECOVERY TIME. This is the amount of time it takes the oil to return to the correct temperature after an item has been cooked. The food absorbs some of the heat, causing the oil's temperature to drop. The more food items in the oil, the lower the temperature drops and the longer the recovery time.

SMOKING POINT. This is the temperature at which fats and oils begin to smoke, indicating that the fat has begun to break down. The higher a particular fat or oil's smoking point, the higher the temperature at which it is safe to cook with that fat or oil.

BLANCHING. This means giving foods a preliminary cooking at a lower temperature, before they are finished at the time of service at a higher temperature. During the initial cooking, the food cooks evenly but the crust does not brown completely. In finishing, the food is reheated to develop the proper color. This procedure is especially useful when it is not possible to cook a food, such as fried chicken, immediately prior to service in a reasonable amount of time.

MISE EN PLACE FOR DEEP FRYING

1. *Main item.* Remove any bones. Bones are usually removed because they slow down the cooking process. Cut the item into the appropriate size. Foods should be fairly thin, with a uniform size and shape so that they can cook rapidly and evenly. Remove the skin (especially from fish), as desired or as indicated in the recipe. Remove any gristle, fat, and silverskin or any inedible shells. Cut the food into chunks or fingers, or butterfly and pound it, depending upon the food's nature and the desired result.

2. *Coating.* Breading may be done up to 1 hour in advance of deep frying and the item may be chilled to allow the breading to firm. For best quality, apply batter or plain flour immediately before cooking. Have available the ingredients for a standard breading, batter or tempura coating, or flour coating.

3. *Cooking medium.* The cooking medium must be able to reach a high temperature without smoking or breaking down. Have available a neutral-flavored oil with a high smoking point. A rendered fat, such as lard, may be used to create a special flavor or effect, as in certain regional dishes such as Southern fried chicken.

4. *Optional components.* This is often a stuffing. A classic example is chicken Kiev, in which the meat is butterflied and pounded to increase its surface area. The appropriate filling, a garlic butter, is encased completely by rolling and folding the meat around the filling. The item is then coated and deep fried.

METHOD FOR DEEP FRYING

1.   Heat the cooking fat to the proper temperature. If a food is added to oil that is too cool, the food's surface will not form a proper seal and the food will become soggy and greasy. In addition, water from the food will be released into the oil, shortening the oil's life.

2.   Add the main item to the hot cooking fat in the proper manner. Use the swimming method for items coated with batter and the basket method for items coated with standard breading.

3.   Turn the items during frying if necessary. Items coated with batter must be turned because the batter will frequently cause the food to float at the surface, with part of the food above the oil level. To ensure even browning, turn the food using tongs or a kitchen fork, being careful not to pierce the item.

4.   Remove the items from the oil as soon as they are fully cooked (see "Determining Doneness and Evaluating Quality," page 50) and blot them on paper towels. They may be seasoned with salt at this point. They must not be suspended over the fryer when they are salted, because salt contributes to the oil's breakdown.

5.   Serve the food immediately on heated plates with the appropriate sauce.

Heat the oil for deep frying to the appropriate temperature prior to adding the foods to be fried. Deep-fried foods will have a nice crust and a tender center.

Fat and Oil Selection and Maintenance

Both fats and oils may be used as a cooking medium for deep frying, although vegetable oil is most commonly used. Fats and oils differ in specific properties but are all basically the same compound and contain a combination of fatty acids, flavor, and glycerin. In general, a neutral flavor and color and a high smoking point (around 425°F/218°C) are the most important considerations in choosing an oil for deep frying. In deep frying, several practices, in addition to selecting the proper oil, will help prolong the oil's life. Follow these ten guidelines:

1.   Store oils in a cool, dry area and keep them away from strong lights, which leach vitamin A.

2.   Use high-quality oils.

3.   Prevent the oil from coming in contact with copper, brass, or bronze, because these metals hasten breakdown.

4.   When frying moist items, dry them as thoroughly as possible before placing them in oil, because water breaks down the oil and lowers the smoking point.

5.   Do not salt items over the pan because salt breaks down the oil.

6.   Fry items at the proper temperature. Do not overheat the oil.

7.   Turn off the fryer after using it and cover it when it is not being used for long periods of time.

8.   Constantly remove any small particles (such as loose bits of breading or batter) from the oil during use.

9.   Filter the kettle's entire contents after each shift, if possible, or at least once a day. After the oil has been properly filtered, replace 20 percent of the original volume with fresh oil to extend the life of the entire amount.

10.   Discard the oil if it becomes rancid, smokes below 350°F/175°C, or foams excessively. As oil is used, it will darken; if it is a great deal darker than when it was fresh, it will brown the food too rapidly. The food may appear properly cooked but actually be underdone.

MOIST-HEAT COOKING

Once man was able to produce cooking vessels of clay or metal that were both watertight and able to withstand direct heat, foods could be prepared by methods other than roasting them over a fire. Moist-heat techniques have traditionally been a frugal way to prepare foods. Often an entire meal—meats, fish, vegetables, and grains—is prepared in a single pot. The classic dishes of many cuisines—the New England boiled dinner and the French pot-au-feu, for example—capitalize on the fact that in addition to producing a moist, tender, and delicately flavored food, these techniques also produce a good quantity of a rich, deeply flavored broth. This broth can be served as a separate course or can form the basis for a sauce. Moist-heat techniques offer you the opportunity to present healthful and appealing dishes with a range of flavors, textures, and appearances not available through other methods. The moist-heat techniques are

Steaming

En papillote

Shallow poaching

Poaching and simmering

Moist-heat cooking methods are used to produce flavorful dishes by cooking the main item in a liquid bath. The amount of liquid varies from one technique to another. Unlike dry-heat methods, moist-heat cookery does not form a seal on the food as an initial step in the cooking process. Without this seal, a certain amount of flavor is transferred from the food into the cooking liquid. For this reason, it is important to either hold the flavor and juices in the food during cooking by wrapping the main item with lettuce or other coverings prior to cooking, or to recapture the flavor by serving the juices as part of the finished dish.

Moist-heat techniques result in products that have a distinctly different flavor, texture, and appearance from those prepared with dry-heat methods. Instead of having a rich color and flavor, steamed, shallow-poached, poached, and simmered foods are generally pale in color and have a delicate flavor. With the exception of simmering, these techniques require the use of naturally tender meat, poultry, or fish; all moist-heat techniques require a flavorful liquid. Careful monitoring of cooking temperatures and times and the ability to determine doneness are critical to a mastery of moist-heat methods.

MISE EN PLACE

1.   *Main items for steaming, shallow poaching, and poaching.* Items to be prepared by steaming, shallow poaching, and poaching should be naturally tender and of a size and shape that will allow them to cook in a short amount of time. Cut the main item into the appropriate sizes. Remove the skin and bones from fish to prepare fillets. Remove the skin and bones from poultry and game birds, if desired. Score whole fish (make shallow cuts at regular intervals), if desired, to promote even cooking and flavor penetration. Leave shellfish in the shells, unless otherwise indicated (scallops are customarily removed from the shell, for example).

2.   *Main items for simmering.* Simmered foods need not be tender, because the process will tenderize them. Both poached and simmered items are usually whole fish or poultry or large pieces of meat. Wrap whole fish in cheesecloth to protect it from breaking apart during cooking. Stuff poultry, if desired, and truss it to help retain its shape. Stuff meats, if desired, and tie them to maintain their shape.

Determining Doneness and Evaluating Quality

Steamed foods should be cooked until they are just done but not overcooked, because they can easily become rubbery and dry. Any juices from the food should be nearly color-less. The flesh of fish and shellfish will lose its translucency when properly cooked, taking on a nearly opaque appearance. The shells of mollusks (mussels, clams, and oysters) will open when properly cooked and the edges of the flesh should curl. Crustaceans (shrimp, crab, and lobster) should have a bright pink or red color. Poultry should take on an evenly opaque appearance and the flesh should offer little resistance when pressed with a fin-gertip. Unlike dry-heat techniques, no initial browning of the food occurs, so the flavor of steamed foods is delicate. Any aromatics used during cooking should be appropriate for the food's flavor and should not be so intense as to overwhelm it. Steamed foods are usually pale in color, and the surface should appear quite moist. Fish, especially salmon, should not have deposits of white albumin on the flesh, which indicate that a fish has been overcooked and/or cooked too quickly. Steamed foods should be moist and plump. Food suitable for this technique is naturally tender, and if not overcooked, it will remain tender. There should be no hint of rubberiness or dryness.

Foods prepared en papillote should be cooked until they are just done. This is dif-ficult to gauge without experience, since you cannot apply the senses of sight and touch in determining doneness. If the item has been cut to the correct size or if it has been partially cooked before being placed en papillote, it should be done when the bag is very puffy and the paper is brown.

Shallow-poached foods should reflect both the flavor of the main item and the cook-ing liquid's ingredients. Because acidic and aromatic ingredients are included, the flavor should be "bright." The beurre blanc or other sauce should add a rich, complementary flavor. Shallow-poached foods should be very tender and exceptionally moist. Because this technique is most often used with delicate foods, the product should have an almost fragile texture. If the item is falling apart or has become dry, it has been overcooked.

Poached and simmered foods should not be overcooked. As with steamed foods, most fish should appear nearly opaque in all areas, particularly near the backbone. Shellfish such as lobster and shrimp should turn a bright pink or red; the shells of mollusks (mus-sels, clams, and oysters) should open and the flesh should begin to curl at the edges.

Poultry and meats should be fork-tender, which means the meat should slide easily from a kitchen fork. Juices that run from the poultry at the point where the thigh meets the breast or from the thickest part of a piece of meat should be nearly clear or have a slight pink blush.

If a poached or simmered item is to be served cold, it should be slightly undercooked. The pot should be removed from the heat and the food allowed to cool in the poaching liquid. The liquid will retain some heat, which will complete the cooking process. Cool the liquid in a cold or ice water bath to prevent bacterial growth. Once it has reached room temperature, the item may be removed for any further preparation. The liquid is custom-arily used in a sauce or as the basis of another dish.

Poached or simmered items should have an appropriate but generally light color. Poultry, especially breast meat, should be almost white. Fish should be opaque, with a delicate color appropriate for the type. For example, turbot should be very white and salmon should be a delicate pink or orange-pink color. However, there should be no de-posits of white albumin on the flesh. Meats should be beige, light brown, or, in the case of white meats such as veal, an ivory color, but never gray. Proper tying or trussing of the item will ensure that its natural shape is preserved. Holding the item correctly once the cooking time is complete is also an important factor in preventing the food from breaking apart. As noted throughout the discussion of this technique, the aim of poaching and simmering is to produce foods that are moist and extremely tender. Any stringiness, dryness, rubberiness, or excessive flaking indicates that the item may have been cooked for too long or at too high a temperature. If the item is not tender or is chewy, it may not have been allowed to cook sufficiently.

Steaming

Steaming cooks food by surrounding it with a vapor bath. Relatively little flavor and moisture are lost, but it is advisable to protect the food in some way during cooking by wrapping or coating it. For example, fish may be wrapped in lettuce leaves or corn husks. The liquid used in steaming often includes herbs, spices, and other aromatics, and these flavors are transferred from the steam to the food during cooking. Foods are placed in a closed vessel, and are above and not touching the liquid. As the liquid comes to a boil, some of it will turn into steam. When the steam comes in contact with the food's surface, the vapor's heat is transferred to the food. Steam circulating around the food provides an even, moist environment, which allows the food to retain most of its natural juices. If an aromatic liquid such as stock, beer, or tea is used or if aromatic ingredients are added to the liquid to make a court bouillon, some flavor transfer from the steam to the food may occur. A flavorful liquid may be served as a broth or it may be further reduced and used as a sauce base. Steamed foods generally contain a greater proportion of nutrients, because water-soluble nutrients are not drawn out of the food as readily. Properly steamed foods do not generally lose much of their original volume, and they are exceptionally moist and tender.

METHOD FOR STEAMING

1.   Bring the liquid to a full boil in a covered vessel. Because the steam is trapped in a covered cooking vessel, a small amount of pressure will build up. Enough liquid should be used to assure that the food will cook completely without requiring the addition of more liquid during cooking. When opening the pot to add the main item, take care to avoid a burn by removing the lid so that the steam will vent away from your face and hands.

2.   Add the main item to the steamer on a rack in a single layer. To ensure even cooking, foods should be placed in a single layer, not touching one another, so that the steam can circulate completely. More than one layer of food may be cooked at a time in a tiered steamer. Foods may be placed on plates or in shallow dishes on the rack in order to collect any juices that might escape.

3.   Replace the lid and allow the steam to build up again. It is a good idea to adjust the heat to maintain even, moderate heat. Even if the liquid is only at a simmer, it can still produce steam, and rapid boiling will cause the liquid to cook away too quickly. Once the food is in the steamer and the cover has been replaced, avoid removing the lid unnecessarily, because the steam can dissipate rapidly, causing cooking to slow down.

4.   Steam the main item to the correct doneness.

5.   Serve the food immediately on heated plates with an appropriate sauce, as desired or as indicated by the recipe.

1. Use flavorful liquids seasoned with aromatic vegetables and/or fresh herbs to infuse the steamed items with flavor.

2. Place the main items, aromatic vegetables, flavorful liquids, and seasonings in parchment paper packages (en papillote), then bake the packages so that the contents cook in their own steam.

En Papillote

In this variation of steaming, the main item and accompanying ingredients are encased in parchment paper (en papillote) and cooked in a hot oven (425° to 450°F/220° to 230°C). The main item rests on a bed of herbs, vegetables, or sauce and the combination of these ingredients and the natural juices serves as the sauce. The steam created by the food's natural juices cooks the food. As the steam volume increases, the paper puffs up.

METHOD FOR EN PAPILLOTE

1.   Cut the parchment paper into a heart shape large enough to hold the main item on one half of the heart, with a 1-inch margin of paper all the way around. Oil or butter the paper on both sides to prevent it from burning.

2.   Place a bed of aromatics, vegetables, or sauce on one half of the heart and top it with the main item.

3.   Fold the empty half of the heart over the main item and fold and crimp the edges of the paper to form a tight seal.

4.   Place the bag on a preheated sizzler platter and put it in a very hot oven.

5.   Bake the food until the bag is highly puffy and the paper is browned. The oven temperature may need to be carefully monitored since delicate foods such as fish fillets can be overcooked quickly at a high temperature. A thicker cut may be best if it is cooked slowly at a moderate temperature (350° to 375°F/175° to 190°C) and then "puffed" in a very hot oven.

6.   Serve en papillote dishes at once. Depending upon the service style of the restaurant, the guest may cut or tear open the packet themselves, or the server may present the dish and then slit it open in front of the guest.

Shallow Poaching

Shallow poaching cooks foods using a combination of steam and a liquid bath. The food is partially submerged in a liquid that often contains an acid, such as wine or lemon juice, and aromatics, such as shallots and herbs. The cooking vessel is covered to capture some of the steam released by the liquid during cooking; the captured steam cooks the portion of the food not directly in the liquid.

In shallow poaching, a significant amount of flavor is transferred between the food and the liquid. In order to retain the flavor released into the liquid, the liquid is reduced and used as a sauce base. The acid in the cooking liquid makes it easier for butter to be emulsified in the sauce; thus, a beurre blanc is often the sauce of choice. Like sautéing and grilling, this is an à la minute technique suited to foods that are cut into portion-size or smaller pieces.

METHOD FOR SHALLOW POACHING

1.   Add a quantity of whole butter or stock to a sauté pan. This will act as the cooking medium to smother the aromatic ingredients.

2.   Make a bed of aromatic ingredients. Smother chopped shallots and julienned vegetables until tender and make them into a bed on the bottom of the pan. This bed will elevate the food item so that it will cook evenly and not stick to the pan.

3.   Add the main item and the cooking liquid. The liquid's level should be no higher than halfway up the item; generally, less liquid is required. If too much is used, either a great deal of time will be needed for it to reduce properly or only part of it will be usable in the sauce. This is undesirable and could result in a flavor loss in both the main item and the sauce.

4.   Bring the liquid to a bare simmer over direct heat. Do not allow the liquid to boil, because it could cause delicate fish flesh to break apart or poultry and game suprêmes to toughen.

5.   Lightly cover the pan with parchment paper. It is not necessary or even desirable to cover the pan tightly. Cooking speed is difficult to monitor, and it is easy for the item to overcook or become tough if it is too tightly covered.

6.   Finish cooking the main item either over direct heat or in a medium-hot oven (350° to 375°F/175° to 190°C). Acceptable results can be achieved by finishing the cooking over direct heat; however, the heat in an oven, which is more even and gentle, is preferable. In addition, finishing shallow poaching in the oven makes burner space available for other purposes.

7.   Transfer the main item to a holding dish and moisten it with a small amount of the cooking liquid. Cover the item and keep it warm while completing the sauce.

8.   Reduce the cooking liquid to a syrupy consistency and prepare a beurre blanc or other sauce, as desired.

9.   Serve the food immediately on heated plates with the sauce.

Poaching and Simmering

Poaching and simmering are techniques that call for a food to be completely submerged in a liquid that is kept at a constant, moderate temperature. The distinction between the two is a slight difference in cooking temperature. Poaching cooks foods at 180° to 185°F/81° to 82°C and is generally associated with tender foods like salmon, chicken breast, and eggs. The surface of a poaching liquid should show some motion, sometimes called "shivering," but no air bubbles should break the surface. Often, poaching is used to partially cook foods in order to make it easy to remove membranes, to help retain shape, or to remove any blood or impurities.

1. Add shallow-poaching liquid to a level no higher than halfway up the main item to properly cook the food and also to infuse the main item with flavor.

2. Lower foods into flavorful liquid that has been brought to the appropriate poaching temperature. Submerge the foods completely in order to cook them properly.

Simmering is generally associated with less tender foods, including cuts of beef or pork or shank meat, which are cooked at a slightly higher temperature, 185° to 200°F/82° to 93°C. There is slightly more action on the liquid's surface, with some air bubbles breaking. Simmered foods are often referred to as being "boiled" (e.g., boiled beef); however, this is not an accurate description of the temperature. In fact, the liquid's temperature should be kept as close to a boil as possible without ever reaching a true boil. Very few foods are truly boiled, because such a vigorous cooking speed causes most meats, fish, and poultry to become tough and stringy.

The liquid used in poaching and simmering should be appropriate for the food and well flavored in order to compensate for any flavor lost during cooking. Stock, broth, or court bouillon are all appropriate, depending upon the type of food and the desired result.

It is important to use good-quality stocks and enough aromatic ingredients, such as herbs, wines, spices, and vegetables, to produce a full, pleasing flavor in both the finished product and in any sauce prepared from the liquid. Poached and simmered items may also be served with a pungent sauce prepared separately, as in the custom of serving "boiled" beef with a horseradish sauce.

METHOD FOR POACHING AND SIMMERING

1.   Bring the cooking liquid to a simmer in a pot. This will both reduce the amount of flavor lost from the main item to the cooking liquid and shorten the cooking time. The pot should be large enough to easily accommodate the main item, with sufficient headroom to allow for both the liquid's expansion as it heats and the displacement of the liquid when the main item is added. A pot that is too large will not produce the most flavorful product because the amount of liquid needed to cover the main item will be greater.

2.   Add the main item. If the item is exceptionally delicate (e.g., turbot or halibut), be sure that precautions have been taken to prevent the flesh from breaking up during cooking (e.g., wrapping the fish in cheesecloth or tying it). In addition, use a rack or trivet to elevate the item from the pot bottom. Be sure that the item is completely submerged in the liquid, which is especially important for poultry. If a part of the food is above the cooking liquid's level, cooking will be uneven, and the finished product will probably not have the properly delicate color.

3.   Maintain the proper cooking speed throughout the poaching or simmering process. Make sure the liquid does not boil. Check the temperature periodically with an instant-read

thermometer and adjust the heat as necessary to stay within 160° to 185°F/71° to 85°C. If a cover is used on a fish poacher, the cooking speed must be monitored. Covering a pot has the effect of creating pressure, which allows the liquid's temperature to become higher. As is true for shallow-poached items, it is sometimes desirable to complete poaching or simmering in an oven, once the proper cooking temperature has been reached over direct heat. Common sense will indicate which items can be placed in an oven and which should remain on the stovetop. For instance, it would be difficult and dangerous to lift a large pot full of hot liquid off the stove and transfer it to an oven.

4. Carefully transfer the main item to a holding container and moisten it with some of the liquid to prevent it from drying.

5. Cut or slice the main item as necessary and serve it immediately on heated plates with the appropriate sauce.

COMBINATION COOKING METHODS

Combination cooking methods are so called because they apply both dry heat and moist heat to the main item. The two major combination techniques are

Braising

Stewing

Because they require less tender (and less expensive) main ingredients than à la minute techniques, braises and stews are often referred to as "peasant" dishes. These dishes traditionally have had a robust, hearty flavor and are often thought of as "winter meals"; however, with some modification, braising and stewing techniques have valid applications year-round. The customary heavy foods are being replaced with poultry, fish, and shellfish, which can be faster to prepare, are lighter in flavor and color, and are appropriate for most contemporary menus.

Combination methods are most often considered appropriate for foods that are flavorful but are too tough to be successfully prepared by any of the à la minute techniques. However, tender foods can also be braised or stewed successfully using less cooking liquid, a lower temperature, and a shorter cooking time.

The first step for most combination methods is to sear the main item. The item is then cooked completely in the presence of a liquid—this may be simply the juices released from the food, which are already present, or a liquid that is added to the pot. Because the cooking vessel is covered during most of the cooking time, these liquids turn to steam and the food cooks by simmering and steaming.

The result of a properly prepared braise or stew is a dish of complexity and flavor concentration that is simply not possible with other cooking techniques. The sauce also has exceptional body, because of the slow cooking needed to dissolve the main item's tough connective tissues. The proteins and other nutrients "lost" from the main item into the cooking liquid are not lost to the dish itself.

Braising and stewing are often associated with regional, home-style cooking. The successful use of these techniques depends, as do all cookery methods, on the proper choice of main ingredients and careful attention to each step of preparation and service. Contemporary renditions of classic dishes, such as a navarin made with lobster instead of mutton, are clear proof that no cooking technique need become outmoded.

Evaluating Quality

The factors for evaluating quality are flavor, appearance, and texture. Braised foods should have an intense flavor as the result of long, gentle cooking. The main item's natural juices, along with the braising liquid, become concentrated, providing both a depth of flavor and a full-bodied sauce. If a braised food does not have a robust flavor, it may have been undercooked or perhaps was allowed to braise at an overly high temperature for an insufficient time. Another possibility is that the main item was not seared properly, with inadequate time allowed for browning the item before liquids were introduced. Finally, if the lid was not removed from the pot during the final stage of cooking, the sauce may not have reduced properly and a glaze may not have been allowed to form on the main item's surface.

Braised foods should have a deep color appropriate for the type of food. They should retain their natural shape, although a significant amount of volume is lost during cooking. To maintain the proper shape throughout the cooking time, the main item should be trussed or tied. It is also important to maintain the proper cooking speed.

Braised foods should be extremely tender, almost to the point at which they can be cut with a fork. They should not, however, fall into shreds; this would indicate that the main item has been overcooked.

Determining Doneness

Properly cooked braised foods are fork-tender. This means that they will slide easily from a kitchen fork inserted at the food's thickest part.

Braising

In braising, the item is first seared in hot oil and then slowly cooked in a liquid medium. This technique is considered appropriate for foods that are portion-size or larger, or cuts from more exercised areas of large animals, mature whole birds, or large fish. Relatively little liquid (stock or jus) is used in relation to the main item's volume. A bed of mirepoix, which lifts the main item away from the pot bottom, also introduces additional moisture and flavor.

One of braising's benefits is that less tender cuts of meat become tender as the moist heat gently penetrates the meat and causes tough connective tissues to soften. Another bonus is that any flavor from the item is released into the cooking liquid, which becomes the accompanying sauce; thus, virtually all flavor and nutrients are retained.

This does not mean that tender foods, even delicate fish and shellfish, cannot be braised. To properly braise these kinds of foods, you use less cooking liquid and must cook the food at a lower temperature and for a shorter time.

The first step for most braises is to sear the main item in a small amount of hot fat. This develops the proper flavor and color and is done in a rondeau or brazier over direct heat on the stovetop. Mirepoix is then allowed to lightly brown or sweat in the same pot and the cooking liquid is added and brought to a simmer. Once these steps are completed, the pot is usually covered and placed in a medium-hot oven (350° to 375°F/175° to 190°C).

Braising in the oven tends to result in a better product without danger of causing the food to scorch from prolonged contact with a pot in direct contact with an open flame. Air is a less efficient conductor than metal, so the result is a gentler transfer of heat. There is also less chance of inadvertently overcooking (and thereby toughening) the item. Finally, burner space is kept open for other needs.

Braised foods gain flavor and tenderness from slow cooking time.

If all the braising is to be done on the stovetop, certain precautions must be taken. The cooking speed must be carefully regulated because the liquid can easily become too hot. If this happens, the portion of the main item covered by the liquid will cook more quickly than any exposed areas and could become tough or stringy. Scorching will also be a problem.

The following is a partial listing of braising techniques and specific names for braised dishes of various types.

DAUBE. A daube is a braise customarily made from red meats, often beef, and including red wine. The main item is often marinated before braising. The name is derived from the French word for the pot used to prepare a daube, the *daubière*, which has an indentation in the lid to hold hot pieces of charcoal.

ESTOUFFADE. This is a French term used to refer to the braising method and the dish itself.

POT ROAST. This common American term for *braise* is also the name of a traditional braised dish.

SWISSING. This is a braising technique often associated with portion-size meat cuts. The main item is repeatedly dredged in flour and pounded to tenderize the flesh (Swiss steak is one example).

METHOD FOR BRAISING

1. Sear the main item in hot oil in a rondeau, brazier, or tilt kettle. White meat and poultry should be seared only to the point at which the skin begins to turn color. Red meats should be seared to a deep brown color. Fish may not require an initial searing.

2. Remove the main item from the pot and add the mirepoix. For white meats, fish, poultry, and game birds, sweat the mirepoix until the onions are translucent. For red meats and large game, sweat until the onions are golden-brown. If a roux is being used as a sauce thickener, it may be added at this point.

3. Place the main item on the bed of mirepoix in the pot. The mirepoix furnishes both moisture and flavor. It also elevates the main item somewhat from the pot bottom and helps to prevent it from sticking.

4. Add the appropriate amount of liquid. There should be just enough liquid to keep the main item moistened throughout the cooking time and to produce an adequate amount of sauce to serve with the finished dish. The more tender the main item, the less liquid will be required, because the cooking time will be shorter and there will be less opportunity for the liquid to reduce properly. In general, the liquid should cover the main item only by one third.

5. Bring the liquid to a simmer over direct heat.

6. Cover the pot and place it in a medium-hot oven (350° to 375°F/175° to 190°C). The more tender the item, the lower the oven's temperature should be. Covering the pot allows the steam to condense on the lid and fall back onto the main item, moistening the food's exposed surfaces. The main item should be turned from time to time during cooking to keep all surfaces evenly moistened with the braising liquid.

7.   Add the sachet d'épices or bouquet garni and vegetable garnish at the appropriate times to assure proper flavor extraction and cooking.

8.   Remove the lid during the final portion of the cooking time. This will cause the braising liquid to reduce adequately so that the sauce will have the proper consistency and flavor. Also, if the main item is turned frequently after the lid has been removed and is thus exposed to hot air, a glaze will form on its surface, providing a glossy sheen and a good flavor.

9.   Remove the main item from the braising liquid when it is fork-tender (see "Determining Doneness," page 64).

10.   Place the pot over direct heat and continue to reduce the sauce to develop its flavor, body, and consistency. This additional reduction fortifies the sauce's flavor and provides an opportunity to skim away any surface fat. Add additional finishing or garnishing ingredients at this point, as appropriate.

11.   Strain the sauce. The mirepoix that is strained out may be either discarded or puréed and returned to the sauce. The sachet d'épices or bouquet garni should be discarded. Return the sauce to the heat and bring it to a boil. Add diluted arrowroot or cornstarch to lightly thicken the sauce, if desired. Add any final finishing or garnishing ingredients. Adjust seasoning with salt and pepper.

12.   Carve or slice the main item and serve it on heated plates with the sauce and an appropriate garnish.

Stewing

Stewing is similar to braising; the same meat cuts are used, but the main item is cut into bite-size pieces. The amount of liquid used in relation to the amount of the item varies from one style of preparation to another. Some stews call for very little additional liquid; others may call for proportionately more liquid than the main item. A stew's components do not differ to any substantial degree from those of a braise.

The technique for stewing is also nearly identical to that for braising, although a few optional steps in stewing allow the chef to vary the results. For example, initial blanching of the main item, instead of searing, results in a pale, almost ivory-colored stew. Because the main item is cut into small pieces, the cooking time for stewing is shorter than for braising.

The following is a partial listing of stews of various types.

BLANQUETTE. This white stew is traditionally made from white meats (veal or chicken) or lamb, and is garnished with mushrooms and pearl onions. The sauce is always white and is finished with a liaison of egg yolks and heavy cream.

BOUILLABAISSE. This is a Mediterranean-style fish stew combining a variety of fish and shellfish.

FRICASSÉE. This is a white stew, often made from veal, poultry, or small game (e.g., rabbit).

GOULASH (GULYÁS). This stew originated in Hungary and is made from beef, veal, or poultry, seasoned and colored with paprika, and generally served with potatoes and dumplings.

NAVARIN. This is a stew traditionally prepared from mutton or lamb, with a garnish of root vegetables, onions, and peas. The name probably derives from the French word for turnips, *navets*, which are the principal garnish.

Sear meat for stews in hot fat before covering it with flavorful liquid and cooking it until tender.

RAGOÛT. A French term for stew, this literally translates as "restores the appetite."

MATELOTE. This is a special type of fish stew, typically prepared with eel, although other fish may be used. Other fish stews that are served as main courses include bouillabaisse, cioppino, and bourride.

METHOD FOR STEWING

1.   Cut the main item into pieces of the desired size. Sear the main item in a skillet or rondeau in hot oil or blanch it by placing it in a pot of cold stock or water and bringing the liquid to a boil. Searing the main item assists in developing color and flavor.

In order to develop a good color, the main item should not be added to the hot oil in quantities so large that the pieces are touching one another. If they are touching, the pan's temperature will be lowered significantly, hindering proper coloring. Instead, the item should be seared in batches, and each batch should be removed when it has developed a good color. The main item is generally dredged in flour prior to searing, to assist in lightly thickening the cooking liquid.

Alternatively, the main item may be blanched instead of seared. Like searing, blanching improves the color and flavor of the finished stew. Skim the surface of the blanching liquid to remove any impurities that could give the stew a gray color or an off flavor. Once a boil is reached, drain the main item.

2.   Remove the main item from the pot and add the mirepoix. Lightly brown the mirepoix, or, for stews that should remain pale in color, sweat it until the vegetables begin to release their juices and become translucent.

3.   Place the main item on the bed of mirepoix in the pot, add the appropriate cooking liquid, and bring it to a simmer. Some stews call for only a small amount of liquid, relying on the main item's natural juices to provide moisture. This is especially true for stews made from naturally tender foods such as fish or shellfish. Other stews may include proportionately more liquid than the main item. See the specific recipes for guidance.

4.   Cover the pot and place it in a medium-hot oven (350° to 375°F/175° to 190°C), or cook it over direct heat on the stovetop.

5.   Add the aromatics and vegetable garnish, if necessary or desired, at the appropriate times to assure proper flavor extraction and cooking.

6.   Stew the food until a piece of the main item is tender to the bite.

7.   Strain the sauce. The mirepoix that is strained out may be either discarded or puréed and returned to the sauce. The sachet d'épices or bouquet garni should be discarded. Return the sauce to the heat and bring it to a boil. Add diluted arrowroot or cornstarch to lightly thicken the sauce, if desired. Add any final finishing or garnishing ingredients. Adjust seasoning with salt and pepper.

8.   Serve the stew on heated plates with the sauce and the appropriate garnish.

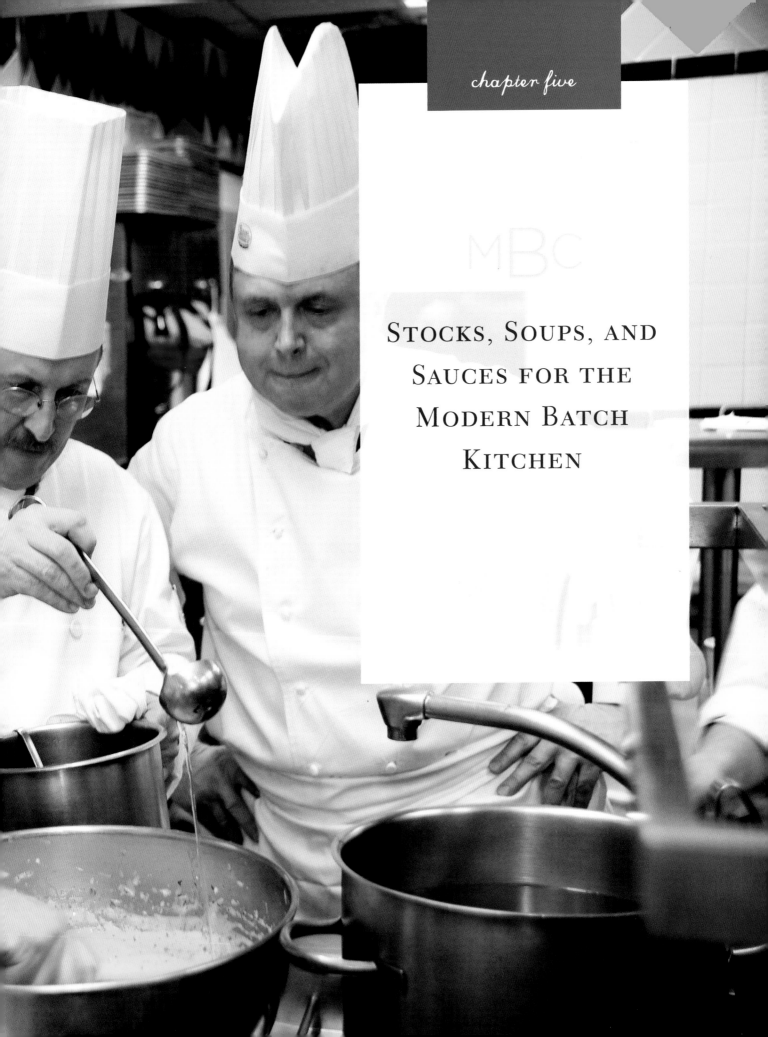

chapter five

STOCKS, SOUPS, AND SAUCES FOR THE MODERN BATCH KITCHEN

STOCKS

You can evaluate stocks on the basis of four criteria: flavor, color, aroma, and clarity. If the correct procedure and ratio of bones, mirepoix, and aromatics to liquid has been followed, the flavor should be well balanced, rich, and full-bodied. The major flavoring ingredient should dominate; for example, chicken stock should taste like chicken. The flavors of the mirepoix and aromatics should be unobtrusive. A stock's flavor should be fresh; all stocks should be checked before they are used in another preparation. To do this, reboil a small amount and taste it.

The recipes included in Chapter 6 indicate the proper ingredients and required amounts for specific stocks. Once you have performed any required preliminary steps (such as blanching, sweating, or browning) with the major flavoring ingredient), you can prepare all stocks, essences, fumets, and court bouillons the same way.

METHOD FOR STOCK

1. Combine the major flavoring ingredient(s) with cold liquid(s) and bring to a simmer. The stock will throw scum to the surface as it develops. This should be skimmed away as necessary throughout the simmering time to develop a clear stock with a good flavor.

2. Add the mirepoix and aromatics at the appropriate point. Add them at the start of cooking time for stocks, fumets, essences, and court bouillons simmered for less than 1 hour. Add them for the last hour of cooking time for stocks simmered for more than 2 hours.

3. Simmer for the appropriate time. Developing a good flavor, aroma, color, and body is important.

4. Drain the stock through a sieve or colander into an appropriate container for cooling. A stock's clarity is better preserved if the major flavoring ingredients and mirepoix are disturbed as little as possible. If the pot does not have a spigot, ladle the stock from the pot rather than pouring it through a sieve. This is a safer procedure, because it is less likely to spill or splash. Discard the bones, mirepoix, and aromatics.

1. Skim the scum from the surface to create a clear stock.

2. Add the mirepoix at the appropriate point to extract the maximum amount of flavor.

3. If not using immediately, cool the stock over an ice water bath.

5.   Cool the stock in an ice water bath. Stirring from time to time helps the stock cool more rapidly.

6.   Store the stock in appropriate containers and hold under refrigeration. Be sure to properly label and date stocks. It is not necessary to remove any fat from the stock surface until after it is thoroughly chilled. The fat will harden and form a protective seal. When the stock is to be used, the fat can easily be lifted away and discarded.

SOUPS

Soup is often the first dish a restaurant's guest will be served. A well-prepared soup will make a positive initial impression. Soups should always be carefully presented—hot soups hot and cold soups cold—in serving dishes that have been properly heated or chilled. Soups are not difficult to make as the techniques are straightforward, but there are many options for major flavoring ingredients and garnishes.

The following are general guidelines that pertain to most soups.

Cooking

1. Stir and skim soup to keep it from sticking and to remove any scum or foam.

2. Place a crouton over a spoon for an attractive but practical presentation that keeps the crouton from becoming soggy.

3. Heat cream prior to adding it to the soup so that it doesn't lower the soup's temperature.

Most soups are cooked at a gentle simmer, just long enough to develop a good flavor and the appropriate body. Vegetables may be added in a staggered manner, according to their cooking times. The soup should be stirred from time to time to prevent starchy ingredients from sticking to the bottom of the pot. Throughout the cooking process, a skimmer or ladle should be used to remove any scum or foam so that the best flavor, texture, and appearance is obtained.

You should also taste the soup frequently as it cooks. When the flavor is fully developed and all of the ingredients are tender, it may be finished or garnished and served right away, or it may be properly cooled and stored. Although some soups may develop a more rounded, mellow flavor if served the day after they are prepared, no soup benefits from hours on the stove. Not only will the flavor become dull and flat, but the nutritive value will be greatly reduced.

1.

2

3.

Finishing

Some soups may be prepared to a specific point and then cooled and stored, using the same techniques appropriate for cooling and storing stocks. When you store soups and finish them later, certain considerations are important. Clear soups should be garnished just before service to prevent them from becoming cloudy and to keep the garnish fresh. Vegetables, for example, should not be overcooked. Some garnishes are added, portion by portion, just prior to service. In other cases, such as for banquet service, the garnish may be added to the entire quantity. See opposite page for more information on garnishing soups.

Cream soups should have the cream added just prior to service for two reasons: The soup will have a fresher flavor, and its shelf life will be greater. Cream should be brought to a boil first to prevent the cream from lowering the soup's temperature.

Many soup bases should be brought back to a full boil before finishing; however, soups that have already been finished with cream, sour cream, butter, or a liaison should not be allowed to come all the way up to a boil (see "Reheating" below).

Final seasoning adjustments should be made after the soup is finished. Seasoning should always be checked just prior to service.

Reheating

If you have prepared soup in advance, reheat only the amount needed for a particular service period. Clear soups should be brought just up to a boil. Seasoning and consistency should be checked and the appropriate garnishes added before serving.

Thick soups, especially creams, purées, and bisques, should be reheated gently. A thin layer of water or stock should be put in a heavy-gauge pot or a steam-jacketed kettle before adding the soup. The soup should be reheated over low heat and stirred frequently until it softens slightly. Then the heat can be increased slightly and the soup may be brought to a simmer. Seasoning and consistency should be checked and any garnishes added just before serving.

Adjusting Consistency

Thick soups, especially those made with starchy vegetables or dried beans, may continue to thicken during cooking and storage. As a general rule, purées, creams, and bisques should be about as thick as heavy cream and liquid enough to pour from a ladle into a bowl. The following steps may be taken to adjust consistency.

For a soup that has become too thick, water or an appropriately flavored stock or broth may be added in small amounts until the proper consistency is reached. Seasoning should be rechecked before serving.

For a soup that is too thin, a small amount of diluted cornstarch or arrowroot may be added. The soup should be at a simmer or slow boil when the starch is added. It should be stirred continuously and should continue simmering for 2 or 3 minutes.

Adjusting Flavor and Seasoning

Meat or poultry glaze may be added to bolster a weak flavor in broth or consommé; however, this will affect the clarity.

Chopped fresh herbs; a few drops of lemon juice, Tabasco sauce, or Worcestershire sauce; or grated citrus rind may be added to brighten a soup's flavor. These items should be added a little at a time and the seasoning carefully checked after each addition.

Salt and pepper may be added just prior to service, when the soup is at the correct temperature.

1. Add warm stock or broth as a more flavorful alternative to thinning an overly thick soup with water.

2. A properly thickened soup should easily coat the spoon.

3. Use paper towels to lift any fat from the surface of a stock, broth, soup, or consommé. Alternatively, refrigerate the finished soup and lift the grease from the surface.

4. Vegetable garnishes should not be overcooked, and should be shocked to maintain their color.

5. Always serve finished soups very hot in heated dishware.

Degreasing

Some soups, especially broth-based ones, may be prepared in advance and cooled and refrigerated properly. You can then easily remove the fat that will congeal on the surface before you reheat the soup. If the soup must be served just after it is prepared, as much surface fat as possible should be skimmed off with a shallow ladle or skimmer. Clear soups may be blotted with strips of absorbent paper to remove any traces of fat before serving. The strips should be floated on the surface and then carefully lifted off. Consommés should be completely fat free. Broths and clear vegetable soups characteristically have some droplets of fat on the surface.

Garnishing

Garnishes can accomplish many things. They may provide contrasts of texture and flavor, introduce a complementary or contrasting flavor, or provide additional or contrasting color. Garnishes should be added just prior to service. If garnishes such as custards or quenelles are prepared in advance, they should be properly cooled and stored separately. Special procedures for preparing large batches of soups include cooking the garnishes separately from the main body of soup and adding the garnish at service time. This will enhance the final appearance of the soup and ensure that the garnish maintains its integrity. Additionally, handling the garnish separately will permit you to accurately portion the garnish for each guest's soup.

Serving

Hot soups should be served very hot, and the thinner the soup, the more important this is. Consommés and broths lose their heat rapidly, so they should be nearly at a boil before they are ladled into heated soup bowls or cups. Cold soups should be thoroughly chilled and served in chilled bowls, cups, or glasses.

SAUCES

Sauces are often considered one of the greatest tests of a chef's skill. Whether they are classic, such as suprême sauce, or contemporary, such as red pepper coulis, good sauces demand the highest technical expertise. The successful pairing of a sauce with a food demonstrates an understanding of the food and an ability to judge and evaluate a dish's flavors, textures, and colors. An understanding of the nuances of pairing a particular sauce with a food develops throughout a chef's career, as lessons are learned about how and why certain combinations have become enduring classics. As you uncover the principles behind these pairings, you will develop an appreciation of sauces in particular and of the skill and artistry of cooking in general.

Uses

Sauces are not just an afterthought—they serve a particular function in a dish's composition. It is in learning to understand why a certain sauce will or will not work with a particular dish that the process of developing culinary judgment begins. Certain sauce combinations endure because the composition is well balanced in all areas: taste, texture, and eye appeal. Once you understand these functions, you can expand your understanding of what a sauce is and why one particular combination of sauce and meat works while the same sauce is not as effective when served with a different meat. Most sauces serve more than one purpose. A sauce that adds a counterpoint flavor may also introduce textural and visual appeal. Sauces introduce several important elements to a dish.

COMPLEMENTARY OR COUNTERPOINT FLAVORS. Some examples of sauces that are classically combined with particular foods illustrate how sauces can provide complementary or counterpoint flavors. Suprême sauce is made by reducing a chicken velouté with chicken stock and finishing it with cream. Correctly made, this ivory-colored sauce has a deep chicken flavor and a velvety texture. When served with chicken meat, the sauce's color and flavor complement the delicate chicken and help to intensify the meat's flavor. The addition of cream to the sauce serves to "round out" the flavors. Robert sauce, on the other hand, is traditionally paired with pork to introduce a counterpoint flavor. The sharpness of the mustard and cornichons tends to cut the meat's richness and introduces a contrast that is pleasing, but not startling, to the palate. This pungent, flavorful sauce brings out the pork's flavor but might overwhelm a more delicate meat, such as veal.

MOISTURE OR SUCCULENCE. Moisture is an important consideration when working with naturally lean foods, such as poultry or fish, or with cooking techniques that tend to have a drying effect, such as grilling or sautéing. For this reason, grilled steaks are commonly served with a compound butter or with a butter-emulsion sauce such as a béarnaise. The same rationale applies to serving beurre blanc with lean white fish that has been shallow poached.

1. Add basil to tomato sauce to introduce additional complementary flavors to the finished sauce.

2. Add broth, stock, wine, or another flavorful liquid to give a sauce moisture that is also flavorful.

3. Whip hollandaise sauce to create a thick texture and lovely sheen.

VISUAL INTEREST. One of the ways a sauce can enhance a dish's appearance is to add luster and sheen. Lightly coating a sautéed medallion of lamb with a jus lié, for example, adds a glossy finish to the lamb that gives the entire plate more eye appeal. Pooling a red pepper coulis beneath a grilled swordfish steak gives a dish a degree of visual excitement by adding an element of color.

TEXTURE. Many sauces receive a final garnish that adds texture. For example, chicken chasseur is enhanced by a sauce finished with tomatoes and mushrooms. Conversely, a smooth sauce may be used to add contrast to a meat that has a distinct texture.

Proper Selection

The variety of flavors and textures available allows you to choose a sauce that makes the best possible sense for the dish being prepared. Here are some of the points to consider when selecting the appropriate sauce.

The sauce should be suitable for the style of service. In a banquet setting, or for any situation where large quantities of food must be served rapidly and at the peak of flavor, it is usually best to rely on the traditional grand sauces or a contemporary sauce that shares some of the same characteristics. One of a grand sauce's fundamental benefits is that it may be prepared in advance and held in large quantities at the correct temperature.

The sauce should be suitable for the main ingredient's cooking technique. A cooking technique that produces flavorful drippings (fond), such as roasting or sautéing, should logically be paired with a pan sauce or gravy that makes use of those drippings. Beurre blancs are suitable for foods that have been shallow poached, because the cooking liquid (cuisson) can become a part of the sauce instead of being discarded.

The sauce's flavor should be appropriate for the flavor of the food with which it is paired. Make sure the flavor of the sauce does not overpower the main ingredient's flavor, and vice versa. Although a delicate cream sauce complements the flavor of Dover sole, it would be overwhelmed by the flavor of grilled tuna steak. By the same token, a sauce flavored by rosemary would completely overpower a delicate fish, but nicely complements lamb.

THE GRAND SAUCES

Because sauces are made in different ways and serve different purposes, depending on when and how they are used, they are grouped in rough categories: grand sauces and contemporary sauces. These categories form a framework for understanding sauces in terms of both technique and application.

The grand sauces—demi-glace, velouté, béchamel, tomato, and hollandaise—were once referred to as the "mother sauces" to indicate that from these basic sauces many others were created. Although they may not be relied upon as heavily as in years past, the grand sauces are still important in a contemporary kitchen. There is some dispute as to how many grand sauces exist. Some argue that because hollandaise cannot be made in advance in a large quantity and stored, and cannot be used to prepare a variety of derivative sauces, it does not qualify. It is included here, however, because the basic technique for preparing hollandaise or a béarnaise does yield a number of variations.

Espagnole Sauce (Brown Sauce)

The classic method of preparing an espagnole sauce, or brown sauce, as written by Antonin Carême, is a lengthy and involved process that calls for Bayonne ham, veal, and partridges. The contemporary version has been greatly simplified and the cooking time reduced. Although it may be served by itself as a sauce, it is also important as an essential component of demi-glace and as a cooking liquid for braises and stews.

Demi-Glace

Demi-glace is a highly flavored, glossy sauce. There are a number of derivatives based on demi-glace that have an important place in the chef's repertoire. A demi-glace of excellent quality will have several characteristics. Demi-glace should have a full, rich flavor. Because the sauce is based on brown veal stock, the flavor should be that of roasted veal. The aromatics, mirepoix, and tomatoes used in the base preparations should not overpower the main flavor. Demi-glace should have a deep brown color. When properly simmered, skimmed, and reduced, demi-glace is translucent and highly glossy. Because it is reduced, and because a roux is used in the espagnole sauce that is one of its components, demi-glace has a noticeable body. However, it should never feel gluey or overly tacky in the mouth. It is the correct consistency when it will evenly coat the back of a spoon (a condition known as nappé). The initial roasting of bones, trimmings, and mirepoix will give the finished sauce a pleasant roasted or caramel aroma, readily discernible when the sauce is heated.

Velouté

Velouté is prepared by thickening a white stock with an appropriate amount of pale roux, then simmering it until the roux is completely "cooked out," leaving no starchy taste. Veloutés may be based on veal, chicken, or fish stock. A common application for veloutés in contemporary kitchens is in cream soup preparation. There are a number of derivatives prepared from velouté.

The finished sauce should be lustrous, with a definite sheen. Velouté should be perfectly smooth, with absolutely no graininess. The sauce should have a noticeable body, thick enough to coat the back of a spoon (nappé), yet still quite liquid. Although a heavy velouté does have applications in the kitchen, such a texture is not appropriate for

Adding a wine-and-peppercorn reduction to the sauce adds great flavor without adding too much additional moisture.

a velouté that is to be used as a sauce. The aroma of a velouté should be that of the base stock. The roux will impart a slight hint of nuttiness, but this should in no way overpower the stock's aroma.

Béchamel

Béchamel is a white sauce made by thickening milk with a white roux and simmering it with aromatics. The first recipes for béchamel sauce included lean veal; however, modern practice rarely includes it. While its importance as a grand sauce has diminished somewhat, béchamel and its derivatives are still important in the contemporary kitchen.

Although béchamel is essentially opaque, with proper cooking and skimming, the finished sauce will be lustrous, with a definite sheen. It should be perfectly smooth, with absolutely no graininess. The sauce should have a noticeable body, thick enough to coat the back of a spoon (nappé), yet still be quite liquid. The aroma should be that of cream. A slight hint of nuttiness from the roux will be apparent, but it should not overpower the cream aroma. The onion, thyme, and nutmeg contribute flavor accents but should not be overly strong.

Tomato Sauce

Although the number of derivative sauces for tomato sauce is not as great as for demiglace, béchamel, or velouté, it is an important sauce. Tomato sauce should have a deep, rich tomato flavor. There should be hints of supporting flavors from any additional ingredients (such as stock or broth, aromatics, or pork products), but these should only have the effect of supporting the tomato. Tomato sauce is opaque, but proper simmering, púreeing, and straining lend it some sheen. This sauce is slightly coarser than the other grand sauces because of the degree of texture that remains even after puréeing and straining the tomatoes. The sauce is still relatively smooth, but thick enough to coat the back of a spoon (nappé) and thin enough to pour easily. Tomato sauce should have a clear tomato smell, with no sour, acid, bitter, or overly sweet (caramel) aromas.

Hollandaise

Hollandaise is an emulsion sauce. An emulsion is formed when one substance is suspended in another—in this case, melted or clarified butter is suspended in partially cooked egg yolks. It is fragile because it is not a true mixture.

Opinions differ on whether to use melted butter or clarified butter. Some chefs prefer clarified butter because they feel that it results in a more stable sauce, whereas others prefer melted butter because they believe that the presence of milk solids gives the sauce a more buttery taste.

There is also a difference of opinion on whether to strain the finished hollandaise. Some chefs, believing that straining causes the sauce to cool too much. Instead, they strain the initial reduction. If the hollandaise becomes too hot as it cooked, the egg yolks might "scramble" in the sauce; in that case, you should strain the finished hollandaise. If you control the heat properly while making the sauce, you should not need to strain it. Unlike the other grand sauces, hollandaise is prepared in a single operation. Its variations, such as béarnaise, Foyot, and Choron, are also made in a single operation. They are not, however, made from a base of hollandaise and finished with other ingredients, as is the case with the other grand sauces.

CONTEMPORARY SAUCES

The broad category of contemporary sauces includes jus lié, beurre blanc, coulis, compound butters, and a variety of miscellaneous sauces, such as relishes, salsas, and compotes. There are several primary factors distinguishing contemporary sauces from the grand sauces. Contemporary sauces usually take less time to prepare and are more likely to be specifically tailored to a given food or technique. In addition, they tend to be lighter in color and body than the grand sauces. They are also more likely to rely on emulsions, reductions, and modified starches for thickening, instead of on roux.

Jus Lié

Jus lié, frequently referred to simply as jus, is a thickened sauce made from stock (usually brown veal stock, although other stocks may be used). It is used in the preparation of many other sauces. Although similar to a demi-glace in appearance and use, jus lié requires less cooking time because it contains a modified starch (e.g., arrowroot) as a thickener. It also has a greater degree of clarity, translucence, and sheen. Jus lié should not be as dark as a demi-glace. A jus lié should have a definite body, similar to that of a demi-glace; it should be thick enough to coat the back of a spoon (nappé). The texture should be smooth and light. A gluey or tacky texture is an indication that the sauce has been allowed to reduce too much or that too much starch has been used.

Beurre Blanc

Beurre blanc is a sauce in which butter forms an emulsion with a reduction. Traditionally, the reduction consists of the cooking liquid (cuisson) used to prepare shallow-poached dishes, but it is also possible to prepare a reduction separately. Although beurre blanc is a fragile sauce, adding a small amount of heavy cream can help to stabilize it so that it may be held during a service period. The sauce should have a distinct sheen. The body should be light and the texture frothy; it should not leave an oily or greasy feeling in the mouth.

Special Problem-Solving Techniques for Warm Emulsion Sauces

The sauce appears to be breaking. This is an indication that the sauce has become too hot. Remove the pot from the heat immediately and place it on a cool surface, such as a stainless-steel worktable. Continue to whip the cool butter in, keeping both the pan and the sauce in motion. When the sauce loses its oily appearance and dulls slightly, place the pan over low heat and continue to work in the butter.

The sauce becomes too thick. This means that the sauce may not be warm enough, which is generally an indication that the butter is being added too quickly. Do not add additional butter until the sauce has warmed and become less thick.

Compound Butters

Flavored compound butters can be considered as sauces used to finish grilled or broiled meats, fish, poultry, game, pastas, or even other sauces. Boiled or steamed vegetables may be tossed in compound butter just before service. Compound butters may be flavored with a wide variety of ingredients, including herbs, nuts, citrus zest, garlic, shallots, ginger, and vegetables.

Coulis

Before the codification of sauces into the grand sauces and their derivatives, any sauce would most likely have gone by the name of coulis. Certain soups were also known as coulis, especially those based on game and game birds. Today, chefs generally use the term *coulis* to identify a sauce that is essentially a purée of a vegetable, such as red peppers, broccoli, or tomatoes. A coulis may be finished with cream or butter. Refer to specific recipes for ingredients and methods.

Miscellaneous Sauces

Several other preparations can be considered sauces because they add moisture, flavor, textural interest, and color to the foods with which they are paired. These include relishes, salsas, compotes, and even beds of vegetables and grains. Various techniques are used to prepare these miscellaneous sauces. Cold vinaigrettes and mayonnaise may be used as a sauce for hot sautéed items or as a marinade. Another cold sauce, salsa, may be used as a sauce for hot foods. Because the vegetables in salsa generally are not cooked, it is considered a "raw" sauce.

Relishes and compotes based on fruits and/or vegetables may be served hot or cold. An example is a confit of red onion, consisting of onions stewed in butter and finished with a small amount of honey and vinegar. Another example is a dried-fruit compote, composed of dried fruits stewed in wine, stock, or a combination of the two. Rice and other grains, such as bulgur and barley, are prepared by the pilaf method and used as a bed for other foods. Rice may also be prepared by the risotto method and used in place of a traditional sauce. Beans and other dried legumes, such as lentils, may be stewed and served in lieu of a standard sauce.

Compound butters can be flavored with a variety of seasonings, and can be finished in an array of shapes, depending on the desired result.

chapter six

RECIPES FOR STOCKS,
SOUPS, SAUCES, AND
BASIC FLAVORINGS

BROWN VEAL STOCK

Makes 5 gallons (20 liters)

Vegetable oil	As needed	As needed
Veal bones, including knuckles and trim	40 lb	18 kg
Cold water	7½ gal	28.4 l
Kosher salt	2 tbsp	30 ml
Mirepoix (page 134), large dice	5 lb	2.25 kg
Tomato paste	20 to 30 oz	570 to 850 g
Sachet d'Epices (page 133)	1 each	1 each

1. Condition the roasting pan. Heat the pan and enough oil to lightly film the pan in the oven. Add the bones to the pan and return to the oven. Roast the bones at 425° to 450°F/220° to 230°C, stirring and turning from time to time, until they are a deep brown, 30 to 45 minutes.

2. Transfer the bones to a stockpot and add all but 1 cup of the cold water and the salt. Deglaze the roasting pan with the remaining 1 cup of water and add the released drippings to the stockpot. Bring the stock to a simmer slowly over low heat. Adjust the heat if necessary to establish an even, gentle simmer and continue to cook, skimming the surface as necessary, for about 5 hours.

3. While the stock is simmering, heat a rondeau over medium-high heat. Add enough oil to film the pan. Add the mirepoix and cook, stirring occasionally, until the onions are a deep golden brown, 15 to 20 minutes. Add the tomato paste and continue to cook, stirring frequently, until the tomato paste turns a rusty brown color and gives off a sweet aroma, 1 to 2 minutes. Add a few ladles of the stock to the rondeau and stir well to release the drippings; add this mixture to the stock after it has simmered for about 5 hours. Add the sachet at the same time.

4. Continue to simmer the stock, skimming as necessary and tasting from time to time, until it has developed a rich flavor and a noticeable body, about 1 hour more.

5. Strain the stock through a fine-mesh sieve.

6. The stock may be used now (degrease by skimming if necessary), or it may be rapidly cooled and held under refrigeration for up to 5 days for later use.

CHICKEN STOCK

Makes 5 gallons (20 liters)

Chicken bones, cut into 3-inch/76-mm lengths	40 lb	18 kg
Cold water	7½ gal	28.4 l
Kosher salt	2 tbsp	30 ml
Mirepoix (page 134), medium dice	5 lb	2.25 kg
Sachet d'Epices (page 133)	1 each	1 each

1. Rinse the bones under cool running water and place them in a stockpot.

2. Add the cold water and salt. (The water should cover the bones by about 2 inches/51 mm.) Slowly bring the stock to a simmer over low heat. Skim the surface as necessary.

3. Simmer for 3 to 4 hours.

4. Add the mirepoix and sachet and continue to simmer the stock for 1 hour more, skimming as necessary and tasting from time to time.

5. Strain the stock through a fine-mesh sieve.

6. The stock may be used now (degrease by skimming if necessary), or it may be rapidly cooled and held under refrigeration for up to 5 days for later use.

FISH STOCK

Makes 5 gallons (20 liters)

Nonoily fish bones (flounder, haddock, cod, halibut, etc.)	55 lb	25 kg
White Mirepoix (page 134), thinly sliced	5 lb	2.25 kg
Cold water	5 gal	19 l
Kosher salt	2 tbsp	30 ml
Sachet d'Epices (page 133)	1 each	1 each

1. Combine the fish bones, mirepoix, cold water, salt, and sachet in a stockpot. Simmer gently over low heat for 40 minutes.

2. Strain the stock through a fine-mesh sieve.

3. The stock may be used now (degrease by skimming if necessary), or it may be rapidly cooled and held under refrigeration for up to 5 days for later use.

   SHELLFISH STOCK: Replace the fish bones with an equal amount of crustacean shells (shrimp, lobster, or crab). Sauté the shells in hot oil until the color deepens. Add a thinly sliced standard Mirepoix (page 134) and sauté until tender. If desired, add 3 oz/85 g tomato paste and cook until the tomato paste turns a deep red color. Add enough water to cover the shells and simmer for 40 minutes, skimming throughout.

FISH FUMET

Makes 1 gallon (3.75 liters)

Vegetable oil	¼ cup	60 ml
Nonoily fish bones (flounder, haddock, cod, halibut, etc.)	11 lb	4.99 kg
White Mirepoix (page 134), thinly sliced	1 lb	450 g
Cold water	5 qt	4.80 l
Dry white wine	1 pt to 1 qt	480 to 950 ml
Kosher salt	2 tsp	10 ml
Sachet d'Epices (page 133)	1 each	1 each

1. Heat the oil in a rondeau and add the bones and mirepoix. Cover the pot and sweat the bones and mirepoix over medium heat until the mirepoix is soft and the bones are opaque, 10 to 12 minutes.

2. Add the water, wine, salt, and sachet and bring to a simmer.

3. Simmer for 40 to 60 minutes, skimming the surface as necessary. Strain the fumet through a fine-mesh sieve.

4. The fumet may be used now (degrease by skimming if necessary), or it may be rapidly cooled and held under refrigeration for up to 5 days for later use.

VEGETABLE STOCK

Makes 5 gallons (20 liters)

Vegetable oil, plus additional as needed for sweating vegetables	5 fl oz	150 ml
Mirepoix (page 134), large dice	15 lb	6.8 kg
Nonstarchy vegetables (leeks, tomatoes, garlic, etc.)	15 lb	6.8 kg
Cold water	6¼ gal	23.6 l
Kosher salt	2 tbsp	30 ml
Sachet d'Epices (page 133)	1 each	1 each

1. Heat the oil in a stockpot over medium-high heat and add the mirepoix and vegetables.

2. Cover and sweat the vegetables for 10 to 12 minutes, stirring occasionally.

3. Add the water and salt, simmer for 15 minutes, and add the sachet. Continue to simmer until the stock is flavorful, about 30 minutes.

4. Strain the stock through a fine-mesh sieve.

5. The stock may be used now (degrease by skimming if necessary), or it may be rapidly cooled and held under refrigeration for up to 5 days for later use.

COURT BOUILLON

Makes 5 gallons (20 liters)

Cold water	5 gal	19 l
White wine vinegar	2½ pt	1.2 l
Kosher salt	2 tbsp	30 ml
Carrots, sliced	3 lb 12 oz	1.7 kg
Onions, sliced	5 lb	2.25 kg
Dried thyme	1 tsp	5 ml
Bay leaves	6 each	6 each
Parsley stems	25 each	25 each
Black peppercorns	1½ tsp	8 ml

1. Combine the water, vinegar, salt, carrots, onions, thyme, bay leaves, and parsley stems in a stockpot. Simmer gently over low heat for 50 minutes.

2. Add the peppercorns and simmer for 10 minutes.

3. Strain the court bouillon through a fine-mesh sieve.

4. The court bouillon may be used now, or it may be rapidly cooled and held under refrigeration for up to 3 days for later use.

ESPAGNOLE SAUCE

Makes 1 gallon (3.75 liters)

Vegetable oil	¼ cup	60 ml
Onions, chopped	8 oz	225 g
Carrots, chopped	4 oz	115 g
Celery, chopped	4 oz	115 g
Tomato paste	2 oz	60 g
Brown Veal Stock (page 82), hot	6 qt	5.75 l
Roux (page 135), cooked until brown	1 lb	450 g
Sachet d'Epices (page 133)	1 each	1 each
Kosher salt, or as needed	1 tbsp	15 ml
Ground black pepper, or as needed	2 tsp	10 ml

1. Heat the oil in a rondeau over medium heat and sauté the onions until translucent. Add the carrots and celery and continue to brown.

2. Add the tomato paste and cook until the tomato paste turns a rusty brown color and gives off a sweet aroma, about 3 minutes.

3. Add the stock and bring it to a simmer.

4. Whisk the roux into the stock. Return to a simmer and add the sachet. Simmer for about 1 hour, skimming the surface as necessary.

5. Strain the sauce through a fine-mesh sieve.

6. Taste the sauce and season with salt and pepper. The sauce is ready to serve now, or it may be rapidly cooled and held under refrigeration for up to 5 days for later use.

DEMI-GLACE

Makes 1 quart (950 milliliters)

Brown Veal Stock (page 82)	1 qt	950 ml
Espagnole Sauce (see above)	1 qt	950 ml

1. Combine the stock and the espagnole sauce in a sauce pot and simmer over low to medium heat until reduced by half. Skim the sauce frequently as it simmers.

2. Strain the sauce through a fine-mesh sieve.

3. The sauce is ready to serve now, or it may be rapidly cooled and held under refrigeration for up to 5 days for later use.

JUS DE VEAU LIÉ

Makes 1 gallon (3.75 liters)

Vegetable oil	¼ cup	60 ml
Lean veal trim	4 lb	1.8 kg
Mirepoix (page 134), medium dice	1 lb	450 g
Tomato purée	4 oz	115 g
Brown Veal Stock (page 82)	9 pt	4.2 l
Sachet d'Epices (page 133)	1 each	1 each
Arrowroot or cornstarch, diluted in an equal amount of cold water	1 oz	30 g
Kosher salt	As needed	As needed
Ground black pepper	As needed	As needed

1. Heat the oil in a rondeau over medium heat. Add the veal trim and mirepoix and sauté, stirring from time to time, until the veal, onions, and carrots have taken on a rich brown color, 25 to 30 minutes.

2. Add the tomato purée and continue to cook over medium heat until the tomato purée turns a rusty brown and gives off a sweet aroma, about 1 minute.

3. Add the stock and bring to a simmer over low heat. Continue to simmer, skimming as necessary, until a good flavor develops, 2 to 3 hours. Add the sachet during the last hour of cooking time.

4. Return the sauce base to a simmer over low heat. Stir the diluted arrowroot or cornstarch to recombine if necessary and gradually add it to the sauce base, adding just enough to achieve a good coating consistency (nappé). The amount of diluted arrowroot or cornstarch needed depends on the batch itself and its intended use.

5. Taste the sauce and season with salt and pepper.

6. Strain the sauce through a fine-mesh sieve.

7. The sauce is ready to serve now, or it may be rapidly cooled and held under refrigeration for up to 5 days for later use.

Jus de Volaille Lié

Makes 1 gallon (3.75 liters)

Vegetable oil	¼ cup	60 ml
Chicken trim	4 lb	1.8 kg
Mirepoix (page 134), medium dice	1 lb	450 g
Tomato purée	4 oz	115 g
Chicken Stock (page 83)	9 pt	4.2 l
Sachet d'Epices (page 133)	1 each	1 each
Arrowroot or cornstarch, diluted in an equal amount of cold water	1 oz	30 g
Kosher salt	As needed	As needed
Ground black pepper	As needed	As needed

1. Heat the oil in a rondeau over medium heat. Add the chicken trim and mirepoix and sauté, stirring from time to time, until the chicken, onions, and carrots have taken on a rich brown color, 25 to 30 minutes.

2. Add the tomato purée and continue to cook over medium heat until the tomato purée turns a rusty brown color and gives off a sweet aroma, about 1 minute.

3. Add the stock and bring to a simmer over low heat. Continue to simmer, skimming as necessary, until a good flavor develops, 2 to 3 hours. Add the sachet during the last hour of cooking time.

4. Return the sauce base to a simmer over low heat. Stir the diluted arrowroot or cornstarch to recombine if necessary and gradually add it to the sauce base, adding just enough to achieve a good coating consistency (nappé). The amount of diluted arrowroot or cornstarch needed depends on the batch itself and its intended use.

5. Taste the sauce and season with salt and pepper.

6. Strain the sauce through a fine-mesh sieve.

7. The sauce is ready to serve now, or it may be rapidly cooled and held under refrigeration for up to 5 days for later use.

CHICKEN VELOUTÉ

Makes 1 gallon (3.75 liters)

Clarified butter or vegetable oil	¼ cup	60 ml
White Mirepoix (page 134), small dice	8 oz	225 g
Roux (page 135), cooked until blond	12 oz	340 g
Chicken Stock (page 83), cold	9 pt	4.2 l
Sachet d'Epices (page 133)	1 each	1 each
Kosher salt	As needed	As needed
Ground white pepper	As needed	As needed

1. Heat the butter or oil in a saucepan over medium heat. Add the mirepoix and cook, stirring from time to time, until the onions are limp and have begun to release their juices into the pan, about 15 minutes. They may take on a light golden color, but should not be allowed to brown.

2. Add the roux to the mirepoix and cook until the roux is very hot, about 2 minutes.

3. Add the stock to the pan gradually, stirring or whisking to work out any lumps. Bring to a full boil, then lower the heat to establish a simmer. (Use a heat diffuser, if desired, to avoid scorching.) Add the sachet and continue to simmer, skimming as necessary, until a good flavor and consistency develop and the starchy feel and taste of the flour have cooked away, 45 minutes to 1 hour.

4. Strain the sauce through a fine-mesh sieve. Strain a second time through doubled cheesecloth, if desired, for the finest texture.

5. Return the sauce to a simmer over low heat. Taste the sauce and season with salt and pepper. Finish the sauce as desired.

6. The sauce is ready to serve now, or it may be rapidly cooled and held under refrigeration for up to 3 days for later use.

BÉCHAMEL SAUCE

Makes 1 gallon (3.75 liters)

Clarified butter or vegetable oil	¼ cup	60 ml
Onions, minced	2 oz	60 g
Roux (page 135), cooked until white	1 lb	450 g
Milk, cold	9 pt	4.2 l
Kosher salt	As needed	As needed
Ground white pepper	As needed	As needed
Ground nutmeg (optional)	As needed	As needed

1. Heat the butter or oil in a saucepan over low to medium heat and add the onions. Sauté, stirring frequently, until the onions are tender and translucent, 6 to 8 minutes.

2. Add the roux to the onions and cook until the roux is very hot, about 2 minutes.

3. Add the milk to the pan gradually, whisking or stirring to work out any lumps. Bring the sauce to a full boil, then reduce the heat and simmer until the sauce is smooth and thickened, about 30 minutes. Stir frequently and skim as necessary throughout the cooking time.

4. Season with salt, pepper, and nutmeg, if using. Strain through doubled cheesecloth.

5. Return the sauce to a simmer. Taste the sauce and adjust seasoning with salt and pepper. Finish the sauce as desired.

6. The sauce is ready to serve now, or it may be rapidly cooled and held under refrigeration for up to 3 days for later use.

ROASTED BUTTERNUT SQUASH SOUP

Makes 3½ gallons (13.25 liters) or 75 portions

Butter	1 lb	450 g
Mirepoix (page 134), medium dice	2 lb	900 g
Shallots, thinly sliced	1 lb 8 oz	680 g
Leeks, white parts, thinly sliced	2 lb	900 g
Ginger, minced	2 oz	60 g
Dry white wine	1 qt	950 ml
Sachet d'Epices (page 133)	1 each	1 each
Chicken Velouté (page 91)	3 gal	11.4 l
Butternut squash, peeled, large dice, roasted	18 lb (raw weight)	8 kg (raw weight)
Heavy cream, hot	¾ cup	180 ml
Kosher salt, or as needed	1 tbsp	15 ml
Cracked white pepper, or as needed	1 tbsp	15 ml
Butter, diced	4 oz	115 g

1. Heat the butter in a soup pot over medium heat. Add the mirepoix, shallots, and leeks and sweat until tender and translucent, 8 to 10 minutes. Add the ginger and wine and cook until the liquid is reduced to nearly dry, about 25 minutes. Add the sachet.

2. Add the velouté and simmer, stirring occasionally, over low heat for 15 minutes. Add the squash and continue to cook, stirring occasionally, until the squash is tender enough to mash with a fork, about 30 minutes.

3. Reserve 2 qt/1.9 l of the soup and purée the remainder.

4. Strain the puréed soup through a fine-mesh sieve and adjust the consistency by adding the reserved soup as desired. The soup is ready to finish and serve now, or it may be rapidly cooled and held under refrigeration for up to 3 days for later service.

5. To finish the soup for service, return it to a simmer. Stir in the cream. Taste the soup and season with salt and pepper. Stir in the butter. Serve the soup in heated bowls or cups.

Soup Sampler: Cream of Asparagus Soup (page 97), Roasted Red Pepper Gazpacho (page 113), and Roasted Butternut Squash Soup

SWEET ONION AND FENNEL SOUP

Makes 2½ gallons (9.5 liters) or 50 portions

Extra-virgin olive oil	5 fl oz	150 ml
Sweet onions, medium dice	9 lb	4.1 kg
Fennel, cored, medium dice	4 lb	1.8 kg
Chicken Stock (page 83)	2 gal	7.5 l
Sachet d'Epices (page 133), including 2 garlic cloves, 4 tbsp fennel seeds	1 each	1 each
Russet potatoes, peeled, large dice	4 lb	1.8 kg
Heavy cream, hot	1 qt	950 ml
Kosher salt, or as needed	2 tbsp	30 ml
Cracked white pepper, or as needed	1½ tsp	8 ml
Dill sprigs	50 each	50 each
Marjoram Oil (see below)	5 fl oz	150 ml
Parmesan crisp	50 each	50 each

1. Heat the olive oil in a soup pot over medium heat. Add the onions and fennel and sweat, stirring from time to time, until tender, about 10 minutes.

2. Add the chicken stock and sachet and simmer over low heat for 20 minutes.

3. Add the potatoes and simmer, stirring occasionally, until tender enough to mash easily, 15 to 20 minutes.

4. Remove from the heat, discard the sachet, and purée the soup. Return the mixture to the soup pot. The soup is ready to finish and serve now, or it may be rapidly cooled and held under refrigeration for up to 3 days for later service.

5. To finish the soup for service, return it to a rapid simmer. Add the heavy cream. Taste the soup and season with salt and pepper. Cook gently for 10 minutes to develop the flavor. Serve the soup in heated bowls or cups, garnished with dill and a drizzle of marjoram oil. Top with a parmesan crisp.

MARJORAM OIL

Makes 12 fluid ounces (360 milliliters)

Marjoram, picked	3 bunches	3 bunches
Extra-virgin olive oil	1¼ cups	300 ml

1. Blanch the marjoram in a pot of boiling water. Drain and place in an ice water bath to halt the cooking. Drain well and pat dry on paper towels.

2. Process the marjoram and the oil in a blender for 2 minutes.

3. Strain through doubled cheesecloth, transfer to a squeeze bottle, and reserve for service. Hold under refrigeration for up to 3 days.

CREAM OF ASPARAGUS SOUP

Makes 2½ gallons (9.5 liters) or 50 portions

Asparagus	8 lb	3.6 kg
Clarified butter or vegetable oil	½ cup	120 ml
White Mirepoix (page 134), medium dice	2 lb	900 g
Chicken Velouté (page 91)	2 gal	7.5 l
Sachet d'Epices (page 133)	1 each	1 each
Heavy cream, hot	1 qt	950 ml
Kosher salt	As needed	As needed
Ground black pepper	As needed	As needed

1. Remove the tough bottom part of the asparagus and discard. (It should snap easily at a certain point toward the bottom of the asparagus.) Slice off the tips, about 1 inch long, and reserve them separately. Slice the asparagus spears thin.

2. Heat the butter or oil in a soup pot and add the mirepoix. Sweat until the onions are translucent, 6 to 8 minutes. Add the sliced asparagus and sweat until slightly tender, about 8 minutes.

3. Add the velouté to the pot and bring to a full boil. Reduce the heat and simmer until the soup is thickened, about 35 minutes. Add the sachet and simmer for 25 minutes more. Stir frequently and skim as needed.

4. Make sure the reserved asparagus tops are no wider than a soupspoon. Blanch them in boiling salted water until tender. Shock the tops in an ice water bath and reserve for service.

5. Strain the soup through a fine-mesh sieve, discard the sachet, and purée the solids until smooth. Add the purée back to the strained soup. Strain again using a fine-mesh sieve or cheesecloth. The soup is ready to finish and serve now, or it may be rapidly cooled and held under refrigeration for up to 2 days for later service.

6. To finish the soup for service, return it to a rapid simmer. Add the heavy cream just before serving. Taste the soup and season with salt and pepper. Serve the soup in heated bowls or cups, garnished with the reserved asparagus tips.

Corn Chowder

Makes 2½ gallons (9.5 liters) or 50 portions

Salt pork, minced	8 oz	225 g
Butter	4 oz	115 g
Onions, small dice	12 oz	340 g
Celery, small dice	12 oz	340 g
Green peppers, small dice	8 oz	225 g
Red peppers, small dice	8 oz	225 g
All-purpose flour	6 oz	170 g
Chicken Stock (page 83)	1 gal	3.75 l
Corn kernels, fresh or frozen	4 lb	1.8 kg
Russet potatoes, peeled, small dice	4 lb	1.8 kg
Bay leaf	1 each	1 each
Heavy cream, hot	1 pt	480 ml
Milk, hot	1 pt	480 ml
Kosher salt	As needed	As needed
Ground white pepper	As needed	As needed
Tabasco sauce	4 tsp	20 ml
Worcestershire sauce	4 tsp	20 ml

1. In a soup pot, render the salt pork and melt the butter over medium heat until the lean portions of the pork are lightly crisp, about 6 minutes.

2. Add the onions, celery, and peppers to the fat mixture and sweat until softened, about 5 minutes.

3. Add the flour and cook, stirring frequently, to make a white roux, about 3 minutes.

4. Remove the pot from the heat and add half of the stock. Stir until combined. Return the pot to medium heat and continue stirring to work out any lumps. Repeat with the remaining half of the stock. Bring the soup to a simmer and cook, stirring periodically to prevent scorching, until the soup thickens, 30 to 40 minutes.

5. Purée half of the corn and add it to the soup with the potatoes. Add the remaining whole corn and bay leaf and simmer, covered, until the corn and potatoes are tender, about 15 minutes.

6. Add the cream and milk to the soup and stir to combine. Heat the soup just until it begins to simmer, about 10 minutes. Remove and discard the bay leaf. The soup is ready to finish and serve now, or it may be rapidly cooled and held under refrigeration for up to 2 days for later service.

7. To finish the soup for service, return it to a boil. Taste the soup and season with salt, pepper, Tabasco, and Worcestershire. Serve the soup in heated bowls or cups.

CHEDDAR CHEESE SOUP

Makes 2½ gallons (9.5 liters) or 50 portions

Butter	4 oz	115 g
Mirepoix (page 134), small dice	2 lb	900 g
Garlic, minced	1 oz	30 g
All-purpose flour	1 lb 4 oz	570 g
Chicken Stock (page 83)	2 gal	7.5 l
Tillamook Cheddar, grated	4 lb	1.8 kg
Dark beer	3 qt	2.8 l
Dry mustard	1 oz	30 g
Worcestershire sauce	¼ cup	60 ml
Tabasco sauce	2 tbsp	30 ml
Heavy cream, hot	3 qt	2.8 l
Kosher salt, or as needed	1 tbsp	15 ml

1. Heat the butter in a soup pot over medium heat, add the mirepoix, and sweat, stirring occasionally, until tender, 10 to 12 minutes. Add the garlic and cook, stirring constantly, until aromatic, about 1 minute. Add the flour and cook, stirring constantly, for 5 minutes.

2. Add the stock and whisk to remove any lumps. Simmer over low heat for 30 minutes.

3. Remove the pot from the heat and stir in the cheese.

4. Combine the beer, mustard, Worcestershire, and Tabasco in a bowl and add to the soup. Strain through a fine-mesh sieve into a clean pot or storage container. The soup is ready to finish and serve now, or it may be rapidly cooled and held under refrigeration for up to 2 days for later service.

5. To finish the soup for service, return it to a simmer. Add the cream and cook the mixture gently for 5 minutes. Taste the soup and season with salt as necessary. Serve the soup in heated bowls or cups.

NEW ENGLAND–STYLE CLAM CHOWDER

Makes 2½ gallons (9.5 liters) or 50 portions

Chowder clams, cleaned	120 each	120 each
Fish Stock (page 84) or water	6 qt	5.6 l
Salt pork, minced to a paste	8 oz	225 g
Clarified butter	1 cup	240 ml
Onions, minced	1 lb	450 g
Celery, small dice	8 oz	225 g
All-purpose flour	8 oz	225 g
Russet potatoes, peeled, small dice	1 lb 8 oz	680 g
Heavy cream, hot	2 qt	1.9 l
Kosher salt	As needed	As needed
Ground white pepper	As needed	As needed
Tabasco sauce, plus additional as needed	2 tsp	10 ml
Worcestershire sauce, plus additional as needed	2 tsp	10 ml

1. In a covered pot, steam the clams in the stock or water until they open.

2. Decant and strain the broth through a coffee filter or cheesecloth and reserve. Remove the meat from the clam shells and chop and reserve the meat.

3. In a stockpot, render the salt pork over medium-low heat. Add the butter, onions, and celery. Sweat until the onions are translucent, 6 to 7 minutes.

4. Add the flour and cook, stirring frequently, to make a blond roux, 5 to 6 minutes.

5. Combine the reserved clam broth and enough additional stock or water to make 6 qt/5.6 l of liquid. Gradually add the stock to the roux and stir to incorporate completely, working out any lumps. Simmer for 30 minutes, skimming the surface as necessary.

6. Add the potatoes and simmer until they are tender. The soup is ready to finish and serve now, or it may be rapidly cooled and held under refrigeration for up to 2 days for later service.

7. To finish the soup for service, return it to a simmer. Add the reserved clams and the cream. Taste the soup and season with salt, pepper, Tabasco, and Worcestershire. Serve the soup in heated bowls or cups.

PURÉE OF SPLIT PEA SOUP

Makes 2½ gallons (9.5 liters) or 50 portions

Bacon, minced	8 oz	225 g
Vegetable oil	½ cup	120 ml
Mirepoix (page 134), small dice	2 lb	900 g
Garlic, minced	4 tsp	20 ml
Chicken Stock (page 83)	1½ gal	5.6 l
Russet potatoes, peeled, large dice	2 lb	900 g
Green split peas	4 lb	1.8 kg
Ham hock	1 each	1 each
Bay leaf	1 each	1 each
Kosher salt	As needed	As needed
Ground black pepper	As needed	As needed
Croutons (page 180)	2 lb	900 g

1. Render the bacon in a soup pot over medium heat. Remove the bits of bacon and reserve for garnish. Add the oil and mirepoix and sweat, stirring occasionally, until the onions are transparent, 10 to 12 minutes. Add the garlic and sauté for 1 minute. Do not brown the garlic.

2. Add the stock, potatoes, split peas, ham hock, and bay leaf and bring to a simmer. Allow the soup to simmer, stirring occasionally, until the peas are tender, about 45 minutes. Remove and discard the bay leaf and ham hock. Dice the lean meat, if desired. Reserve the meat.

3. Purée the soup using a food mill, blender, or food processor until it is smooth. Add the ham hock meat, if desired. Taste and season with salt and pepper. The soup is ready to finish and serve now, or it may be rapidly cooled and held under refrigeration for up to 3 days for later service.

4. To finish the soup for service, return it to a boil. Serve the soup in heated bowls or cups, garnished with croutons and reserved bacon bits.

GAZPACHO ANDALUZ (ANDALUSIAN GAZPACHO)

Makes 2½ gallons (9.5 liters) or 50 portions

Plum tomatoes, peeled, seeded, medium dice	16 lb	7.25 kg
Green peppers, medium dice	2 lb	900 g
Cucumbers, peeled seeded, medium dice	2 lb	900 g
Garlic cloves, crushed	16 each	16 each
Red wine vinegar	1 pt	480 ml
Olive oil	1 qt	950 ml
Kosher salt	As needed	As needed
Ground black pepper	As needed	As needed
GARNISH		
Tomatoes, small dice	8 oz	225 g
Green peppers, small dice	8 oz	225 g
Cucumbers, small dice	8 oz	225 g
White bread, small dice	2 oz	60 g

1. Combine the plum tomatoes, peppers, cucumbers, garlic, vinegar, oil, salt, and pepper in a nonreactive container. Cover and marinate under refrigeration overnight.

2. Purée the marinated ingredients in a blender or food mill, working in batches if necessary. Strain through a fine-mesh sieve. Taste the soup and adjust seasoning with salt and pepper.

3. Chill the soup for at least 4 hours and up to 24 hours before serving.

4. Serve the soup in chilled bowls or cups, garnished with tomatoes, peppers, cucumbers, and bread.

VEGETABLE SOUP EMILIA-ROMAGNA-STYLE (MINESTRONE ALLA EMILIANA)

Makes 2½ gallons (9.5 liters) or 50 portions

Olive oil	1 pt	480 ml
Butter	8 oz	225 g
Onions, thinly sliced	2 lb	900 g
Carrots, small dice	2 lb	900 g
Celery, small dice	2 lb	900 g
Russet potatoes, peeled, small dice	2 lb 4 oz	1 kg
Zucchini, small dice	3 lb	1.4 kg
Green beans, small dice	1 lb 8 oz	680 g
Savoy cabbage, shredded	4 lb	1.8 kg
Chicken Stock (page 83)	2 gal	7.5 l
Parmesan rinds, cut into 3-inch/76-mm squares	4 each	4 each
Canned whole plum tomatoes, seeded, coarsely chopped, with juices	2 lb	900 g
Kosher salt	As needed	As needed
Ground black pepper	As needed	As needed
Great northern or navy beans, cooked	1 lb 4 oz	570 g
GARNISH		
Parmesan, grated, plus additional as needed	4 oz	115 g
Extra-virgin olive oil, plus additional as needed	1 cup	240 ml

1. In a soup pot, heat the olive oil and melt the butter over low heat. Add the onions and sweat until wilted and soft. Add the carrots and cook for 3 minutes.

2. Add the vegetables in the following sequence, allowing each to soften before adding the next: celery, potatoes, zucchini, green beans, and cabbage. Do not brown the vegetables.

3. Add the broth, cheese rind pieces, and tomatoes with their juices.

4. Partially cover and cook at a low simmer for at least 3 hours. Remove and discard the Parmesan rind pieces. Add more broth as necessary to maintain the soup's level in the pot. The soup is ready to finish and serve now, or it may be rapidly cooled and held under refrigeration for up to 3 days for later service.

5. To finish the soup for service, return it to a boil. Taste the soup and season with salt and pepper. Add the cooked beans. Serve the soup in heated bowls or cups, garnished with cheese and a drizzle of extra-virgin olive oil.

NOTE *To make banquet service more efficient, add garnish vegetables to heated cups. Ladle the hot broth into them at the table.*

LOBSTER BISQUE

Makes 2½ gallons (9.5 liters) or 50 portions

Olive oil	¾ cup	180 ml
Onions, small dice	2 lb 4 oz	1 kg
Carrots, small dice	2 lb 4 oz	1 kg
Celery, small dice	2 lb 4 oz	1 kg
Leeks, thinly sliced	1 lb	450 g
Fennel, small dice	4 lb 8 oz	2 kg
Garlic cloves, crushed	12 each	12 each
Lobster shells, crushed, roasted	12 lb 10 oz	5.7 kg
Tomato paste	8 oz	225 g
Brandy	½ cup	120 ml
Dry white wine	1½ pt	720 ml
Fish Stock (page 84)	6 qt	5.6 l
Water	3 qt	2.8 l
Arborio or Carnaroli rice	8 oz	225 g
Roux (page 135), cooked until blond, cold	10 oz	285 g
Heavy cream, hot	3 pt	1.4 l
Kosher salt	As needed	As needed
Cayenne	As needed	As needed
Lemon juice	¼ cup	60 ml
Tarragon, chopped	2 oz	60 g

1. In a soup pot, heat the oil over medium heat. Add the onions and sweat for 5 minutes. Add the carrots, celery, leeks, fennel, and garlic and sweat for an additional 5 minutes.

2. Add the lobster shells and sweat for 10 minutes, until the shells are very fragrant and the liquid is released.

3. Add the tomato paste and cook until the tomato paste turns a rusty brown color. Add the brandy and continue to cook until the brandy is nearly cooked away (you may ignite the brandy to burn it off, if desired).

4. Add the wine and cook over high heat until it is reduced by half, about 5 minutes. Add the stock and water and bring to a boil. Add the rice and cook, covered, over medium-low heat until the rice is tender enough to mash, about 45 minutes.

5. When the rice is very soft, strain the soup through a fine-mesh sieve, return it to the pot, and bring it to a boil.

6. Add the roux and cook, stirring out any lumps, until the soup thickens, about 10 minutes.

7. Add the cream and cook until the soup is reduced to the desired consistency. Taste the soup and season with salt, cayenne, and lemon juice. Pass through a sieve again if necessary. The soup is ready to finish and serve now, or it may be rapidly cooled and held under refrigeration for up to 2 days for later service.

8. To finish the soup for service, return it to a simmer. Taste the soup and adjust seasoning as necessary. Serve the soup in heated bowls or cups, garnished with tarragon.

CHICKEN AND SHRIMP GUMBO

Makes 2½ gallons (9.5 liters) or 50 portions

Vegetable oil	2 tbsp	30 ml
Andouille sausage, small dice	8 oz	225 g
Chicken breasts, boneless, skinless, medium dice	1 lb	450 g
Onions, medium dice	1 lb	450 g
Green peppers, medium dice	10 oz	285 g
Celery, medium dice	10 oz	285 g
Jalapeños, minced	4 oz	115 g
Green onions, thinly sliced on the diagonal	6 oz	170 g
Garlic, chopped	1 oz	30 g
Okra, sliced	10 oz	285 g
Plum tomatoes, peeled, seeded, medium dice	1 lb	450 g
All-purpose flour, baked until dark brown	10 oz	285 g
Chicken Stock (page 83)	6 qt	5.6 l
Bay leaves	2 each	2 each
Dried oregano	2 tsp	10 ml
Onion powder	2 tsp	10 ml
Dried thyme	2 tbsp	30 ml
Dried basil	2 tbsp	30 ml
Kosher salt	As needed	As needed
Ground black pepper	As needed	As needed
Shrimp, peeled, deveined, chopped	2 lb 8 oz	1.15 kg
Rice, long-grain, cooked	1 lb 10 oz	740 g
Filé powder	2 tbsp	30 ml

1. Heat the oil over medium-high heat in a soup pot and add the sausage. Sauté, stirring occasionally, until the sausage starts to become firm, about 1 minute.

2. Add the chicken and sear until it begins to lose its raw appearance, 2 to 3 minutes.

3. Add the onions, peppers, celery, jalapeños, green onions, garlic, okra, and tomatoes. Sauté, stirring occasionally, until the vegetables are tender and the onions are translucent, 5 to 7 minutes.

4. Add the flour to the mixture and cook, stirring constantly, for 1 minute. Add the stock and stir constantly to work out any lumps.

5. Add the bay leaves, oregano, onion powder, thyme, basil, salt, and pepper and simmer for 30 minutes.

6. Add the shrimp and rice, simmer for 2 minutes, and whisk in the filé powder. Be sure to blend well. Do not allow the soup to return to a boil. The soup is ready to finish and serve now, or it may be rapidly cooled and held under refrigeration for up to 3 days for later service.

7. To finish the soup for service, return it to a simmer. Taste the soup and adjust seasoning with salt and pepper if necessary. Serve the soup in heated bowls or cups.

Roasted Red Pepper Gazpacho

Makes 2½ gallons (9.5 liters) or 50 portions

White bread, dry, crust removed	1 lb 4 oz	570 g
Tomato juice	3 pt	1.4 l
Tomatoes, peeled, seeded	4 lb	1.8 kg
Cucumbers, peeled, seeded	2½ lb	1.15 kg
Green peppers, roasted, peeled	1 lb 4 oz	570 g
Red peppers, roasted, peeled	1 lb 4 oz	570 g
Red onions, sliced	2 lb	900 g
Garlic cloves, mashed	8 each	8 each
Tomato purée	4 oz	115 g
Extra-virgin olive oil	¼ cup	60 ml
Red wine vinegar	¾ cup	180 ml
Limes, juiced	6 each	6 each
Kosher salt, or as needed	4 tsp	20 ml
Cracked black pepper, or as needed	4 tsp	20 ml
GARNISH		
Cucumbers, short julienne	2 each	2 each
Celery Seed Croutons (page 180)	1 tbsp	15 ml
Safron Aïoli (page 177)	5 tbsp	75 mL

1. Soak the bread in the tomato juice for 30 minutes.

2. Grind the tomatoes, cucumbers, peppers, and onions through a grinder with a coarse die directly into a bowl set over ice.

3. In a blender, purée the soaked bread, garlic, and any tomato juice that has not been absorbed by the bread. Fold the mixture into the ground vegetables. Add the tomato purée, oil, vinegar, lime juice, salt, and pepper. Taste the soup and adjust seasoning.

4. Place in a clean stainless-steel bowl and refrigerate overnight. Taste the soup and adjust seasoning the next day if necessary.

5. Serve the soup in chilled bowls or cups, garnished with julienned cucumbers and croutons.

Venetian Bean and Potato Soup

Makes 2½ gallons (9.5 liters) or 50 portions

Olive oil	¼ cup	60 ml
Pancetta, small dice	1 lb	450 g
Onions, peeled, small dice	12 oz	340 g
Cannellini beans, cooked	4 lb	1.8 kg
Zucchini, small dice	1 lb	450 g
Yukon gold potatoes, peeled, small dice	2 lb	900 g
Spinach, julienned	1 lb	450 g
Carrots, small dice	2 lb	900 g
Tomato purée	2 lb	900 g
Chicken Stock (page 83)	5 qt	4.7 l
Sachet d'Epices (page 133), including marjoram and omitting pepper and garlic	1 each	1 each
Kosher salt	1 tbsp	15 ml
Ground black pepper	½ tsp	3 ml
Parmesan, grated	12 oz	340 g

1. Heat the oil in a soup pot over medium-high heat and add the pancetta.

2. Cook the pancetta until lightly browned, stirring frequently, 5 to 6 minutes. Remove with a slotted spoon and set aside to drain on paper towels. Remove the excess fat from the pan, leaving about ¼ cup/60 ml.

3. Reduce the heat to low, add the onions to the pan, and cook until slightly softened, 3 to 4 minutes.

4. Add the beans, zucchini, potatoes, spinach, carrots, tomato purée, stock, sachet, salt, pepper, and pancetta and simmer for 20 minutes.

5. Remove the sachet. The soup is ready to finish and serve now, or it may be rapidly cooled and held under refrigeration for up to 3 days for later service.

6. To finish the soup for service, return it to a simmer. Stir in the cheese. Serve the soup in heated bowls or cups.

Tomato Sauce

Makes 1 gallon (3.75 liters)

Olive oil	¼ cup	60 ml
Onions, minced	12 oz	340 g
Garlic, minced	1 oz	30 g
Tomatoes, fresh or canned, with juice	12 lb (fresh) or 9 lb (canned)	5.4 kg (fresh) or 4 kg (canned)
Basil sprigs (optional)	5 or 6 each	5 or 6 each
Kosher salt	As needed	As needed
Ground black pepper	As needed	As needed

1. Heat the oil in a sauce pot over medium-high heat. Add the onions and garlic and cook, stirring from time to time, until the onions are tender and translucent, but with no browning, 6 to 8 minutes.

2. Add the tomatoes and basil, if using. Simmer the sauce over low heat until the flavor is fully developed, 1½ to 2 hours. The sauce will thicken and reduce slightly as it simmers. Remove and discard the basil sprigs. Taste the sauce and season with salt and pepper as necessary. Purée the sauce through a food mill or with an immersion blender, if desired.

3. The sauce is ready to serve now, or it may be rapidly cooled and held under refrigeration for up to 5 days for later use.

1. Mise en place for tomato sauce.

2. Simmer the tomato sauce to develop and concentrate the flavor.

3. The finished sauce can be served as a thick, chunky sauce, or it can be puréed for a smoother texture.

Tomato Coulis

Makes 1 quart (950 milliliters)

Olive oil	2 tbsp	30 ml
Onions, minced	4 oz	115 g
Garlic, minced	2 tsp	10 ml
Tomato purée	4 oz	115 g
Dry red wine	¾ cup	180 ml
Plum tomatoes, peeled, seeded, medium dice	1 lb 4 oz	570 g
Chicken Stock (page 83)	1 pt	480 ml
Basil leaves	5 each	5 each
Thyme sprig	1 each	1 each
Bay leaf	1 each	1 each
Kosher salt	As needed	As needed
Ground black pepper	As needed	As needed

1. Heat the oil in a sauce pot over medium-high heat and sauté the onions until they are translucent, 6 to 8 minutes. Add the garlic and sauté, stirring constantly, until aromatic, about 1 minute. Add the tomato purée and cook until the tomato purée turns a rusty brown color and gives off a sweet aroma, about 5 minutes.

2. Add the wine, tomatoes, stock, basil, thyme, and bay leaf. Simmer until the sauce has a good flavor and is lightly thickened, about 45 minutes. Remove and discard the herbs.

3. Pass the mixture through a food mill fitted with a coarse disk. Adjust the consistency if necessary by thinning a heavy coulis with additional stock or reducing a thin coulis by simmering over medium heat.

4. Taste the coulis and season with salt and pepper.

5. The coulis is ready to serve now, or it may be rapidly cooled and held under refrigeration for up to 5 days for later use.

Marsala Sauce

Makes 3¾ quarts (3.6 liters)

Shallots, minced	3¾ oz	110 g
Thyme sprigs	7 each	7 each
Bay leaves	4 each	4 each
Black peppercorns	1½ tsp	8 ml
Dry red wine	1 qt	950 ml
Jus de Veau Lié (page 89) or Demi-Glace (page 88)	3¾ qt	3.5 l
Marsala	1 qt	950 ml
Kosher salt	As needed	As needed
Ground black pepper	As needed	As needed
Butter, diced	15 oz	425 g

1. In a saucepan, combine the shallots, thyme, bay leaves, peppercorns, and wine. Cook over medium-high heat until the liquid is reduced by half.

2. Add the jus lié or demi-glace and continue to simmer until the sauce has developed a good flavor and consistency, about 25 minutes. Add the Marsala and return to a simmer. Taste the sauce and season with salt and pepper. Strain the sauce through a fine-mesh sieve into a clean saucepan or storage container. The sauce is ready to finish and serve now, or it may be rapidly cooled and held under refrigeration for up to 5 days for later use.

3. To finish the sauce for service, return it to a simmer in individual portions or batches and swirl in the butter.

SALSA VERDE

Makes 1 quart (950 milliliters)

Tomatillos, husked	1 lb 8 oz	680 g
Serranos, stemmed	4 each	4 each
Cilantro, chopped	¾ oz	20 g
Onions, small dice	12 oz	340 g
Garlic cloves, roughly chopped	2 each	2 each
Lard	½ oz	15 g
Chicken Stock (page 83)	1½ pt	720 ml
Kosher salt	As needed	As needed

1. Boil the tomatillos and serranos in salted water to cover until tender, 10 to 15 minutes. Drain.

2. Place the tomatillos and serranos in a blender, along with the cilantro, onions, and garlic. Process until almost smooth.

3. Heat the lard in a medium skillet over medium-high heat. When the skillet is hot, pour in the purée and stir constantly until the purée is darker and thicker, 4 to 5 minutes. Add the stock and bring the sauce to a boil. Reduce the heat to medium and simmer until the sauce is thick enough to coat the back of a spoon, about 20 minutes. Taste the salsa and season with salt.

4. The salsa is ready to serve now, or it may be rapidly cooled and held under refrigeration for up to 3 days for later use.

   NOTE *To make a vegetarian salsa verde, substitute vegetable oil for the lard, and water or vegetable stock for the chicken stock.*

SALSA FRESCA

Makes 1 quart (950 milliliters)

Tomatoes, peeled, seeded, small dice	18 oz	510 g
Onions, minced	3 oz	85 g
Green peppers, small dice	2²/₃ oz	75 g
Garlic, minced	2 tsp	10 ml
Cilantro, chopped	1 tbsp	15 ml
Oregano, chopped	1 tsp	5 ml
Lime juice	2 fl oz	60 ml
Jalapeños, small dice	1 oz	30 g
Olive oil	2 tbsp	30 ml
Kosher salt, or as needed	2 tsp	10 ml
Ground black pepper, or as needed	¼ tsp	1 ml

Combine all the ingredients in a bowl. Taste the salsa and adjust seasoning. The salsa is ready to serve now, or it may be held under refrigeration for up to 2 days for later use.

ROASTED TOMATO SALSA

Makes 1 quart (950 milliliters)

Tomatoes, roasted, peeled, seeded, small dice	18 oz	510 g
Onions, minced	3 oz	85 g
Red peppers, roasted, peeled, seeded, small dice	2²/₃ oz	75 g
Garlic, minced	2 tsp	10 ml
Cilantro, chopped	1 tbsp	15 ml
Lime juice	¼ cup	60 ml
Jalapeño, seeded and minced	1 each	1 each
Kosher salt, or as needed	2 tsp	10 ml
Ground black pepper, or as needed	¼ tsp	1 ml

Combine all the ingredients in a bowl. Taste the salsa and adjust seasoning. The salsa is ready to serve now, or it may be held under refrigeration for up to 2 days for later use.

SPICED SWEET-SOUR BLACKBERRY KETCHUP

Makes 2½ quarts (2.4 liters)

Red wine vinegar	1 pt	480 ml
Blackberries, fresh or frozen	3 lb	1.4 kg
Brown sugar	1 lb 4 oz	570 g
Ground cloves	⅛ tsp	⅛ tsp
Ground ginger	1 tsp	5 ml
Ground cinnamon	1 tsp	5 ml
Cayenne	½ tsp	3 ml
Kosher salt	1 tsp	5 ml
Butter	2 tbsp	30 ml

1. Bring the vinegar to a boil in a rondeau and simmer until it is reduced by half.

2. Purée the blackberries in a blender. If desired, strain the blackberries through a fine-mesh sieve and discard the seeds.

3. Bring to a boil, then reduce the heat and add the brown sugar, cloves, ginger, cinnamon, cayenne, and salt. Simmer until thickened and flavorful, about 20 minutes.

4. Remove from the heat and finish by swirling in the butter.

5. The ketchup is ready to serve now, or it may be rapidly cooled and held under refrigeration for up to 3 days for later service.

1. In a rondeau, simmer the vinegar to reduce it and concentrate the flavor.

2. Add the puréed blackberries to the reduced vinegar.

3. Season the mixture with brown sugar, cloves, ginger, cinnamon, cayenne, and salt.

4. Bring the ketchup to a boil, then reduce the heat and allow to simmer. This will thicken the ketchup and further develop the flavor.

POBLANO CHILE DRESSING

Makes 1½ quarts (1.4 liters)

Basic Mayonnaise (page 390)	1½ pt	720 ml
Buttermilk	1 cup	240 ml
Oven-Roasted Tomatoes (page 300), puréed	8 oz	225 g
Dried poblanos, puréed (see Note)	8 oz	225 g
Garlic, roasted, puréed	1 tsp	5 ml
Oregano, chopped	1 tbsp	15 ml
Chives, cut into short pieces	¼ cup	60 ml
White wine vinegar	½ cup	120 ml
Worcestershire sauce	½ tsp	3 ml
Kosher salt, plus as needed	1 tsp	5 ml
Cracked black pepper, or as needed	1 tsp	5 ml

1. In a bowl, combine the mayonnaise, buttermilk, puréed oven-roasted tomatoes, puréed poblanos, garlic, oregano, chives, vinegar, and Worcestershire. Mix well.

2. Taste the dressing and season with salt and pepper.

3. The dressing is ready to serve now, or it may be held under refrigeration for up to 3 days for later service.

   NOTE *Dried chiles should be toasted in a hot dry pan, placed in a bowl, covered with hot water, and rehydrated for at least 30 minutes before puréeing.*

ZESTY CHIPOTLE AND BACON RANCH DIP

Makes 2½ quarts (2.4 liters)

Sour cream	1 lb	450 g
Basic Mayonnaise (page 390)	1 pt	480 ml
Buttermilk	1 cup	240 ml
Lemon juice	¼ cup	60 ml
Red wine vinegar	2 tbsp	30 ml
Garlic cloves, roasted, crushed	4 each	4 each
Worcestershire sauce	2 tsp	10 ml
Chives, cut into short pieces	1 tbsp	15 ml
Cilantro, chopped	1 tbsp	15 ml
Parsley, chopped	1 tbsp	15 ml
Shallots, roasted, minced	2 tbsp	30 ml
Dijon mustard	2 tbsp	30 ml
Celery seeds	2 tsp	10 ml
Chipotles in adobo sauce, minced	4 oz	115 g
Bacon, cooked, crumbled	4 oz	115 g
Kosher salt, or as needed	1 tbsp	15 ml
Cracked black pepper, or as needed	1½ tsp	8 ml

Combine all the ingredients in a stainless-steel bowl and mix well. Taste the dip and adjust seasoning. Serve immediately or hold, covered, under refrigeration for up to 3 days for later service.

Romesco Sauce

Makes 1 quart (950 milliliters)

Anchos	4 each	4 each
Marinated Roasted Peppers (page 301)	4 each	4 each
Olive oil	1¼ cups	300 ml
Garlic cloves, minced	6 each	6 each
Red wine vinegar	¼ cup	60 ml
Spanish paprika	¾ oz	20 g
Cayenne	½ tsp	3 ml
Tomato paste	4 oz	115 g
Hazelnuts, ground	1 lb	450 g
Kosher salt	As needed	As needed

1. Put the anchos in a small saucepan and cover with water. Bring to a boil, then turn off the heat and let steep for 20 minutes.

2. Drain the anchos, combine with the remaining ingredients in a blender or food processor, and purée to a smooth consistency.

3. Allow the sauce to rest overnight under refrigeration to develop a full flavor. Hold under refrigeration for up to 6 days for later service. Taste the sauce and adjust seasoning with salt before using.

Latin Citrus Marinade (Mojo)

Makes 1 quart (950 milliliters)

Orange juice	18 fl oz	540 ml
Lemon juice	9 fl oz	270 ml
Lime juice	3 fl oz	90 ml
Ground annatto	3 tbsp	45 ml
Garlic, chopped	2 tsp	10 ml
Kosher salt	1 tbsp	15 ml
Dried oregano	2 tsp	10 ml
Ground cumin	2 tsp	10 ml
Ground cloves	½ tsp	3 ml
Ground cinnamon	½ tsp	3 ml
Ground black pepper	½ tsp	3 ml

1. Combine all the ingredients in a bowl and mix well.

2. Use immediately or hold under refrigeration for up to 4 days for later use.

3. Use as a marinade for poultry or fish.

ARUGULA PESTO

Makes 2½ quarts (2.4 liters)

Garlic cloves, peeled, roasted	12 each	12 each
Arugula leaves, chopped	10 oz	285 g
Basil leaves, chopped	4 oz	115 g
Parsley, chopped	4 oz	115 g
Parmesan, grated	12 oz	340 g
Pine nuts, toasted	8 oz	225 g
Extra-virgin olive oil	1 cup	240 ml
Butter	4 oz	115 g
Kosher salt, or as needed	1 tbsp	15 ml
Cracked black pepper, or as needed	1½ tsp	8 ml

1. Combine the garlic, arugula, basil, parsley, cheese, and pine nuts in a food processor. Pulse the mixture until finely chopped.

2. Add the oil in a thin stream and process until the oil is fully incorporated and a paste forms.

3. Add the butter and mix well until a smooth, creamy paste is formed.

4. Taste the pesto and season with salt and pepper.

5. Use immediately or hold under refrigeration for up to 2 days for later service.

1. Mise en place for arugula pesto.

2. Combine the garlic, arugula, basil, parsley, cheese, and pine nuts in a food processor fitted with a steel blade. Chop until relatively fine.

3. With the machine running, add the oil in a thin stream.

4. The pesto will thicken and become a smooth paste that still has some texture.

SEASONING MIX FOR SPIT-ROASTED MEATS AND POULTRY

Makes 12 ounces (350 grams)

Kosher salt	6¼ oz	175 g
Dry mustard	4 oz	115 g
Ground black pepper	1 oz	30 g
Dried thyme	¼ oz	7 g
Dried oregano	¼ oz	7 g
Ground coriander	½ oz	15 g
Celery seeds	½ oz	15 g

1. Combine all the ingredients in a bowl and stir to blend evenly.

2. Use immediately or place in a tightly sealed container, store in a cool, dark area, and use within 1 month.

BARBECUE SPICE MIX

Makes 14½ ounces (425 grams)

Spanish paprika	2½ oz	75 g
Chili Powder (on facing page)	2½ oz	75 g
Kosher salt	2½ oz	75 g
Ground cumin	1½ oz	45 g
Sugar	1½ oz	45 g
Dry mustard	¾ oz	20 g
Ground black pepper	¾ oz	20 g
Dried thyme	¾ oz	20 g
Dried oregano	½ oz	15 g
Curry powder	¾ oz	20 g
Cayenne	½ oz	15 g

1. Combine all the ingredients in a bowl and stir until evenly blended.

2. Use immediately or place in a tightly sealed container, store in a cool, dark area, and use within 1 month.

CHILI POWDER

Makes 2 ounces (57 grams)

Dried chiles, such as ancho, pasilla, poblano	1½ oz	45 g
Ground cumin	½ oz	15 g
Dried oregano	1 tsp	5 ml
Garlic powder	½ tsp	3 ml
Ground coriander	¼ tsp	1 ml
Ground cloves (optional)	¼ tsp	1 ml

1. Toast the dried chiles in a dry sauté pan over medium-high heat until they puff and soften, about 1 minute. Let the chiles cool slightly. Grind the chiles to a powder in a food processor.

2. Add the remaining spices, including the cloves, if using, and pulse once or twice to blend evenly.

3. Use immediately or place in a tightly sealed container, store in a cool, dark area, and use within 1 month.

LIAISON

Makes 10½ fluid ounces (315 milliliters), enough to thicken 24 fluid ounces (720 milliliters) of liquid

Heavy cream	1 cup	240 ml
Egg yolks, large	3 each	3 each

Blend the cream and eggs yolks together in a bowl until evenly blended. Before adding the liaison to a dish, the liaison must be tempered as follows: Add about the same amount of hot liquid as liaison to the bowl and blend well. Repeat twice more to gradually heat up the liaison. At this point, the tempered liaison may be added to the entire batch.

Maître d'Hôtel Butter

Makes 1 pound (450 grams)

Unsalted butter, room temperature	1 lb	450 g
Parsley, minced	2 oz	60 g
Lemon juice	1 tbsp	15 ml
Kosher salt, plus additional as needed	¼ tsp	1 ml
Ground black pepper, plus additional as needed	¼ tsp	1 ml

1. Working either by hand with a wooden spoon or in a stand mixer with a paddle attachment, soften the butter and then add the remaining ingredients and blend well. Taste the butter and adjust seasoning with salt and pepper.

2. The compound butter is ready to use, or it may be rolled into a log or piped into shapes and held under refrigeration up to 2 weeks for later use.

   Sun-Dried Tomato and Oregano Butter: Add 1 tbsp/15 ml minced oregano and 1 oz/30 g minced sun-dried tomatoes.

   Tarragon Butter: Replace the parsley with an equal amount of minced tarragon.

   Lobster Butter: Add 2 oz/60 g lobster coral and 2 oz/60 g very finely minced lobster meat to the butter.

   Pimiento Butter: Replace the parsley with an equal amount of minced pimientos.

   Green Onion Butter: Add 1 tbsp/15 ml soy sauce and ½ tsp/3 ml minced garlic, and replace the parsley with an equal amount of minced green onions.

   Dill Butter: Replace the parsley with an equal amount of minced dill.

   Basil Butter: Replace the parsley with an equal amount of minced basil.

BOUQUET GARNI

Makes 1 bouquet, enough to flavor 1 gallon (3.75 liters) of liquid

Thyme sprig	1 each	1 each
Parsley stems	3 or 4 each	3 or 4 each
Bay leaf	1 each	1 each
Leek leaves	2 or 3 each	2 or 3 each
Celery stalk, cut crosswise in half	1 each	1 each

Encase the thyme, parsley, and bay leaf inside the leek leaves and celery. Tie the ingredients into a bundle with a piece of string, leaving a long enough tail of string to tie onto the pot handle for easy removal. Add the bouquet at the point recommended in your recipe or during the final 30 minutes of simmering time.

SACHET D'EPICES

Makes 1 sachet, enough to flavor 1 gallon (3.75 liters) of liquid

Thyme sprig	1 each	1 each
Parsley stems	3 or 4 each	3 or 4 each
Bay leaf	1 each	1 each
Cracked black peppercorns	1 tsp	5 ml
Garlic clove (optional)	1 each	1 each

Cut a square of cheesecloth about 4 inches/10 cm square. Place the thyme, parsley, bay leaf, peppercorns, and garlic, if using, on the cheesecloth. Gather the cheesecloth around the spices to make a bundle. Tie the bundle shut with a piece of string, leaving a long enough tail of string to tie onto the pot handle for easy removal. Add the sachet at the point recommended in your recipe or during the final 30 minutes of simmering time.

MIREPOIX

Makes 2 pounds (900 grams)

Onions or the white parts of leeks, chopped	1 lb	450 g
Celery root or hearts, chopped	8 oz	225 g
Carrots, chopped	8 oz	225 g

Chop the ingredients to the size directed by the specific recipe, or according to the overall cooking time (the longer the dish cooks, the larger the cut). Add to recipes as directed.

WHITE MIREPOIX

Makes 2 pounds (900 grams)

Onions or the white parts of leeks, chopped	1 lb	450 g
Celery root or hearts, chopped	8 oz	225 g
Parsnips, chopped	8 oz	225 g

Chop the ingredients to the size directed by the specific recipe, or according to the overall cooking time (the longer the dish cooks, the larger the cut). Add to recipes as directed.

CAJUN TRINITY

Makes 2 pounds (900 grams)

Onions, chopped	1 lb	450 g
Green peppers, chopped	8 oz	225 g
Celery, chopped	8 oz	225 g

Chop the ingredients to the size directed by the specific recipe, or according to the overall cooking time (the longer the dish cooks, the larger the cut). Add to recipes as directed.

MATIGNON

Makes 1 pound 13 ounces (825 grams)

Ham, chopped	7 oz	200 g
Onions, chopped	9 oz	255 g
Carrots, chopped	9 oz	255 g
Celery, chopped	4 oz	115 g
Thyme sprig	1 each	1 each
Bay leaf	1 each	1 each

Chop the ham, onions, carrots, and celery to the size directed by the specific recipe, or according to the overall cooking time (the longer the dish cooks, the larger the cut). Add the chopped ingredients, thyme, and bay leaf to recipes as directed.

ROUX

Makes 2 pounds 8 ounces (1.15 kilograms)

Butter	1 lb	450 g
All-purpose flour	1 lb 8 oz	680 g

1. Heat the butter in a rondeau over medium heat and add the flour, stirring to combine. The roux should be very smooth and moist, with a glossy sheen, not dry or greasy. Adjust the roux's texture by adding more flour or butter if needed.

2. Stir the roux as it cooks to keep it from scorching, and continue to cook it to the desired color: white (barely colored or chalky), about 8 minutes; blond (golden straw color with a slightly nutty aroma), about 10 minutes; brown (deep brown with a strong nutty aroma), about 12 minutes; and dark (dark brown with a pronounced nutty flavor and aroma), about 14 minutes. To reduce the chances of scorching, large quantities of roux may be placed in a medium oven (350° to 375°F/175° to 190°C) to complete cooking.

3. Once the roux is cooked to its desired doneness, it is ready to use, or it may be cooled and held under refrigeration for up to 1 week for later use.

   NOTES *Roux can be combined with a liquid in order to thicken it in three ways. Cool roux may be added to a hot liquid, cool liquid may be added to a hot roux, or warm roux may be added to a liquid of the same temperature.*

chapter seven

RECIPES FOR
BREAKFAST AND
BRUNCH

HARD-COOKED EGGS

Makes 50 portions (100 eggs)

Eggs, cold	100 each	100 each

1. Place the eggs in a large pot. Fill the pot with enough cold water to cover the eggs.

2. Bring the water to a gentle boil and immediately lower the temperature to a simmer. Begin timing the cooking at this point.

3. Cook small eggs for 12 minutes, medium eggs for 13 minutes, large eggs for 14 to 15 minutes, and extra-large eggs for 15 minutes.

4. Serve the eggs, 2 per portion, hot in the shell, or cool them quickly in cool water and peel as soon as possible for cold preparations.

POACHED EGGS

Makes 50 portions

Water	As needed	As needed
Distilled white vinegar	As needed	As needed
Eggs	100 each	100 each

1. In a large, shallow pot, bring a mixture of water and vinegar to 200°F/95°C. Use a ratio of 1 qt/950 ml of water to 1 tbsp/15 ml of vinegar.

2. Break the eggs, one at a time, into cups, being careful not to break the yolks.

3. Slide the eggs into the simmering water and simmer them until the whites are completely set and the yolks have thickened slightly, 3 to 4 minutes. (Poached eggs should feel soft when touched; if they feel hard, they are overcooked.)

4. Remove the eggs carefully with a skimmer and drop them into an ice water bath to stop the cooking process.

5. Remove the eggs from the cold water and trim any excess white.

6. For service, reheat the poached eggs in slightly salted, 120° to 140°F/50° to 60°C water. Remove the eggs with a skimmer and dry before serving. Serve immediately, 2 eggs per portion, on heated plates.

POACHED EGGS WITH SMOKED SALMON

Makes 50 portions

Poached Eggs (page 139)	100 each	100 each
Bagels, split, toasted, buttered	50 each	50 each
Smoked salmon, sliced	100 slices	100 slices
Chives, chopped	As needed	As needed

1. If the eggs have been poached in advance, reheat them in simmering water until warmed through. Blot on paper towels and trim away any ragged edges if necessary.

2. Top each bagel half with a slice of smoked salmon and a poached egg.

3. Serve immediately, 2 bagel halves per portion, on heated plates, garnished with chopped chives.

POACHED EGGS FARMER-STYLE
Makes 50 portions

Poached Eggs (page 139)	50 each	50 each
Toast rounds or ovals	50 each	50 each
Unsalted butter, melted	1 lb 4 oz	570 g
Tomatoes, peeled, sliced	50 slices	50 slices
Boiled ham, sliced	50 slices	50 slices
Creamed Mushrooms (page 309)	4 lb 8 oz	2 kg
Mornay Sauce (see below), warm	5 pt	2.4 l
Gruyère, grated	15 oz	425 g

1. If the eggs have been poached in advance, reheat them in simmering water until warmed through. Blot on paper towels and trim away any ragged edges if necessary.

2. Place the toast on a sheet pan. Brush with butter and top each piece with a tomato slice, a ham slice, mushrooms, and a poached egg. Coat with Mornay sauce and sprinkle with cheese.

3. Brown lightly under a broiler or salamander until the Mornay sauce is very hot and lightly browned, about 2 minutes.

4. Serve immediately on heated plates.

MORNAY SAUCE
Makes 1 gallon (3.75 liters)

Béchamel Sauce (page 92)	1 gal	3.75 l
Gruyère, grated	20 oz	570 g
Parmesan, grated	12 oz	360 g
Kosher salt, or as needed	2 tsp	10 ml
Ground white pepper, or as needed	½ tsp	3 ml

1. Combine the béchamel sauce and the cheeses in a large pot over low heat.

2. Heat gently until the cheeses are melted, stirring constantly, about 10 minutes. Remove the sauce from the heat as soon as the cheeses melt, to prevent it from becoming stringy.

3. Taste the sauce and season with salt and pepper. The sauce can be held warm or it may be properly cooled and stored under refrigeration for up to 4 days.

POACHED EGGS ON HASH

Makes 50 portions

Poached Eggs (page 139)	50 each	50 each
Parsley sprigs (optional)	50 each	50 each
Toast rounds or ovals	50 each	50 each
Unsalted butter, melted	1 lb 4 oz	570 g
Corned Beef Hash (page 261)	50 portions	50 portions
Mornay Sauce (page 142), warm	5 pt	2.4 l
Gruyère, grated	15 oz	425 g

1. If the eggs have been poached in advance, reheat them in simmering water until warmed through. Blot on paper towels and trim away any ragged edges if necessary.

2. To deep fry the parsley, place the sprigs in a fryer basket and fry at 325°F/165°C until crisp, about 1 minute. Blot on paper towels and reserve.

3. Place the toast on a sheet pan. Brush with butter and top each piece with corned beef hash and a poached egg. Coat with Mornay sauce and sprinkle with cheese.

4. Brown lightly under the broiler or salamander until the Mornay sauce is very hot and lightly browned, about 2 minutes.

5. Serve immediately on heated plates, garnished with a sprig of deep-fried or fresh parsley if using.

FRIED EGGS (SUNNY-SIDE UP, BASTED, OR OVER)

Makes 10 portions

Eggs	20 each	20 each
Clarified butter or vegetable oil or bacon fat, rendered	As needed	As needed
Kosher salt	As needed	As needed
Ground black pepper	As needed	As needed

1. Break the eggs into a container without damaging the yolks.

2. Working in batches as needed, heat the butter or oil in a skillet over medium-high heat until it is very hot but not smoking and the foaming has subsided. Crack the eggs directly into the hot butter or oil and reduce the heat to medium-low or low. Fry the eggs, shaking the pan occasionally to keep the eggs from sticking. Season the eggs with salt and pepper.

3. Fry for about 2 minutes for "runny" yolks, 3 minutes for medium yolks, and 3½ to 4 minutes for hard yolks. Sunny-side-up eggs are not turned.

4. To prepare basted eggs, tilt the skillet, allow the fat to collect at the side of the pan, and baste the eggs with the fat as they cook, or add a small amount of water and cover the pan to steam the eggs.

5. For "over" eggs, turn the eggs near the end of their cooking time and cook them to the desired doneness (20 to 30 seconds more for over light, 1 minute more for over hard).

6. Serve immediately, 2 eggs per portion, on heated plates.

Huevos Rancheros

Makes 50 portions

Corn tortillas, 6 inches / 15 cm	50 each	50 each
Vegetarian Refried Beans (page 323)	3 qt	2.8 l
Clarified butter or vegetable oil	As needed	As needed
Eggs	100 each	100 each
Kosher salt	As needed	As needed
Ground black pepper	As needed	As needed
Monterey Jack, grated	3 lb 2 oz	1.5 kg
Avocados	12½ each	12½ each
Limes, juiced	3 each	3 each
Salsa Fresca (page 121)	3 pt 2 fl oz	1.5 l
Sour cream	3 lb 2 oz	1.5 kg
Cilantro sprigs	50 each	50 each

1. Heat the tortillas by toasting them one at a time in a dry cast-iron skillet over medium-high heat until lightly toasted. Place the tortillas on a sheet pan, spread each tortilla with ¼ cup/60 ml of the refried beans, and cover to keep warm.

2. Working in batches as needed, heat the butter or oil in a skillet over medium-high heat until it is very hot but not smoking and the foaming has subsided. Crack the eggs directly into the hot butter or oil and reduce the heat to medium-low or low. Fry the eggs, shaking the pan occasionally to keep the eggs from sticking. Season the eggs with salt and pepper. Fry for about 2 minutes for sunny-side up, 3 minutes for medium yolks, and 3½ to 4 minutes for hard yolks.

3. Top each prepared tortilla with 2 fried eggs and 1 oz/30 g of the cheese. Slide the tortillas under the broiler to melt the cheese.

4. Meanwhile, dice the avocados and toss with the lime juice to prevent the avocados from discoloring. Divide the avocados among the tortillas.

5. Top each serving with 2 tbsp/30 ml of the salsa and 1 oz/30 g of the sour cream. Serve immediately on heated plates, garnished with cilantro sprigs.

"Spit in the Eye" with Turkey Hash

Makes 50 portions

Vegetable oil or bacon fat, rendered	½ cup	120 ml
Onions, large dice	2 lb 8 oz	1.15 kg
Parsnips, large dice	1 lb 9 oz	710 g
Carrots, large dice	15 oz	425 g
Red-skin potatoes, peeled if desired	7 lb 8 oz	3.4 kg
Smoked turkey, cut into 1-inch cubes	10 lb	4.5 kg
Tomato purée	8 oz	225 g
Kosher salt	As needed	As needed
Ground black pepper	As needed	As needed
Toast rounds or ovals	50 each	50 each
Unsalted butter, melted	10 oz	285 g
Fried Eggs, cooked sunny-side up (page 146)	50 each	50 each

1. Heat a roasting pan over medium heat. Add ¼ cup/60 ml of the oil or fat to the pan. Add the onions and sweat until they are soft, 5 to 6 minutes. Add the parsnips, carrots, potatoes, and turkey to the pan and cover with foil.

2. Place the pan of vegetables in a 375°F/190°C oven and roast until they are fully cooked and tender, about 1 hour. Remove the foil, stir in the tomato purée, and return the pan, uncovered, to the oven. Cook until the tomato purée has browned, about 15 minutes. Taste the vegetables and season with salt and pepper. Cool slightly.

3. Grind the mixture through the medium die of a meat grinder. Form into patties, 2 to 3 oz/60 to 85 g each, by hand or using a circular mold. Hold under refrigeration up to 2 days.

4. Place the toast on a sheet pan. Brush with butter and toast lightly under the broiler or salamander. Reserve for service.

5. When ready to serve, heat 2 tbsp/30 ml of the oil or fat in a heavy sauté pan or griddle over medium-high heat. Working in batches if necessary, pan fry the patties until they are crispy on each side and hot in the center, about 2 minutes per side.

6. Assemble the "spit in the eye" by placing 1 egg on each slice of toast on heated plates. Serve immediately with a turkey hash patty.

FARMER-STYLE OMELET

Makes 50 portions

Bacon, minced, or vegetable oil	3 lb 2 oz bacon or 25 fl oz oil	1.4 kg bacon or 740 ml oil
Onions, minced	3 lb 2 oz	1.4 kg
Potatoes, diced, cooked	3 lb 2 oz	1.4 kg
Eggs	150 each	150 each
Kosher salt, or as needed	2 tbsp	30 ml
Ground white pepper, or as needed	2 tsp	10 ml

1. For each serving, render 1 oz/30 g of the bacon in a skillet until crisp, or heat 1 tbsp/15 ml of the oil over medium heat.

2. Add 1 oz/30 g of the onions and sauté, stirring occasionally, until light golden brown, 10 to 12 minutes.

3. Add 1 oz/30 g of the potatoes and sauté until lightly browned, about 5 minutes.

4. Meanwhile, beat 3 eggs together with a pinch of salt and pepper. Pour the eggs over the ingredients in the skillet and stir gently.

5. Reduce the heat to low, cover the skillet, and cook until the eggs are nearly set.

6. Remove the cover and place the skillet under the broiler to brown the eggs lightly.

7. Serve immediately on a heated plate.

OVEN-ROASTED POTATO AND SPINACH FRITTATA

Makes 50 portions

Olive oil	1 cup	240 ml
Vidalia onions, diced	4 lb 8 oz	2 kg
Yukon gold potatoes, diced, roasted	4 lb 8 oz	2 kg
Spinach, blanched, squeezed, and chopped	3 lb	1.4 kg
Green onions, sliced on the diagonal	12 oz	340 g
Tomatoes, peeled, seeded, chopped	2 lb 4 oz	1 kg
Eggs	96 each	96 each
Kosher salt	1 tbsp	15 ml
Ground black pepper	1 tsp	5 ml
Thyme, chopped	1 oz	30 g
Parsley, chopped	2 oz	60 g
Manchego cheese, grated	2 lb 4 oz	1 kg

1. Heat the oil in a skillet over medium-high heat, add the Vidalia onions, and sauté for 5 to 8 minutes. Add the potatoes and continue to sauté until they are hot, about 5 minutes.

2. Add the spinach, green onions, and tomatoes and continue to cook until heated through. Divide the mixture into 2 full hotel pans that have been lightly oiled.

3. In a mixing bowl, beat the eggs with the salt and pepper. Stir in the thyme, parsley, and cheese. Pour the eggs over the vegetable mixture in each pan. Cover the pans and bake at 325°F/165°C until the eggs are set, 15 to 20 minutes.

4. Remove the covers and brown the eggs lightly under the broiler or salamander.

5. Serve immediately on heated plates.

SAUSAGE AND ROASTED VEGETABLE FRITTATA

Makes 50 portions

Sausage, cooked, small dice	4 lb 12 oz	2.15 kg
Onions, minced	4 lb 8 oz	2 kg
Red peppers, roasted, peeled, seeded, small dice	1 lb 12 oz	800 g
Yellow peppers, roasted, peeled, seeded, small dice	1 lb 12 oz	800 g
Zucchini, roasted, small dice	1 lb 12 oz	800 g
Eggs	100 each	100 each
Kosher salt	1 tbsp	15 ml
Ground black pepper	1 tbsp	15 ml

1. Heat a large skillet or rondeau over high heat, add the sausage, and cook until the sausage is heated and some of the fat has been rendered, about 3 minutes. Pour off the excess fat, leaving enough in the skillet to coat it. Add the onions and sauté them for 1 minute. Add the peppers and zucchini and continue to sauté until the zucchini is tender and starting to release moisture, about 5 minutes. Reserve the sausage and pepper mixture.

2. Beat the eggs and season with salt and pepper. Working in batches, combine the egg mixture with the vegetables and sausage. Pour the mixture into a heated skillet and stir gently to combine.

3. Reduce the heat to low, cover the skillet, and cook until the eggs are nearly set, about 5 minutes. Or, finish the frittatas in a 325°F/165°C oven.

4. Remove the cover and place the skillet under the broiler to brown the eggs lightly, 1 to 2 minutes. Cut the frittata into wedges.

5. Serve immediately on heated plates.

RANCHERO EGG AND AVOCADO CASSEROLE

Makes 50 portions

Corn tortillas, 6 inches/15 cm	50 each	50 each
Vegetarian Refried Beans (page 323)	4 lb	1.8 kg
Eggs	64 each	64 each
Kosher salt	1 tbsp	15 ml
Ground black pepper	1 tsp	5 ml
Monterey Jack, grated	12 oz	340 g
Avocados, diced	2 lb 4 oz	1 kg
Green onions, thinly sliced	12 oz	340 g
Lime juice	¾ cup	180 ml
Vegetable oil	¾ cup	180 ml
Salsa Fresca (page 121)	3 qt	2.8 l
Sour cream	8 oz	225 g
Cilantro sprigs	50 each	50 each

1. Heat the tortillas by toasting them one at a time in a dry cast-iron skillet over medium-high heat or directly over a gas flame until lightly toasted. Place the tortillas on a sheet pan, spread each tortilla with 3 tbsp/45 ml of the refried beans, and cover to keep warm.

2. In a large bowl, whisk the eggs with the salt, pepper, cheese, avocados, green onions, and lime juice.

3. Heat the oil in a skillet over medium heat. Add the egg mixture, working in batches as necessary, and cook, stirring frequently, until the eggs are set, 4 to 5 minutes. Remove from the heat.

4. Divide the egg mixture among the tortillas with beans and top each with salsa fresca and sour cream.

5. Serve immediately on heated plates, garnished with cilantro sprigs.

MUSHROOM, TOMATO, AND EGG WRAP

Makes 50 portions

Vegetable oil	¼ cup	60 ml
White mushrooms, sliced	5 lb	2.25 kg
Eggs, beaten	100 each	100 each
Tomatoes, peeled, seeded, chopped	3 lb	1.4 kg
Flour tortillas, 10 inches/25 cm	50 each	50 each
Green onions, sliced on the diagonal	1 lb	450 g
Cheddar, grated	4 lb	1.8 kg
Sour cream	3 lb 4 oz	1.5 kg

1. Heat the oil in a tilt skillet set at medium-high heat, add the mushrooms, and sauté until cooked, 5 to 8 minutes. Reduce the heat and add the eggs and tomatoes. Scramble the eggs and cook until they are set. Reserve.

2. Heat the tortillas by toasting them one at a time in a dry cast-iron skillet over medium-high heat or directly over a gas flame until lightly toasted.

3. Divide the egg mixture among the warm tortillas and top each with green onions, cheese, and sour cream.

4. Roll up the wraps individually in parchment paper and hold warm for service.

WARM GOAT CHEESE CUSTARD

Makes 50 portions

Unsalted butter, softened, for coating molds	As needed	As needed
Cream cheese, room temperature	1 lb 14 oz	850 g
Goat cheese, room temperature	2 lb 13 oz	1.25 kg
Kosher salt, plus additional as needed	½ oz	14 g
Ground black pepper	As needed	As needed
Eggs	45 each	45 each
Heavy cream	3¾ qt	3.5 l
Chives, sliced	5 oz	140 g
Green grapes, seedless	200 each	200 each

1. Butter 50 timbale molds (2 fl oz/60 ml each).

2. Combine the cream cheese with two-thirds of the goat cheese, reserving the remaining one-third for garnish. Season to taste with salt and pepper. Mix with the paddle attachment of a mixer until the mixture is very smooth.

3. Add the eggs, one third of the cream, half of the chives, and the ½ oz/14 g salt. Mix on low speed until the ingredients are just blended. Divide the mixture among the timbale molds and cover the molds with buttered parchment paper.

4. Place the timbale molds in a bain-marie and bake in a 325°F/165°C oven until a knife inserted near the center of a timbale comes away clean, 25 to 30 minutes.

5. Reduce the remaining cream by half in a sauce pot over medium heat. Season with salt and pepper. Add the remaining chives and the grapes to the cream just before service.

6. Unmold the timbales onto heated plates and coat with the sauce. Serve immediately, garnished with the reserved goat cheese.

QUICHE LORRAINE

Makes 50 portions

Basic Pie Dough (page 360)	2½ to 2¾ lb	1.13 to 1.25 kg
Unsalted butter or vegetable oil	5 oz	140 g
Slab bacon, small dice	2 lb 8 oz	1 kg
Heavy cream	30 fl oz	890 ml
Milk	30 fl oz	890 ml
Eggs	15 each	15 each
Kosher salt	5 tsp	25 ml
Ground black pepper	1¼ tsp	6 ml
Ground nutmeg	A pinch	A pinch
Emmantaler cheese, grated	1 lb 4 oz	570 g

1. Roll the dough out to fit an 8- or 9-inch/20- or 23-cm quiche, tart, or pie pan. Bake blind as directed on page 360.

2. Heat the butter or oil in a skillet over medium-high heat. Add the bacon when the butter stops foaming and sauté the bacon, stirring frequently, until browned, 4 to 5 minutes. Remove the bacon with a slotted spoon and drain. Discard the rendered fat, or save for another use.

3. Whisk together the cream, milk, and eggs. Season with salt, pepper, and nutmeg.

4. Scatter the bacon and cheese evenly over the pie crust. Add the custard mixture gradually, stirring it gently with the back of a fork to distribute the filling ingredients evenly.

5. Set the quiche pan on a sheet pan and bake in a 350°F/175°C oven until a knife blade inserted in the center comes out clean, 40 to 45 minutes. Allow the quiche to set for at least 15 minutes before cutting into wedges.

6. Serve hot or at room temperature.

BANANAS FOSTER FRENCH TOAST

Makes 50 portions

CARAMELIZED BANANAS

Bananas	25 each	25 each
Brown sugar	1 lb 8 oz	680 g
Ground cinnamon	1½ oz	45 g
Vanilla extract	2 tbsp	30 ml
Orange juice	1½ pt	720 ml

FRENCH TOAST

Eggs	50 each	50 each
Ground cinnamon	2 tbsp	30 ml
Vanilla extract	2 tbsp	30 ml
Clarified butter	1 lb 8 oz	680 g
Whole-grain bread, sliced	100 slices	100 slices
Confectioners' sugar	8 oz	225 g
Blueberry Sauce (page 166; optional)	3¼ qt	3 l

1. To prepare the caramelized bananas, cut the bananas into quarters (cut in half lengthwise and then in half crosswise). Combine the brown sugar, cinnamon, vanilla, and orange juice in a rondeau. Bring to a boil over high heat and continue to boil to reduce the liquid until syrupy, about 5 minutes. Place the banana quarters into the syrup. Heat for 3 minutes, turning to ensure they are coated on all sides. Allow the bananas to cool in the syrup.

2. To prepare the French toast, whisk together the eggs, cinnamon, and vanilla in a mixing bowl. Reserve.

3. Heat the clarified butter in a tilt skillet set at medium-high heat. Place 2 pieces of the caramelized bananas in between 2 slices of the bread. Repeat with the remaining bananas and bread.

4. Dip the banana sandwiches into the egg mixture and sauté in the clarified butter until golden brown, about 2 minutes per side.

5. Serve immediately on heated plates dusted with confectioners' sugar and topped with the blueberry sauce, if using.

BLUEBERRY SAUCE

Makes 50 portions

Sugar	2 lb	900 g
Orange juice	½ cup	120 ml
Lemon juice	½ cup	120 ml
Blueberries, frozen	4 lb 12 oz	2.15 kg
Cornstarch, diluted in an equal amount of cold water	1 oz	30 g

1. Combine the sugar, orange juice, lemon juice, and blueberries in a nonreactive sauce pot. Marinate at room temperature for 30 minutes.

2. Bring the mixture to a boil over medium-high heat. Reduce the heat to low to establish a simmer. Continue to simmer until the blueberries have turned a deep reddish-purple and are very tender, about 15 minutes.

3. Stir the diluted cornstarch to recombine if necessary and stir into the blueberry mixture all at once. Return to a simmer, cook for 2 minutes, and remove from the heat.

4. The sauce is ready to serve (hot or cold) at this point, or it may be rapidly cooled and held under refrigeration for up to 5 days for later service.

SUNRISE SMOOTHIE

Makes 2 portions

Orange juice	½ cup	120 ml
Pomegranate juice	½ cup	120 ml
Ice cubes	1 pt	480 ml
Lime, sliced	2 slices	2 slices

Purée the juices and ice in a blender until smooth and frothy. Serve immediately in chilled glasses, garnished with a lime slice.

chapter eight

RECIPES FOR SALAD DRESSINGS, SALADS, SANDWICHES, AND APPETIZERS

Red Wine Vinaigrette

Makes 1 quart (950 milliliters)

Red wine vinegar	1 cup	240 ml
Dijon mustard (optional)	2 tsp	10 ml
Shallots, minced	2 each	2 each
Mild olive oil or canola oil	1½ pt	720 ml
Sugar (optional)	2 tsp	10 ml
Kosher salt, plus additional as needed	2 tsp	10 ml
Ground black pepper, plus additional as needed	½ tsp	3 ml
Minced herbs, such as chives, parsley, tarragon (optional)	3 tbsp	45 ml

1. Combine the vinegar, mustard, if using, and shallots.

2. Whisk in the oil gradually.

3. Taste the vinaigrette and season with sugar, if using, salt, and pepper. Add the herbs, if using.

4. Serve immediately or hold under refrigeration up to 5 days for later service.

NOTE *This vinaigrette can easily be adapted for a variety of situations by substituting a different-flavored vinegar for the red wine vinegar, or a different oil for the olive or canola oil.*

BALSAMIC VINAIGRETTE

Makes 1 quart (950 milliliters)

Red wine vinegar	½ cup	120 ml
Balsamic vinegar	½ cup	120 ml
Dijon mustard (optional)	2 tbsp	30 ml
Mild olive oil or canola oil	1½ pt	720 ml
Kosher salt, plus additional as needed	2 tsp	10 ml
Ground black pepper, plus additional as needed	½ tsp	3 ml
Minced herbs, such as chives, parsley, tarragon (optional)	3 tbsp	45 ml

1. Combine the vinegars and mustard, if using.

2. Whisk in the oil gradually.

3. Season with salt and pepper. Add the herbs, if using.

4. Serve immediately or hold under refrigeration up to 5 days for later service.

   PORT WINE BALSAMIC VINAIGRETTE: Substitute ½ cup/120 ml ruby port for the red wine vinegar.

HERB AND TRUFFLE VINAIGRETTE

Makes 1 quart (950 milliliters)

Red wine vinegar	1½ cups	360 ml
Balsamic vinegar	½ cup	120 ml
Water	¼ cup	60 ml
Dijon mustard	2 tsp	10 ml
Minced herbs, such as chives, tarragon, dill, or chervil	1 oz	30 g
Shallots, minced	2 each	2 each
Mild olive oil	1¾ cups	420 ml
Truffle oil	3 tbsp	45 ml
Sugar as needed	2 tsp	10 ml
Kosher salt, plus additional as needed	2 tsp	10 ml
Ground black pepper, plus additional as needed	½ tsp	3 ml
Black or white truffle, chopped (optional)	1 tsp	5 ml

1. Mix together the vinegars, water, mustard, herbs, and shallots.

2. Whisk in the oils gradually.

3. Taste the vinaigrette and season with sugar, salt, and pepper.

4. Serve immediately or hold under refrigeration up to 5 days for later service. Add the truffle just before serving, if using.

ALMOND-FIG VINAIGRETTE

Makes 1½ quarts (1.4 liters)

Balsamic vinegar	½ cup	120 ml
Dry red wine, such as Zinfandel or Merlot	½ cup	120 ml
Shallots, minced	4 each	4 each
Almonds, blanched, roasted, chopped	4 oz	115 g
Kosher salt, plus additional as needed	2 tsp	10 ml
Ground black pepper, plus additional as needed	½ tsp	3 ml
Almond oil	1½ cups	360 ml
Extra-virgin olive oil	1 pt	480 ml
Dried figs, chopped	5¼ oz	150 g
Lemon juice	¼ cup	60 ml
Tabasco sauce	As needed	As needed

1. Combine the vinegar, wine, shallots, and almonds. Season with salt and pepper.

2. Whisk in the oils gradually.

3. Stir in the figs, lemon juice, and Tabasco sauce. Taste and adjust seasoning with salt and pepper.

4. Serve immediately or hold under refrigeration up to 5 days for later service.

CHIPOTLE-SHERRY VINAIGRETTE

Makes 1 quart (950 milliliters)

Sherry vinegar	1 cup	240 ml
Lime juice	¼ cup	60 ml
Chipotles, in adobo sauce, minced	5 each	5 each
Shallots, minced	2 each	2 each
Garlic cloves, minced	2 each	2 each
Piloncillo or brown sugar	2 tbsp	30 ml
Kosher salt, plus additional as needed	As needed	As needed
Ground black pepper	As needed	As needed
Extra-virgin olive oil	1½ pt	720 ml
Fines Herbes (page 234), minced	1 oz	30 g

1. Combine the vinegar, lime juice, chipotles, shallots, garlic, and piloncillo or brown sugar. Season with salt and pepper.

2. Whisk in the oil gradually.

3. Stir in the fines herbes. Taste and adjust seasoning with salt, pepper, and piloncillo or brown sugar if necessary.

4. Serve immediately or hold under refrigeration up to 5 days for later service.

FIRE-ROASTED TOMATO VINAIGRETTE

Makes 1 quart (950 milliliters)

Plum tomatoes	10 each	10 each
Olive oil	1 pt	480 ml
Red wine vinegar	¾ cup	180 ml
Thyme leaves, chopped	1 tbsp	15 ml
Basil, chopped	2 tbsp	30 ml
Tabasco sauce	As needed	As needed
Kosher salt, plus additional as needed	2 tsp	10 ml
Ground black pepper, plus additional as needed	½ tsp	3 ml

1. Wash and core the tomatoes and lightly coat them with some of the oil. Char them over an open flame. Peel the skin, crush the tomatoes with a wooden spoon or potato masher, and then strain the tomatoes through a fine-mesh sieve.

2. Combine the strained tomato purée and vinegar. Whisk in the remaining oil gradually.

3. Stir in the thyme, basil, and Tabasco. Season with salt and pepper.

4. Serve immediately or hold under refrigeration up to 5 days for later service.

EXTRA-VIRGIN CAESAR DRESSING

Makes 1 quart (950 milliliters)

Anchovy fillets	3 oz	85 g
Mild mustard	1 tbsp	15 ml
Garlic, mashed to a paste	2 tsp	10 ml
Worcestershire sauce	1 tbsp	15 ml
Red wine vinegar	¾ cup	180 ml
Parmesan, grated	2 oz	60 g
Kosher salt	As needed	As needed
Ground black pepper	As needed	As needed
Extra-virgin olive oil	18 fl oz	530 ml
Lemon juice, plus additional as needed	2 tbsp	30 ml
Tabasco sauce, plus additional as needed	½ tsp	3 ml

1. Blend the anchovies, mustard, garlic, and Worcestershire in a bowl to form a paste. Add the vinegar, cheese, salt, and pepper. Gradually whisk in the oil.

2. Add the lemon juice and Tabasco. Taste the dressing and adjust seasoning with salt, pepper, lemon juice, and Tabasco.

3. Serve immediately or hold under refrigeration for up to 3 days for later service.

1. Mise en place for Caesar dressing.

2. Transfer the blended dressing to another receptacle for tasting and final seasoning.

Aïoli

Makes 1 quart (950 milliliters)

Pasteurized egg yolks	2½ oz	70 g
Water	1 tbsp	15 ml
White wine vinegar	2 tbsp	30 ml
Dijon mustard	2 tsp	10 ml
Garlic, mashed to a paste	2½ tsp	13 ml
Vegetable oil	1¾ cups	420 ml
Extra-virgin olive oil	1¼ cups	300 ml
Kosher salt, plus additional as needed	As needed	As needed
Ground white pepper	As needed	As needed
Lemon juice	As needed	As needed

1. Combine the egg yolks, water, vinegar, mustard, and garlic in a bowl. Mix well with a balloon whisk until the mixture is slightly foamy.

2. Gradually add the oils in a thin stream, constantly beating with the whisk, until the oils are incorporated and the aïoli is smooth and thick.

3. Season with salt, pepper, and lemon juice.

4. Serve immediately or hold under refrigeration up to 3 days for later service.

   SAFFRON AÏOLI: Add 2 tsp/10mL crushed saffron to the egg yolks in step 1.

Baby Spinach, Avocado, and Grapefruit Salad

Makes 50 portions

Avocados, sliced	7½ each	7½ each
Grapefruits, cut into suprêmes	15 each	15 each
Baby spinach	5 lb	2.25 kg
Balsamic Vinaigrette (page 171)	1 pt 9 fl oz	750 ml
Kosher salt, plus additional as needed	As needed	As needed
Ground black pepper	As needed	As needed

1. For each serving, combine 1¼ oz/35 g of the avocado (2 or 3 pieces) with 1½ oz/40 g of the grapefruit suprêmes (about 3 pieces).

2. Toss 1½ oz/40 g of the spinach with 1 tbsp/15 ml of the vinaigrette. Taste and then season with salt and pepper.

3. Arrange the spinach on a chilled plate. Top it with the avocados and grapefruit. Serve immediately.

Wilted Spinach Salad with Warm Bacon Vinaigrette

Makes 50 portions

Bacon, medium dice	2 lb 8 oz	1.15 kg
Shallots, minced	7½ oz	215 g
Garlic, minced	1 oz	30 g
Brown sugar	1 lb 4 oz	570 g
Cider vinegar	15 fl oz	450 ml
Vegetable oil	1 pt 9 fl oz	750 ml
Kosher salt, plus additional as needed	As needed	As needed
Cracked black pepper	As needed	As needed
Spinach	7 lb 8 oz	3.4 kg
Hard-Cooked Eggs (page 138), small dice	25 each	25 each
White mushrooms, sliced	1 lb 14 oz	850 g
Red onions, thinly sliced	15 oz	425 g
Croutons (page 180)	1 lb 4 oz	570 g

1. To prepare the vinaigrette, render the bacon in a skillet over medium-low heat. When the bacon is crisp, remove it from the pan, drain, and reserve.

2. Add the shallots and garlic to the bacon fat and sweat, stirring occasionally, until soft, 6 to 8 minutes. Blend in the brown sugar. Remove the pan from the heat. Whisk in the vinegar and oil. Taste and then season with salt and pepper.

3. Toss the spinach with the eggs, mushrooms, onions, croutons, and reserved bacon. Add the warm vinaigrette and toss once.

4. Serve immediately.

CROUTONS

Makes 1 pound (455 grams)

White bread, fine crumb, crust removed if desired	1 lb	450 g
Unsalted butter, melted	½ cup	120 ml
Kosher salt, plus additional as needed	1 tsp	5 ml
Ground black pepper (optional)	As needed	As needed

1. Slice and cube the bread into the desired size (from small cubes to garnish soups served in cups, to large slices to garnish salads). If the bread is very fresh, let the bread cubes dry out in the oven for 5 minutes before continuing.

2. Toss the bread together with the butter. Taste and then season with salt and pepper. Transfer to a sheet pan.

3. Bake in a 350°F/175°C oven until lightly golden, 8 to 10 minutes.

4. Serve immediately or store in an airtight container at room temperature for up to 3 days.

NOTES *For smaller batches, the croutons can be cooked on top of the stove in a skillet or sauté pan. Deep-fat frying is not recommended for croutons, because they absorb too much oil and become greasy.*

GARLIC-FLAVORED CROUTONS: Add 2 tsp/10 ml very finely minced garlic (garlic paste) to the oil or butter before tossing with the bread cubes.

CHEESE CROUTONS: After the bread cubes have been tossed with the butter, sprinkle generously with grated Parmesan, Romano, or other hard grating cheese and toss to combine evenly.

HERB-FLAVORED CROUTONS: Add 2 tbsp/30 ml chopped fresh herbs or dried herbs (such as oregano or rosemary) to the bread cubes along with the butter.

CELERY SEED CROUTONS: Add 2 tsp/10 ml celery seeds to the bread cubes along with the butter.

*Wilted Spinach Salad with Warm
Bacon Vinaigrette (page 179)*

Mushrooms, Beets, and Baby Greens with Robiola Cheese and Walnuts

Makes 50 portions

Red beets, medium	3 lb 12 oz	1.7 kg
Golden beets, medium	3 lb 12 oz	1.7 kg
Kosher salt, plus as needed	2 tsp	10 ml
Extra-virgin olive oil as needed	1¼ cups	300 ml
Cremini mushrooms, trimmed and sliced	1 lb 9 oz	710 g
White mushrooms, trimmed and sliced	1 lb 9 oz	710 g
Assorted wild mushrooms, trimmed	3 lb 7 oz	1.55 kg
Herb and Truffle Vinaigrette (page 172)	3 pt	1.4 l
Frisée hearts	1 lb 4 oz	570 g
Baby arugula	10 oz	285 g
Mesclun greens	1 lb 4 oz	570 g
Baguettes, sliced thin on an angle	50 slices	50 slices
Robiola cheese	3 lb 2 oz	1.4 kg
Ground black pepper (optional) as needed	1 tsp	5 ml
Walnuts, toasted, roughly chopped	1 lb 9 oz	710 g
Truffle oil	As needed	As needed

1. Remove the tops from the beets. Place the red and golden beets in separate pots with enough cold water to cover them by about 2 inches/51 mm. Add 2 tsp/10 ml salt and cook until the beets are tender, 30 to 40 minutes. Drain the beets and cool.

2. Peel the beets with the back of a paring knife and cut into a medium dice. (Keep the beet colors separate, if desired.) Coat the beets with 1 cup/240 ml of the olive oil and reserve. (The beets may be held under refrigeration for up to 2 days for later service.)

3. Heat a large sauté pan over medium heat. Add 2 tbsp/30 ml of the remaining olive oil to the pan. Add the cremini and white mushrooms in batches, being careful not to overcrowd the pan. Sauté in batches until golden brown and tender, 4 to 5 minutes. Remove the mushrooms and cool in a half hotel pan. Repeat with the wild mushrooms, adding the remaining olive oil if needed. Toss all the mushrooms with 7½ fl oz/220 ml of the vinaigrette and reserve.

4. Combine the frisée, arugula, and mesclun and reserve.

5. Brush each baguette slice with olive oil, place on a sheet pan, and bake in a 350°F/175°C oven until golden brown on the first side, about 2½ minutes. Turn the slices over and bake until golden brown on the opposite side, about 2½ minutes more.

6. Spread 1 oz/30 ml of the cheese on 1 side of each baguette slice. Season with salt and pepper and melt under a salamander or broiler.

7. For each portion, place 2½ oz/70 g of the mushroom salad on a chilled plate. Toss 1 oz/30 g of the baby greens with 1 tsp/5 ml of the vinaigrette and arrange on the plate. Arrange 2 oz/60 g of the beets around the greens and sprinkle with ½ oz/15 g of the walnuts. Place 1 toasted baguette slice on the plate. Drizzle a few drops of truffle oil around the greens and serve immediately.

Borlotti Bean, Onion, and Celery Heart Salad

Makes 50 portions

Borlotti beans, dried	5 lb	2.25 kg
Yellow onions, small, halved	2 each	2 each
Carrots, halved	2 each	2 each
Bay leaves	3 each	3 each
Garlic cloves, crushed	4 each	4 each
Celery rib	1 each	1 each
Rosemary sprig	1 each	1 each
Thyme sprig	1 each	1 each
Extra-virgin olive oil	1 pt plus 2 tbsp	510 ml
Red onions, small dice	8 oz	225 g
Celery heart, ribs and leaves, small dice	8 oz	225 g
Parsley, chopped	2 oz	60 g
Savory, chopped	2 oz	60 g
Mint, chopped	1 oz	30 g
Red wine vinegar	1 cup	240 ml
Kosher salt, plus additional as needed	2 tbsp	30 ml
Cracked black pepper	2 tbsp	30 ml

1. Sort the beans to remove stones or debris and rinse well. Soak the beans for 4 to 6 hours in enough cold water to cover by 3 inches/76 mm. Discard any beans that are floating on the surface. Drain the beans and discard the water. (For a short-soak alternative, place the beans in a large pot, add enough water to cover generously, and bring to a boil over high heat. As soon as the water boils, remove the pot from the heat and cover. Drain after 1 hour and continue with the next step.)

2. Place the onions, carrots, bay leaves, garlic, celery rib, rosemary, thyme, and 2 tbsp/30 ml oil in a stockpot. Add the beans and enough cold water to cover them. Bring just to a simmer over medium heat. Cover and continue cooking until the beans are tender, about 1 hour. Check the beans during the cooking time; they should be firm but not mushy when fully cooked. If necessary, add additional water to keep the beans from drying out. Cooking time will vary depending on the freshness of the beans.

3. Combine the red onions; diced celery, parsley, savory, mint, and 1 pt/480 ml oil in a stainless-steel bowl. Set aside.

4. Once the beans are cooked, drain them and discard the herbs and vegetables. Transfer the beans to a clean stainless-steel bowl and toss with the onion, celery, and herb mixture. Stir in the vinegar. Allow the flavors to mature for 30 minutes. Taste

the salad and season with salt and pepper. Serve at once or hold under refrigeration for up to 3 days for later service.

NOTE *Other beans such as large corona beans, small white navy beans, and cannellini beans can be prepared in the same manner, but these beans would need to soak in water overnight under refrigeration.*

Warm Bavarian Potato Salad

Makes 50 portions

Vegetable oil	1 cup	240 ml
Bacon, small dice	1 lb 8 oz	680 g
Onions, small dice	1 lb 8 oz	680 g
White wine vinegar	1 pt	480 ml
Chicken Stock (page 83)	2½ pt	1.2 l
Sugar	1½ oz	40 g
Kosher salt, plus additional as needed	2 tbsp	30 ml
Ground black pepper	1½ tsp	8 ml
Waxy potatoes, cooked, peeled, sliced ¼ inch/6 mm thick	15 lb	6.8 kg
Parsley or chives, chopped	1 oz	30 g

1. Heat the oil in a skillet over medium-high heat. Render the bacon in the oil until it is slightly crisp, about 8 minutes. Remove the bacon with a slotted spoon and reserve. Return the pan with the oil to the heat.

2. Add the onions to the oil and sauté until translucent, 5 to 6 minutes.

3. Add the vinegar, stock, sugar, salt, pepper, and reserved bacon. Bring to a boil. As soon as the boil is reached, remove the skillet from the heat.

4. Pour the dressing over the potatoes, toss gently, cover, and let stand for 30 minutes before serving. Add the parsley or chives, toss, and serve.

ROASTED PEPPER SALAD

Makes 50 portions

Yellow peppers	4 lb	1.8 kg
Red peppers	4 lb	1.8 kg
Extra-virgin olive oil	1 cup	240 ml
Kosher salt, plus additional as needed	1 tbsp	15 ml
Basil, chiffonade	¼ cup	120 ml
Parsley, chopped	¼ cup	120 ml
Garlic cloves, thinly sliced	8 each	8 each
Capers, drained, rinsed, chopped	3 oz	85 g
Red wine vinegar	½ cup	120 ml
Cracked black pepper	1 tbsp	15 ml

1. Place the peppers on a sheet pan, rub them with a little of the oil, and season them with some of the salt. Place the pan in a 350°F/175°C oven and roast until the skins of the peppers are blistered, about 12 minutes. Place the peppers in a mixing bowl and cover tightly with plastic wrap. Allow the peppers to steam until they are cool enough to handle.

2. When cool, peel the peppers (wearing gloves), remove the seeds, and cut the peppers into ¼-inch/6-mm julienne strips.

3. Place the cut peppers in a large clean mixing bowl. Add the basil, parsley, garlic, capers, the remaining oil, and the vinegar. Taste and then season with salt and pepper and gently mix.

4. Hold the mixture under refrigeration for at least 1 hour and up to 24 hours.

5. Use a slotted spoon to lift the salad out of its dressing just before serving.

Scallop and Shrimp Salad

Makes 50 portions

Shrimp (16/20 count), cooked, peeled, deveined, halved	2 lb	900 g
Sea scallops (60 count), muscle tabs removed, cooked, halved	2 lb	900 g
Black olives, pitted, quartered	8 oz	225 g
Carrots, julienned	8 oz	225 g
Red peppers, julienned	8 oz	225 g
Green peppers, julienned	8 oz	225 g
Celery, julienned	8 oz	225 g
Tarragon, chopped	2 oz	60 g
Rice wine vinegar	¾ cup	180 ml
Extra-virgin olive oil	1 cup	240 ml
Lime juice	¼ cup	60 ml
Kosher salt, plus additional as needed	1 tbsp	15 ml
Cracked black pepper	1 tbsp	15 ml

1. Combine the cooked shrimp and scallops in a large clean mixing bowl. Cover with plastic wrap and refrigerate.

2. In a separate bowl, combine the olives, carrots, peppers, celery, and tarragon and toss gently.

3. Add the vinegar and oil. Combine the vegetable and dressing mixture with the shrimp and scallops. Mix using gloves.

4. Add the lime juice. Taste and then season with salt and pepper. Cover the salad and hold under refrigeration for at least 1 hour and up to 24 hours before service.

Fajita Cobb Salad

Makes 50 portions

Lime juice	4½ fl oz	135 ml
Vegetable oil	¾ cup	180 ml
Garlic, minced	3 oz	85 g
Ground cumin	2 tbsp	30 ml
Kosher salt, plus additional as needed	2 tbsp	30 ml
Red pepper flakes	1½ tsp	8 ml
Beef tenderloin medallions (about 3 oz/85 g each)	100 each	100 each
Oven-Roasted Tomatoes (page 300), fine dice	6 lb 4 oz	2.8 kg
Barbecue Sauce (page 191)	1½ pt	720 ml
Cilantro, minced	3 oz	85 g
Mixed greens	3 lb 4 oz	1.5 kg
Avocados, sliced	3 lb 4 oz	1.5 kg
Corn, grilled, cut off cob	3 lb 4 oz	1.5 kg
Green onions, thinly sliced	1 lb 8 oz	680 g
Crisp bacon, small dice	3 lb 4 oz	1.5 kg
Blue cheese, crumbled	1 lb 8 oz	680 g
Hard-Cooked Eggs (page 138), quartered	50 each	50 each
Corn tortillas, 8 inches/20 cm, julienned, toasted	12½ oz	355 g

1. Combine the lime juice, oil, garlic, cumin, salt, and red pepper to create the fajita marinade.

2. Coat the beef medallions with the marinade. Cover and marinate under refrigeration for 1 to 4 hours.

3. Remove the medallions from the marinade when ready to grill, allowing any excess marinade to drain away. Grill the medallions to the desired doneness, 3 to 4 minutes per side for medium. Hold warm for service.

4. Combine the oven-roasted tomatoes, barbecue sauce, and cilantro for the salad dressing.

5. Mix the greens, avocados, corn, and green onions in a large bowl. Add the dressing and toss. Arrange on plates.

6. Divide the bacon, cheese, and hard-cooked eggs among the plates. Place 2 grilled beef fajita medallions on each plate. Top each plate with toasted corn tortillas and serve.

Fajita Cobb Salad (page 189)

BARBECUE SAUCE

Makes 2 quarts (1.9 liters)

Vegetable oil	2 tbsp	30 ml
Onions, medium dice	8 oz	225 g
Garlic, minced	1 oz	30 g
Jalapeños, minced	1 oz	30 g
Tomato paste	1 lb	450 g
Chili Powder (page 131)	1 oz	30 g
Coffee, brewed	1 pt	480 ml
Worcestershire sauce	¾ cup	180 ml
Cider vinegar	1½ cups	360 ml
Brown sugar	12 oz	340 g
Apple cider	1½ cups	360 ml
Kosher salt, plus additional as needed	1½ tsp	8 ml

1. Heat the oil in a sauce pot over medium-high heat. Add the onions, garlic, and jalapeños and cook, stirring frequently, until the onions are translucent, about 5 minutes. Add the tomato paste and sauté until the tomato paste turns a rusty brown color. Add the remaining ingredients and bring to a boil. Lower the heat and simmer until thickened and flavorful, about 15 minutes.

2. The sauce is ready to use now, or it may be rapidly cooled and held under refrigeration for up to 2 weeks for later use.

SHRIMP ESCABÈCHE

Makes 50 portions (150 pieces)

Shrimp (10/15 count), peeled, deveined, tails removed	150 each	150 each
Extra-virgin olive oil	¾ cup	180 ml
Garlic, minced	2 oz	60 g
Lemon juice	1½ cups	360 ml
Manzilla olives, pitted, minced	8 oz	225 g
Green peppers, finely minced	8 oz	225 g
Onions, finely minced	8 oz	225 g
Plum tomatoes, small dice	8 oz	225 g
Parsley, minced	8 oz	225 g

1. Combine the shrimp, oil, garlic, and ¼ cup/60 ml lemon juice and marinate under refrigeration for at least 30 minutes and up to 3 hours.

2. Heat a skillet over high heat. Add the shrimp and pan sear until the shrimp turn a bright red or pink color, about 3 minutes. Immediately remove the shrimp from the heat and set aside in hotel pans.

3. In the same skillet, add the olives, green peppers, onions, tomatoes, and parsley. Sweat over medium heat until tender, about 5 minutes.

4. Add the remaining 1¼ cups/300 ml lemon juice and immediately remove the pan from the heat.

5. Pour the olive mixture over the shrimp in the hotel pans.

6. Serve at room temperature or chilled.

CURRIED SHRIMP WITH PASTA

Makes 50 portions

Shrimp (21/25 count), peeled, deveined, tails removed	7 lb	3.2 kg
Kosher salt	As needed	As needed
Ground black pepper	As needed	As needed
Vegetable oil	As needed	As needed
Butter	1 lb	450 g
Shallots, minced	8 oz	225 g
Curry powder	1 oz	30 g
Brandy	1 pt	480 ml
Fish Fumet (page 85)	3 qt	2.8 l
Heavy cream, reduced by half	3 pt	1.4 l
Fresh Egg Pasta (page 282), cut into linguini	4 lb	1.8 kg
Green onions, sliced on the diagonal	1 lb	450 g
Lobster Butter (page 132), diced	1 lb	450 g

1. Season the shrimp with salt and pepper. Divide the ingredients into batches of the appropriate size. To prepare one batch at a time, heat some of the oil in a sauté pan over high heat and add the shrimp. Sauté until the shrimp are just cooked through, 4 to 5 minutes. Remove the shrimp from the pan, leaving the oil in the pan, and reserve the shrimp.

2. Add the butter to the oil in the pan and heat until very hot. Add the shallots and sauté, stirring frequently, until they are translucent, 2 to 3 minutes. Add the curry powder. Deglaze with the brandy and reduce until the liquid cooks away. Add the fumet and cream. Let the mixture reduce until it lightly coats the back of a spoon. Keep warm until ready to combine with the pasta.

3. Bring a large pot of salted water to a rolling boil. Add the pasta and stir a few times to separate the strands. Cook the pasta until it is tender to the bite but still retains some texture, about 3 to 4 minutes. Drain the pasta immediately in a colander.

4. Return the shrimp to the sauté pan and add the green onions. Stir or swirl in the lobster butter.

5. Add the drained pasta and toss or stir gently over medium heat until the pasta is coated and heated through, 2 to 3 minutes. Taste and adjust seasoning with salt if necessary.

6. Serve immediately on heated plates.

Lobster Tortellini in Coconut-Curry Broth

Makes 50 portions

Lobsters (1 lb/450 g each)	10 each	10 each
Egg whites, lightly beaten	8 each	8 each
Heavy cream	1½ cups	360 ml
Shallots, minced, smothered	1 oz	30 g
Garlic, minced, smothered	1 oz	30 g
Chives, minced	1½ oz	40 g
Saffron Pasta dough (page 282)	5 lb 4 oz	2.4 kg
Fish Stock or Shellfish Stock (page 84)	4½ qt	4.25 l
Chicken Stock (page 83)	4½ qt	4.25 l
Coconut milk	3½ qt	3.3 l
Lemongrass, thinly sliced	12 oz	340 g
Red curry paste	2 oz	60 g
Kale, torn into bite-size pieces	3 lb	1.4 kg
Kosher salt, plus additional as needed	1 tbsp	15 ml
Ground black pepper	1 tsp	5 ml
Red or yellow peppers, peeled, julienned	3 lb	1.4 kg
Radishes, thinly sliced	12½ oz	355 g
Mint, minced	10 oz	285 g

1. Cook the lobsters by boiling or steaming until they are cooked through, 10 to 12 minutes. Remove them from the pot and cool. Remove the meat from the tail and claw sections. Slice the tail sections in half lengthwise. Remove the vein from each tail section. Reserve the claw and tail meat.

2. To prepare the filling, coarsely chop the lobster tail meat. Purée it to a coarse paste in a food processor.

3. Add the egg whites and cream and process to a fine paste. Add the shallots, garlic, and chives and pulse the machine on and off a few times to incorporate them into the lobster mixture. Remove the filling from the food processor and refrigerate.

4. Roll out the pasta dough into thin sheets and cut into 2-inch/51-mm squares. Place 1 tsp/5 ml of the lobster filling on each square. Fold the squares diagonally in half to make triangles and overlap the two corners to form tortellini. Bring a large pot of salted water to a boil, reduce to a simmer, and add the tortellini. Simmer the tortellini until tender, about 5 minutes. Drain immediately in a colander and set aside.

5. To prepare the coconut-curry broth, combine the stocks, coconut milk, lemongrass, and red curry paste in a saucepan over medium heat. Bring to a simmer and cook

for 5 to 10 minutes. Add the kale and cook until the kale is just heated through, 2 to 3 minutes. Taste the broth and then season with salt and pepper.

6. To serve, ladle the broth into heated bowls and add 5 or 6 tortellini to each bowl. Garnish with the reserved claw meat, peppers, radishes, and a sprinkle of mint.

Fresh Vegetable Kebobs with Orzo and Tomato Relish

Makes 50 portions

Tomatoes, peeled, seeded, chopped	12 lb 8 oz	5.65 kg
Red onions, minced	1 lb 8 oz	680 g
Basil, julienned	1 lb 8 oz	680 g
Red wine vinegar	1½ pt	720 ml
Olive oil	1½ pt	720 ml
Kosher salt, plus additional as needed	1 tbsp	15 ml
Ground black pepper, plus additional as needed	1 tsp	5 ml
KEBOBS		
White mushrooms, quartered	12 lb 8 oz	5.65 kg
Yellow squash, large dice	6 lb 4 oz	2.8 kg
Zucchini, large dice	6 lb 4 oz	2.8 kg
Red onions, large dice	6 lb 4 oz	2.8 kg
Red bell peppers, large dice	6 lb 4 oz	2.8 kg
Olive oil, or as needed	5 tbsp	75 ml
Kosher salt, plus additional as needed	1 tbsp	15 ml
Ground black pepper	1 tsp	5 ml
ORZO		
Extra-virgin olive oil	1½ pt	720 ml
Orzo pasta, cooked	12 lb 8 oz	5.65 kg

1. Combine the tomatoes, onions, basil, vinegar, and olive oil. Season with salt and pepper. Evenly divide the mixture into two batches. Purée one batch to use as the tomato relish. Bring the other batch to a simmer over low heat and cook for 15 minutes. Reserve hot.

2. To prepare the kebobs. thread the mushrooms, yellow squash, zucchini, red onions, and peppers onto 100 skewers.

3. Brush the vegetable kebobs with olive oil, and season with salt and pepper. Grill over medium heat until the vegetables are tender, 10 to 15 minutes.

4. To prepare the orzo, heat the extra-virgin olive oil in a tilt skillet set at medium. Add the cooked orzo and sauté until the orzo is very hot, about 6 minutes. Add the cooked tomato mixture. Taste and then season with salt and pepper.

5. Divide the orzo among heated plates and top with 2 kebobs per plate. Spoon the tomato relish onto the kebobs and serve.

Vegetable Panini with Tomato Chutney and Aïoli

Makes 50 portions

TOMATO CHUTNEY

Tomatoes, peeled, seeded, chopped	12 lb 8 oz	5.65 kg
Capers, drained, rinsed	3¼ oz	90 g
Black olives, pitted, sliced	1 lb 8 oz	680 g
Garlic, minced	1 tbsp	15 ml
Basil, julienned	1½ oz	40 g
Kosher salt, plus additional as needed	2 tbsp	30 ml

VEGETABLE PANINI

Extra-virgin olive oil	2¼ qt	2.12 l
Eggplants, sliced ¼ inch/6 mm thick	6 lb 4 oz	2.8 kg
Red and/or green peppers, sliced into ¼-inch/6-mm rings	6 lb 4 oz	2.8 kg
Red onions, sliced ¼ inch/6 mm thick	6 lb 4 oz	2.8 kg
Yellow squash, sliced ¼ inch/6 mm thick	6 lb 4 oz	2.8 kg
Zucchini, sliced ¼ inch/6 mm thick	6 lb 4 oz	2.8 kg
Kosher salt, plus additional as needed	3 tbsp	45 ml
Ground black pepper	1 tbsp	15 ml
Italian bread, sliced ½ inch/13 mm thick	100 slices	100 slices
Aïoli (page 177)	14 oz	400 g
Parmigiano-Reggiano, shredded	3 lb 4 oz	1.5 kg

1. To prepare the tomato chutney, combine the tomatoes, capers, olives, garlic, basil, and 2 tbsp/30 ml salt in a saucepan and cook over medium heat until thickened, 10 to 15 minutes. Reserve.

2. To prepare the vegetable panini, toss the oil with the eggplants, peppers, onions, yellow squash, and zucchini. Season with salt and pepper. Grill the vegetables over medium-high heat until tender, about 8 minutes for the eggplants, yellow squash, and zucchini and 12 to 15 minutes for the peppers and onions. Hold warm.

3. Brush one side of each bread slice very lightly with aïoli.

4. Sprinkle the dry side of 50 of the bread slices with the cheese and top with the grilled vegetables. Top with the tomato chutney. Top each sandwich with one of the remaining bread slices, aïoli side up. Place the sandwiches on a panini grill or a hot griddle. Cook until golden brown, 3 to 4 minutes per side.

5. Serve at once.

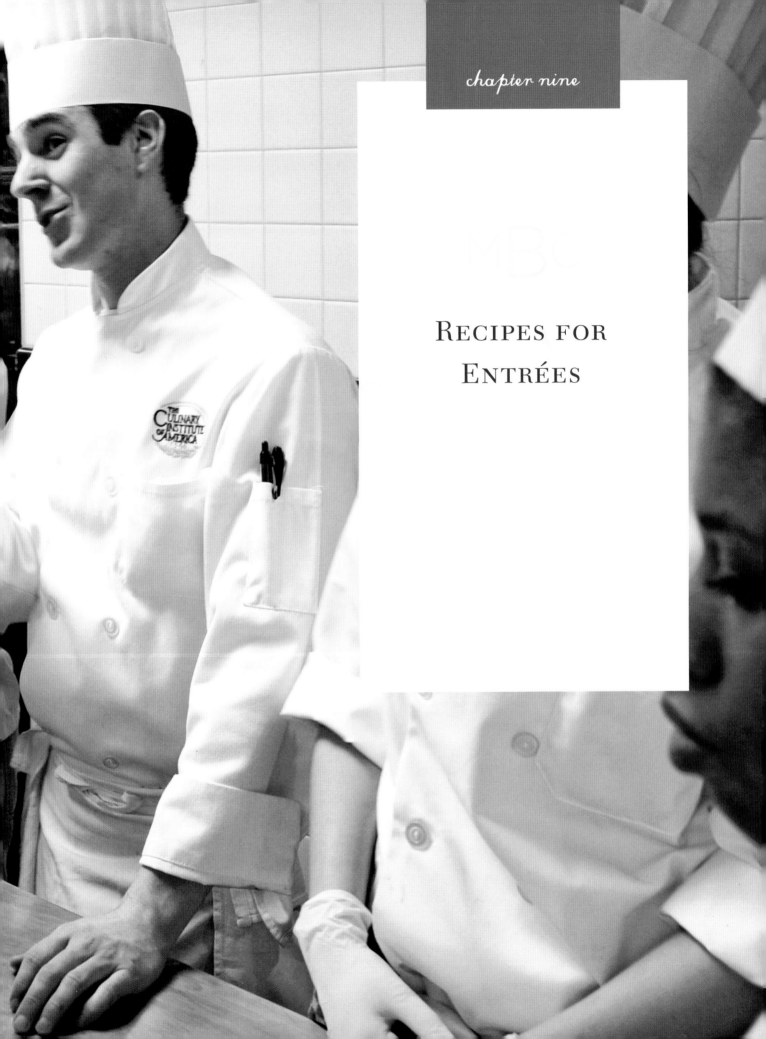

chapter nine

RECIPES FOR
ENTRÉES

Grilled or Broiled Chicken Breasts with Sun-Dried Tomato and Oregano Butter

Makes 50 portions

Chicken breast portions (about 5 oz / 140 g each), boneless, skin on	50 each	50 each
Kosher salt, plus additional as needed	5 tsp	25 ml
Ground black pepper, plus additional as needed	1 tbsp	15 ml
Vegetable oil	15 fl oz	450 ml
Sun-Dried Tomato and Oregano Butter (page 132), piped or sliced into fifty 1-oz/30-g portions	3 lb 2 oz	1.5 kg

1. Season the chicken with salt and pepper and lightly brush with oil.

2. Place the chicken presentation side down on the grill or broiler rods. Grill or broil undisturbed for about 2 minutes. (If desired, give each breast a quarter turn after the first minute of grilling to achieve grill marks.)

3. Turn the chicken over and continue to cook until it is cooked through and the internal temperature reaches 165°F/73°C, 6 to 8 minutes more.

4. Top each chicken breast with a portion of the sun-dried tomato and oregano butter and heat under the broiler or salamander until the butter begins to melt.

5. Serve the chicken on heated plates.

GRILLED OR BROILED PAILLARDS OF CHICKEN WITH TARRAGON BUTTER

Makes 50 portions

Chicken breast portions (5 to 6 oz / 140 to 170 g), boneless, skinless	50 each	50 each
Vegetable oil	1¼ cups	300 ml
Kosher salt, plus additional as needed	2 tbsp	30 ml
Ground black pepper, plus additional as needed	1 tbsp	15 ml
Lemon juice	1¼ cups	300 ml
Tarragon leaves, chopped	10 tsp	50 ml
Tarragon Butter (page 132), piped or sliced into fifty 1-oz/30-g portions	3 lb 2 oz	1.5 kg

1. Trim and pound the chicken to an even thickness, about ¼ inch/6 mm, to shape them into paillards.

2. Combine the oil, salt, pepper, lemon juice, and tarragon and add the chicken. Marinate under refrigeration for at least 30 minutes and up to 24 hours.

3. Just before grilling, remove the chicken from the marinade, allow any excess marinade to drain away, and blot if necessary.

4. Place the chicken presentation side down on the grill or broiler rods. Grill undisturbed for about 2 minutes. (If desired, give each breast a quarter turn after the first minute of grilling to achieve grill marks.)

5. Turn the chicken over and continue to cook until it is cooked through and the internal temperature reaches 165°F/73°C, 2 to 3 minutes more.

6. Top each paillard with a portion of the tarragon butter. Serve the chicken on heated plates.

GRILLED OR BROILED CHICKEN BREASTS WITH HONEY-MARSALA SAUCE

Makes 50 portions

Extra-virgin olive oil, plus as needed for brushing chicken	1 tbsp	15 ml
Red onions, fine dice	8 oz	225 g
Garlic, minced	2 tsp	10 ml
Tomatoes, peeled, seeded, chopped	10 oz	285 g
Demi-Glace (page 88)	6¼ pt	3 l
Honey	4 tsp	20 ml
Marsala	1 cup	240 ml
Kosher salt, plus additional as needed	2 tbsp	30 ml
Ground black pepper, plus additional as needed	1 tbsp	15 ml
Chicken suprême portions (7 to 8 oz/200 to 225 g each)	50 each	50 each

1. In a rondeau, heat 1 tbsp/15 ml extra-virgin olive oil over medium-high heat and add the onions and garlic. Cook, stirring frequently, until the onions are tender but not brown, about 6 minutes.

2. Add the tomatoes, demi-glace, honey, and Marsala. Bring to a gentle boil, then reduce the heat and simmer for 40 minutes over low heat. Season with salt and pepper and blend with an immersion blender. Return the sauce to a simmer for service and hold hot.

3. Just before grilling or broiling, season the chicken with a little salt and pepper and brush lightly with olive oil.

4. Place the chicken presentation side down on the grill or broiler rods. Grill undisturbed for about 2 minutes. (If desired, give each breast a quarter turn after the first minute of grilling to achieve grill marks.)

5. Turn the chicken over and continue to cook until it is cooked through and the internal temperature reaches 165°F/73°C, 6 to 8 minutes more.

6. Serve each chicken portion with 2 oz/60 ml sauce on heated plates.

GRILLED OR BROILED PORK CHOPS WITH SHERRY VINEGAR SAUCE

Makes 50 portions

Pork chop portions (about 12 oz/340 g each, 2 inches/51 mm thick), bone in	50 each	50 each
Kosher salt, plus additional as needed	2 tbsp	30 ml
Ground black pepper, plus additional as needed	2 tsp	10 ml
Olive oil	1¼ cups	300 ml
Sherry Vinegar Sauce (below), hot	4¾ pt	2.4 l

1. Season the pork chops with salt and pepper and lightly brush with oil.

2. Place the pork chops presentation side down on the grill or broiler rods. Grill or broil undisturbed for 8 to 10 minutes. (If desired, give each chop a quarter turn halfway through the grilling time to achieve grill marks.)

3. Turn the pork chops over and continue to cook until the internal temperature reaches 145°F/63°C for medium or 160°F/70°C for well done, 8 to 10 minutes more.

4. Remove the pork chops from the grill or broiler and allow them to rest for about 5 minutes.

5. Serve each pork chop with 3 tbsp/45 ml of the sauce on heated plates.

SHERRY VINEGAR SAUCE

Makes 2½ quarts (2.4 liters)

Sherry vinegar	1¼ cups	300 ml
Dark brown sugar	7 oz	200 g
Jus de Veau Lié (page 89) or Demi-Glace(page 88)	2½ qt	2.4 l
Kosher salt, plus additional as needed	2 tsp	10 ml
Ground black pepper, plus additional as needed	1 tsp	5 ml

1. Prepare a gastrique as follows: Cook the vinegar and brown sugar in a saucepan over medium-high heat until the mixture comes to a boil and the sugar is completely dissolved, 4 to 6 minutes.

2. Remove the saucepan from the heat and add the jus lié or demi-glace to the gastrique. Stir to combine and return to a simmer over medium heat. Reduce the sauce until it coats the back of a spoon, about 15 minutes.

3. Taste and season with salt and pepper. Strain the sauce through a fine-mesh sieve. The sauce is ready to serve now, or it may be rapidly cooled and refrigerated up to 3 days for later service.

BARBECUED STEAK WITH HERB CRUST

Makes 50 portions

HERB CRUST

Garlic, minced	2½ oz	70 g
Parsley, chopped	5 oz	140 g
Fresh bread crumbs	4 lb	1.8 kg
Butter, melted	4 lb	1.8 kg
Kosher salt	1 tbsp	15 ml
Ground black pepper	2 tsp	10 ml
BARBECUED STEAK		
Sirloin steak portions (about 10 oz/285 g each)	50 each	50 each
Kosher salt, plus additional as needed	1 tbsp	15 ml
Ground black pepper, plus additional as needed	1 tsp	5 ml
Garlic, minced	1½ oz	45 g
Vegetable oil	15 fl oz	445 ml
Barbecue Sauce (page 191)	4¾ pt	2.4 l

1. To prepare the herb crust, combine the garlic, parsley, bread crumbs, butter, salt, and pepper and blend well.

2. To make the barbecued steak, season the steaks with salt and pepper, rub with the garlic, and lightly brush with oil.

3. Place the steaks presentation side down on the grill or broiler rods. Grill or broil the steaks undisturbed for about 4 minutes. (If desired, give each steak a quarter turn halfway through the grilling time to achieve grill marks.)

4. Turn the steaks over and continue to cook to the desired doneness: about 2 minutes more for rare (internal temperature of 120°F/49°C), 4 minutes for medium rare (130°F/55°C), 6 minutes for medium (140°F/60°C), 7 minutes for medium well (150°F/65°C), and 8 minutes for well done (160°F/70°C).

5. Top the steaks with the herb crust and brown the topping under the broiler or salamander.

6. Serve each steak with 3 tbsp/45 ml of the barbecue sauce on heated plates.

GRILLED PORTOBELLO WITH BARLEY PILAF AND STEAMED SPINACH

Makes 50 portions

Portobello caps (about 5 oz/140 g each)	50 each	50 each
Garlic, roasted, puréed	6 oz	170 g
Balsamic vinegar	1 cup	240 ml
Extra-virgin olive oil	1½ pt	720 ml
Chicken Stock (page 83)	15 fl oz	445 ml
Dry mustard	4 tsp	20 ml
Thyme, minced	3 tbsp	45 ml
Kosher salt	2 tbsp	30 ml
Cracked black pepper	2 tbsp	30 ml
Barley Pilaf (page 216)	13¼ lb	6 kg
Spinach, steamed	6¼ lb	2.8 kg

1. Use a soupspoon to carefully remove and discard the gills from the mushroom caps. Very lightly spread the puréed garlic on all sides of the mushroom caps.

2. Combine the vinegar, oil, stock, mustard, thyme, salt, and pepper and add the mushrooms. Marinate at room temperature for at least 30 minutes or up to 4 hours under refrigeration.

3. Just before grilling, remove the mushrooms from the marinade and allow any excess marinade to drain away. Reserve the marinade.

4. Place the mushrooms smooth side down on the grill. Grill on the first side until they are golden and marked from the grill rods, about 3 minutes. Turn the mushrooms once and continue to cook on the second side until the mushrooms are very hot, 2 minutes more.

5. Place the mushrooms in 2-inch/51-mm hotel pans and add the reserved marinade. Cover with foil and bake in a 350°F/175°C oven until tender, about 15 minutes.

6. Serve the mushrooms with 4 oz/115 g barley pilaf and 2 oz/60 g steamed spinach on heated plates.

BARLEY PILAF

Makes 50 portions

Extra-virgin olive oil	½ cup	120 ml
Onions, small dice	1 lb 4 oz	570 g
Barley	4 lb	1.8 kg
Chicken Stock (page 83)	6 qt	5.6 l
Kosher salt, plus additional as needed	4 tsp	20 ml
Ground black pepper, plus additional as needed	1 tsp	5 ml
Parsley, minced	3 oz	85 g
Chives, cut into short pieces	3 oz	85 g
Thai basil, finely snipped	3 oz	85 g

1. Heat the oil in a rondeau over medium-high heat, add the onions, and sauté for approximately 4 minutes. Do not let the onions brown.

2. Add the barley, chicken stock, salt, and pepper. Bring the mixture to a boil and cover. Place in a 325°F/165°C oven. Cook for approximately 45 minutes, until the barley is tender.

3. Remove the lid and fold in the parsley, chives, and basil. Taste and adjust seasoning with salt and pepper. The barley is ready to serve now or it may be held hot.

Roast Turkey with Pan Gravy and Chestnut Stuffing

Makes 50 portions

Whole turkeys (about 15 lb/6.8 kg each)	5 each	5 each
Kosher salt, plus additional as needed	2 tbsp	30 ml
Ground black pepper, plus additional as needed	1 tbsp	15 ml
Onions, quartered	10 each	10 each
Parsley stems	60 to 75 each	60 to 75 each
Clarified butter or vegetable oil	1 pt 9 fl oz	750 ml
Mirepoix (page 134), medium dice	3 lb 12 oz	1.7 kg
All-purpose flour	10 oz	285 g
Chicken Stock (page 83), hot	1½ gal	5.75 l
Chestnut Stuffing (page 218)	13 lb 12 oz	6.25 kg

1. Season the cavity of each turkey with salt and pepper. Place the quartered onions and parsley stems inside the cavities. Rub the skins of the turkeys with butter or oil and truss each turkey with twine.

2. Place each turkey breast side up on a rack in a roasting pan.

3. Roast at 350°F/175°C for 3 hours, basting from time to time. Scatter the mirepoix around the turkeys and continue to roast until the thigh meat reaches an internal temperature of 165°F/73°C, 30 to 40 minutes more.

4. Remove the turkeys from the roasting pans and allow them to rest while you prepare the gravy.

5. Place the roasting pans on the stovetop over medium-high heat and cook until the mirepoix is browned and the fat is clear, about 5 minutes. Pour off all but 1 cup/240 ml of the fat from one pan and combine all the mirepoix in the same pan. Add the flour and cook the roux, stirring constantly, until smooth and golden brown, 4 to 5 minutes. Whisk in the stock until completely smooth.

6. Simmer the gravy until it reaches the proper consistency and flavor, 20 to 30 minutes. Degrease the gravy by skimming away as much fat from the surface as possible. Taste the gravy and adjust seasoning with salt and pepper. Strain the gravy through a fine-mesh sieve and hold hot for service.

7. Carve the turkey into portions and serve each portion with 3 fl oz/90 ml pan gravy and 4 oz/115 g chestnut stuffing on heated plates.

Continued

Chestnut Stuffing

Makes 13 pounds 12 ounces (6.25 kg)

Bacon fat or butter	1 lb 4 oz	570 g
Onions, minced	1 lb 4 oz	570 g
Day-old bread, cubed	7 lb 8 oz	3.4 kg
Chicken Stock (page 83), hot	2½ pt	1.2 l
Eggs	5 each	5 each
Parsley, chopped	10 tbsp	150 ml
Sage, chopped	5 tsp	25 ml
Chestnuts, peeled, roasted, chopped	2 lb 8 oz	1.15 kg
Kosher salt	5 tsp	25 ml
Ground black pepper	2½ tsp	13 ml

1. Heat the bacon fat or butter in a skillet over medium-high heat. Add the onions and sauté until they are tender, about 10 minutes. Transfer the onions, along with the fat in the pan, to a mixing bowl.

2. Combine the bread, stock, and eggs and add to the onions. Add the parsley, sage, chestnuts, salt, and pepper. Mix well.

3. Place the stuffing in a buttered hotel pan and cover it with parchment paper. Bake the stuffing at 350°F/175°C for 5 minutes. Serve very hot.

Roast Turkey with Pan Gravy and Chestnut Stuffing

ROAST CHICKEN WITH PAN GRAVY

Makes 50 portions

Chickens (about 3 lb 8 oz/1.6 kg each), wing tips removed and reserved	25 each	25 each
Kosher salt, plus additional as needed	10 oz	285 g
Ground white pepper, plus additional as needed	3½ fl oz	105 ml
Thyme sprigs	25 each	25 each
Rosemary sprigs	25 each	25 each
Bay leaves	25 each	25 each
Clarified butter or vegetable oil	1 pt 9 fl oz	750 ml
Mirepoix (page 134), medium dice	3 lb 12 oz	1.7 kg
All-purpose flour	10 oz	285 g
Chicken Stock (page 83), hot	6¼ qt	5.9 l

1. Season the cavity of each chicken with salt and pepper. Place 1 sprig each of thyme and rosemary and 1 bay leaf inside each cavity. Rub the skins of the chickens with butter or oil and truss each chicken with twine.

2. Place the chickens breast side up on racks in roasting pans. Scatter the wing tips in the pans.

3. Roast the chickens in a 350°F/175°C oven, basting from time to time, for 40 minutes. Scatter the mirepoix around the chickens and continue to roast until the thigh meat reaches an internal temperature of 165°F/73°C, 30 to 40 minutes more.

4. Remove the chickens from the roasting pans and hold warm while you prepare the gravy.

5. Place the roasting pans on the stovetop over medium-high heat and cook until the mirepoix is browned and the fat is clear, about 5 minutes. Pour off all but 1 cup/ 240 ml of the fat from one pan and combine all the mirepoix in the same pan. Add the flour and cook the roux, stirring constantly, until smooth and golden brown, 4 to 5 minutes. Whisk in the stock until completely smooth.

6. Simmer the gravy until it reaches the proper consistency and flavor, 20 to 30 minutes. Degrease the gravy by skimming away as much fat from the surface as possible. Taste the gravy and adjust seasoning with salt and pepper. Strain the gravy through a fine-mesh sieve and hold hot for service.

7. Cut the chickens into portions (halves, quarters, or eighths) and serve each portion with 3 fl oz/90 ml of the pan gravy on heated plates.

TRI-TIP BEEFSTEAK WITH DARK ONION SAUCE

Makes 50 portions

Tri-tip beefsteak portions (about 6 oz/170 g each), trimmed	50 each	50 each
Kosher salt	3 tbsp	45 ml
Cracked black pepper	3 tbsp	45 ml
Extra-virgin olive oil	1 pt	480 ml
Onions, medium dice	6 lb	2.7 kg
Tomato paste	12 oz	340 g
Dark brown sugar	8 oz	225 g
Dark beer (12-fl-oz/360-ml bottles)	6 bottles	6 bottles
Brown Veal Stock (page 82)	2 qt	1.9 l
Dijon mustard	8 oz	225 g
Balsamic vinegar	1 cup	240 ml
Parsley, chopped	3 oz	85 g
Chives, cut into short pieces	3 oz	85 g

1. Season the steaks with salt and pepper. Heat the oil in a tilt skillet or rondeau over high heat, add the steaks, and sear on both sides.

2. Remove the steaks and set aside. Add the onions to the tilt skillet or rondeau and cook, stirring frequently, until the onions are caramelized, about 20 minutes. Add the tomato paste and cook until aromatic, about 3 minutes. Add the brown sugar.

3. Deglaze the pan with the beer and cook until the liquid is reduced by half, about 8 minutes. Add the stock, mustard, and vinegar.

4. Return the steaks and any accumulated juices to the rondeau or tilt skillet. Cover and braise the steaks gently in a rondeau in a 300°F/150°C oven or at 200°F/95°C in a tilt skillet until tender, about 1½ hours.

5. Remove the steaks, place in serving pans, and hold hot until ready for service.

6. Return the rondeau to the stovetop. Reduce the sauce over medium-high heat until it coats the back of a spoon, about 10 minutes. Add the parsley and chives.

7. Serve each steak portion with 2 fl oz/60 ml sauce on heated plates.

Pork Roast with Jus Lié

Makes 50 portions

Pork loin roast, bone in	22 lb 8 oz	10.2 kg
Garlic, minced	2½ oz	70 g
Rosemary, minced	5 tsp	25 ml
Kosher salt, plus additional as needed	2 tbsp	30 ml
Ground black pepper, plus additional as needed	1 tbsp	15 ml
Mirepoix (page 134), small dice	2 lb 8 oz	1.15 kg
Dry white wine	20 fl oz	590 ml
Tomato paste	5 oz	140 g
Brown Veal Stock (page 82)	5 qt	4.7 l
Thyme sprigs	10 each	10 each
Bay leaves	5 each	5 each
Arrowroot, diluted in an equal amount of cold water, plus additional as needed	1 oz	30 g

1. Trim the pork loin and tie with twine. Rub the pork with the garlic, rosemary, salt, and pepper. Place the pork on a rack in a roasting pan.

2. Roast at 375°F/190°C for 1 hour, basting from time to time. Scatter the mirepoix around the pork and continue to roast to an internal temperature of 160°F/70°C, 30 to 45 minutes more.

3. Remove the pork from the roasting pan and hold warm while you prepare the jus lié.

4. Place the roasting pan on the stovetop over medium-high heat and cook until the mirepoix is browned and the fat is clear, about 5 minutes. Pour off all the fat. Deglaze the pan with the wine. Add the tomato paste and cook, stirring frequently, until the tomato paste turns a deep brick red color and gives off a sweet aroma, 30 to 45 seconds.

5. Add the stock and any juices that accumulate as the pork rests, stirring to release the fond completely. Add the thyme and bay leaves and simmer the jus until it reaches the proper consistency and flavor, 20 to 30 minutes.

6. Stir the diluted arrowroot to recombine if necessary. Add the diluted arrowroot and cook, stirring constantly, until the sauce has thickened enough to coat the back of a spoon. Degrease the sauce by skimming away as much fat from the surface as possible. Taste the sauce and adjust seasoning with salt and pepper. Strain the jus lié through a fine-mesh sieve and hold it hot for service.

7. Carve the pork loin into 7-oz/200-g portions (with bone) and serve each portion with 2 fl oz/60 ml jus lié on heated plates.

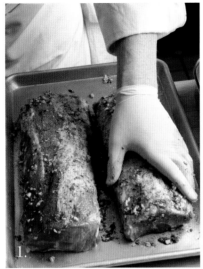

1. Rub the pork loin with the garlic, rosemary, salt, and pepper.

2. After roasting for 1 hour, scatter the mirepoix in the bottom of the roasting pan, place the pork roast on top, and continue to roast for 30 to 45 minutes more.

3. Slice the pork after it rests and serve with the jus lié.

Lacquer-Roasted Pork Ribs (Kao Paigu)

Makes 50 portions

Dark soy sauce	7½ fl oz	220 ml
Sherry	7½ fl oz	220 ml
Pork sparerib racks, St. Louis–style (about 3 lb/1.3 kg each), trimmed	25 each	25 each
MARINADE		
Hoisin sauce	2½ pt	1.2 l
Black bean sauce	30 fl oz	890 ml
Ketchup	3¾ pt	1.75 l
Chinese rice wine (Shaoxing)	1¼ cups	300 ml
Sesame oil	5 fl oz	150 ml
Garlic, minced	1½ oz	45 g
Ginger, minced	1 oz	30 g
Ground white pepper	5 tsp	25 ml
Green onions, thinly sliced	2½ oz	70 g
Kosher salt	1½ oz	45 g
Sugar	1 lb 2 oz	510 g
LACQUER COATING		
Honey	1¼ pt	590 ml
Sesame oil	5 tbsp	75 ml

1. Combine the soy sauce and sherry and brush the mixture on the ribs.

2. To prepare the marinade, combine the hoisin sauce, black bean sauce, ketchup, rice wine, sesame oil, garlic, ginger, pepper, green onions, salt, and sugar. Pour the mixture over the ribs and massage it into the meat. Cover and marinate under refrigeration overnight, turning occasionally.

3. Remove the ribs from the marinade and wipe off the excess. Place the ribs in a roasting pan on a wire rack.

4. Fill a pan with water, place it in a cold oven, and then preheat the oven to 325°F/165°C. Place the ribs in the oven and roast, turning occasionally, until they reach an internal temperature of 150°F/65°C, about 1½ hours.

5. To prepare the lacquer coating, combine the honey and sesame oil. During the last 20 minutes of roasting, brush the ribs on all sides with the mixture.

6. Remove the ribs from the oven and allow them to rest for 10 minutes. Cut the racks in half or into individual ribs before serving.

1. Brush the marinade onto the ribs and massage it into the meat.

2. During the last 20 minutes of roasting, brush the ribs with the prepared lacquer mixture.

3. Cut the racks in half or into individual ribs before serving.

Pan-Roasted Duck with Potato Gratin, Spicy Greens, and Coriander Sauce

Makes 50 portions

Long Island duck breast portions (about 5 oz/140 g each)	50 each	50 each
Kosher salt	3 tbsp	45 ml
Cracked black pepper	1 tbsp	15 ml
CORIANDER SAUCE		
Jus de Volaille Lié (page 90)	6¾ pt	2.4 l
Coriander seeds	1 oz	30 g
Butter, cubed, room temperature	6 oz	170 g
Spicy Greens (follows)	50 portions	50 portions
Potato Gratin (follows)	50 portions	50 portions

1. Score the skin on the duck breasts with a sharp knife to promote drying. Place on sheet pans. Dry the breasts, uncovered, in a cooler for 1 day.

2. Season the duck breasts with salt and pepper. Heat a sauté pan over medium-low heat, add the duck breasts skin side down, and cook to render out the fat, 10 to 12 minutes. Continue to cook until the duck breasts are golden brown on the fat side.

3. Place the duck breasts on sheet pans with racks and bake in a 375°F/190°C oven until medium rare (135°F/58°C), 12 to 15 minutes.

4. To prepare the coriander sauce, combine the jus lié and the coriander seeds and simmer until the sauce is flavored with the coriander. Strain into a clean pot and divide into batches of the desired size. To finish the coriander sauce, return it to a simmer and whisk in the butter.

5. Serve each duck breast with 2 fl oz/60 ml coriander sauce, accompanied with 2½ oz/75 g spicy greens and 3½ oz/100 g potato gratin.

Spicy Greens

Makes 9 pounds (4 kilograms) or 50 portions

Olive oil	5 fl oz	150 ml
Red onions, minced	2 lb	900 g
Watercress, stemmed	20 bunches	20 bunches
Arugula, stemmed	4 lb	1.8 kg
Mizuna, stemmed	3 lb	1.4 kg
Chicken Stock (page 83)	5 fl oz	150 ml

1. Divide the prepared ingredients into batches of the desired size. Heat the oil in a tilt skillet or rondeau over medium-high heat, add the onions, and sweat, stirring from time to time, until they are tender and translucent, about 10 minutes.

2. Add the watercress, arugula, and mizuna and cook until the greens are wilted, about 5 minutes. Add the stock. Hold hot in hotel pans for service.

Potato Gratin

Makes 12 pounds (5.5 kilograms)

Shallots, minced	12 each	12 each
Heavy cream	2 qt	1.9 l
Milk	2 qt	1.9 l
Kosher salt	1 tbsp	15 ml
Cracked black pepper	1 tbsp	15 ml
Russet potatoes, peeled	12 lb	5.5 kg
White cheddar, grated	1 lb	450 g
Parmesan, grated	1 lb	450 g

1. Combine the shallots, cream, milk, salt, and pepper in a large rondeau.

2. Slice the potatoes on a mandoline, 1/16 inch/2 mm thick. Do not wash or soak the potatoes after they are sliced. This will help to preserve the starch in the potatoes so that they hold together after cooking. Add the potatoes to the milk and cream mixture as they are sliced to prevent oxidation.

3. Once all the potatoes have been added to the rondeau, slowly bring the mixture to a simmer over low heat. Simmer, stirring constantly, for 3 minutes.

Continued

4. Remove the rondeau from the heat and add three-fourths of the cheeses to the potato mixture and mix well. Pour into 4 buttered 2-inch/51-mm shallow hotel pans until half full. Cover the top of the potatoes with the remaining cheese.

5. Bake, covered, in a 300°F/150°C convection oven until the potatoes are nearly done, about 1 hour. Continue baking, uncovered, until golden brown, about 15 minutes.

6. Let the potatoes rest for at least 15 minutes before cutting into 3½ oz/100 g portions and serving.

Pan-Roasted Duck with Potato Gratin,
Spicy Greens, and Coriander Sauce
(page 228)

Pan-Roasted Center Cut Pork with Marinated Peppers

Makes 50 portions

Pork loin roast, center cut, boneless	20 lb	9 kg
Garlic, minced	2½ oz	70 g
Rosemary, minced	5 tsp	25 ml
Kosher salt, plus additional as needed	5 tbsp	75 ml
Ground black pepper, plus additional as needed	7 tsp	35 ml
Mirepoix (page 134), small dice	2 lb 8 oz	1.15 kg
Dry white wine	20 fl oz	590 ml
Tomato paste	5 fl oz	150 ml
Brown Veal Stock (page 82)	3 qt	2.8 l
Thyme sprigs	10 each	10 each
Bay leaves	5 each	5 each
Arrowroot, diluted in equal amount of cold water, plus additional as needed (optional)	1 oz	30 g
Roasted Pepper Salad (page 187)	3 lb	1.4 kg

1. Trim the pork loin and tie with twine. Rub the pork with the garlic, rosemary, salt, and pepper. Place the pork on a rack in a roasting pan.

2. Roast the pork loin in a 325°F/165°C oven, basting from time to time, for 1 hour. Scatter the mirepoix around the pork and continue to roast until a thermometer inserted in the center of the meat registers 160°F/70°C, 30 to 45 minutes more.

3. Remove the pork from the roasting pan and hold warm while you prepare the jus lié.

4. Place the roasting pan on the stovetop over medium-high heat and cook until the mirepoix is browned and the fat is clear. Pour off all the fat. Deglaze the pan with the wine. Add the tomato paste and cook, stirring frequently, until the tomato paste turns a deep brick red color and gives off a sweet aroma, 30 to 45 seconds.

5. Add the stock and any accumulated juices from the resting pork, stirring to release the fond completely. Add the thyme and bay leaves and simmer the jus until it reaches the proper consistency and flavor, 20 to 30 minutes. Stir the diluted arrowroot to recombine if necessary. Add the diluted arrowroot, and cook, stirring constantly, until the sauce has thickened enough to coat the back of a spoon. Strain the sauce and then degrease it by skimming away as much fat from the surface as possible. Taste the sauce and adjust seasoning with salt and pepper.

6. Add the roasted pepper salad (marinated peppers) to the jus lié and hold it hot for service.

Continued

7. Carve the pork loin into 6-oz/170-g portions and serve each portion with 2 fl oz/60 ml jus lié.

Pan-Roasted Center Cut Pork with
Marinated Peppers (page 231)

Sautéed Chicken with Fines Herbes Sauce

Makes 50 portions

Chicken suprême portions (7 to 8 oz/200 to 225 g each)	50 each	50 each
Kosher salt, plus additional as needed	2 tbsp	30 ml
Ground black pepper, plus additional as needed	1 tbsp	15 ml
All-purpose flour (optional)	15 oz	425 g
Clarified butter or olive oil	1¼ cups	300 ml
Shallots, minced	3¾ oz	110 g
Dry white wine	1¼ pt	590 ml
Fines Herbes Sauce (page 234)	6¼ pt	2.95 l
Fines Herbes (page 234)	4 oz	115 g

1. Blot the chicken dry and season with salt and pepper. Dredge in flour, if using, and shake off any excess.

2. Working in batches of the desired size, heat the butter or oil in a large sauté pan over medium-high heat until it is almost smoking. Sauté the chicken on the presentation side until golden brown, about 4 minutes. Turn the chicken and continue to sauté until it is cooked through and the internal temperature reaches 165°F/73°C, 4 to 5 minutes more. Remove the chicken from the pan and keep warm while completing the sauce.

3. To prepare the sauce, pour off the excess fat from the pan. Add the shallots and sauté them until they are translucent, about 1 minute.

4. Deglaze the pan with the wine and reduce until it is almost dry, about 3 minutes. Add the fines herbes sauce and any accumulated juices from the resting chicken, simmer briefly, and strain through a fine-mesh sieve into a clean saucepan.

5. Return the sauce to a simmer over medium heat. Stir in the fines herbes. Taste the sauce and then season with salt and pepper.

6. Serve each chicken suprême with 2 fl oz/60 ml sauce on heated plates.

FINES HERBES SAUCE
Makes 2 quarts (1.9 liters)

Clarified butter	¼ cup	60 ml
Shallots, minced	1½ oz	45 g
Dry white wine	18 fl oz	540 ml
Fines Herbes (see below)	6 oz	170 g
Jus de Volaille Lié (page 90), Jus de Veau Lié (page 89), or Demi-Glace (page 88)	2 qt	1.9 l
Heavy cream	18 fl oz	540 ml
Kosher salt	½ oz	15 g
Ground black pepper	2 tsp	10 ml

1. Heat the butter in a saucepan over medium-high heat. Add the shallots and sweat until they are translucent, 2 to 3 minutes. Add the wine and fines herbes and simmer until nearly dry, about 15 minutes.

2. Add the jus lié or demi-glace, bring to a simmer, and simmer until flavorful and slightly reduced, about 10 minutes. Add the cream and continue to simmer the sauce, skimming as necessary, until it reaches the proper consistency and flavor, about 10 minutes.

3. Taste and season with salt and pepper and strain the sauce through a fine-mesh sieve.

4. The sauce is ready to use now, or it may be rapidly cooled and held under refrigeration for up to 2 days for later use.

FINES HERBES
Makes 6 ounces (180 grams)

Chervil leaves, chopped	1½ oz	45 g
Chives, chopped	1½ oz	45 g
Parsley leaves chopped	1½ oz	45 g
Tarragon leaves chopped	1½ oz	45 g

Combine all the herbs and mix well. Use immediately or place in a tightly sealed container and hold under refrigeration up to 8 hours for later use.

NOTES *Add burnet, marjoram, savory, lavender, or watercress to the herb mixture to adjust the flavor, if desired. Add fines herbes near the end of cooking time because they do not hold their flavor long. Fine herbes are typically used as a flavoring for omelettes or crêpes, or as the final addition to soups and consommés.*

Sautéed Chicken with Fines Herbes Sauce (page 233)

CHICKEN PROVENÇAL

Makes 50 portions

Chicken suprême portions (7 to 8 oz/200 to 225 g each)	50 each	50 each
Kosher salt, plus additional as needed	2 tbsp	30 ml
Ground black pepper, plus additional as needed	2 tsp	10 ml
All-purpose flour (optional)	15 oz	425 g
Clarified butter or olive oil	1¼ cups	300 ml
PROVENÇAL SAUCE		
Garlic, minced	1 oz	30 g
Anchovy fillets, mashed to a paste	15 each	15 each
Tomatoes, peeled, seeded, chopped	3 lb 12 oz	1.7 kg
Dry white wine	3 pt	1.4 l
Jus de Volaille Lié (page 90), Jus de Veau Lié (page 89), or Demi-Glace (page 88)	3¾ qt	3.5 l
Black olives, pitted, sliced or julienned	1 lb 4 oz	570 g
Basil, chiffonade	5 oz	140 g

1. Blot the chicken dry and season with salt and pepper. Dredge in flour, if using, and shake off any excess.

2. Working in batches of the desired size, heat the butter or oil in a large sauté pan over medium-high heat until it is almost smoking. Sauté the chicken on the presentation side until golden brown, about 4 minutes. Turn the chicken and continue to sauté until it is cooked through and the internal temperature reaches 165°F/73°C, about 5 minutes more. Remove the chicken from the pan and keep warm while completing the sauce.

3. To prepare the Provençal sauce, pour off the excess fat from the pan. Add the garlic and anchovies and sauté until their aroma is released, 30 to 40 seconds. Add the tomatoes and continue to sauté until any juices they release have cooked down, about 5 minutes.

4. Add the wine to deglaze the pan and simmer until the wine has nearly cooked away, about 5 minutes. Add the jus lié or demi-glace and any juices released by the chicken. Reduce until the sauce coats the back of a spoon, about 15 minutes.

5. Strain through a fine-mesh sieve into a clean saucepan and return to a simmer. Add the olives and basil and return to a simmer. Taste and then season with salt and pepper. Return the chicken to the pan and turn it in the sauce to coat evenly.

6. Serve each chicken suprême with 3 fl oz/90 ml of the sauce on heated plates.

Portobello Stuffed with Corn and Roasted Tomatoes

Makes 50 portions

Plum tomatoes, peeled, seeded, halved	6½ lb	3 kg
Extra-virgin olive oil	1½ cups	360 ml
Onions, fine dice	1 lb	450 g
Zucchini, small dice	3 lb 4 oz	1.5 kg
Corn, grilled, kernels cut from cob	6½ lb	3 kg
Kosher salt, plus additional as needed	2 tbsp	30 ml
Ground black pepper	2 tsp	10 ml
Thyme, chopped	2 tbsp	30 ml
Parsley, chopped	5 tbsp	75 ml
Balsamic vinegar	1½ cups	360 ml
Portobello caps (about 5 oz/140 g each)	50 each	50 each
CRUMB MIXTURE		
Panko bread crumbs, toasted	1 lb 8 oz	680 g
Extra-virgin olive oil	¾ cup	180 ml

1. Preheat a roasting pan in a 400°F/205°C oven. Add the tomatoes and roast until the juices they release begin to brown, 15 to 20 minutes. Purée the tomatoes in a food processor until chunky, 30 to 60 seconds.

2. Heat the oil in a skillet or rondeau over medium-high heat, add the onions, and sauté until tender and translucent, 5 to 6 minutes. Add the zucchini and continue to sauté until tender, 6 to 8 minutes. Add the corn and sauté until all of the vegetables are fully cooked and very hot, 4 to 5 minutes more. Add the roasted tomato purée, salt, pepper, thyme, parsley, and vinegar.

3. Use a soupspoon to carefully remove and discard the gills from the mushroom caps and arrange on sheet pans. Bake the mushrooms at 350°F/175°C until partially cooked, 5 to 6 minutes. Fill each cap with the corn mixture and set aside.

4. To prepare the crumb mixture, combine the toasted panko bread crumbs with the oil. Top the mushrooms with the crumb mixture. Return the mushrooms to the oven and bake until heated thorough, 10 to 12 minutes.

5. Serve the mushrooms on heated plates.

SALMON STEAK WITH HERB CRUST AND WHITE BEANS

Makes 50 portions

Fresh white bread crumbs	12 oz	340 g
Parsley, minced	2 oz	60 g
Horseradish, grated	3 oz	85 g
Grana Padano cheese, grated	12 oz	340 g
Extra-virgin olive oil	1½ cups	360 ml
Salmon steak portions (about 7 oz/200 g each), center cut	50 each	50 each
Kosher salt	3 oz	85 g
Ground black pepper	½ oz	15 g
Southwest White Bean Stew (page 322)	12 lb	5.5 kg

1. Combine the bread crumbs, parsley, horseradish, Grana Padano, and oil until evenly moistened.

2. Season the salmon with salt and pepper. Lightly press ¾ oz/20 g of the bread crumb mixture onto each salmon steak.

3. Bake the salmon on a sheet pan at 325°F/165°C until the salmon is medium-rare (125°F/52°C), about 8 minutes. Remove from the oven and place under a salamander to toast the bread crumb mixture.

4. Serve each salmon portion on 3½ oz/100 g of the Southwest white bean stew.

SALMON FILLET WITH SMOKED SALMON AND HORSERADISH CRUST

Makes 50 portions

Salmon fillet portions (about 6 oz/170 g each)	50 each	50 each
Lime juice	1¼ cups	300 ml
Garlic, minced	2 oz	60 g
Shallots, minced	1½ oz	45 g
Cracked black peppercorns	10 tsp	50 ml
Butter	15 oz	425 g
Fresh bread crumbs	1 lb 4 oz	570 g
Smoked salmon, minced	1 lb 4 oz	570 g
Prepared horseradish, drained	5 oz	140 g
Beurre Blanc (see below), warm	6¼ pt	2.95 l

1. Place the salmon fillets in a hotel pan. Rub them with the lime juice and sprinkle with 1½ oz/45 g garlic, 1 oz/30 g shallots, and the peppercorns.

2. To prepare the crumb mixture, heat the butter in a sauté pan over medium heat. Add the remaining shallots and garlic and sauté until they are aromatic, about 1 minute.

3. Combine the sautéed shallots and garlic with the bread crumbs, smoked salmon, and horseradish in a food processor and process to a fine consistency.

4. Portion about 1 oz/30 g of the crumb mixture on top of each fillet and press it onto the surface so it will adhere.

5. Bake the salmon (in batches of the desired size) in a 350°F/175°C oven until it is opaque pink on the outside and just beginning to flake, 6 to 7 minutes.

6. Serve each portion of salmon with 2 fl oz/60 ml of the warm beurre blanc on heated plates.

BEURRE BLANC

Makes 2 quarts (1.9 liters)

Shallots, minced	1 oz	30 g
Black peppercorns	6 to 8 each	6 to 8 each
Dry white wine	1 pt	480 ml
Lemon juice	½ cup	120 ml
Cider vinegar or white wine vinegar	¾ cup	180 ml
Heavy cream, reduced by half (optional)	1 pt	480 ml
Butter, cubed, chilled	3 lb	1.3 kg

Kosher salt, plus additional as needed	1 tbsp	15 ml
Ground white pepper, plus additional as needed	1 tsp	5 ml
Lemon zest, grated (optional)	½ oz	15 g

1. Combine the shallots, peppercorns, wine, lemon juice, and vinegar in a saucepan. Reduce over medium-high heat until nearly dry, about 5 minutes.

2. Add the reduced cream, if using, and simmer the sauce to reduce slightly, 2 to 3 minutes.

3. Add the butter a few pieces at a time, whisking constantly to blend the butter into the reduction. The heat should be quite low as you work. Continue adding butter until the full amount has been incorporated.

4. Taste the sauce and season with salt and pepper. Finish the sauce by adding the lemon zest, if using. The sauce may be strained through a fine-mesh sieve, if desired.

5. The sauce is ready to serve now or it may be held warm for up to 2 hours.

Beef Tournedos Provençal

Makes 50 portions

Beef tournedos portions (7 to 8 oz/200 to 225 g each)	50 each	50 each
Kosher salt, plus additional as needed	2 tbsp	30 ml
Ground black pepper, plus additional as needed	2 tsp	10 ml
Clarified butter or olive oil	1¼ cups	300 ml
PROVENÇAL SAUCE		
Garlic, minced	1 oz	30 g
Anchovy fillets, mashed to a paste	15 each	15 each
Tomatoes, peeled, seeded, chopped	3 lb 12 oz	1.7 kg
Dry red wine	3 pt	1.4 l
Jus de Volaille Lié (page 90), Jus de Veau Lié (page 89), or Demi-Glace (page 88)	3¾ qt	3.5 l
Black olives, pitted, sliced or julienned	1 lb 4 oz	570 g
Basil, chiffonade	5 oz	140 g

1. Blot the beef dry and season with salt and pepper. Divide the ingredients into batches of the desired size.

2. Heat the butter or oil in a large sauté pan over medium-high heat until it is almost smoking. Sauté the desired number of tournedos to the desired doneness: 2 minutes per side for rare (internal temperature of 120°F/49°C), 3 minutes per side for medium rare (130°F/55°C), 4½ minutes per side for medium (140°F/60°C), 6 minutes per side for medium well (150°F/65°C), and 7 minutes per side for well done (160°F/70°C). Remove the beef from the pan and keep warm while completing the sauce.

3. To prepare the Provençal sauce, pour off the excess fat from the pan. Add the garlic and anchovies and sauté until their aroma is released, 30 to 40 seconds. Add the tomatoes and continue to sauté until any juices they release have cooked down, about 5 minutes.

4. Add the wine to deglaze the pan and simmer until it has nearly cooked away, about 5 minutes. Add the jus lié or demi-glace and any juices released by the beef. Reduce until the sauce lightly coats the back of a spoon, about 15 minutes. Strain through a fine-mesh sieve into a clean saucepan and return to a simmer. Add the olives and basil and return to a simmer. Taste the sauce and season with salt and pepper.

5. Serve each tournedos with 2 fl oz/60 ml of the sauce on heated plates.

VEAL SCALOPPINE MARSALA

Makes 50 portions

Veal top round portions (about 6 oz / 170 g each), boneless	50 each	50 each
Kosher salt, plus additional as needed	2 tbsp	30 ml
Ground black pepper, plus additional as needed	2 tsp	10 ml
All-purpose flour (optional)	15 oz	425 g
Clarified butter or olive oil	1¼ cups	300 ml
Shallots, minced	2½ oz	70 g
Dry white wine	30 fl oz	890 ml
Marsala Sauce (page 119)	3¾ qt	3.5 l
Butter (optional)	1 lb 9 oz	710 g

1. Pound each portion of veal between sheets of parchment paper or plastic wrap to a thickness of ¼ inch/6 mm. Blot dry and season with salt and pepper. Dredge in flour, if using, and shake off any excess.

2. Working in batches of the desired size, heat the butter or oil in a large sauté pan over medium-high heat until it is almost smoking. Sauté the veal to the desired doneness, about 2 minutes per side for medium (internal temperature of 140°F/60°C). Remove the veal from the pan and keep warm while completing the sauce.

3. Pour off the excess fat from the pan. Add the shallots and sauté until they are translucent, about 1 minute.

4. Add the wine to deglaze the pan and simmer until it has nearly cooked away, about 5 minutes. Add the Marsala sauce and any accumulated juices from the resting veal, simmer briefly, and strain through a fine-mesh sieve into a clean saucepan.

5. Return the sauce to a simmer. Taste and adjust seasoning with salt and pepper. Swirl in the butter, if using, to finish the sauce.

6. Serve each portion of veal with 2 fl oz/60 ml of the sauce on heated plates.

SWISS-STYLE SHREDDED VEAL

Makes 50 portions

Veal top round or tender leg cut, cut into émincé	18 lb 12 oz	8.5 kg
Kosher salt, plus additional as needed	2 tbsp	30 ml
Ground black pepper, plus additional as needed	2 tsp	10 ml
All-purpose flour (optional)	15 oz	425 g
Clarified butter or olive oil	1¼ cups	300 ml
Shallots, chopped	15 oz	425 g
White mushrooms, sliced	1 lb 9 oz	710 g
Dry white wine	3 pt	1.4 l
Jus de Veau Lié (page 89) or Demi-Glace (page 88)	3 pt	1.4 l
Heavy cream	20 fl oz	590 ml
Brandy	5 fl oz	150 ml
Lemon juice, plus additional as needed	2 tbsp	30 ml
Spätzle (page 334), hot	6 lb	2.75 kg

1. Blot the veal dry and season with salt and pepper. Dredge in flour, if using, and shake off any excess.

2. Working in batches of the desired size, heat the butter or oil in a large sauté pan over medium-high heat until it is almost smoking. Sauté the veal, stirring from time to time, until it is just cooked through, about 5 minutes. Remove the veal from the pan and keep warm while completing the sauce.

3. Pour off the excess fat from the pan. Add the shallots and mushrooms and sauté until the shallots are softened and translucent, about 5 minutes.

4. Add the wine to deglaze the pan and simmer until it has nearly cooked away, about 5 minutes. Add the jus lié or demi-glace, cream, brandy, and any juices released by the veal. Reduce until the sauce reaches the proper consistency and flavor, 4 to 5 minutes.

5. Taste the sauce and adjust seasoning with the lemon juice, salt, and pepper.

6. Combine the veal with the sauce by batches. Serve each 8-oz/225-g portion with 2 oz/60 g spätzle on heated plates.

MARINATED SEA BASS FILLET

Makes 50 portions

Extra-virgin olive oil, plus additional as needed for sautéing	5 fl oz	150 ml
Lemon juice	¼ cup	60 ml
Cracked black pepper	1 tbsp	15 ml
Ginger, minced	1 tbsp	15 ml
Tabasco sauce	1 tbsp	15 ml
Sea bass portions (about 5 oz / 140 g each), cleaned, trimmed	50 each	50 each
Zucchini Provençal (page 313), hot	6¼ lb	2.8 kg
Green Beans with Walnuts (page 297), hot	6¼ lb	2.8 kg

1. Combine the oil, lemon juice, pepper, ginger, and Tabasco to make a marinade.

2. Place the sea bass in a shallow container, pour the marinade over the fish, and turn the pieces to coat them evenly. Marinate under refrigeration for at least 1 hour and up to 3 hours before sautéing.

3. Heat a sauté pan over high heat. Add enough oil to film the pan. Sauté the sea bass on the presentation side until firm and golden, about 2 minutes. Turn the sea bass and continue to sauté until cooked through, 2 to 3 minutes more.

4. Serve each portion of sea bass with 2 oz/60 g zucchini provençal and 2 oz/60 g green beans on heated plates.

ANCHO-CRUSTED SALMON WITH YELLOW MOLE

Makes 50 portions

Anchos, chopped	10 each	10 each
Cumin seeds	1 oz	30 g
Fennel seeds	1 oz	30 g
Coriander seeds	1½ oz	45 g
Black peppercorns	1 oz	30 g
Dried thyme	½ oz	15 g
Dried oregano	½ oz	15 g
Kosher salt	2½ oz	75 g
Dry mustard	1½ oz	45 g
Salmon fillet portions (about 6 oz / 170 g each), skinless	50 each	50 each
Clarified butter or olive oil	7½ fl oz	220 ml
Yellow Mole (see below), hot	6¼ pt	3 l

1. Toast the anchos, cumin seeds, fennel seeds, and coriander seeds on a sheet pan in a 300°F/150°C oven until fragrant, about 5 minutes. Remove and cool to room temperature.

2. In a spice grinder, combine the toasted spices with the peppercorns, thyme, and oregano. Grind to a coarse powder. Stir in the salt and mustard.

3. Lightly coat each salmon fillet with the spice mixture to form a crust.

4. Heat the butter or oil in a large sauté pan over medium-high heat. Sauté the salmon on the first side until the spices start to brown, 1 to 2 minutes. Turn the salmon and continue to sauté over medium heat, or transfer to a 350°F/175°C oven and bake, until the salmon reaches the desired doneness, 4 to 6 minutes, depending on the thickness of the cut.

5. Serve each salmon fillet with 2 fl oz/60 ml of the mole on heated plates.

YELLOW MOLE

Makes 6¼ pt (3 liters)

Olive oil	3 fl oz	90 ml
Onions, sliced	2 lb 4 oz	1 kg
Garlic, sliced	1 tbsp	15 ml
Fennel, chopped	1 lb	450 g
Cinnamon sticks (2 inches/51 mm each)	3 each	3 each
Ground allspice	¾ tsp	4 ml
Dried epazote	4½ tsp	23 ml

Sugar	2¼ oz	65 g
Water	1 pt 9 fl oz	750 ml
Yellow peppers, chopped	4 lb 12 oz	2.15 kg
Tomatillos, quartered	9¼ oz	260 g
Lime juice, plus additional as needed	⅓ cup	80 ml
Kosher salt, plus additional as needed	1 tbsp	15 ml

1. Heat the oil in a pot over medium-high heat. Add the onions and garlic and cook until the onions are translucent, about 8 minutes.

2. Add the fennel, cinnamon, allspice, epazote, sugar, and water. Bring to a simmer and add the peppers.

3. Cover the pot and simmer on low heat until the peppers are soft, about 25 minutes.

4. Remove and discard cinnamon sticks. Transfer the mixture to a blender and purée with the tomatillos until very smooth. Strain through a large-mesh sieve.

5. Taste the mole and season with lime juice and salt. The sauce is ready to serve now, or it may be rapidly cooled and held under refrigeration up to 2 days for later service.

1. Simmer the mixture until the peppers have softened. Season with lime juice and salt.

2. Purée the mole in a blender until it is smooth. The finished mole will be thick and will still have some texture.

3. After coating the salmon in ground spices, sauté it until the spices on each side begin to brown.

4. The finished salmon will have browned evenly on both sides.

FRIED FISH CAKES

Makes 50 portions

Whitefish fillets	6 lb 4 oz	2.8 kg
Shallots, minced	7½ oz	215 g
Garlic cloves	10 each	10 each
Cilantro, including roots	2½ oz	70 g
Galangal, chopped	1½ oz	45 g
Kosher salt	2 tbsp	30 ml
Fish sauce (nuoc mam)	5 fl oz	150 ml
Peanut oil	5 qt	4.7 l
Yard-long beans, cooked, drained	6 lb 4 oz	2.8 kg
Cucumber Salad (see below)	6 lb 4 oz	2.8 kg
Optional garnish: chopped hard cooked eggs and capers	as needed	as needed

1. Keep the whitefish and all grinding equipment very cold. Grind the fish through the fine die of a meat grinder or chop in a food processor to form a paste.

2. Transfer the whitefish mixture to a clean bowl. Use a spoon to fold in the shallots, garlic, cilantro, galangal, salt, and fish sauce.

3. Wearing gloves, form the mixture into patties, 2 oz/60 g each, by hand or using a circular mold. Hold under refrigeration up to 24 hours until service.

4. When ready to serve, heat enough of the oil in a skillet over medium-high heat to coat it liberally, add the patties, working in batches if necessary, and cook until browned on both sides and cooked through, about 4 minutes.

5. Serve each fish cake with 2 oz/60 g yard-long beans and 2 oz/60 g cucumber salad.

CUCUMBER SALAD

Makes 50 portions

Rice wine vinegar	20 fl oz	590 ml
Sugar	18 oz	510 g
Kosher salt	1½ oz	45 g
Seedless cucumbers, halved lengthwise, very thinly sliced	15 each	15 each
Red onions, quartered lengthwise, very thinly sliced	5 each	5 each
Red jalapeños, halved, very thinly sliced	1½ oz	45 g
Mint, roughly chopped or torn	2 oz	60 g
Cilantro leaves	3 oz	85 g

1. Combine the vinegar, sugar, and salt in a saucepan. Warm over low heat, whisking constantly, until the sugar and salt are dissolved. Do not boil.

2. Cool the mixture and pour over the cucumbers, onions, and jalapeños. Marinate at room temperature for 30 minutes. The salad is ready to serve now or it may be held up to 2 days under refrigeration.

3. Drain the salad and serve, garnished with mint and cilantro.

Fried Fish Cakes (page 255)

BUTTERMILK FRIED CHICKEN

Makes 50 portions

Chickens (3 lb 8 oz / 1.6 kg each), whole	20 each	20 each
Buttermilk	5 pt	2.4 l
Dijon mustard	1 lb 4 oz	570 g
Old Bay seasoning	2½ oz	70 g
Tarragon, minced	2 oz	60 g
All-purpose flour	2 lb	900 g
Poultry seasoning	2 tbsp	30 ml
Cayenne	4 tsp	20 ml
Vegetable shortening as needed for frying	2 qt	1.9 l
Country Gravy (page 258)	6¼ pt	2.95 l

1. Cut the chicken into pieces (2 wing portions, 2 drumsticks, 2 thighs, and 4 breast portions). Combine the chicken pieces with the buttermilk, mustard, Old Bay, and tarragon. Mix well and marinate under refrigeration overnight.

2. Combine the flour with the poultry seasoning and cayenne. Mix well.

3. Drain the buttermilk mixture from the chicken on wire racks. Dredge the chicken in the flour mixture and let it sit for about 15 minutes.

4. Heat the shortening in a large cast-iron pan over high heat. Dredge the chicken in the flour again. Working in batches, pan fry the chicken until golden brown on both sides.

5. Place the chicken rack on a sheet pan and bake at 350°F/175°C until it reaches an internal temperature of 165°F/73°C.

6. Serve each chicken portion with 2 fl oz/60 ml gravy on heated plates.

COUNTRY GRAVY

Makes 2 quarts (1.9 liters)

Clarified butter	½ cup	120 ml
Slab bacon, rind removed, minced	1 lb	450 g
Onions, minced	1 lb	450 g
Celery, minced	4 oz	115 g
Garlic, minced	1 tbsp	15 ml
All-purpose flour	5 oz	140 g
Chicken Stock (page 83)	2 qt	1.9 l
Chicken wings, browned	24 oz	680 g
Bay leaf	1 each	1 each
Kosher salt, plus additional as needed	2 tbsp	30 ml
Ground black pepper, plus additional as needed	2 tsp	10 ml
Milk	¾ cup	180 ml
Heavy cream	¾ cup	180 ml

1. Heat the butter in a rondeau or sauce pot over medium-low heat. Add the bacon and cook until the fat is released from the bacon and the bacon bits are crispy, about 8 minutes.

2. Add the onions, celery, and garlic and sweat until the onions are translucent, 4 to 6 minutes. Pour off the excess fat, leaving about ½ cup/120 ml.

3. Stir in the flour and cook over medium heat, stirring constantly, to make a pale roux, about 8 minutes.

4. Add the stock, wings, and bay leaf. Season with some of the salt and pepper.

5. Simmer the gravy, skimming as necessary, for 30 to 40 minutes. Add the milk and cream and return the gravy to a simmer.

6. Strain the gravy through a fine-mesh sieve. Taste the gravy and then adjust seasoning with salt and pepper.

7. The gravy is ready to serve now, or it may be rapidly cooled and held under refrigeration for up to 3 days for later service.

Buttermilk Fried Chicken (page 257)

Corned Beef Hash

Makes 50 portions

Vegetable oil or bacon fat, plus additional for frying	1¼ cups	300 ml
Onions, large dice	2 lb 8 oz	1.15 kg
Parsnips, large dice	1 lb 9 oz	710 g
Carrots, large dice	15 oz	425 g
Red-skin potatoes, peeled if desired	7 lb 8 oz	3.4 kg
Corned beef, cooked, cut into 1-inch/25-mm cubes	10 lb	4.5 kg
Tomato purée	5 fl oz	140 ml
Kosher salt, plus additional as needed	2 tbsp	30 ml
Ground black pepper, plus additional as needed	2 tsp	10 ml

1. Heat a roasting pan over medium heat. Add 2½ fl oz/75 ml of the oil or the fat to the pan. Add the onions and sweat until they are soft, 5 to 6 minutes. Add the parsnips, carrots, potatoes, and corned beef to the pan and cover with foil.

2. Place the pan in a 375°F/190°C oven and roast until the vegetables are fully cooked and tender, about 1 hour. Remove the foil, stir in the tomato purée, and return the pan, uncovered, to the oven. Cook until the tomato purée has browned, about 15 minutes. Taste the mixture and then season with salt and pepper. Cool slightly.

3. Grind the mixture through the medium die of a meat grinder. Form into patties, 2 to 3 oz/60 to 85 g each, by hand or using a ring mold. Hold under refrigeration up to 24 hours until service.

4. When ready to serve, heat enough oil in a sauté pan or griddle to coat it liberally. Working in batches if necessary, cook the patties until they are crispy on each side and hot in the center.

5. Serve the corned beef hash on heated plates.

Boston Scrod with Cream, Capers, and Tomatoes

Makes 50 portions

Scrod fillet portions (about 6 oz/170 g each)	50 each	50 each
Kosher salt, plus additional as needed	2 tbsp	30 ml
Ground black pepper, plus additional as needed	2 tsp	10 ml
Butter, cold	1 lb 4 oz	570 g
Shallots, minced	1½ oz	45 g
Dry white wine	1 pt 9 fl oz	750 ml
Fish Fumet (page 85)	1 pt 9 fl oz	750 ml
Heavy cream	30 fl oz	890 ml
Tomatoes, peeled, seeded, chopped	1 lb 4 oz	570 g
Capers, drained, rinsed	2½ oz	75 g
White mushrooms, sliced, sautéed	1 lb 4 oz	570 g
Lemon juice	5 fl oz	150 ml

1. Season the scrod with some of the salt and pepper.

2. Rub or brush sauté pans or hotel pans (depending upon the size of your batch) with enough of the butter to lightly coat the pan and sprinkle the shallots evenly in the pan. Place the scrod on top of the shallots. Add the wine and fumet.

3. Bring the liquid to just under a simmer over low heat. Cover the scrod with a piece of buttered parchment paper (cartouche). Transfer the pan with the covered scrod to a 325°F/165°C oven. Poach the scrod until the flesh is opaque and gives under slight pressure, 10 to 12 minutes.

4. Transfer the scrod to a half hotel pan, cover with the cartouche, and hold warm. (Reserve the sauté pan and the cooking liquid to finish the sauce in step 6.)

5. Place the cream in a sauce pot over medium heat and cook until the liquid is reduced by half.

6. Place the sauté pan with the cooking liquid on the stovetop over high heat and reduce by two-thirds, 10 to 12 minutes. Add the cream and simmer for 1 to 2 minutes. Add the tomatoes, capers, mushrooms, and any accumulated juices from the resting fish and simmer until the sauce reaches the proper consistency and flavor, 3 to 4 minutes. Whisk or swirl in the remaining butter and add the lemon juice. Taste the sauce and season with salt and pepper.

7. Serve each scrod fillet with 2 fl oz/60 ml of the sauce on heated plates.

Pescado à la Veracruzana

Makes 50 portions

Red snapper fillet portions (about 6 oz/140 g each)	50 each	50 each
Kosher salt, plus additional as needed	2 tbsp	30 ml
Ground black pepper. plus additional as needed	2 tsp	10 ml
Lime juice	30 fl oz	890 ml
Olive oil	15 fl oz	445 ml
Onions, minced	5 lb	2.25 kg
Garlic cloves, minced	15 each	15 each
Tomatoes, peeled, seeded, medium dice	15 lb	6.8 kg
Green olives, pitted, chopped	65 each	65 each
Capers, drained, rinsed	2 oz	60 g
Pickled jalapeños, julienned	25 each	25 each
Bay leaves	15 each	15 each
Marjoram or oregano, chopped	2½ tsp	13 ml
Thyme, chopped	2½ tsp	13 ml
Fish Stock (page 84)	5 qt	4.7 l
GARNISH		
Parsley, chopped	2½ oz	75 g
Capers, drained, rinsed	3 oz	85 g
Green olives	150 to 200 each	150 to 200 each

1. Cut a shallow crisscross into the skin of all the snapper fillets with a boning knife. Season the snapper with some of the salt and pepper. Marinate it in the lime juice under refrigeration for at least 1 and up to 12 hours.

2. Meanwhile, prepare the sauce. Heat ¼ cup/60 ml of the oil in a saucepan or rondeau over medium-high heat. Add the onions and garlic and sauté, stirring frequently, until they start to turn golden, 6 to 8 minutes. Add the tomatoes, olives, capers, jalapeños, bay leaves, marjoram or oregano, thyme, and stock. Bring the sauce to a simmer and cook until the tomatoes are soft and the flavors have blended, about 20 minutes. Taste the sauce and season with salt and pepper. Reserve.

3. Lightly grease sauté pans or hotel pans with the remaining oil. Place the snapper in the pans. Pour the sauce over and around the snapper.

4. Bring the liquid to just under a simmer over low heat. Cover the snapper with a piece of buttered parchment paper (cartouche). Transfer the entire pan to a 350°F/175°C oven. Shallow poach the snapper until cooked through, about 12 minutes. Remove the snapper from the oven.

5. Serve each snapper fillet with 2 fl oz/60 ml of the sauce on heated plates, garnished with parsley, capers, and olives.

PORK IN GREEN CURRY SAUCE

Makes 50 portions

Coconut milk, chilled	3 gal	11.5 l
Green Curry Paste (see below)	2½ pt	1.2 l
Pork butt, cut into 2-inch/51-mm cubes	20 lb	9 kg
Kaffir lime leaves (single leaves), bruised	60 each	60 each
Fish sauce (nuoc mam)	20 fl oz	590 ml
Palm sugar	12½ oz	355 g
Thai eggplants, quartered	5 lb	2.25 kg
Thai basil leaves	250 each	250 each
Steamed jasmine rice	12 lb	5.5 kg
Thai bird chiles, finely julienned	15 to 20 each	15 to 20 each

1. Skim the thick coconut cream from the top of the coconut milk and place the cream in a large pot over medium-high heat, reserving the remaining milk to add in step 3. Cook the cream, stirring constantly, until it begins to separate, about 10 minutes.

2. Add the curry paste to the cream, stirring well to dilute the paste and blend it evenly into the cream. Simmer until aromatic, at least 2 minutes. Add the pork and lime leaves and mix well to coat the pork.

3. Add the fish sauce, sugar, and the reserved coconut milk. Bring the mixture to a simmer, add the eggplants, and continue to simmer until the pork is tender and cooked through, 20 to 25 minutes. Remove the pot from the heat, add the basil, and mix well.

4. Serve 8-oz/225-g portions of the curry with 3½ oz/100 g steamed rice. Garnish with chiles.

GREEN CURRY PASTE

Makes 2½ pints (1.2 liters)

Cumin seeds	5 tsp	25 ml
Coriander seeds	¼ cup	120 ml
White peppercorns	5 tsp	25 ml
Shallots, thinly sliced	10 oz	285 g
Garlic cloves, thinly sliced	2½ oz	70 g
Green Thai chiles, seeded	25 each	25 each
Cilantro root, minced	2½ oz	70 g
Lemongrass, thinly sliced	2½ oz	70 g
Galangal, sliced	1¼ oz	35 g
Grated kaffir lime zest	1¼ oz	35 g
Kaffir lime leaves (single leaves), chopped	20 each	20 each

Shrimp paste	1¼ oz	35 g
Kosher salt	1¼ oz	35 g

1. Toast the cumin and coriander seeds in a dry sauté pan over medium-high heat until golden brown and aromatic, about 2 minutes. Keep the pan in constant motion as the spices toast. Transfer to a small bowl.

2. In the same pan, toast the peppercorns in the same manner and combine with the cumin and coriander.

3. Using a spice grinder, grind the toasted cumin, coriander, and peppercorns to a medium-fine powder and set aside.

4. Place the remaining ingredients, except the ground spices, in a blender and grind into a fine paste.

5. Combine the paste with the ground spices and blend together until smooth.

6. Use immediately or place in a tightly sealed container and hold under refrigeration up to 5 days for later use.

GRILLED SQUASH JAMBALAYA

Makes 50 portions

Peanut oil	¾ cup	180 ml
Onions, minced	3 lb	1.4 kg
Green peppers, small dice	2 lb	900 g
Celery, small dice	2 lb	900 g
Garlic cloves, minced	4 each	4 each
Ground black pepper	2 tsp	10 ml
Cayenne	½ tsp	3 ml
Bay leaves	2 each	2 each
Kosher salt, plus additional as needed	2 tbsp	30 ml
Tomatoes, peeled, seeded, chopped	5 lb	2.25 kg
White mushrooms, quartered	2 lb	900 g
Vegetable Stock (page 86)	1 gal	3.75 l
Dried oregano	½ cup	120 ml
Basil, chiffonade	1 oz	30 g
Thyme, chopped	½ oz	15 g
Tabasco sauce	1 tbsp	15 ml
Long-grain white rice	4 lb	1.8 kg
Yellow squash or zucchini, sliced, grilled	8 lb	3.6 kg
Red peppers, roasted, peeled	2 lb	900 g
Green onions, thinly sliced	8 oz	225 g

1. Heat the oil in a rondeau over medium-high heat. Add the onions, green peppers, celery, garlic, pepper, cayenne, bay leaves, and salt. Cook until the vegetables begin to soften, about 10 minutes.

2. Add the tomatoes with their juice and the mushrooms. Stir in the stock and oregano and simmer for 20 minutes. Stir in the basil, thyme, and Tabasco.

3. Add the rice to the jambalaya and bring to a simmer. Cover the rondeau, transfer to a 350°F/175°C oven, and bake for 20 minutes.

4. Serve the jambalaya in heated bowls garnished with 2½ oz/70 g grilled squash, ½ oz/15 g roasted peppers, and a sprinkle of green onions.

Chicken Mole Poblano

Makes 50 portions

Chicken suprême portions (about 8 oz/225 g each)	50 each	50 each
Kosher salt, plus additional as needed	2 tbsp	30 ml
Olive oil	1½ cups	360 ml
MOLE SAUCE		
Onions, fine dice	1 lb 8 oz	680 g
Green peppers, fine dice	3 lb 4 oz	1.5 kg
Jalapeños, minced	3 oz	85 g
Almonds, blanched, chopped	1¼ lb	570 g
Garlic, minced	2 tbsp	30 ml
Chili Powder (page 131)	12 oz	340 g
Thyme, minced	½ oz	15 g
Ground cinnamon	3 tbsp	45 ml
Tomatoes, peeled, seeded, chopped	4 lb 12 oz	2.15 kg
Chicken Stock (page 83)	3¼ qt	3 l
Mexican chocolate, chopped	1 lb 10 oz	740 g
Kosher salt, plus additional as needed	2 oz	60 g
Ground black pepper, plus additional as needed	1 tbsp	15 ml
Sesame seeds, toasted	1 cup	240 ml

1. Season the chicken with salt.

2. Heat the oil in a rondeau over medium-high heat, add the chicken suprêmes, and brown on both sides. Remove the chicken and keep warm.

3. To prepare the mole poblano, add the onions to the pan and sauté until browned, 6 to 8 minutes. Add the green peppers, jalapeños, almonds, and garlic. Sauté until the peppers are tender, 6 to 8 minutes.

4. Add the chili powder, thyme, and cinnamon. Sauté, stirring frequently, until aromatic, 2 to 3 minutes.

5. Add the tomatoes and stock. Bring to a simmer and return the chicken to the pan.

6. Transfer the pan to a 325°F/165°C oven, cover, and braise for 25 minutes.

7. Remove the chicken from the pan and set aside. Return the pan to the stovetop. Heat the sauce over low heat and stir in the chocolate until melted. Taste and then season with salt and pepper. Add the chicken to the sauce and simmer gently for 2 to 3 minutes.

8. The chicken is ready to serve now or it may be held warm. Serve the chicken on heated plates, topped with 2 fl oz/60 ml sauce and a sprinkling of sesame seeds (scant ½ tsp/3 ml) before serving.

BRAISED BEEF SHORT RIBS WITH POLENTA AND ROASTED CREMINI

Makes 50 portions

Beef short ribs, cleaned, trimmed	40 lb	18 kg
Kosher salt	3 tbsp	45 ml
Cracked black pepper	1 tbsp	15 ml
Vegetable oil	½ cup	120 ml
Mirepoix (page 134), large dice	5 lb	2.25 kg
Tomato paste	¼ cup	60 ml
Dry red wine	2 bottles (1 l each)	2 bottles (1 l each)
Brown Veal Stock (page 82)	6 gal	22.7 l
Sachet d'Epices (page 133)	2 each	2 each
Soft Polenta with Rosemary (see opposite page), hot	6¼ lb	2.8 kg
Roasted Cremini Mushrooms (see opposite page), hot	6¼ lb	2.8 kg

1. Split the ribs lengthwise and season with salt and pepper.

2. Heat enough oil in a braising pan to coat it well and place over high heat. Add the ribs and sear, turning the ribs as necessary until both sides of the ribs are golden brown, 10 to 12 minutes total. Remove the ribs from the pan and keep warm.

3. Add the mirepoix to the pan and cook, stirring frequently, until the onions begin to brown, about 10 minutes. Add the tomato paste and cook, stirring frequently, until the tomato paste turns a deep brick red color and gives off a sweet aroma, 30 to 45 seconds. Add the wine, stir well to release the fond from the pan, and continue to cook until the liquid is reduced by half, about 10 minutes.

4. Return the ribs to the pan and add enough stock to cover them by three-fourths. Add the sachet.

5. Cover the pan and braise the ribs in a 325°F/165°C oven until fork-tender, 2 to 2½ hours. Make sure to turn the ribs every 15 minutes while they braise.

6. Remove the ribs from the braising liquid and keep warm. Return the pan with the braising liquid to the stovetop. Reduce the liquid over high heat until it thickens, about 15 minutes. Strain the sauce through a fine-mesh sieve and hold it hot for service.

7. Serve a 12-oz/340-g portion of ribs with 2 fl oz/60 ml sauce, 3½ oz/100 g polenta, and 2 oz/60 g cremini on heated plates.

Soft Polenta with Rosemary
Makes 50 portions

Extra-virgin olive oil	¾ cup	180 ml
Garlic, thinly sliced	2 oz	60 g
Rosemary, minced	4 tsp	20 ml
Chicken Stock (page 83)	1 gal	3.75 l
Milk	2 qt	1.9 l
Coarse yellow cornmeal	1¾ lb	800 g
Parmigiano-Reggiano, grated	1 lb	450 g
Kosher salt	3 tbsp	45 ml
Cracked black pepper	2 tbsp	30 ml

1. Heat the oil in a heavy-bottomed pot over medium heat and add the garlic and rosemary. Sauté until the garlic is soft but not brown, about 1 minute. Add the stock and milk and bring the mixture to a boil. Add the cornmeal in a gradual stream, whisking constantly. Turn the heat down and simmer gently, stirring frequently, until the polenta is creamy, 20 to 30 minutes. Stir in the cheese.

2. Before serving, stir the polenta thoroughly, and season with salt and pepper. The polenta is ready to serve now, or it may be held hot for later service.

Roasted Cremini Mushrooms
Makes 6¼ pounds (2.8 kilograms)

Cremini mushrooms, trimmed	12 lb	5.5 kg
Extra-virgin olive oil	¾ cup	180 ml
Garlic, thinly sliced	2 oz	60 g
Rosemary, minced	4 tsp	20 ml
Kosher salt	3 tbsp	45 ml
Cracked black pepper	2 tsp	10 ml

1. Combine the mushrooms, olive oil, garlic, rosemary, salt, and pepper and toss until the mushrooms are evenly coated.

2. Roast the mushrooms on sheet pans in a 450°F/230°C oven until the mushrooms are tender and browned, about 20 minutes.

3. The mushrooms are ready to serve now or they may be held under refrigeration for up to 4 days. If necessary, warm the mushrooms in a 200°F/95°C oven for 15 minutes.

Braised Veal Shanks with Braising Greens and Polenta

Makes 50 portions

Osso buco (veal shank), crosscut portions (about 1 lb/450 g each, 1½ inches/38 mm thick)	50 each	50 each
Kosher salt, plus additional as needed	2 tbsp	30 ml
Cracked black pepper, plus additional as needed	2 tbsp	30 ml
All-purpose flour	4 oz	115 g
Vegetable oil as needed for searing	¾ cup	180 ml
Onions, small dice	2 lb	900 g
Garlic, minced	8 oz	225 g
Dry red wine	1 qt	950 ml
Brown Veal Stock (page 82)	4 gal	15 l
Canned tomatoes, drained, seeded, chopped	6 lb	2.7 kg
Lemon juice	3 fl oz	90 ml
Gremolata (page 277), optional	14 oz	400 g
Braising Greens (page 308), hot	8 lb	3.6 kg
Basic Polenta (page 330), hot	12 lb	5.5 kg

1. Season the veal shanks with salt and pepper and tie a string around them to keep them together. Lightly dredge in flour. Shake off any excess flour.

2. Heat about enough of the oil in a braising pan over high heat to coat generously. When the oil is nearly smoking, add the shanks and sear on all sides to a deep brown, about 10 minutes total. Transfer the shanks to a hotel pan and keep warm.

3. In the same pan, heat additional oil if necessary (there should be enough to coat the pan liberally) over medium-high heat. Add the onions and garlic and cook, stirring frequently, until the onions are tender and translucent, about 10 minutes. Add the wine, stir well to release the fond from the pan, and continue to cook until the liquid is reduced by three-quarters, about 10 minutes. Add the stock and bring to a boil.

4. Return the shanks and any juices that have accumulated to the pan (there should be enough liquid to cover them halfway). Cover the pan and braise the shanks in a 325°F/165°C oven until fork-tender, 2 to 2½ hours.

5. Carefully remove the shanks from the roasting pan, making sure that they hold together, and shingle into hotel pans. Hold hot for service.

Continued

Braised Veal Shanks with Braising Greens and
Polenta (page 275)

6. Pour the sauce from the braising pan into a saucepan or rondeau. Degrease the sauce by skimming away as much fat from the surface as possible. Add the tomatoes and simmer over medium heat until the sauce is reduced by half. Taste the sauce and season with salt, pepper, and lemon juice. The shanks and sauce are ready to serve now, or they may be rapidly chilled and held under refrigeration for up to 2 days for later service.

7. Reheat the shanks in the sauce in a 325°F/165°C oven if made in advance. Serve each shank with 2 fl oz/60 ml of the sauce on heated plates, garnished with 2 tsp/10 ml gremolata, if using, and accompanied by 2½ oz/70 g greens and 3½ oz/100 g polenta.

GREMOLATA

Makes 14 ounces (400 grams)

Panko bread crumbs	10 oz	285 g
Orange zest, blanched, minced	1 oz	30 g
Lemon zest, blanched, minced	1 oz	30 g
Garlic, minced	1 oz	30 g
Parsley, chopped	1 oz	30 g
Kosher salt	2 tsp	10 ml
Ground black pepper	½ tsp	3 ml

1. Process the bread crumbs in a food processor for 5 seconds and spread thinly on a dry sheet pan. Toast them in a 500°F/260°C oven until lightly browned, about 7 minutes. Transfer to a bowl and reserve.

2. Add the orange and lemon zests, garlic, parsley, salt, and pepper to the bread crumbs. Toss to combine.

3. The gremolata is ready to serve now, or it may be held under refrigeration up to 24 hours for later service. If refrigerated, bring up to room temperature before serving.

OSSO BUCO MILANESE

Makes 50 portions

Osso buco (veal shank), crosscut portions (about 1 lb/450 g each, 1½ inches/38 mm thick)	50 each	50 each
Kosher salt, plus additional as needed	3 tbsp	45 ml
Ground black pepper, plus additional as needed	2 tbsp	30 ml
All-purpose flour	10 oz	285 g
Olive oil	1¼ cups	300 ml
Mirepoix (page 134), small dice	3 lb 12 oz	1.7 kg
Garlic, minced	2 tbsp	30 ml
Tomato paste	15 oz	425 g
Dry white wine	2½ pt	1.2 l
Brown Veal Stock (page 82)	2½ gal	9.5 l
Bouquet Garni (page 133)	1 each	1 each
Arrowroot, diluted in equal amount of cold water	As needed	As needed
Gremolata (page 277)	5 oz	140 g

1. Season the veal shanks with salt and pepper and tie a string around them to keep them together. Lightly dredge them in flour and shake off any excess flour.

2. Heat the oil over medium-high heat in a rondeau or brazier until it starts to shimmer. Place the shanks carefully in the oil and sear until deep brown on all sides. Transfer the shanks to a hotel pan and keep warm.

3. Add the mirepoix, and the garlic to the rondeau or brazier and cook, stirring from time to time, until the onions are golden brown, about 10 minutes. Add the tomato paste and cook until the tomato paste turns a deep brick red color and gives off a sweet aroma, about 1 minute. Add the wine, stir well to release the fond from the pan, and continue to cook until the liquid is reduced by half, about 10 minutes. Return the shanks to the pan along with any juices they may have released. Add enough stock to cover the shanks by two-thirds. Bring to a gentle simmer over medium-low heat.

4. Cover the pan and transfer it to a 350°F/175°C oven. Braise the shanks for 45 minutes and then add the bouquet garni. Degrease the liquid if necessary by skimming away as much fat from the surface as possible. Continue to braise the shanks until fork-tender, 1 to 1½ hours more.

5. Transfer the shanks to a hotel pan and moisten with some of the cooking liquid. Keep warm while finishing the sauce.

6. Pour the sauce from the braising pan into a saucepan or rondeau. Degrease the sauce by skimming away as much fat from the surface as possible. Simmer over high heat until the sauce lightly coats the back of a spoon, about 15 minutes. If necessary, the sauce can be thickened lightly with diluted arrowroot. (Stir the diluted arrowroot

to recombine if necessary.) Taste the sauce and then season with salt and pepper. Strain the sauce through a fine-mesh sieve and hold it hot for service.

7. Remove the strings from the shanks before serving with 2 fl oz/60 ml of the sauce, garnished with 2 tsp/10 ml gremolata, on heated plates.

PASTA PRIMAVERA WITH PESTO CREAM

Makes 50 portions

Campanelle (or similar short pasta shape)	6 lb	2.7 kg
Olive oil	1½ cups	360 ml
Leeks, white and light green parts, medium dice	3 lb 8 oz	1.8 kg
Zucchini, cut into short sticks	5 lb	1.6 kg
Red and yellow peppers, cut into short sticks	3 lb 8 oz	1.6 kg
Kale, rinsed and coarsely chopped	2 lb	900 g
Heavy cream	3 qt	2.8 l
Arugula Pesto (page 128)	12 oz	340 g
Parmesan, grated	12 oz	340 g
Kosher salt, plus additional as needed	2 tbsp	30 ml
Ground black pepper	2 tsp	10 ml

1. Bring a large pot of salted water to a rolling boil. Add the pasta and boil until it is tender to the bite but still retains some texture. Cooking time may vary by brand; follow package directions. Drain the pasta immediately in a colander. (If the pasta is cooked in advance of service, rinse the pasta well in cold water and rub a small amount of oil into the pasta to keep the strands separated.)

2. While the pasta is cooking, heat the oil in a large sauté pan over medium-high heat. Add the leeks and sauté until bright green and tender, 7 to 10 minutes. Add the asparagus, peas, and mushrooms and sauté until the vegetables are tender and the moisture has cooked away, 5 to 10 minutes.

3. Add the cream, pesto, and Parmesan and stir well. Gently bring to a simmer, cooking just until the sauce begins to thicken.

4. Reheat the pasta, in batches if necessary, in boiling salted water for 1 or 2 minutes. Drain before combining the pasta with the sauce. Add the cooked pasta to the sauté pan with the vegetables and cream sauce and toss together. Taste and season with salt and pepper.

5. Serve 6-oz/170-g portions of pasta on heated plates.

Fresh Egg Pasta

Makes 4 pounds 8 ounces (2 kilograms)

All-purpose flour, plus additional as needed	4 lb	1.8 kg
Kosher salt	½ oz	15 g
Eggs	16 each	16 each
Water, plus additional as needed	½ cup	120 ml
Vegetable oil or olive oil (optional)	½ cup	120 ml

1. Combine the flour and salt in a large bowl, making a well in the center. Place the eggs, water, and oil, if using, in the center of the well. With a fork, gradually pull the dry ingredients into the egg mixture. Stir until a loose mass forms. As the dough is mixed, adjust the consistency with additional flour or water.

2. Turn the dough out onto a lightly floured work surface and knead until the texture becomes smooth and elastic, 4 to 5 minutes. Gather and smooth the dough into a ball, cover, and let the dough relax at room temperature for 1 hour before rolling. The dough may be wrapped and stored under refrigeration for up to 2 days, if it is not being rolled immediately.

3. Roll the pasta dough into thin sheets and cut into desired shapes by hand or by using a pasta machine. The pasta is ready to cook now, or it may be covered and held under refrigeration for up to 2 days.

WHOLE WHEAT PASTA: Substitute whole wheat flour for half of the all-purpose flour.

BUCKWHEAT PASTA: Substitute 14 oz/400 g buckwheat flour for an equal amount of the all-purpose flour.

SPINACH PASTA: Purée 24 oz/680 g spinach leaves, squeeze dry in cheesecloth, and add to the eggs. Adjust the dough with additional flour as needed.

SAFFRON PASTA: Steep ¼ to ½ oz/8 to 15 g pulverized saffron threads in 2 tbsp/30 ml hot water and add to the eggs. Adjust the dough with additional flour as needed.

CITRUS PASTA: Add 1½ oz/45 g finely grated lemon or orange zest to the eggs. Substitute ½ cup/120 ml lemon or orange juice for the water. Adjust the dough with additional flour as needed.

CURRIED PASTA: Add ½ to ¾ oz/15 to 20 g curry powder to the flour.

HERBED PASTA: Add 6 oz/170 g chopped fresh herbs to the eggs. Adjust the dough with additional flour as needed.

BLACK PEPPER PASTA: Add ½ oz/15 g cracked black peppercorns to the flour.

RED PEPPER PASTA: Sauté 24 oz/680 g puréed roasted red peppers until reduced and dry. Cool and add to the eggs. Adjust the dough with additional flour as needed.

TOMATO PASTA: Sauté 12 oz/340 g tomato purée until reduced and dry. Cool and add to the eggs. Adjust the dough with additional flour as needed.

PUMPKIN, CARROT, OR BEET PASTA: Sauté 24 oz/680 g puréed cooked pumpkin, carrots, or beets until reduced and dry. Cool and add to the eggs. Adjust the dough with additional flour as needed.

MUSHROOMS AND ARTICHOKES WITH BLACK PEPPER PASTA

Makes 25 portions

Butter	3 oz	85 g
Shallots, minced	3 oz	85 g
Assorted mushrooms, sliced	2 lb	900 g
Dry white wine	1¼ cups	300 ml
Heavy cream	2½ pt	1.2 l
Artichoke bottoms, cooked, cut into wedges or sliced	2 lb 4 oz	1 kg
Tomatoes, peeled, seeded, chopped	2 lb 8 oz	1.15 kg
Black Pepper Pasta (page 282)	2 lb 8 oz	1.15 kg
Kosher salt, plus additional as needed	2 tsp	10 ml
Parsley, chopped, for garnish	As needed	As needed

1. Melt the butter in a sauté pan over medium-high heat, add the shallots, and sauté until they are translucent, about 2 minutes. Add the mushrooms and sauté until they are tender and very hot, about 4 minutes. Add the wine and reduce until the pan is nearly dry, about 5 minutes. Add the cream and reduce until the liquid is slightly thickened, 5 minutes more.

2. Add the artichoke bottoms and tomatoes and heat until warmed through, about 3 minutes.

3. Bring a large pot of salted water to a rolling boil. Add the pasta and stir a few times to separate the strands. Cook the pasta until al dente, about 3 to 4 minutes. Drain the pasta immediately in a colander. Add the pasta to the artichoke mixture and toss together in the sauté pan over medium-high heat until the pasta is evenly coated and very hot. Taste and then season with salt.

4. Serve 6-oz/170-g portions of pasta on heated plates, garnished with parsley.

Orecchiette with Italian Sausage, Broccoli Rabe, and Parmesan

Makes 50 portions

Broccoli rabe	11 lb 4 oz	5.1 kg
Olive oil	3 pt	1.4 l
Onions, minced	3 lb 12 oz	1.7 kg
Tomato paste	2 lb 13 oz	1.25 kg
Italian sausage, bulk or removed from casings	6 lb 4 oz	2.8 kg
Orecchiette pasta, dry	11 lb 4 oz	5.1 kg
Garlic cloves, sliced	10 each	10 each
Red pepper flakes	½ tsp	3 ml
Chicken Stock (page 83) or water	5 fl oz	150 ml
Parsley, chopped	1 oz	30 g
Basil, chiffonade	1 oz	30 g
Oregano, chopped	1 oz	30 g
Chives, minced	1 oz	30 g
Parmesan, grated	1 lb 9 oz	710 g

1. Clean the broccoli rabe by cutting off 1 inch/25 mm from the bottom of each stem. Blanch the broccoli rabe in boiling salted water until 90 percent cooked, about 4 minutes. Remove and shock in an ice water bath. Drain and set aside.

2. In a large sauté pan or rondeau, heat 1 cup/240 ml of the oil over medium heat. Add the onions and cook until tender, about 4 minutes. Add the tomato paste and sausage. Crumble the sausage with a whisk in the pan. Let the mixture cook until the sausage resembles a Bolognese-style sauce, about 5 minutes. Remove from the heat and reserve.

3. Bring a large pot of salted water to a rolling boil. Add the pasta and boil until it is tender to the bite but still retains some texture, about 6 minutes. (Cooking time may vary by brand; follow package directions.) Drain the pasta in a colander.

4. While the pasta is cooking, heat a large sauté pan or rondeau over medium heat and add the remaining oil. Add the garlic, red pepper, stock or water, and reserved sausage mixture. Cook, stirring to combine, for 1 minute. Add the parsley, basil, oregano, chives, and broccoli rabe and cook until the broccoli rabe is very hot, about 3 minutes. Add the cooked pasta and 15 oz/425 g of the cheese and toss to mix.

5. Serve 6-oz/170-g portions of pasta on heated plates, garnished with the remaining cheese.

PAELLA VALENCIANA

Makes 50 portions

Shrimp (16/20 count)	100 each	100 each
Extra-virgin olive oil	9 fl oz	270 ml
Saffron, crushed	2 tbsp	30 ml
Chicken Stock (page 83)	11 qt 1 pint	10.8 l
Chicken legs, separated	50 each	50 each
Kosher salt, plus additional as needed	1 tbsp	15 ml
Ground black pepper, plus additional as needed	1 tsp	5 ml
Onions, large dice	1 lb 14 oz	850 g
Red peppers, large dice	1 lb 14 oz	850 g
Green peppers, large dice	1 lb 14 oz	850 g
Garlic, minced	7½ oz	215 g
Dry Spanish chorizo, sliced ⅛ inch/3 mm thick	1 lb 14 oz	850 g
Spanish rice	7 lb 8 oz	3.4 kg
Tomatoes, peeled, seeded, large dice	1 lb 14 oz	850 g
Clams, cleaned	100 each	100 each
Mussels, cleaned, debearded	15 lb	6.8 kg
Green peas, cooked	1 lb 14 oz	850 g
Green onions, thinly sliced	7½ oz	215 g
Piquillo chiles, julienned	20 each	20 each

1. Peel and devein the shrimp, reserving the shells. Sauté the shells in ¼ cup/60 ml of the oil in a rondeau over high heat until they turn pink, about 4 minutes. Add the saffron and stock and simmer for 30 minutes. Strain the stock through a fine-mesh sieve and hold hot.

2. Season the chicken with salt and pepper. Add ¼ cup/60 ml of the oil to a tilt skillet and heat until the oil is almost smoking. Add the chicken and brown on all sides. Remove from the pan and reserve.

3. Add the remaining oil and the onions and peppers to the pan. Sauté for 2 to 3 minutes, add the garlic, and sauté for 1 minute more. Add the chorizo and rice and stirr to coat the rice with the oil.

4. Add the tomatoes, reserved stock, chicken, and clams to the pan. Cover, reduce the heat, and cook until all the clams are open, about 5 minutes. Do not stir the rice during the cooking process.

5. Add the mussels and shrimp to the pan. Cover and cook until the shrimp is fully cooked and the mussels open, 5 to 7 minutes. During the last minute of cooking, add the peas. (If necessary, add more stock during cooking so that the rice does not dry out.)

6. Serve the paella (5 oz/140 g rice mixture, 1 chicken leg, 2 shrimp, 2 clams, and 2 mussels per portion) garnished with green onions and chiles.

Cioppino

Makes 50 portions

Olive oil	5 fl oz	150 ml
Onions, fine dice	3 lb 12 oz	1.7 kg
Green onions, sliced on the diagonal	5 bunches	5 bunches
Green peppers, small dice	3 lb 12 oz	1.7 kg
Fennel, small dice	3 lb 12 oz	1.7 kg
Kosher salt, plus additional as needed	2 tbsp	30 ml
Ground black pepper, plus additional as needed	2 tsp	10 ml
Garlic, minced	1½ oz	45 g
Tomatoes, peeled, seeded, chopped	20 lb	9 kg
Dry white wine	2½ pt	1.2 l
Tomato Sauce (page 116)	5 pt	2.4 l
Bay leaves	10 each	10 each
Fish Fumet (page 85)	5 qt	4.7 l
Manila clams, cleaned	12 lb 8 oz	5.65 kg
Mussels, cleaned, debearded	12 lb 8 oz	5.65 kg
Shrimp (16/20 count), peeled, deveined	7 lb 8 oz	3.4 kg
Cod, large dice	12 lb 8 oz	5.65 kg
Sea scallops, muscle tabs removed	3 lb 12 oz	1.7 kg
Garlic-Flavored Croutons (page 180)	50 each	50 each
Basil, chiffonade	3 lb 12 oz	1.7 kg

1. Heat the oil in a large soup pot over medium heat. Add the onions, green onions, peppers, fennel, salt, and pepper. Sauté until the onions are translucent, 7 to 8 minutes. Add the garlic and sauté until aromatic, about 1 minute more.

2. Add the tomatoes, wine, tomato sauce, bay leaves, and fumet. Cover the pot and simmer gently until flavorful, about 20 minutes. Add more stock if necessary. Remove and discard the bay leaves.

3. Add the clams, mussels, shrimp, cod, and scallops to the pot and simmer until the shrimp, cod, and scallops are cooked and the clams and mussels are open, 7 to 8 minutes.

4. Serve the cioppino in heated bowls, garnished with a crouton and basil.

DUCK CONFIT

Makes 50 portions

Kosher salt	12½ oz	355 g
Curing salt	1¼ tsp	6 ml
Ground black pepper, plus additional as needed	1¼ tsp	6 ml
Juniper berries, crushed	10 each	10 each
Bay leaves, crushed	5 each	5 each
Garlic, chopped	2½ tsp	13 ml
Ducks (about 6 lb/2.75 kg each)	5 each	5 each
Duck fat, rendered	3¾ qt	3.5 l

1. Mix the salt, curing salt, pepper, juniper berries, bay leaves, and garlic together.

2. Disjoint the duck and trim the excess fat from the legs. Reserve the fat for rendering. Coat the duck with the seasoning mixture. Place the duck in a container with a weighted lid and press it for 72 hours in the refrigerator.

3. Place the duck fat in a rondeau over low heat. Cook slowly until the fat melts and becomes very clear. Strain the fat through a fine-mesh sieve to remove any solids. Measure out 3¾ qt/3.5 liters of duck fat; reserve any additional duck fat to use in other preparations.

4. Brush off the excess seasoning mixture, rinse with cool water, and blot dry. Place the duck in a rondeau or brazier and cover it with the rendered duck fat. Stew the meat in the fat over medium-low heat until it is very tender, about 2 hours.

5. Cool the duck in the cooking fat. Transfer the duck pieces to storage containers and pour the duck fat over them to completely submerge the pieces. Cover and hold under refrigeration up to 2 weeks. When ready to use the confit, scrape away any excess fat and broil the duck on a rack until the skin is crisp, about 2 minutes. Use as needed.

chapter ten

RECIPES FOR SIDE DISHES

Pecan Carrots

Makes 12½ pounds/5.7 kilograms or 50 portions (about 4 ounces/115 grams each)

Carrots, sliced ¼ inch/6 mm thick	12 lb 8 oz	5.65 kg
Butter	1 lb	450 g
Honey	5 oz	140 g
Shallots, minced	4 oz	115 g
Pecans, toasted, chopped	15 oz	425 g
Chives, minced	5 tsp	25 ml
Kosher salt, plus additional as needed	2 tbsp	30 ml
Ground black pepper, plus additional as needed	2 tsp	10 ml

1. Add about 5 inches/13 cm of salted water to a large pan and bring to a boil over high heat. Add the carrots to the water, adding more water if necessary to barely cover the carrots. Return to a boil. Cover the pan tightly and reduce the heat slightly.

2. Pan steam the carrots until they are fully cooked and tender to the bite, 5 to 6 minutes. When done, drain the excess water from the pan. Return the carrots to the heat and add the butter, honey, shallots, pecans, and chives. Taste the carrots and season with salt and pepper. Stir or toss until the carrots are evenly coated and very hot.

3. Serve immediately on heated plates.

Green Beans with Walnuts

Makes 12½ pounds/5.7 kilograms or 50 portions (about 4 ounces/115 grams each)

Haricots verts	12 lb 8 oz	5.65 kg
Butter	10 oz	285 g
Shallots, minced	10 oz	285 g
Garlic, minced	5 tsp	25 ml
Chicken Stock (page 83), hot	2½ pt	1.2 l
Kosher salt, plus additional as needed	2 tbsp	30 ml
Ground black pepper, plus additional as needed	2 tsp	10 ml
Walnut oil	5 fl oz	150 ml
Walnuts, chopped	15 oz	425 g
Chives, minced	2½ oz	70 g

1. Cut the green beans on the diagonal into 2-inch/51-mm lengths, if desired.

2. Heat the butter in a small rondeau over medium heat. Add the shallots and garlic and sauté until the shallots are translucent, 2 to 3 minutes. Add the green beans in an even layer and add the hot stock. Season with salt and pepper.

3. Bring the stock to a simmer, cover the pan, and pan steam the beans until tender, 10 to 12 minutes. The cooking liquid should reduce during this time and thicken slightly to coat the beans. If necessary, remove the cover and continue simmering until the liquid is almost fully reduced, 1 to 2 minutes more.

4. Toss the green beans with the oil, walnuts, and chives. Taste the green beans and adjust seasoning with salt and pepper.

5. Serve immediately on heated plates.

GRILLED SHIITAKES WITH SOY-SESAME GLAZE

Makes 12½ pounds/5.7 kilograms or 50 portions (about 4 ounces/115 grams each)

Soy sauce or tamari	20 fl oz	590 ml
Water	1¼ cups	300 ml
Peanut oil or corn oil	1¼ cups	300 ml
Tahini	10 oz	285 g
Sesame oil	2½ fl oz	75 ml
Garlic, minced	2½ oz	70 g
Ginger, minced	1 oz	30 g
Red pepper flakes (optional)	1½ tsp	8 ml
Shiitakes, stems removed	12 lb 8 oz	5.65 kg
Green onions	50 each	50 each
Sesame seeds, toasted	1½ oz	45 g

1. Combine the soy sauce or tamari, water, peanut or corn oil, tahini, sesame oil, garlic, ginger, and red pepper, if using. Hold up to 2 days under refrigeration until ready to use.

2. If desired, slice any large mushroom caps in half.

3. Add the mushrooms and green onions to the glaze and marinate for at least 15 minutes or up to 1 hour.

4. Remove the mushrooms and green onions from the glaze, letting the excess drain away.

5. Grill the mushrooms and green onions until they are marked on all sides and cooked through, about 2 minutes per side.

6. Scatter with the sesame seeds and serve immediately.

OVEN-ROASTED TOMATOES

Makes 10 pounds/4.5 kilograms

Tomatoes	22 lb 8 oz	10.2 kg
Extra-virgin olive oil	15 fl oz	450 ml
Garlic, minced	2½ oz	70 g
Shallots, minced	2½ oz	70 g
Basil, chopped	3 tbsp	45 ml
Oregano, chopped	3 tbsp	45 ml
Thyme, chopped	2 tbsp	30 ml
Kosher salt	2 tbsp	30 ml
Ground black pepper	2 tsp	10 ml

1. Remove the cores from the tomatoes and cut the tomatoes into the desired shape (halves, quarters, wedges, or slices).

2. Combine the oil, garlic, shallots, basil, oregano, thyme, salt, and pepper. Drizzle this mixture over the tomatoes and turn carefully to coat them.

3. Arrange the tomatoes on racks set in sheet pans. Roast in a 275°F/135°C oven until the tomatoes are dried and lightly browned, 1 to 1½ hours.

4. The tomatoes are ready to serve now or use as an ingredient in another dish, or they may be cooled on the racks and held, covered, under refrigeration up to 5 days for later use.

Marinated Roasted Peppers

Makes 12½ pounds/5.7 kilograms or 50 portions (about 4 ounces/115 grams each)

Red peppers, cored, seeded, roasted, and peeled	12 lb	5.5 kg
Olive oil	20 fl oz	590 ml
Golden raisins	10 oz	285 g
Pine nuts, toasted	10 oz	285 g
Parsley, chopped	5 oz	140 g
Garlic, minced	2½ oz	70 g
Kosher salt	2 tbsp	30 ml
Ground black pepper	2 tsp	10 ml

1. Cut the roasted peppers into ¼-inch/6-mm slices and drain in a sieve or colander for 2 hours.

2. Combine the peppers with the rest of the ingredients.

3. Serve immediately or hold under refrigeration up to 5 days for later service.

Roasted Carrots

Makes 12½ pounds/5.7 kilograms or 50 portions (about 4 ounces/115 grams each)

Duck fat or lard	10 oz	285 g
Carrots, oblique cut	12 lb 8 oz	5.65 kg
Kosher salt, plus additional as needed	2 tbsp	30 ml
Ground black pepper, plus additional as needed	2 tsp	10 ml

1. Preheat a roasting pan in a 350°F/175°C oven. Add the duck fat or lard and melt it in the pan.

2. Add the carrots and season with salt and pepper. Return the pan to the oven and roast the carrots until tender and golden brown, about 20 minutes. Taste and then adjust seasoning with salt and pepper.

3. Serve immediately on heated plates.

Marinated Grilled Vegetables Provençal

Makes 50 portions, about 4 ounces/115 grams each

Vegetable oil	2½ pt	1.2 l
Soy sauce	1¼ cups	300 ml
Lemon juice	5 fl oz	150 ml
Garlic, minced	1 oz	30 g
Fennel seeds	2½ tsp	13 ml
Zucchini, sliced ¾ inch/19 mm thick (either on the diagonal or lengthwise)	6 lb 4 oz	2.8 kg
Eggplants, sliced ¾ inch/19 mm thick (either on the diagonal or lengthwise)	6 lb 4 oz	2.8 kg
Onions, sliced ¾ inch/19 mm thick	2 lb 8 oz	1.15 kg
Kosher salt, plus additional as needed	2 tbsp	30 ml
Ground black pepper, plus additional as needed	2 tsp	10 ml
Green peppers	1 lb 14 oz	850 g
Red peppers	1 lb 14 oz	850 g
Tomatoes, peeled, seeded, medium dice	1 lb 4 oz	570 g
Balsamic vinegar	2½ fl oz	75 ml
Basil, chiffonade	5 oz	140 g

1. Combine 2 pt/1 l of the oil, the soy sauce, the lemon juice, ½ oz/15 g of the garlic, and the fennel. Add the zucchini, eggplants, and onions and marinate for 1 hour.

2. Drain the vegetables and season with salt and pepper.

3. Place the zucchini, eggplants, and onions on the grill and cook on the first side until browned. Turn once and complete cooking on the second side until the vegetables are tender, about 3 minutes total or more. Remove from the grill.

4. Grill or broil the peppers until evenly charred on all sides, about 5 minutes. Remove from the grill and let the peppers cool. Remove the skin, core, seeds, and ribs.

5. Pour enough of the remaining oil into a rondeau or tilt skillet to coat it generously and heat over medium heat. Add the remaining garlic and cook until tender but not brown, about 1 minute. Add the grilled vegetables and tomatoes and stir gently to finish heating the vegetables and blending the flavors, 4 to 5 minutes. Add additional oil if needed to coat the vegetables evenly. Add the vinegar, taste, and then adjust seasoning with salt and pepper. Fold in the basil or use it to garnish individual servings.

6. Serve at room temperature or store up to 5 days under refrigeration for later service.

Broccoli Rabe with Garlic and Peppers

Makes 12½ pounds/5.7 kilograms or 50 portions (about 4 ounces/115 grams each)

Broccoli rabe	16 lb	7.25 kg
Kosher salt, plus additional as needed	3 tbsp	45 ml
Extra-virgin olive oil, plus additional as needed	1½ cups	360 ml
Garlic, thinly sliced	1½ oz	45 g
Jalapeños, minced	4 tbsp	60 ml
Chicken Stock (page 83), plus additional as needed	1 pt	480 ml
Red pepper flakes, plus additional as needed	1 tbsp	15 ml
Lemon juice	3 tbsp	45 ml
Tarragon, snipped	2 tbsp	30 ml

1. Wash the broccoli rabe thoroughly and separate into stems and florets. Bring a large pot of water to a boil. Add 2 tbsp/30 ml salt and blanch the broccoli rabe stems and florets until tender, about 5 minutes. Shock in an ice water bath, drain well, and reserve.

2. Heat ¾ cup/180 ml of the oil in a skillet over medium-high heat and add the broccoli rabe (work in batches if necessary to avoid overcrowding the pan). Sauté, stirring frequently, until the broccoli rabe is very hot, about 3 minutes. Transfer to a hotel pan and keep warm.

3. In a rondeau, heat the remaining oil over medium heat. Add the garlic and jalapeños and sauté, stirring frequently, until aromatic and lightly golden, about 2 minutes.

4. Add the broccoli rabe to the rondeau with enough stock to barely moisten (about ¼ inch/6 mm deep). (This may be done all at once for a large batch, or divided into smaller batches.) Cook over medium heat, mixing thoroughly to distribute the garlic and peppers evenly. Cook gently until the liquid evaporates, about 3 minutes.

5. Taste and then season with the red pepper, salt, lemon juice, tarragon, and additional oil if needed.

6. Serve immediately on heated plates.

Whipped Potatoes

Makes 12½ pounds/5.7 kilograms or 50 portions (about 4 ounces/115 grams each)

Russet potatoes	20 lb	9 kg
Butter, room temperature	30 to 40 oz	850 g to 1.12 kg
Milk, hot	3¾ pt	1.75 l
Heavy cream, hot	3¾ pt	1.75 l
Kosher salt, plus additional as needed	3 tsp	45 ml
Ground white pepper, plus additional as needed	1 tbsp	15 ml

1. Scrub, peel, and cut the potatoes into large pieces. Boil or steam until they are tender enough to mash easily, about 20 minutes. Drain and dry them over low heat or on a sheet pan in a 300°F/150°C oven until no more steam rises from them. While the potatoes are still hot, purée them through a food mill or potato ricer into a heated bowl.

2. Add the butter and mix into the potatoes by hand or in an electric mixer with a paddle or wire whip attachment until just incorporated. Add the milk, cream, salt, and pepper and whip by hand or with the mixer until smooth and light.

3. Spoon the potatoes onto heated plates or transfer them to a piping bag and pipe into the desired shapes for service.

Ratatouille

Makes 12½ pounds/5.7 kilograms or 50 portions (about 4 ounces/115 grams each)

Olive oil, plus additional as needed for sautéing	15 fl oz	450 ml
Onions, medium dice	3 lb 12 oz	1.7 kg
Garlic, minced	3¾ oz	110 g
Tomato paste	5 oz	140 g
Green peppers, medium dice	1 lb 4 oz	570 g
Eggplants, medium dice	5 lb	2.25 kg
Zucchini, medium dice	3 lb 12 oz	1.7 kg
White mushrooms, quartered or sliced	1 lb 14 oz	850 g
Tomatoes, peeled, seeded, medium dice	2 lb 8 oz	1.15 kg
Chicken Stock (page 83) or Vegetable Stock (page 86), plus additional as needed for stewing	20 fl oz	590 ml
Kosher salt	As needed	As needed
Ground black pepper, plus additional as needed	2 tsp	10 ml
Chopped herbs, such as basil, parsley, oregano	5 oz	140 g

1. Heat the oil in a rondeau over medium heat or in a tilt skillet. Add the onions and sauté until translucent, 4 to 5 minutes. Add the garlic and sauté until soft, about 1 minute.

2. Turn the heat to medium-low. Add the tomato paste and cook until it completely coats the onions and develops a deeper color, 1 to 2 minutes.

3. Add the vegetables in the following sequence: peppers, eggplants, zucchini, mushrooms, and tomatoes. Cook each vegetable until it softens (2 to 3 minutes each) before adding the next.

4. Add the stock and turn the heat to low, allowing the vegetables to stew. The vegetables should be moist but not soupy.

5. Stew until the vegetables are tender and flavorful, about 25 minutes. Taste and then season with the salt, pepper, and fresh herbs.

6. Serve immediately on heated plates.

1. Add the vegetables from firmest to softest (peppers, eggplants, zucchini, mushrooms, tomatoes) and allow each to cook until they have softened prior to adding the next vegetable.

2. Cover the pot and simmer until the vegetables are tender and good flavor has developed.

3. The finished ratatouille.

BRAISING GREENS

Makes 12½ pounds/5.7 kilograms or 50 portions (about 4 ounces/115 grams each)

Mixed braising greens (collards, mustard, dandelion, etc.), stemmed and cleaned	8 lb	3.6 kg
Rainbow Swiss chard, stemmed and cleaned	10 lb	4.5 kg
Bacon, small dice	2 lb	900 g
Olive oil, plus additional as needed for sautéing	3 fl oz	90 ml
Shallots, minced	12 oz	340 g
Chicken Stock (page 83)	¾ cup	180 ml

1. Chop the greens and chard coarsely.

2. Cook the bacon in a rondeau over medium heat until the fat is rendered and the bacon is crisp. Remove the crisp bacon with a slotted spoon and reserve. Pour the rendered bacon fat into a container and reserve.

3. Add equal parts olive oil and bacon fat to a sauté pan; there should be enough to liberally coat the pan. Add the shallots and sauté, stirring frequently, until they are tender and translucent, about 2 minutes. The dish may be completed in one large batch or several smaller batches.

4. Add the greens and chard and sauté, stirring frequently, until wilted, about 5 minutes. Add the chicken stock and bring to a simmer over low heat. Continue to simmer until the greens are tender, about 15 minutes.

5. Serve the greens immediately, garnished with the reserved bacon pieces.

CREAMED MUSHROOMS

Makes 12½ pounds/5.7 kilograms or 50 portions (about 4 ounces/115 grams each)

Olive oil, plus additional as needed for sautéing	1 cup	240 ml
Shallots, minced	1 lb	450 g
White mushrooms, sliced	15 lb	6.8 kg
Thyme, chopped	¼ cup	60 ml
Dry white wine	1½ pt	720 ml
Heavy cream	1½ pt	720 ml
Butter, cubed, cold	6 oz	170 g
Kosher salt, plus additional as needed	2 tbsp	30 ml
Ground black pepper, plus additional as needed	1 tbsp	15 ml

1. Heat a rondeau over medium-high heat. Add the oil and heat until shimmering but not smoking. Add the shallots to the pan and sauté until tender, about 2 minutes. Increase the heat to high, add the mushrooms and thyme (work in batches to avoid overcrowding the pan and lowering the temperature), and sauté until the mushrooms are lightly browned, about 2 minutes.

2. Add the wine and stir to deglaze the pan, scraping up any browned bits from the pan bottom. Add the cream and simmer over high heat until the liquid has reduced by about half, 6 to 7 minutes.

3. Swirl in the butter to thicken the cream slightly (this may be done by batch as you heat up the mushrooms for service). Taste and then season with salt and pepper.

4. Serve the mushrooms on heated plates.

Baked Potatoes with Deep-Fried Onions

Makes 50 portions (1 potato and about 1 ounce/30 grams fried onions each)

Russet potatoes	50 each	50 each
Sour cream	3 pt	1.4 l
Chives, minced	10 tbsp	150 ml
Kosher salt, plus additional as needed	1 tbsp	15 ml
Ground black pepper, plus additional as needed	1 tsp	5 ml
Onions, sliced thin, deep fried	3 lb 2 oz	1.4 kg

1. Scrub the potatoes and blot dry. Pierce the skins in a few places with a paring knife.

2. Bake the potatoes on a rack in a 400°F/205°C oven until very tender and cooked through, about 1 hour.

3. Meanwhile, blend the sour cream and chives. Taste and then season with salt and pepper.

4. Cut an X into the top of each potato and pinch the potato open. Place 2 tbsp/30 ml of the sour cream on top of each, and top with the onions.

5. Serve immediately on heated plates.

Roasted Tuscan-Style Potatoes

Makes 12½ pounds/5.7 kilograms or 50 portions (about 4 ounces/115 grams each)

Chef's potatoes	16 lb 9 oz	7.5 kg
Olive oil	15 fl oz	450 ml
Garlic, thinly sliced	10 oz	285 g
Rosemary needles	¼ cup	60 ml
Sage leaves, cut into ribbons	3 tbsp	45 ml
Kosher salt, plus additional as needed	2 tbsp	30 ml
Ground black pepper, plus additional as needed	2 tsp	10 ml

1. Scrub, peel, and cut the potatoes into a large dice. Place in a pot, cover with cold water, and bring to a boil over medium-high heat. Simmer until the potatoes are partially cooked, about 20 minutes. Drain, being careful not to break the potatoes.

2. Heat a large roasting pan in a 400°F/205°C oven. Add 12 fl oz/360 ml oil and the potatoes, stir to coat the potatoes with oil, and add the garlic, rosemary, and sage. Season with salt and pepper. Roast until the potatoes are tender, 25 to 30 minutes. Stir occasionally to brown the potatoes evenly.

3. Serve 4-oz/115-g portions immediately on heated plates.

POTATOES AU GRATIN

Makes 12½ pounds/5.7 kilograms or 50 portions (about 4 ounces/115 grams each)

Chef's potatoes	12½ lb	5.5 kg
Garlic cloves	25 each	25 each
Milk	3¾ qt	3.8 l
Ground nutmeg	A pinch	A pinch
Kosher salt	2 tbsp	30 ml
Ground black pepper	2 tsp	10 ml
Heavy cream	3¾ pt	1.75 l
Butter, cut into small pieces	1 lb 4 oz	570 g

1. Scrub, peel, and thinly slice the potatoes using a mandoline.

2. Place the garlic in a saucepan with the milk and bring to a boil over medium heat. Season the milk with nutmeg, salt, and pepper and add the sliced potatoes.

3. Bring the milk to a simmer and cook the potatoes, taking care that the milk does not boil over, for 10 to 12 minutes. Discard the garlic cloves.

4. Transfer the potatoes and milk to a buttered hotel pan, pour the cream over the top, and dot with the butter.

5. Bake in a 375°F/190°C oven until the top is golden brown and the potatoes have absorbed the milk, about 45 minutes.

6. Allow the potatoes to rest for 10 to 15 minutes before slicing into servings.

Zucchini Provençal

Makes 12½ pounds/5.7 kilograms or 50 portions (about 4 ounces/115 grams each)

Extra-virgin olive oil	1¼ cups	300 ml
Garlic, minced	3 oz	85 g
Red onions, small dice	1 lb 8 oz	680 g
White mushrooms, quartered	1 lb 4 oz	570 g
Zucchini, medium dice	7 lb	3.15 kg
Plum tomatoes, seeded, medium dice	1 lb 12 oz	800 g
Black olives, pitted, quartered	10 oz	285 g
Basil, chopped	½ oz	15 g
Oregano, chopped	½ oz	15 g
Kosher salt, plus additional as needed	2 tbsp	30 ml
Ground black pepper, plus additional as needed	1 tbsp	15 ml

1. In a large rondeau, heat the oil over medium-high heat. Add the garlic and onions and sauté, stirring frequently, until the onions are tender and just turning golden, about 12 minutes.

2. Add the mushrooms and zucchini and sauté until the mushrooms start to release their juices and the zucchini is nearly translucent, about 10 minutes.

3. Add the plum tomatoes and olives and simmer gently until all of the ingredients are tender and the dish has a good flavor, about 20 minutes. (It may be cooled and stored under refrigeration for up to 2 days before reheating and serving.)

4. Taste and then season with the basil, oregano, salt, and pepper.

5. Serve immediately on heated plates.

GNOCCHI PIEDMONTESE

Makes 12½ pounds/5.7 kilograms or 50 portions (about 4 ounces/115 grams each)

Russet potatoes	15 lb	6.8 kg
Butter, room temperature	5 oz	140 g
Eggs	15 each	15 each
Kosher salt, plus additional as needed	3 tbsp	45 ml
Ground black pepper, plus additional as needed	1 tbsp	15 ml
Ground nutmeg (optional)	A pinch	A pinch
All-purpose flour, plus additional as needed	5 lb	2.25 kg
Butter	10 oz	285 g
Parmesan, grated	15 oz	425 g
Parsley, chopped	5 oz	140 g
Tomato Sauce (page 116; optional)	3½ qt	3.9 l

1. Scrub, peel, and cut the potatoes into large pieces. Boil or steam them until they are tender enough to mash easily, about 20 minutes. Drain and dry them over low heat or on a sheet pan in a 300°F/150°C oven until no more steam rises from them. While the potatoes are still hot, purée them through a food mill or potato ricer into a heated bowl.

2. Add the butter, eggs, salt, pepper, and nutmeg, if using. Mix well. Incorporate enough of the flour to make a stiff dough.

3. Roll out the dough into cylinders about 1 inch/25 mm wide. Cut the cylinders into pieces about 1 inch/25 mm long. Roll each piece over the tines of a fork, pressing and rolling the dough in with your thumb.

4. Bring a large pot of salted water to a boil, reduce to a simmer, and add the gnocchi. Cook the gnocchi until they rise to the surface, 2 to 3 minutes. Lift the gnocchi from the water with a slotted spoon or spider or drain in a colander. Shock the finished gnocchi in an ice water bath if you are holding them for later service. Reheat them in simmering salted water, about 2 minutes, and then drain before finishing.

5. Working in batches, heat the butter in a sauté pan over medium-high heat, add the gnocchi, and toss until very hot and coated with butter. Add the cheese and parsley. Taste and then season with salt and pepper.

6. Serve immediately on heated plates with the tomato sauce, if using.

See photos on page 316

1. Add the butter, eggs, salt, pepper, and nutmeg to the riced potatoes. Gently add flour to make the dough come together as a shaggy mass.

2. Roll the dough into cylinders about 1 inch/25 mm in diameter.

3. Cut the cylinders into pieces about 1 inch/25 mm long.

4. Add the formed gnocchi to simmering salted water.

5. Cook the gnocchi until they rise to the surface, 2 to 3 minutes. Shock the finished gnocchi in an ice water bath.

MACAIRE POTATOES

Makes 12½ pounds/5.7 kilograms or 50 portions (about 4 ounces/115 grams each)

Russet potatoes	15 lb	6.8 kg
Butter, room temperature	10 oz	285 g
Kosher salt	3 tbsp	45 ml
Ground black pepper	1 tbsp	15 ml
Eggs	5 each	5 each
Clarified butter or vegetable oil	5 fl oz	150 ml

1. Scrub the potatoes and blot dry. Pierce the skins in a few places with a paring knife.

2. Bake the potatoes in a 400°F/205°C oven until very tender and cooked through, about 1 hour.

3. Halve the potatoes, scoop out the flesh while it is still very hot, and transfer the flesh to a heated bowl. Mash the potato flesh, butter, salt, pepper, and eggs together with a fork or wooden spoon until evenly blended. Form into patties, 2 oz/60 g each, about ¾ inch/19 mm thick.

4. Heat the clarified butter or oil in a large sauté pan over medium-high heat. Working in batches if necessary, sauté the patties until golden on both sides and very hot, 2 to 3 minutes per side.

5. Serve immediately on heated plates.

Potato and Parsnip Purée

Makes 12½ pounds/5.7 kilograms or 50 portions (about 4 ounces/115 grams each)

Russet potatoes, peeled, quartered	14 lb	6.4 kg
Kosher salt, plus additional as needed	3 tbsp	45 ml
Butter, softened	1 lb 12 oz	800 g
Parsnips, cores removed if necessary, sliced	4 lb	1.8 kg
Milk, hot	18 fl oz	530 ml
Heavy cream, hot	2½ pt	1.2 l
Ground black pepper, plus additional as needed	1 tbsp	15 ml
Nutmeg, grated	⅛ tsp	⅛ tsp

1. Put the potatoes in a large pot and add enough cold water to cover them. Add salt to taste and bring the water to a simmer over medium heat. Continue to simmer until the potatoes are tender, about 20 minutes. Drain the potatoes in a colander and keep hot.

2. While the potatoes are cooking, heat 8 oz/225 g of the butter in a skillet over medium-low heat. Add the parsnips, stir to coat well, cover the pan, and sweat gently until tender, about 20 minutes.

3. While the cooked potatoes and parsnips are still very hot, purée them through a food mill into the bowl of an electric mixer (warm the bowl by rinsing in hot water for the best results). Immediately incorporate the remaining butter in a mixer with a paddle attachment.

4. Add the hot milk, then the hot cream, and mix until the potatoes are smooth and light.

5. Taste and season with salt, pepper, and nutmeg.

6. Serve immediately on heated plates.

CELERY ROOT MASHED POTATOES

Makes 12½ pounds/5.7 kilograms or 50 portions (about 4 ounces/115 grams each)

Yukon gold potatoes, peeled	6¼ lb	2.8 kg
Kosher salt, plus additional as needed	2 tbsp	30 ml
Heavy cream	2 qt	1.9 l
Butter	1½ lb	680 g
Celery root	6¼ lb	2.8 kg
Milk	2 qt	1.9 l
Ground white pepper, plus additional as needed	1 tbsp	15 ml

1. Cut the potatoes in half. Put the potatoes in a large pot and add enough cold water to cover them. Add 1 tbsp/15 ml salt and bring the water to a simmer over medium heat. Continue to simmer until the potatoes are tender, about 20 minutes.

2. Meanwhile, combine the cream and butter in a pot over medium-high heat and bring to a simmer.

3. Peel the celery root. Cut into large dice and place in a large pot. Add the milk and enough cold water to cover them. Add 1 tbsp/15 ml salt and bring the water to a simmer over medium heat. Continue to simmer until the potatoes are tender, about 20 minutes.

4. Drain the cooked potatoes and celery root in a colander and air-dry until steam is no longer rising from them.

5. Purée the potatoes and the celery root through a food mill while they are still very hot into a warmed mixing bowl. Add the hot cream and butter and stir until the purée is very smooth and light. Taste and then season with salt and pepper.

6. Serve the purée very hot.

Boiled White Beans

Makes 10 pounds/4.5 kilograms or 50 portions (about 3 ounces/85 grams each)

Dried white beans (navy or cannellini)	5 lb	2.25 kg
Vegetable oil	2 tbsp	30 ml
Onions, medium dice	18 oz	510 g
Vegetable Stock (page 86)	5 pt	2.4 l
Ham hock (optional)	1 each	1 each
Sachet d'Epices (page 133)	1 each	1 each

1. Sort the beans to remove stones or debris and rinse well. Soak the beans for 8 to 12 hours in enough cold water to cover by 3 inches/76 mm. Discard any beans that are floating on the surface. Drain the beans and discard the water. (For a short-soak alternative, place the beans in a large pot, add enough water to cover generously, and bring to a boil over high heat. As soon as the water boils, remove the pot from the heat and cover. Drain after 1 hour and continue with the next step.)

2. Heat the oil in a pot over medium heat. Add the onions and sweat until the onions are translucent, about 8 minutes. Add the drained beans and enough of the stock to cover the beans by 2 inches/51 mm. Add the ham hock, if using, and sachet. Simmer until the beans are nearly tender, 45 minutes to 1 hour. Cooking time will vary depending on the variety and freshness of the beans.

3. Remove the ham hock and sachet. The meat from the ham hock can be diced to use as a garnish in another dish.

4. The beans are ready to serve now or to use as an ingredient in another dish, or they may be cooled and held under refrigeration in their cooking liquid for up to 5 days for later use.

BLACK BEANS WITH PEPPERS AND CHORIZO

Makes 10 pounds/4.5 kilograms or 50 portions (about 3 ounces/85 grams each)

Dried black beans	3 lb 12 oz	1.7 kg
Water or Chicken Stock (page 83)	3¾ gal	14.2 l
Kosher salt, plus additional as needed	2 tbsp	30 ml
Vegetable oil	1 cup	240 ml
Bacon, minced	15 oz	425 g
Onions, medium dice	1 lb 14 oz	850 g
Garlic, minced	1 oz	30 g
Dry Spanish chorizo, sliced ¼ in/6 mm thick	1 lb 4 oz	570 g
Red peppers, medium dice	15 oz	425 g
Green peppers, medium dice	15 oz	425 g
Green onions, sliced thin	10 oz	285 g
Oregano, chopped	2½ oz	70 g
Cilantro, chopped	2½ oz	70 g
Ground black pepper, plus additional as needed	2 tsp	10 ml
Sour cream (optional)	1 lb 9 oz	710 g

1. Sort the beans to remove stones or debris and rinse well. Soak the beans for at least 6 and up to 12 hours in enough cold water to cover by 3 inches/76 mm. Discard any beans that are floating on the surface. Drain the beans and discard the water. (For a short-soak alternative, place the beans in a large pot, add enough water to cover generously, and bring to a boil over high heat. As soon as the water boils, remove the pot from the heat and cover. Drain after 1 hour and continue with the next step.)

2. Combine the beans and water or stock in a pot over medium-high heat. Simmer for 1 hour. Add the salt and continue to simmer until the beans are tender to the bite, 20 to 30 minutes. (Cooking time will vary depending on the freshness of the beans.) Set the beans aside in their cooking liquid.

3. In a large saucepan, heat the oil over medium-high heat and add the bacon. Cook until the bacon is rendered. Add the onions and sauté until tender and lightly browned, about 8 minutes. Add the garlic and cook, stirring frequently, for 1 minute more.

4. Add the chorizo and peppers and sauté, stirring frequently, until the peppers are tender, 6 to 8 minutes.

5. Drain the beans and add them to the saucepan with enough cooking liquid to keep them moist (the consistency should be that of a thick stew). Simmer the beans until all the flavors are developed and all the ingredients are heated through, about 15 minutes.

6. Add the green onions, oregano, and cilantro. Taste and then season with salt and pepper.

7. Serve on heated plates, garnished with sour cream, if using.

SOUTHWEST WHITE BEAN STEW

Makes 12½ pounds/5.7 kilograms or 50 portions (about 4 ounces/115 grams each)

Boiled White Beans (page 320), drained	10 lb	4.5 kg
Vegetable oil	¼ cup	60 ml
Onions, chopped	1 lb 14 oz	850 g
Red peppers, small dice	1 lb 4 oz	570 g
Jalapeños, minced	10 oz	285 g
Garlic, minced	5 oz	140 g
Sherry vinegar	1¼ cups	300 ml
Tomatoes, peeled, seeded, chopped	1 lb 4 oz	570 g
Cilantro, chopped	1 oz	30 g
Kosher salt, plus additional as needed	2 tbsp	30 ml
Ground black pepper, plus additional as needed	2 tsp	10 ml

1. Purée half of the cooked beans and combine the puréed beans with the whole beans.

2. Heat the oil in a saucepan over medium-high heat. Add the onions, peppers, jalapeños, and garlic. Sauté until the onions are translucent, 5 to 6 minutes.

3. Add the beans and sauté, stirring constantly, until they are heated through, about 10 minutes.

4. Add the vinegar and tomatoes and continue to sauté until very hot, 2 or 3 minutes.

5. Stir in the cilantro. Taste and then season with salt and pepper.

6. Serve immediately or hold hot for service.

Vegetarian Refried Beans

Makes 12½ pounds/5.7 kilograms or 50 portions (about 4 ounces/115 grams each)

Dried pinto beans	5 lb	2.25 kg
Vegetable Stock (page 86)	5 pt	2.4 l
Vegetable oil	2 tbsp	30 ml
Onions, small dice	18 oz	510 g
Garlic, minced	2½ oz	70 g
Kosher salt, plus additional as needed	1 tbsp	15 ml
Cumin seeds, toasted, cracked	1 tbsp	15 ml
Chili Powder (page 131)	3 tbsp	45 ml

1. Sort the beans to remove stones or debris and rinse well. Soak the beans for at least 6 and up to 12 hours in enough cold water to cover by 3 inches/76 mm. Discard any beans that are floating on the surface. Drain the beans and discard the water. (For a short-soak alternative, place the beans in a large pot, add enough water to cover generously, and bring to a boil over high heat. As soon as the water boils, remove the pot from the heat and cover. Drain after 1 hour and continue with the next step.)

2. Place the beans in a pot and pour in just enough of the stock to cover the beans by 2 inches/51 mm. Simmer over medium heat until the beans are tender to the bite, 45 to 50 minutes. (Cooking time will vary depending on the freshness of the beans.) Set the beans aside in their cooking liquid.

3. Heat the oil in a large sauté pan over medium heat. Add the onions and garlic and sweat until the onions are translucent, 6 to 7 minutes. Drain the cooked beans, reserving their cooking liquid. Add the beans to the pan and simmer over low heat, stirring constantly, until very hot, 10 to 12 minutes more. Mash about one-third of the beans against the side of the pot with a wooden spoon, and add enough of the reserved liquid to keep the beans moist. Taste and then season with salt, cumin, and chili powder.

4. Hold hot for service.

Young Green Beans and Leeks

Makes 12½ pounds/5.7 kilograms or 50 portions (about 4 ounces/115 grams each)

Haricots verts, trimmed	10 lb	4.5 kg
Celery stalks, sliced on the diagonal	1 lb 8 oz	680 g
Extra-virgin olive oil	½ cup	120 ml
Leeks, white parts, julienned	1 lb 8 oz	680 g
Plum tomatoes, peeled, seeded, julienned	1 lb 8 oz	680 g
Basil, chopped	¼ cup	60 ml
Kosher salt, plus additional as needed	2 tbsp	30 ml
Ground black pepper, plus additional as needed	1 tbsp	15 ml

1. Bring a large pot of water to a rolling boil over high heat. Add enough salt to flavor the water. Add the haricots verts (working in batches) and cook until the beans are bright green and barely tender, about 4 minutes. Use a slotted spoon or wire basket to lift the beans from the water. Immediately drop them into an ice water bath. Continue until all of the haricots verts have been blanched. Blanch the celery in the same manner. Blot the haricots verts and celery dry or let them drain until dry.

2. Heat the oil in a large skillet over medium-high heat and sauté the leeks and the blanched haricots verts and celery until the leeks are tender, about 4 minutes.

3. Add the tomatoes and continue to sauté until very hot, 2 to 3 minutes more.

4. Taste and then season with basil, salt, and pepper.

5. Serve immediately on heated plates.

BASIC BOILED RICE

Makes 12½ pounds/5.7 kilograms or 50 portions (about 4 ounces/115 grams each)

Long-grain white rice	4 lb 6 oz	1.98 kg
Water	3¾ gal	14.2 l
Kosher salt	3 tbsp	45 ml

1. Rinse the rice under cold water in a strainer until the water runs clear. Drain the rice well before using.

2. Bring the water to a rolling boil in a pot and add the salt.

3. Add the rice in a thin stream, stirring it with a fork to prevent the grains from clumping as they are added. (There should be enough water to cover the rice.) When the water returns to a boil, reduce the heat to a simmer.

4. Simmer the rice until tender, about 15 minutes. Drain immediately in a colander and set the colander in the pot. Return to the heat to steam the rice dry for 5 minutes. The rice should no longer be sticky.

5. Fluff the rice with a fork.

6. Serve immediately on heated plates or hold hot for service.

Rice Pilaf

Makes 12½ pounds/5.7 kilograms or 50 portions (about 4 ounces/115 grams each)

Long-grain white rice	4 lb 6 oz	1.98 kg
Clarified butter or vegetable oil	5 fl oz	150 ml
Onions, minced	3¾ oz	110 g
Chicken Stock (page 83), hot	3¾ qt	3.5 l
Bay leaves	2 each	2 each
Thyme sprigs	5 each	5 each
Kosher salt, plus additional as needed	2 tbsp	30 ml
Ground black pepper, plus additional as needed	2 tsp	10 ml

1. Rinse the rice under cold water in a strainer until the water runs clear, if desired. Drain the rice well before using.

2. Heat the butter or oil in a heavy-gauge pot over medium heat. Add the onions and cook, stirring frequently, until they are tender and translucent, 5 to 6 minutes.

3. Add the rice and sauté, stirring frequently, until the rice is coated with butter or oil and heated through, 2 to 3 minutes.

4. Add the heated stock to the rice and bring to a simmer, stirring to prevent the rice from clumping together or sticking to the bottom of the pot.

5. Add the bay leaves, thyme, salt, and pepper. Cover the pot and simmer over low heat on the stovetop or in a 350°F/175°C oven until the grains are tender to the bite, 14 to 16 minutes. Allow the rice to rest for 5 minutes and fluff with a fork. Remove and discard the bay leaves and thyme sprigs. Taste and then adjust seasoning with salt and pepper.

6. Serve immediately on heated plates or hold hot for service.

Risotto

Makes 12½ pounds/5.7 kilograms or 50 portions (about 4 ounces/115 grams each)

Butter	1 lb	450 g
Onions, minced	10 oz	285 g
Arborio rice	4 lb 6 oz	1.98 kg
Chicken Stock (page 83), hot	7½ qt	7 l
Parmesan, grated	1½ lb	680 g
Kosher salt, plus additional as needed	2 tbsp	30 ml
Ground black pepper, plus additional as needed	2 tsp	10 ml

1. Heat 10 oz/285 g of the butter in a deep pot over medium-high heat. Add the onions and sweat, stirring occasionally, until softened and translucent, 6 to 8 minutes.

2. Add the rice and mix thoroughly with the butter. Cook, stirring constantly, until the mixture gives off a toasted aroma, about 1 minute.

3. Add one-third of the stock to the rice and cook, stirring constantly, until the rice has absorbed the stock, 5 to 6 minutes. Repeat, adding the remaining stock in two more portions, allowing each to be absorbed before adding the next. Risotto should be tender and creamy.

4. Away from the heat, stir in the remaining butter until completely smooth. Add the cheese and stir to blend well. Taste and season with salt and pepper.

5. Serve immediately on heated plates or hold hot for service.

LOBSTER RISOTTO

Makes 12½ pounds/5.7 kilograms or 50 portions (about 4 ounces/115 grams each)

Extra-virgin olive oil	1 cup	240 ml
Red onions, minced	1 lb	450 g
Portobello mushrooms, medium dice	3 lb	1.4 kg
Arborio rice	4 lb	1.8 kg
Chicken Stock (page 83), hot, plus additional as needed	7½ qt	7 l
Dry white wine	1 pt	480 ml
Kosher salt, plus additional as needed	2 tbsp	30 ml
Ground black pepper, plus additional as needed	1 tbsp	15 ml
Butter, room temperature	8 oz	225 g
Parmesan, grated	1½ lb	680 g
Chives, cut into short pieces	2 oz	60 g
Lobster meat, cooked, medium dice	2 lb	900 g

1. Heat the olive oil in a large rondeau over medium-high heat. Add the onions and sweat until translucent, 6 to 8 minutes.

2. Add the mushrooms and sauté until the juices released by the mushrooms cook away, 7 to 8 minutes more. Add the rice and stir to coat with oil. Cook, stirring constantly, until the mixture gives off a toasted aroma, about 1 minute. Stir in the stock and wine and season with 1 tbsp/15 ml salt and 1 tsp/5 ml pepper.

3. Cover the rondeau and bake in a 350°F/175°C oven until the rice is tender, 30 to 35 minutes. Stir the rice every 5 minutes as it bakes to produce a creamy consistency and to prevent it from sticking. If necessary, add a bit more stock as the risotto bakes; it should be creamy like a porridge when properly cooked.

4. Fold in the butter, cheese, and chives. Taste and then adjust seasoning with salt and pepper.

5. Just before service, fold the lobster pieces into the hot risotto and serve on heated plates.

BASIC POLENTA

Makes 12½ pounds/5.7 kilograms or 50 portions (about 4 ounces/115 grams each)

Water	5 qt	4.75 l
Kosher salt, plus additional as needed	3 tbsp	45 ml
Coarse yellow cornmeal	2 lb	900 g
Butter, room temperature	10 oz	285 g
Ground black pepper, plus additional as needed	2 tsp	10 ml

1. Bring the water to a boil in a deep pot over high heat and season with salt.

2. Pour the cornmeal into the water in a stream, stirring constantly until it has all been added. Return to a simmer, cover, and place in a 325°F/165°C oven. Cook until the polenta is fully cooked and creamy, about 30 minutes. Stir the polenta once or twice while it cooks. The polenta is ready to finish for service, or it may be stored as follows: Pour the polenta onto an oiled sheet tray or shallow hotel pan, spread it in an even layer, and cover with plastic wrap. Store under refrigeration for up to 2 days.

3. Remove the pot from the oven and blend in the butter. Taste and then season with salt and pepper.

4. To reheat cold polenta, cut the firmed polenta into squares, rounds, or other shapes. Reheat the polenta by broiling, grilling, baking, or sautéing until very hot.

5. Serve immediately on heated plates or hold hot for service.

PAN-FRIED POLENTA WITH PARMESAN AND ROSEMARY

Makes 12½ pounds/5.7 kilograms or 50 portions (about 4 ounces/115 grams each)

Butter, softened	7 oz	200 g
Extra-virgin olive oil	7 fl oz	200 ml
Garlic cloves, thinly sliced	8 each	8 each
Rosemary needles, chopped	2 tbsp	30 ml
Chicken Stock (page 83)	4¼ qt	4 l
Coarse yellow cornmeal	2 lb	900 g
Parmesan, grated	12 oz	340 g
Kosher salt, plus additional as needed	3 tbsp	45 ml
Ground black pepper, plus additional as needed	2 tbsp	30 ml
Olive oil, or as needed for frying	6 fl oz	180 ml

1. Heat the butter and oil in a rondeau over medium-high heat. Add the garlic and rosemary and sweat, stirring constantly, until the garlic is slightly golden, about 3 minutes. Add the stock and bring to a boil.

2. Pour the cornmeal into the mixture in a stream, stirring constantly, until it has all been added. Simmer the mixture gently, stirring constantly with a wooden spoon, until the polenta pulls away from the sides of the pot, about 45 minutes.

3. Remove the pot from the heat and stir in the cheese. Taste and then season with salt and pepper. Pour the polenta into buttered hotel pans to a depth of 1 inch/25 mm and refrigerate at least 3 hours or until firm. Cut the polenta into the desired shapes and pan fry in olive oil as needed for service.

4. Serve immediately on heated plates.

Toasted Quinoa and Sweet Pepper Pilaf

Makes 12½ pounds/5.7 kilograms or 50 portions (about 4 ounces/115 grams each)

Vegetable oil	¼ cup	60 ml
Shallots, minced	3 oz	85 g
Garlic cloves, minced	8 each	8 each
Quinoa	2½ pt	1.2 l
Chicken Stock (page 83)	5 pt	2.4 l
Bay leaves	4 each	4 each
Thyme, fresh or dried	4 sprigs fresh or 2 tsp dried	4 sprigs fresh or 10 ml dried
Kosher salt, plus additional as needed	2 tbsp	30 ml
Red peppers, roasted, peeled, seeded, small dice	1 qt	950 ml
Yellow peppers, roasted, peeled, seeded, small dice	1 qt	950 ml
Ground black pepper, plus additional as needed	2 tsp	10 ml

1. Heat the oil in a rondeau over medium heat. Add the shallots and garlic and sauté until aromatic and tender, 2 to 3 minutes. Add the quinoa and stir while the grain toasts, about 1 minute; it will have a "popped corn" aroma and some kernels may pop.

2. Add the stock, toasted quinoa, bay leaves, thyme, and 1 tbsp/15 ml salt. Stir well with a fork and bring the broth to a simmer over medium heat. Reduce the heat to low.

3. Cover the pot and simmer the quinoa over low heat on the stovetop or in a 325°F/165°C oven until tender and very fluffy, about 15 minutes.

4. Remove and discard the bay leaves and thyme sprigs. Fluff the grains with a fork to break up any clumps and fold in the peppers. Taste the quinoa and adjust seasoning with salt and pepper.

5. Serve immediately on heated plates.

Bread Dumplings

Makes 12½ pounds/5.7 kilograms or 50 portions (about 4 ounces/115 grams each)

White bread or rolls, with crust, small dice	5 lb	2.25 kg
Butter	10 oz	285 g
Onions, minced	1 lb 4 oz	570 g
All-purpose flour	1 lb 4 oz	570 g
Milk, plus additional as needed	2½ pt	1.2 l
Eggs	20 each	20 each
Parsley, minced	2½ oz	70 g
Kosher salt	2 tbsp	30 ml
Ground white pepper	2 tsp	10 ml
Ground nutmeg (optional)	As needed	As needed
Chicken Stock (page 83), hot, or as needed	1 qt	950 ml

1. Dry the bread on a sheet pan in a 300°F/150°C oven for 10 to 12 minutes.

2. Heat the butter in a sauté pan over medium-high heat, add the onions, and sauté until lightly browned, 8 to 10 minutes. Remove from the pan and cool.

3. Combine the dried bread, flour, and sautéed onions in a large bowl.

4. Combine the milk, eggs, parsley, salt, pepper, and nutmeg, if using, in another bowl.

5. Pour the liquid mixture into the dry mixture and blend together lightly. Let stand for 30 minutes. Add more milk if the bread is very dry. Shape the mixture into 2-inch/51-mm dumplings by hand.

6. Bring about 4 inches/10 cm salted water to a gentle simmer over low heat. Add the dumplings, working in batches, and poach until the dumplings are cooked through and firm, about 15 minutes. Transfer the dumplings to perforated pans with a slotted spoon or skimmer and let them drain briefly.

7. Serve immediately on heated plates, or hold, lightly moistened with stock and covered, in a hotel pan for service.

Spätzle

Makes 12½ pounds/5.7 kilograms or 50 portions (about 4 ounces/115 grams each)

Eggs	30 each	30 each
Milk	1 pt 9 fl oz	750 ml
Water	2½ pt	1.2 l
Kosher salt, plus additional as needed	2 tbsp	30 ml
Ground white pepper, plus additional as needed	2 tsp	10 ml
Nutmeg, grated	A pinch	A pinch
All-purpose flour	5 lb	2.25 kg
Butter	1 lb 4 oz	570 g

1. Combine the eggs, milk, and water in a 20-qt/18.75-l mixing bowl. Season with salt, pepper, and nutmeg. Add the flour and beat with the paddle attachment on medium speed until smooth. Allow the mixture to rest for 1 hour.

2. Bring a large pot of salted water to a simmer over medium-high heat. Work the batter through a spätzle maker into the simmering water. When the spätzle comes to the top of the pot, remove it with a spider. The spätzle is ready to finish now or it may be cooled in an ice water bath, drained, and held under refrigeration up to 2 days for later service.

3. Heat the butter in a rondeau or tilt skillet over medium-high heat. Add the spätzle and sauté until very hot, about 3 minutes. Taste and then adjust seasoning with salt and pepper.

4. Serve immediately on heated plates.

1. The finished spätzle batter will be thick and smooth.

2. Work the batter through a spätzle maker into salted simmering water.

3. Sauté the cooked spätzle in hot oil until lightly brown.

Baked Acorn Squash with Hazelnut-Maple Glaze

Makes 50 portions (2 wedges per portion, about 4 ounces/115 grams)

Hazelnuts, roasted, chopped	1½ lb	680 g
Butter, softened	1½ lb	680 g
Maple syrup	1 qt	950 ml
Kosher salt	2 tbsp	30 ml
Ground black pepper	2 tsp	10 ml
Acorn squash, cut into 100 wedges, seeds removed	15 lb	6.8 kg
Water	1 pt	480 ml

1. Combine the hazelnuts, butter, maple syrup, salt, and pepper in the bowl of a mixer with a paddle attachment.

2. Brush the squash with the hazelnut butter and place into hotel pans. Add enough water to barely coat the bottoms of the pans and cover tightly with foil.

3. Bake at 325°F/165°C for 10 minutes. Uncover the squash and baste the wedges with the cooking liquid. Continue to bake until the squash is very tender and has a rich, golden color, 8 to 10 minutes more. Baste the squash once or twice more as it finishes baking.

4. Serve immediately or hold hot for service.

Orzo and Pecan Sauté

Makes 12½ pounds/5.7 kilograms or 50 portions (about 4 ounces/115 grams each)

Butter	1 lb	450 g
Orzo pasta, cooked	4 lb 12 oz	2.15 kg
Brown rice, cooked	4 lb 12 oz	2.15 kg
Pecans, chopped, toasted	1½ lb	680 g
Parsley, chopped	¼ cup	60 ml
Kosher salt, plus additional as needed	2 tbsp	30 ml

1. Heat the butter over medium-high heat. Add the orzo and brown rice and sauté until heated thoroughly, 8 to 10 minutes.

2. Add the pecans and parsley. Mix thoroughly. Taste and then season with salt.

3. Serve immediately on heated plates.

SAVORY BREAD PUDDING WITH ROASTED GARLIC AND ASIAGO

Makes 12½ pounds/5.7 kilograms or 50 portions (about 4 ounces/115 grams each)

Pullman loaves, crust removed, medium dice	3 lb	1.4 kg
Olive oil	½ cup	120 ml
Ground black pepper	4 tsp	20 ml
CUSTARD		
Heavy cream	1 gal	3.75 l
Eggs	30 each	30 each
Roasted garlic, puréed	8 oz	225 g
Asiago, finely grated	1 lb	450 g
Blue cheese, crumbled	8 oz	225 g
Chives, chopped	¼ cup	120 ml
Tarragon, chopped	¼ cup	120 ml
Thyme, chopped	4 tsp	20 ml
Kosher salt	1 tbsp	15 ml
Ground black pepper	2 tsp	10 ml

1. Toss the bread with the oil and pepper. Bake on a sheet pan in a 350°F/175°C oven, tossing occasionally, until golden brown, 8 to 10 minutes. Transfer to a bowl.

2. To make the custard, combine the cream, eggs, garlic purée, cheeses, chives, tarragon, thyme, salt, and pepper in a stainless-steel mixing bowl. Mix until smooth and then pour the custard over the toasted bread cubes. Let the bread soak in the custard for at least 1 hour (or up to 12 hours under refrigeration).

3. Divide the mixture into lightly oiled 3-fl-oz/90-ml aluminum molds and place into hotel pans. (The molds may touch each other.)

4. Set the pans on oven racks and then add enough hot water to come up to the level of the pudding inside the molds to make a hot water bath.

5. Bake in a water bath in a 325°F/165°C oven until the custard is set and the tops are golden brown, 40 to 45 minutes. Let the puddings rest at room temperature for at least 15 minutes before unmolding and serving. (The puddings may be cooled and then held under refrigeration still in their molds for up to 24 hours before serving. Reheat the puddings in a 325°F/165°C oven for 10 to 12 minutes.)

6. Unmold the puddings before serving on heated plates.

chapter eleven

MBC

RECIPES FOR BAKED GOODS AND DESSERTS

FOCACCIA

Makes 16 loaves (1 pound/450 grams each)

Bread flour	5 lb	2.25 kg
Instant dry yeast	½ oz	15 g
Water, warm (105°F/41°C)	3 pt 5 fl oz	1.6 l
Salt	1¾ oz	50 g
Olive oil	As needed	As needed
Toppings, such as minced herbs, sautéed onions, sliced tomatoes, coarse salt	As needed	As needed

1. Combine the flour and yeast in the bowl of an electric mixer. Add the water and salt and mix with a dough hook attachment on low speed for 2 minutes. Mix on medium speed until the dough is smooth and elastic, about 3 minutes.

2. Transfer the dough to a clean oiled bowl, cover, and let it rise until nearly doubled in volume, about 30 minutes. Fold the dough over on itself gently. Cover the dough and let it rise until nearly doubled, about 30 minutes more.

3. Turn the dough out onto a lightly floured work surface. Scale the dough into pieces, 1 lb/450 g each. For each loaf, shape the dough into a round. Let the dough rest, covered, until relaxed, 15 to 20 minutes. (Work sequentially, starting the next step with the first piece of dough you divided and rounded.)

4. To shape the focaccia, flatten and stretch each round of dough into a rectangle (about 4 by 10 inches/10 by 25 cm) or a disk, and place it on a liberally oiled sheet pan. Let the loaves rise until doubled, 30 to 40 minutes. Just before baking, dimple the focaccia with your fingertips. Brush generously with oil and scatter the desired topping over each focaccia.

5. Bake in a 450°F/235°C oven until the top crust has a rich golden color, about 30 minutes.

6. Transfer the focaccia to racks and allow them to cool completely.

1. Spread a layer of olive oil across a sheet pan.

2. Flatten and stretch each round of dough into a rectangle.

3. After the foccacia dough has doubled in size, use your fingertips to dimple the foccacia.

CIABATTA

Makes 10 loaves (1½ pounds/670 grams each)

Water (68° to 76°F/20° to 25°C)	7¼ pt	3.4 l
Compressed fresh yeast	½ oz	15 g
Bread flour	10 lb	4.5 kg
Salt	3½ tsp	18 ml
Olive oil for brushing ciabatta (optional)	As needed	As needed
Kosher salt (optional)	As needed	As needed

1. Combine the water and yeast in the bowl of an electric mixer and blend until the yeast is fully dissolved. Add the flour and salt and mix with a dough hook attachment on low speed until just incorporated. Mix on medium speed until the dough is smooth and elastic, 10 to 12 minutes.

2. Transfer the dough to a clean oiled bowl, cover, and let it rise until doubled in volume, about 1 hour 15 minutes.

3. Turn the dough out onto a well-floured work surface. Scale the dough into pieces, 1 lb 8 oz/670 g each, and gently stretch each piece into a rectangle about 4 by 10 inches/10 by 25 cm. Place on an oiled sheet pan.

4. Bake in a 450°F/235°C oven until the top crust has a rich golden color, about 30 minutes.

5. Remove the ciabatta from the pan and, if using, immediately brush with oil and scatter salt over the surface. Transfer to racks and cool completely.

BUTTERMILK BISCUITS

Makes 80 biscuits (about 2 ounces/60 grams each)

All-purpose flour	7 lb	3.2 kg
Sugar	8 oz	225 g
Baking powder	6 oz	170 g
Salt	2 oz	60 g
Butter, cold	2 lb	900 g
Eggs	1 lb	450 g
Buttermilk	3 pt	1.4 l
EGG WASH		
Eggs	2 each	2 each
Cold water	2 tbsp	30 ml

1. Combine the flour, sugar, baking powder, and salt.

2. Add the butter and rub together until the mixture has the appearance of a coarse meal.

3. Combine the eggs and buttermilk in a separate bowl. Add to the flour mixture, tossing to combine. Gather the dough into a ball and knead a few times on a floured surface.

4. Roll out the dough on a lightly floured work surface to a thickness of 1 inch/25 mm. Using a 2-inch/51-mm cutter, cut out the biscuits. Place the biscuits on parchment paper–lined sheet pans. Gather any scraps and press them together into a ball. Reroll the dough and cut additional biscuits until all of the dough is used.

5. To prepare the egg wash, blend the eggs with the water until smooth. Use a pastry brush to lightly coat the tops of the biscuits with egg wash.

6. Bake at 400°F/205°C until golden brown, about 15 minutes.

7. Transfer the biscuits to racks and allow them to cool completely.

HAM AND CHEESE SCONES

Makes 60 scones (about 3 ounces/85 grams each)

Bread flour	5 lb 10 oz	2.5 kg
Sugar	1 lb 5 oz	595 g
Baking powder	5¼ oz	150 g
Salt	2¼ oz	65 g
Ham, medium dice	3 lb	1.4 kg

Green onions, chopped	3 bunches	3 bunches
Cheddar, medium dice	1 lb 8 oz	680 g
Heavy cream, cold	2¼ qt	2.12 l

1. Combine the flour, sugar, baking powder, and salt in the bowl of an electric mixer and mix with a paddle attachment on medium speed until well blended, about 5 minutes. Add the ham, green onions, and cheese and mix until just incorporated. Add the cream and mix until just combined.

2. Scale the dough into six portions, 2 lb 5 oz/1.1 kg each, and pat each portion by hand into a cake pan or ring 10 inches/25 cm in diameter. Remove the dough from the rings, place it on a parchment paper–lined sheet pan, wrap well, and freeze thoroughly, at least 2 hours and up to 3 days.

3. Cut each disk into 10 equal wedges and place the wedges on parchment paper–lined sheet pans.

4. Bake the scones in a 350°F/175°C oven until golden brown, 20 to 25 minutes.

5. Cool the scones on the pans for a few minutes, then transfer them to racks to cool completely.

PROFITEROLES

Makes 50 profiteroles (about 2½ ounces/75 grams each)

Pâte à Choux (see opposite page)	4 lb	1.8 g
Eggs	4 each	4 each
Almonds, sliced	8 oz	225 g
Sugar	4 oz	115 g
Pastry Cream (page 370)	3 pt	1.4 l
Heavy cream, whipped to medium peaks (sweetened lightly with sugar if desired)	1 lb 2 oz	510 g
Confectioners' sugar	As needed	As needed

1. Using a pastry bag fitted with a No. 5 plain piping tip, pipe the pâte à choux into bulbs 1½ inches/38 mm in diameter on parchment paper–lined sheet pans. Blend the eggs with about 2 tbsp/30 ml cold water until smooth. Use a pastry brush to lightly coat the tops of the profiteroles with the egg wash.

2. Stick several almond slices into the top of each profiterole so that they protrude from the top and sprinkle each profiterole lightly with the sugar.

3. Bake at 360°F/180°C until the cracks formed in the pastries are no longer yellow, about 50 minutes. Transfer to racks and allow the profiteroles to cool to room temperature. Slice the top off each of the baked profiteroles.

4. Using a No. 5 plain piping tip, pipe the pastry cream into the bases, being careful not to overfill them.

5. Using a No. 5 star tip, pipe a double rosette of whipped cream on top of the pastry cream.

6. Place the tops of the pastries on the whipped cream and lightly dust with confectioners' sugar. Serve immediately.

Pâte à Choux

Makes 6½ pounds (2.95 kilograms)

Milk	1 pt	480 ml
Water	1 pt	480 ml
Butter	1 lb	450 g
Sugar	2 tsp	10 ml
Salt	2 tsp	10 ml
Bread flour	1 lb 8 oz	680 g
Eggs	2 lb 4 oz	1 kg

1. Bring the milk, water, butter, sugar, and salt to a boil in a sauce pot over medium heat, stirring constantly. Remove from the heat, add the flour all at once, and stir vigorously to combine. Return the pan to medium heat and cook, stirring constantly, until the mixture pulls away from the sides of the pan, about 3 minutes.

2. Transfer the mixture to the bowl of an electric mixer and mix briefly with a paddle attachment on medium speed. Add the eggs 2 at a time and mix until smooth after each addition.

3. The pâte à choux is ready to be piped and baked.

   NOTE *For a drier pâte à choux that is lighter in color, substitute an equal amount of water for the milk.*

CHERRY–CHOCOLATE CHUNK COOKIES

Makes 12 dozen cookies

All-purpose flour	4 lb 5 oz	1.95 kg
Salt	1½ oz	40 g
Baking soda	1 oz	30 g
Butter, softened	2 lb 14 oz	1.3 kg
Sugar	1 lb 14 oz	850 g
Light brown sugar	1 lb 6 oz	620 g
Eggs	9 each	9 each
Vanilla extract	2 tbsp	30 ml
Semisweet chocolate chunks	4 lb 5 oz	1.95 kg
Unsweetened dried cherries, chopped	2 lb	900 g

1. Sift together the flour, salt, and baking soda.

2. Cream the butter and sugars in the bowl of an electric mixer with a paddle attachment on medium speed, scraping down the bowl as needed, until the mixture is smooth and light in color, about 5 minutes.

3. Combine the eggs and vanilla in a separate bowl. Add the egg mixture to the butter and sugar mixture in 3 additions, mixing on medium speed until fully incorporated after each addition and scraping down the bowl as needed. On low speed, mix in the sifted dry ingredients, chocolate chunks, and cherry pieces until just incorporated.

4. Scoop (using a No. 24 scoop) or scale the dough into portions, 1½ oz/40 g each, and place the pieces on parchment paper–lined sheet pans in even rows. Alternatively, the dough may be scaled into larger pieces, 2 lb/900 g each, shaped into logs 16 inches/41 cm long, wrapped tightly in parchment paper, and refrigerated until firm enough to slice. Slice each log into 16 pieces and arrange on parchment paper–lined sheet pans in even rows.

5. Bake at 375°F/190°C until golden brown around the edges, 12 to 14 minutes.

6. Cool the cookies completely on the pans.

MUDSLIDE COOKIES

Makes 12½ dozen cookies

Cake flour	10½ oz	300 g
Baking powder	1 oz	30 g
Salt	2 tsp	10 ml
Espresso, brewed	½ cup	120 ml
Vanilla extract	1 tbsp	15 ml
Unsweetened chocolate, chopped	1 lb 4 oz	570 g
Bittersweet chocolate, chopped	4 lb	1.8 kg
Butter, softened	10½ oz	300 g
Eggs	22 each	22 each
Sugar	4 lb	1.8 kg
Walnuts, chopped	1 lb 5 oz	595 g
Semisweet chocolate chips	4 lb 8 oz	2 kg

1. Sift together the flour, baking powder, and salt.

2. Blend the espresso and vanilla.

3. Melt the chocolates together with the butter over low heat in a saucepan.

4. Beat the eggs, sugar, and coffee mixture in the bowl of an electric mixer with a whip attachment on high speed until light and thick, 6 to 8 minutes. Blend in the chocolate mixture on medium speed. On low speed, mix in the dry ingredients until just blended. Blend in the walnuts and chocolate chips until just incorporated.

5. Scale or scoop (using a No. 20 scoop) the dough into portions, 2 oz/60 g each, and place the pieces on parchment paper–lined sheet pans in even rows. Alternatively, the dough may be scaled into larger pieces, 2 lb/900 g each, shaped into logs 16 inches/41 cm long, wrapped tightly in parchment paper, and refrigerated until firm enough to slice. Slice each log into 16 pieces and arrange them on parchment paper–lined sheet pans in even rows.

6. Bake at 350°F/175°C until the cookies are cracked on top but still appear slightly moist, about 12 minutes.

7. Cool the cookies on the pans for a few minutes, then transfer them to racks to cool completely.

MACERATED STRAWBERRIES ON LEMON POUND CAKE

Makes 6 large cakes (2 pounds/900 grams each), 8 portions per cake

LEMON POUND CAKE

Cake flour	3 lb 4 oz	1.5 kg
Baking powder	1½ oz	40 g
Lemons, grated zest and juice	3 each	3 each
Butter, softened	2 lb 4 oz	1 kg
Sugar	2 lb 4 oz	1 kg
Salt	½ oz	15 g
Eggs	3 lb 12 oz	1.7 kg
Macerated Strawberries (see opposite page)	As needed	As needed

1. Sift together the flour and baking powder.

2. Cream the lemon zest and juice, butter, sugar, and salt in the bowl of an electric mixture with a paddle attachment on medium speed, scraping down the bowl as needed, until the mixture is smooth and light in color, about 5 minutes.

3. Whisk the eggs until the yolks and whites are blended in a separate bowl. Add the eggs to the butter and sugar mixture in 3 additions, mixing on medium speed until fully incorporated after each addition and scraping down the bowl as needed. Add the sifted dry ingredients and mix on low speed, scraping down the bowl as needed, until just blended.

4. Coat 6 loaf pans (9 by 5 by 3 inches/23 by 13 by 8 cm) with a light film of oil or butter. Scale 2 lb/900 g of the batter into each loaf pan.

5. Bake the cakes in a 350°F/175°C oven until a wooden skewer inserted near the center of a cake comes out clean, about 50 minutes.

6. Cool the cakes in the pans for a few minutes, then transfer them to racks to cool completely.

7. Just before serving, garnish the cakes with the macerated strawberries.

MACERATED STRAWBERRIES
Makes 50 portions

Strawberries	9 lb	4 kg
Sugar	8 oz	225 g
Orange juice	1 pt	480 ml
Vanilla extract	2½ fl oz	75 ml

Trim the tops off the strawberries and slice or quarter the berries. Toss the strawberries with the sugar, orange juice, and vanilla in a large bowl. Macerate under refrigeration for at least 30 minutes and up to 4 hours before using.

ENGLISH TRIFLE

Makes 50 portions

Currant jelly	2 lb	900 g
Rum-Flavored Simple Syrup (page 367)	1½ pt	720 ml
Dry sherry	1½ cups	360 ml
Vanilla Sponge Cake (page 358), cut into ½-inch/13-mm cubes	2 lb 4 oz	1 kg
Fresh fruit (peaches, bananas, plums, berries, cherries, etc.), cut into ½-inch/13-mm cubes	4 lb 8 oz	2 kg
Diplomat Cream (page 371), made without gelatin	4 lb	1.8 kg
Heavy cream, whipped to medium peaks	1 lb 6 oz	620 g
Chocolate curls or shavings	As needed	As needed

1. Divide the jelly evenly among 50 stemmed glasses or other containers (9-fl-oz/270-ml capacity).

2. Combine the syrup and sherry.

3. Place the sponge cake cubes in a bowl, add the syrup mixture, and toss to moisten evenly. Divide half of the sponge cake cubes evenly among the glasses. Top with half of the fruit, dividing evenly.

4. Using a pastry bag fitted with a No. 5 plain piping tip, pipe a layer of diplomat cream on top of the fruit. Divide the remaining sponge cake cubes among the glasses, then divide the remaining fruit among them. Pipe the remaining diplomat cream on top; the glasses should be filled to within ¼ inch/6 mm of the top. The trifles are ready to garnish and serve now, or they may be held under refrigeration for up to 2 days.

5. To garnish the trifles, use a No. 4 star tip to pipe a rosette of whipped cream on top of each trifle. Garnish each with chocolate curls or shavings and serve.

Vanilla Sponge Cake

Makes 6 cakes (8 inches/20 centimeters and 12 ounces/340 grams each)

Butter, melted	9 fl oz	270 ml
Vanilla extract	2 tbsp	30 ml
Eggs	13 each	13 each
Egg yolks	13 each	13 each
Sugar	1 lb 11 oz	765 g
Cake flour, sifted	1 lb 11 oz	765 g

1. Blend the butter with the vanilla. Reserve.

2. Combine the eggs, egg yolks, and sugar in the bowl of an electric mixer. Set the bowl over a pan of barely simmering water and whisk constantly until the mixture reaches 110°F/43°C.

3. Transfer the bowl to a mixer with a wire whip attachment and whip on high speed until the foam has tripled in volume and is no longer increasing in volume. Fold in the flour. Fold the butter and vanilla into the batter.

4. Coat six 8-inch/20-cm cake pans with a light film of oil or butter. Scale 1 lb/450 g of the batter into each cake pan.

5. Bake at 375°F/190°C until the tops of the cakes spring back when lightly touched, about 30 minutes.

6. Cool the cakes in the pans for a few minutes, then transfer them to racks to cool completely.

   Chocolate Sponge Cake: Replace 4 oz/115 g of the flour with Dutch-process cocoa powder. Sift the cocoa together with the flour.

FLOURLESS DARK CHOCOLATE CAKE WITH FRANGELICO WHIPPED CREAM

Makes 50 portions

Hazelnuts, whole, toasted, skinned	15 oz	425 g
Sugar	15 oz	425 g
Olive oil	3 fl oz	90 ml
Heavy cream	1½ cups	360 ml
Butter	1 lb 2 oz	510 g
Bittersweet chocolate, chopped	1 lb 8 oz	680 g
Semisweet chocolate, chopped	1 lb 8 oz	680 g
Eggs, separated	18 each	18 each
WHIPPED CREAM		
Heavy cream	1 qt	950 ml
Sugar, plus additional as needed	4 oz	115 g
Frangelico liqueur	½ cup	120 ml
Confectioners' sugar, or as needed	3 oz	85 g

1. Grind half of the nuts and half of the sugar in a food processor until very fine. Grind the other half of the nuts with the oil until pasty.

2. Heat the cream and butter together in a saucepan over low heat until simmering. Remove the pot from the heat and stir in the chocolates until melted. Cool slightly.

3. Whisk the egg yolks until pale and ribbony, then stir in the chocolate and nuts.

4. Beat the egg whites in a separate bowl until soft peaks form, add the remaining sugar, and beat until stiff. Fold the whites into the chocolate mixture in 3 additions.

5. Lightly butter fifty 3-fl-oz/90-ml ramekins and dust with flour. Pour the batter evenly into the prepared ramekins and bake at 350°F/175°C until a wooden skewer inserted in the center of a cake comes out slightly moist, about 12 minutes.

6. Let the cakes cool in the ramekins on racks until ready to serve. The cakes may be held under refrigeration up to 2 days before service.

7. To prepare the whipped cream, whip the cream to soft or medium peaks and sweeten to taste with the sugar. Add the Frangelico and continue to whip until the Frangelico is blended into the cream.

8. When ready to serve, dust the cakes with confectioners' sugar. Serve the chocolate cake in the ramekins with the whipped cream.

BASIC PIE DOUGH (3-2-1)

Makes 6 pounds 6 ounces (2.89 kilograms)

All-purpose flour	3 lb	1.4 kg
Salt	1 oz	30 g
Butter, cut into pieces, chilled	2 lb	900 g
Cold water	1 pt	480 ml

1. Combine the flour and salt thoroughly. Gently rub the butter into the flour using your fingertips until the mixture forms large flakes for an extremely flaky crust, or until the mixture has the appearance of coarse meal for a finer crumb.

2. Add the water all at once and mix until the dough just comes together. It should be moist enough to hold together when pressed into a ball.

3. Turn the dough out onto a lightly floured work surface and shape into an even rectangle. Wrap the dough with plastic wrap and refrigerate for 20 to 30 minutes. The dough is ready to roll out now or it may be held under refrigeration for up to 3 days or frozen for up to 6 weeks. (Thaw frozen dough in the refrigerator before rolling it out.)

4. Scale the dough as necessary, using about 1 oz/30 g of dough per 1 inch/25 mm of pie pan diameter.

5. To roll out the dough, work on a lightly floured surface and roll the dough into the desired shape and thickness using smooth, even strokes. Transfer the dough to a pie, tart, or tartlet pan. The shell is ready to fill or bake blind now.

6. To blind bake the dough, dock the dough in several places and line with parchment paper. Add pie weights or beans and bake the crust at 375°F/190°C until the crust is set and the rim looks dry, but not colored, 18 to 20 minutes. Remove the paper and the weights or beans. If necessary (check your recipe), return the crust to the oven and bake until the bottom looks dry and the rim is a light golden color, another 5 minutes.

BERRY COBBLER

Makes 40 portions (20 cobblers, ½ cobbler per portion)

Strawberries, hulled and halved	4 lb	1.8 kg
Raspberries	3 lb	1.4 kg
Blueberries	4 lb	1. 8 kg
Sugar	1 lb	450 g
Cornstarch	5 oz	140 g
Basic Pie Dough (see above)	5 lb	2.25 kg
Eggs	2 each	2 each

1. Combine the berries in a bowl and toss with the sugar and cornstarch.

2. Divide the mixture evenly among twenty 12-fl-oz/360-ml ramekins.

3. Roll out the pie dough ¼ inch/6 mm thick. Cut the dough into 20 rounds big enough to cover the ramekins, about 4 inches/10 cm in diameter. Top the filled ramekins with the pie dough rounds.

4. Blend the eggs with about 2 tbsp/30 ml cold water until smooth. Use a pastry brush to lightly coat the tops of the pie dough with egg wash.

5. Bake at 325°F/165°C until the tops are golden brown, about 20 minutes.

6. Serve the cobbler warm in the ramekin.

FRUIT CRISP

Makes 50 portions (6 ounces/170 grams each)

Raspberries	3 lb	1.4 kg
Blackberries	3 lb	1.4 kg
Blueberries	3 lb	1.4 kg
Orange zest, grated	2 tbsp	30 ml
Cornstarch	3 fl oz	90 ml
Sugar	1½ lb	680 g
Orange juice	1½ pt	720 ml
Cake flour	4 lb 12 oz	2.15 kg
Confectioners' sugar	3 lb	1.4 kg
Brown sugar	12½ oz	355 g
Salt	1½ tsp	8 ml
Butter, room temperature	3 lb	1.4 kg
Vanilla extract	¼ cup	60 ml

1. Combine the berries, orange zest, cornstarch, and sugar in a stainless-steel mixing bowl; toss well to combine. Add the orange juice and set aside to macerate at room temperature for 30 minutes.

2. Combine the flour, sugars, and salt in a mixing bowl and blend evenly. Add the butter and vanilla and mix until crumbly.

3. Divide the macerated berries between two hotel pans or baking pans about 2 inches/51 mm deep and cover generously with the vanilla streusel mixture.

4. Bake in a 375°F/190°C oven until the streusel topping is golden brown, about 20 minutes.

5. Let the crisp rest at least 15 minutes before cutting into portions and serving.

BREAD AND BUTTER PUDDING

Makes 50 portions

Raisins	15 oz	425 g
Rum	20 fl oz	590 ml
Brioche or challah	2 lb 13 oz	1.25 kg
Butter, melted, plus as needed for brushing molds	15 oz	425 g
Milk	5 qt	4.7 l
Sugar	1 lb 14 oz	850 g
Eggs, beaten	30 each	30 each
Egg yolks, beaten	20 each	20 each
Vanilla extract	2½ tsp	13 ml
Ground cinnamon	2½ tsp	13 ml
Salt	2½ tsp	13 ml

1. Place the raisins in a bowl and add the rum. Set them aside to plump for 20 minutes, then drain.

2. Cut the bread into ½-inch/13-mm cubes. Place them on a sheet pan and drizzle with the butter. Toast in a 350°F/175°C oven, stirring once or twice, until golden brown, 8 to 10 minutes.

3. Combine the milk and 15 oz/425 g of the sugar in a saucepan and bring to a boil over medium heat.

4. Meanwhile, blend the eggs, egg yolks, vanilla, and the remaining 15 oz/425 g of sugar to make the liaison. Temper the liaison by gradually adding about one-third of the hot milk and sugar mixture, whipping constantly. Add the remaining hot milk and sugar mixture and strain the custard through a fine-mesh sieve into a bowl.

5. Add the bread, cinnamon, salt, and drained raisins to the custard. Soak over an ice water bath for 1 hour to allow the bread to absorb the custard.

6. Lightly brush fifty 6-fl-oz/180-ml ramekins with melted butter. Ladle the mixture into the ramekins, filling them three-fourths full.

7. Place the ramekins in a water bath and bake in a 350°F/175°C oven until just set, 45 to 50 minutes.

8. Remove the puddings from the water bath and wipe the ramekins dry.

9. Refrigerate the puddings until fully chilled, at least 3 hours and up to 3 days before serving.

Bread and Butter Pudding with
Macadamia Nuts and White Chocolate
(page 366)

Bread and Butter Pudding with Macadamia Nuts and White Chocolate

Makes 50 portions (6 fluid ounces/180 milliliters each)

Raisins	15 oz	425 g
Rum	20 fl oz	590 ml
Brioche or challah	2 lb 13 oz	1.25 kg
Butter, melted, plus additional for brushing molds	15 fl oz	445 ml
Milk	5 qt	4.7 l
Sugar	1 lb 14 oz	850 g
Eggs, beaten	30 each	30 each
Egg yolks, beaten	20 each	20 each
Vanilla extract	2½ tsp	13 ml
Ground cinnamon	2½ tsp	13 ml
Salt	2½ tsp	13 ml
Macadamia nuts, salted, coarsely chopped	1 lb	450 g
White chocolate, chopped	1 lb 8 oz	680 g

1. Place the raisins in a bowl and add the rum. Set them aside to plump for 20 minutes, then drain.

2. Cut the bread into ½-inch/13-mm cubes. Place them on a sheet pan and drizzle with the butter. Toast the bread cubes in a 350°F/175°C oven, stirring once or twice, until golden brown, 8 to 10 minutes.

3. Combine the milk and 15 oz/425 g of the sugar in a saucepan and bring to a boil over medium heat.

4. Meanwhile, blend the eggs, egg yolks, vanilla, and the remaining 15 oz/425 g of sugar to make the liaison. Temper the liaison by gradually adding about one-third of the hot milk and sugar mixture, whipping constantly. Add the remaining hot milk and sugar mixture and strain the custard through a fine-mesh sieve into a bowl.

5. Add the bread, cinnamon, salt, and drained raisins to the custard. Soak over an ice water bath for 1 hour to allow the bread to absorb the custard. Lightly brush fifty 6-fl-oz/180-ml ramekins with melted butter. Just before filling the ramekins, stir the macadamia nuts and chocolate into the batter. Ladle the mixture into the ramekins, filling them three-fourths full.

6. Bake in a hot water bath at 350°F/175°C until just set, 45 to 50 minutes. Remove the custards from the water bath and wipe the ramekins dry.

7. Refrigerate the custards until fully chilled, at least 3 hours and up to 3 days before serving.

SIMPLE SYRUP

Makes 2 quarts (1.9 liters)

Sugar	2 lb	900 g
Water	1 qt	950 ml

Combine the sugar and water in a saucepan and stir to ensure all the sugar is moistened. Bring to a boil over high heat, stirring to dissolve the sugar. The syrup is ready to use now or it may be cooled and held under refrigeration in covered containers for up to 3 weeks.

RUM-FLAVORED SIMPLE SYRUP: Replace 8 fl oz/240 ml of the water with rum.

1. Combine the sugar and water in a saucepan and stir to moisten the sugar completely. Bring the mixture to a boil.

2. The finished syrup will be clear and all the sugar will be dissolved.

Vanilla ice cream with Dried Cherry Sauce

DRIED CHERRY SAUCE

Makes 1 pound 10 ounces (735 grams)

Sugar	3 oz	85 g
Dry red wine	13 fl oz	390 ml
Water	¾ cup	180 ml
Orange juice	2 tbsp	30 ml
Lemon juice	2 tbsp	30 ml
Vanilla bean	1 each	1 each
Unsweetened dried cherries	4 oz	115 g
Cornstarch	½ oz	15 g

1. Combine the sugar, 12 fl oz/360 ml of the wine, the water, orange juice, and lemon juice in a stainless-steel saucepan. Split the vanilla bean, scrape the seeds into the pan, add the pod, and bring the mixture to a boil over high heat. Remove from the heat and add the cherries.

2. Cover and refrigerate overnight.

3. Strain the sauce through a fine-mesh sieve into a saucepan, reserving the cherries. Bring the sauce to a boil over medium-high heat.

4. Meanwhile, dilute the cornstarch with the remaining 1 fl oz/30 ml of wine. Gradually whisk the diluted cornstarch into the sauce and bring back to a boil, whisking until the sauce thickens enough to coat the back of a spoon.

5. Allow the sauce to cool to room temperature.

6. Add the reserved cherries and serve immediately.

HARD GANACHE

Makes 6 pounds (2.75 kilograms)

Dark chocolate, finely chopped	4 lb	1.8 kg
Heavy cream	1 qt	950 ml

1. Place the chocolate in a stainless-steel bowl.

2. Bring the cream just to a simmer in a saucepan over low heat. Pour the hot cream over the chocolate, allow it to stand for 1 minute, and stir until the chocolate is thoroughly melted.

3. The ganache can be used immediately, or it may be covered and held under refrigeration up to 5 days, then rewarmed over simmering water until softened.

WHOLE-BEAN VANILLA SAUCE

Makes 1 quart (950 milliliters)

Milk	1 pt	480 ml
Heavy cream	1 pt	480 ml
Vanilla bean, split, scraped	1 each	1 each
Sugar	8 oz	225 g
Egg yolks	14 each	14 each

1. Heat the milk, cream, vanilla bean pod and seeds, and half of the sugar in a saucepan over medium heat until the mixture reaches the boiling point.

2. Combine the egg yolks and the rest of the sugar in a bowl to make a liaison. Temper the liaison by gradually adding about one-third of the hot milk and sugar mixture, whipping constantly. Add the remaining hot milk and sugar mixture and return the sauce to the saucepan.

3. Stirring constantly, heat slowly to 180°F/82°C.

4. Remove the sauce from the heat immediately and strain it through a fine-mesh sieve into a clean container (set the container in an ice water bath if you are planning to store the sauce).

5. The sauce is ready to serve or use now, or it may be held in covered containers under refrigeration for up to 3 days.

PASTRY CREAM

Makes 1 quart (950 milliliters)

Milk	1 qt	950 ml
Sugar	8 oz	225 g
Eggs	6 to 8 each	6 to 8 each
Cornstarch	3 oz	85 g
Vanilla extract	3 tbsp	45 ml
Butter	3 oz	85 g

1. Combine the milk with half of the sugar in a saucepan and bring it to a boil over medium-high heat.

2. Whisk about one-fourth of the hot milk mixture into the eggs to temper them. Combine the remaining sugar with the cornstarch in a bowl. Add the eggs and mix until smooth.

3. Add the egg mixture to the hot milk mixture gradually while stirring constantly. Bring the mixture to a full boil over medium heat, continuing to stir constantly.

4. Remove the pan from the heat and stir in the vanilla and butter. Transfer the pastry cream to a clean container, place a piece of plastic wrap directly on the pastry cream, and let it cool.

5. The pastry cream is ready to use now, or it may be cooled quickly over an ice bath and held under refrigeration up to 3 days for later use.

DIPLOMAT CREAM

Makes 3 quarts (2.8 liters)

Heavy cream	1 qt	950 ml
Water	½ cup	120 ml
Gelatin	½ oz	15 g
Pastry Cream (see opposite page), warm	1 qt	950 ml

1. Whip the cream to soft peaks. Cover and hold under refrigeration until ready to add to the diplomat cream.

2. Put the water in a small bowl and sprinkle the gelatin over the water. Let the gelatin soften and absorb the water, about 10 minutes. Warm the softened gelatin over barely simmering water or in a microwave on a low power setting until the mixture is clear and liquid enough to pour.

3. Stir about 1 pt/480 ml of the warm pastry cream into the gelatin and stir until blended. Add the gelatin mixture to the rest of the pastry cream and stir to blend. Cool over an ice water bath to 75°F/24°C.

4. Add the whipped cream to the cooled pastry cream mixture in 2 additions, folding in the cream after each addition until the mixture is smooth and homogeneous.

5. Use the diplomat cream immediately to fill pastries or pipe into molds as directed by specific recipes. Cover the molded cream desserts or filled pastries and refrigerate until the cream completely sets, at least 3 hours and up to 24 hours before serving.

Chocolate Mousse, garnish with whipped cream, chocolate "strings" and a cookie.

CHOCOLATE MOUSSE

Makes 50 portions (4 fluid ounces/120 milliliters each)

Bittersweet chocolate, finely chopped	3 lb 2 oz	1.4 kg
Butter	7½ oz	215 g
Eggs, separated (see Note)	25 each	25 each
Water	5 fl oz	150 ml
Sugar	10 oz	285 g
Heavy cream, whipped to medium peaks	2½ pt	1.2 l
Rum (optional)	3 fl oz	90 ml

1. Combine the chocolate and butter and melt over a hot water bath.

2. Combine the egg yolks with the water and half of the sugar and whisk over a hot water bath until the mixture reaches 145°F/63°C, about 5 minutes. Remove from the heat and whip until cool.

3. Using a large rubber spatula, fold the chocolate mixture into the egg yolks.

4. Combine the egg whites with the remaining sugar in a separate bowl and whisk over a hot water bath until the mixture reaches 145°F/63°C, about 5 minutes. Remove the whites from the heat and beat to full volume. Continue beating until cool.

5. Fold the egg white mixture into the egg yolk and chocolate mixture.

6. Fold in the whipped cream and add the rum, if using. Pipe the mixture into fifty 4-fl-oz/120-ml molds.

7. Refrigerate the mousse until fully chilled, at least 3 hours. They may be held under refrigeration up to 3 days. Serve directly in the ramekin.

NOTE *To avoid possible salmonella contamination, substitute 2 lb/900 g pasteurized egg whites and 1 lb/450 g pasteurized egg yolks.*

CRÈME BRÛLÉE

Makes 50 portions (6 fluid ounces/180 milliliters each)

Heavy cream	5 qt	4.7 l
Sugar	3 lb 4 oz	1.5 kg
Salt	A pinch	A pinch
Vanilla beans	3 each	3 each
Egg yolks, beaten	1 lb 12 oz	800 g
Confectioners' sugar	1 lb 6 oz	620 g

1. Combine the cream, 1 lb 4 oz/570 g of the sugar, and the salt in a saucepan and bring to a simmer over medium heat, stirring gently with a wooden spoon. Remove from the heat. Split the vanilla beans, scrape the seeds into the pan, add the pods, cover, and steep for 15 minutes.

2. Return the pan to the heat and bring the cream to a boil over medium heat.

3. Combine the egg yolks and 10 oz/285 g of the remaining sugar. Stir a portion of the hot cream into the egg yolks to temper them, then stir the egg yolk mixture back into the hot cream. Strain the custard through a fine-mesh sieve and ladle it into fifty 6-fl-oz/180-ml crème brûlée ramekins, filling them three-fourths full.

4. Place the ramekins in a water bath and bake in a 325°F/163°C oven until just set, 20 to 25 minutes.

5. Remove the custards from the water bath and wipe the ramekins dry.

6. Refrigerate until fully chilled, at least 3 hours. The custards may be held under refrigeration up to 3 days for later service.

Sprinkle a thin layer of sugar evenly on top of each baked custard's surface.

Use a propane torch to melt and caramelize the sugar.

The finished crème brûlée will have a caramelized sugar crust.

7. To finish the crème brûlées, evenly coat each custard's surface with a thin layer of the remaining sugar. Use a propane torch to melt and caramelize the sugar. Lightly dust the surface with confectioners' sugar and serve immediately.

Crème Caramel

Makes 50 portions (4 fluid ounces/120 milliliters each)

CARAMEL		
Water	1¼ cups	300 ml
Sugar	1 lb 4 oz	570 g
CUSTARD		
Milk	1¾ cups	420 ml
Sugar	1 lb 14 oz	850 g
Vanilla extract	3 tbsp	45 ml
Eggs, lightly beaten	20 each	20 each
Egg yolks	15 each	15 each

1. To prepare the caramel, combine the water and 2½ oz/70 g of the sugar in a saucepan over medium heat. Allow the sugar to melt.

2. Add the remaining sugar in small increments, allowing it to melt before each new addition. Continue this process until all the sugar has been added. Cook the caramel to the desired color.

3. Divide the caramel equally among fifty 4-fl-oz/120-ml ramekins, swirling the caramel to coat the bottoms. Place the ramekins into one or more roasting pans and reserve.

4. To prepare the custard, combine the milk with 1 lb 4 oz/570 g of the sugar in a saucepan over medium heat and cook, stirring occasionally, until the mixture reaches the boiling point. Stir in the vanilla extract.

5. Combine the eggs and egg yolks with the remaining 10 oz/285 g sugar in a bowl to make a liaison. Temper the liaison by gradually adding about one-third of the hot milk and sugar mixture, whipping constantly. Add the remaining hot milk and sugar mixture and return the sauce to the saucepan. Remove the pan from the heat immediately and strain the custard through a fine-mesh sieve into the caramel-coated ramekins, filling them three-fourths full. Bake the ramekins in a hot water bath at 325°F/163°C until fully set, about 1 hour.

6. Remove the custards from the water bath and wipe the ramekins dry. Allow the custards to cool.

7. Wrap each custard individually and refrigerate for at least 24 hours before unmolding and serving. The custards may be held under refrigeration for up to 3 days.

8. To unmold the custards, run a small sharp knife between the custard and the ramekin, invert each one onto a serving plate, and tap it lightly to release.

Frozen Grand Marnier Soufflé

Makes 50 portions (about 6 fluid ounces/180 milliliters each)

Water	6¼ fl oz	185 ml
Gelatin	1 oz	30 g
Eggs	2 lb 1 oz	940 g
Egg yolks	1 lb 9 oz	710 g
Sugar	1 lb 2 oz	510 g
Grand Marnier liqueur	1 pt	480 ml
Heavy cream, whipped to soft peaks	2 qt	1.9 l

1. Cut 50 strips, 2 by 11 inches/5 by 28 cm each, of parchment paper or acetate. Wrap each strip around the inside of a 4½-fl-oz/135-ml ramekin and fasten with tape. Place the ramekins on a sheet pan and place in the freezer until fully chilled.

2. Put the water in a small bowl and sprinkle the gelatin over the water. Let the gelatin soften and absorb the water, about 10 minutes.

3. Combine the eggs, egg yolks, sugar, and Grand Marnier in the bowl of an electric mixer. Set the bowl over a pan of simmering water and whisk constantly until the mixture reaches and holds 165°F/75°C for 1 minute.

4. Transfer the bowl to a mixer with a wire whip attachment and whip on high speed until the foam has tripled in volume and is no longer increasing in volume.

5. Warm the softened gelatin over barely simmering water or in a microwave on a low power setting until the mixture is clear and liquid enough to pour.

6. Fold the gelatin mixture into the egg mixture. Fold in the whipped cream.

7. Pour or pipe the mixture into the prepared ramekins, level each even with the top of the paper collar, cover, and freeze at least 3 hours before serving. The soufflés may be held in the freezer for up to 10 days. Remove collars just before serving and serve in the ramekins.

1. Pour or pipe the soufflé mixture into ramekins lined with parchment paper or acetate.

2. Gently remove the lining and serve the finished soufflés immediately.

GRAND MARNIER SOUFFLÉ WITH WHOLE-BEAN VANILLA SAUCE

Makes 50 portions (4-ounce/115-gram soufflés with 1½ ounces/45 grams sauce)

Butter, plus additional as needed for coating ramekins	8 oz	225 g
Sugar, plus additional as needed for dusting ramekins	12 oz	340 g
Grand Marnier liqueur	¾ cup	180 ml
Egg yolks	1 lb	450 g
Pastry Cream (page 370)	2½ qt	2.4 l
Egg whites	2 lb	900 g
Confectioners' sugar for dusting	As needed	As needed
Whole-Bean Vanilla Sauce (page 370)	2½ qt	2.4 l

1. Coat the inside of fifty 4-fl-oz/120-ml ramekins with a film of softened butter, making sure to coat the rims as well as the insides, and dust with sugar.

2. To prepare the soufflé base, melt the butter in a bowl over a pan of barely simmering water, gently stirring to blend. Add the Grand Marnier and egg yolks. Blend the mixture into the pastry cream and set aside.

3. To prepare the meringue, whip the egg whites to soft peaks in the bowl of an electric mixer with a wire whip attachment on high speed.

4. Gradually sprinkle in the sugar while continuing to whip, then whip the meringue to medium peaks.

5. Gently blend about one third of the meringue into the soufflé base. Fold in the remaining meringue, thoroughly incorporating it.

6. Divide the soufflé mixture among the prepared ramekins.

7. Bake at 350°F/175°C until fully risen, about 20 minutes, and then immediately dust with confectioners' sugar and serve with the whole-bean vanilla sauce.

1. Whip the egg whites to soft peaks in an electric mixer.

2. Gently blend one third of the meringue into the soufflé base.

3. After this addition, the soufflé base will be thick and smooth.

4. Gently fold in the remaining meringue.

5. Gently divide the soufflé mixture among the prepared ramekins.

6. Lightly dust the finished soufflés with confectioners' sugar.

7. Serve the finished soufflés with whole-bean vanilla sauce.

TANGERINE SOUP WITH PINEAPPLE SORBET

Makes 50 portions (3 fluid ounces/90 milliliters soup with 1½ ounces/45 grams sorbet)

Tangerine juice, strained	4¾ qt	4.5 l
Arrowroot	4 oz	115 g
Water, cold	½ cup	120 ml
Pineapple sorbet	4 lb 8 oz	2 kg
Mint sprigs	50 each	50 each

1. Bring the tangerine juice to a simmer in a saucepan over medium heat.

2. Combine the arrowroot and cold water and stir until smooth. Whisk into the simmering tangerine juice. Return to a simmer to thicken lightly, then remove from the heat and refrigerate until fully chilled, at least 2 hours. The soup may be held under refrigeration for up to 2 days before serving.

3. Divide the tangerine soup among small chilled bowls or cups. Place a scoop of sorbet in each bowl or cup of soup and garnish with a mint sprig. Serve immediately.

chapter twelve

RECIPES FOR RECEPTION FOODS

GORGONZOLA AND PEAR SANDWICH

Makes 50 portions

Cream cheese	10 oz	285 g
Gorgonzola	1 lb 9 oz	710 g
Heavy cream	1¼ cups	300 ml
Salt	As needed	As needed
Ground black pepper	As needed	As needed
Honey	1¼ cups	300 ml
White wine vinegar	5 fl oz	150 ml
Pears	5 lb	2.25 kg
Raisin pumpernickel, sliced ⅛ inch/3 mm thick, 1 inch/25 mm wide, 3 inches/75	100 slices	100 slices

1. Blend the cream cheese and Gorgonzola with enough cream to get a smooth, spreadable consistency. Taste and season with salt and pepper.

2. Combine the honey and vinegar. Peel and thinly slice the pears and brush them with the honey and vinegar mixture to prevent oxidation.

3. For each sandwich, spread the cheese mixture on 2 slices of bread. Place about 1¼ oz/35 g of the pears on the cheese side of 1 slice of the bread. Top with the second slice of bread, cheese side down.

4. Serve immediately or hold, covered, under refrigeration for no more than 2 hours.

ROASTED PEPPER AND GOAT CHEESE CANAPÉS

Makes 50 canapés

Red peppers	1½ each	1½ each
Yellow peppers	1½ each	1½ each
Green peppers	1½ each	1½ each
Olive oil. plus additional as needed	⅔ cup	160 ml
Salt	1½ tsp	8 ml
Freshly ground pepper	¾ tsp	4 ml
Baguettes, cut on an angle into ¼-inch/6-mm slices (1½ baguettes)	50 slices	50 slices
Garlic cloves, halved	4½ each	4½ each
Goat's milk cheese log	1 lb 2 oz	510 g
Thyme, chopped	2 tbsp	30 ml
Basil, chiffonade	3 tbsp	45 ml

1. Cut the peppers in half and remove and discard the seeds and ribs. Rub each pepper half lightly with oil and place the peppers cut side down on a sheet pan. Roast in a 400°F/205°C oven until the skin blisters and darkens, about 20 minutes.

2. Remove the peppers from the oven and cover tightly with foil or a second sheet pan turned upside down. Let the peppers steam until they are cool enough to handle, at least 1 hour. Pull away the skin and discard (use a paring knife to help with any pieces that don't come away easily).

3. Cut the peppers into a fine, short julienne, transfer to a container, and add ⅔ cup/160 ml oil, the salt, and ¼ tsp/1 ml of the pepper. Stir to coat the peppers evenly. Cover and marinate under refrigeration for at least 3 hours or up to 8 hours before using.

4. Brush the baguette slices lightly with oil on both sides, place on a sheet pan, and bake at 325°F/165°C until the crostini are dry and lightly toasted (a light golden brown), about 15 minutes.

5. While the crostini are still hot, pierce half of a garlic clove with a fork and rub the crostini with the garlic, replacing the piece of garlic as it is used up.

6. Brush the cheese log with oil and roll in a mixture of the thyme and the remaining ½ tsp/3 ml of black pepper. Slice the cheese thinly.

7. Top each crostini with a slice of cheese and 1 tsp/5 ml of the roasted peppers. Scatter the basil over the crostini and serve.

Crostini with Oven-Roasted Tomatoes

Makes 50 canapés

Canned plum tomatoes	13 lb	6 kg
Extra-virgin olive oil	1 pt	480 ml
Onions, small dice	1 lb	450 g
Garlic cloves, sliced	10 each	10 each
Thyme, picked	½ cup	120 ml
Oregano, picked	½ cup	120 ml
Kosher salt, plus additional as needed	2 tbsp	30 ml
Cracked black pepper, plus additional as needed	2 tbsp	30 ml
Baguette, sliced into rounds and toasted, or melba toast	50 slices or pieces	50 slices or pieces

1. Drain the tomatoes through a sieve and reserve the liquid for another use. Carefully remove the tomatoes from the sieve to avoid breakage.

2. In a large rondeau, heat the oil over medium-high heat. Add the onions and sauté, stirring frequently, until the onions are tender and translucent, 5 to 6 minutes. Add the garlic and sauté until the aroma is released but the garlic is not browned, about 4 minutes. Remove from the heat.

3. Carefully place the tomatoes in the pan and season with thyme, oregano, salt, and pepper.

4. Place the rondeau, uncovered, in a 250°F/120°C oven and roast the tomatoes until they have a rich, roasted flavor, about 2 hours.

5. Drain the tomatoes on a perforated hotel pan. Reserve the oil for later use.

6. Place the tomatoes in a food processor and pulse gently to a coarse texture.

7. Transfer the tomato mixture to a clean stainless-steel container and cool to room temperature. (The tomatoes may be held under refrigeration for up to 3 days for later service.)

8. Add the reserved olive oil to the tomatoes. Taste and adjust seasoning with salt and pepper.

9. Spread about 2 teaspoons of the tomatoes onto each slice of toasted baguette or piece of melba toast and serve.

CHESAPEAKE-STYLE CRAB CAKES

Makes 100 cakes (2½ ounces/70 grams each)

Vegetable oil	5 fl oz	150 ml
Shallots, minced	50 each	50 each
Basic Mayonnaise (page 390)	2 qt	1.9 l
Eggs, beaten	10 each	10 each
Pommery mustard	25 oz	700 g
Tabasco sauce	2 tbsp	30 ml
Parsley, chopped	1 cup	240 ml
Chives, minced	10 bunches	10 bunches
Old Bay seasoning	10 oz	285 g
Blue crab meat, picked	12 lb 8 oz	5.65 kg
Saltine cracker crumbs	1 lb 2 oz	510 g
Salt	As needed	As needed
Ground black pepper	As needed	As needed
Peanut oil	As needed	As needed
Roasted Pepper Salad (page 187)	5 pt	2.5 l

1. Heat the vegetable oil over medium-high heat, add the shallots, and sweat until they are translucent, about 6 minutes. Remove from the heat and cool.

2. Combine the mayonnaise, eggs, mustard, Tabasco, parsley, chives, and Old Bay with the shallots. Fold the mayonnaise mixture into the crabmeat without shredding. Fold in the cracker crumbs. Season with salt and pepper.

3. Divide the mixture into 2½-oz/70-g servings and form into small cakes 1½ inches/ 38 mm in diameter and ¾ inch/19 mm thick.

4. Heat the peanut oil in a skillet over medium-high heat, add the crab cakes, and sauté until golden brown and cooked through, about 2 minutes per side.

5. Garnish each crab cake with 2 tsp/10 ml of the roasted pepper salad and serve immediately.

BASIC MAYONNAISE

Makes 2 quarts (1.9 liters)

Pasteurized egg yolks	6 oz	170 g
White vinegar	¼ cup	60 ml
Water	¼ cup	60 ml
Dry mustard	2 tbsp	30 ml
Vegetable oil	3 pt	1.4 l
Kosher salt, plus additional as needed	2 tbsp	30 ml
Ground white pepper, plus additional as needed	1 tsp	5 ml
Lemon juice	2 fl oz	60 ml

1. Whisk the egg yolks, vinegar, water, and mustard together until slightly foamy.

2. Add the oil gradually in a thin stream, whipping constantly, until all the oil is incorporated and the mayonnaise is thick.

3. Taste and season the mayonnaise with salt, pepper, and lemon juice.

4. Refrigerate the mayonnaise immediately. Use as needed. Mayonnaise may be held under refrigeration for up to 4 days.

   GREEN MAYONNAISE (SAUCE VERT): Mince 2 oz/60 g cooked spinach. Squeeze it in a piece of cheesecloth to extract the juice. (Reserve the spinach for another use or discard.) Add the juice to the mayonnaise. Add additional chopped herbs, such as parsley, basil, chives, and dill.

Chesapeake-Style Crab Cakes

LOBSTER SALAD WITH BEETS, MANGOS, AVOCADOS, AND ORANGE OIL

Makes 50 portions

Live lobsters (1 lb/450 g each)	25 each	25 each
Red beets, cooked, peeled	15 to 20 each	15 to 20 each
Ripe mangos	15 to 20 each	15 to 20 each
Ripe avocados	15 to 20 each	15 to 20 each
Salt as needed	2 tbsp	30 ml
Ground black pepper, plus additional as needed	2 tsp	10 ml
Orange Oil (see below) as needed	1 pt	480 ml
Tomatoes, peeled, seeded, small dice	1 lb 9 oz	710 g

1. Cook the lobsters by boiling or steaming until they are cooked through, 10 to 12 minutes. Remove them from the pot and cool. Remove the meat from the tail and claw sections. Slice the tail sections in half lengthwise. Remove the vein from each tail section. Reserve the claw and tail meat.

2. Slice the beets about ½ inch/13 mm thick. Use a round cutter to shape into circles, if desired.

3. Peel the mangos and avocados as close to service time as possible. Slice them about ½ inch/13 mm thick.

4. Arrange 2 or 3 slices each of the beets, avocados, and mangos on chilled plates and season with salt and pepper. Top with the lobster, using half of a tail and one claw section per salad. Drizzle a few drops of orange oil over each salad.

5. Garnish each salad with ½ oz/15 g of the diced tomatoes. Brush the lobster with additional oil and serve immediately.

ORANGE OIL

Makes 1 pint (480 milliliters)

Olive oil	1½ cups	360 ml
Extra-virgin olive oil	¾ cup	180 ml
Oranges, zest only, cut into strips	3 each	3 each

1. Combine the oils in a saucepan over low heat and heat to 140°F/60°C. Be extremely careful not to overheat the oil. Remove the oil from the heat and add the zest.

2. Cool the oil to room temperature and infuse it overnight in the refrigerator.

3. Strain the oil through a fine-mesh sieve and then transfer into a bottle or other container.

4. Close the bottle and hold under refrigeration. Use as needed. The oil may be held for up to 5 days.

ADOBO CHICKEN QUESADILLA WITH ROASTED TOMATO SALSA

Makes 50 portions

Garlic, minced	1½ oz	40 g
Salt	2 tbsp	30 ml
Oregano, preferably Mexican, picked	3 oz	85 g
Ground cumin	2 tbsp	30 ml
Cilantro, chopped	3 oz	85 g
Cider vinegar	1 qt 6 fl oz	1.12 l
Lime juice	1½ cups	360 ml
Olive oil	1½ cups	360 ml
Chicken breasts, boneless, skinless	6 lb 4 oz	2.8 kg
Jack cheese, shredded	3 lb	1.4 kg
Green onions, minced	2 oz	60 g
Jalapeños, minced	1½ oz	40 g
Flour tortillas, 5 inches/13 cm	50 each	50 each
Olive oil spray	As needed	As needed
Sour cream	1½ lb	680 g
Roasted Tomato Salsa (page 121)	1½ qt	1.4 l

1. Combine the garlic, salt, oregano, cumin, cilantro, vinegar, lime juice, and oil. Add the chicken and marinate under refrigeration for 1 hour.

2. Grill the chicken on the first side until golden, about 3 minutes. Turn once and grill on the second side until cooked through, 2 to 3 minutes more. Allow the chicken to cool. Shred the chicken and reserve.

3. Combine the cheese, green onions, jalapeño, and shredded chicken. Mix well. Top each tortilla with 3 oz/85 g of the mixture and fold the tortilla in half to enclose the filling.

4. Brush a griddle or skillet with oil and cook the filled tortillas until browned, about 4 minutes per side. Cut into wedges.

5. Top each quesadilla with the sour cream and salsa and serve.

TEQUILA-ROASTED OYSTERS WITH SALSA FRESCA

Makes 50 portions (4 oysters each)

CILANTRO-POBLANO BUTTER		
Butter, room temperature	3 lb	1.4 kg
Poblanos, minced	6 oz	170 g
Cilantro, chopped	1½ oz	40 g
Garlic powder	1 tbsp	15 ml
Salt	2 tbsp	30 ml
Tequila	12½ fl oz	370 ml
Lime juice, fresh	¾ cup	180 ml
ROASTED OYSTERS		
Oysters, cleaned	200 each	200 each
Coarse salt	As needed for a bed	As needed for a bed
Salsa Fresca (page 121)	1½ qt	1.4 l

1. To prepare the cilantro-poblano butter, combine the butter, poblanos, cilantro, garlic powder, salt, tequila, and lime juice in a food processor. Purée until smooth.

2. To make the roasted oysters, remove the top of each shell and run a knife under each oyster to loosen it. Spread coarse salt on sheet pans to a depth of ¼ inch/6 mm. Nestle the oysters in the salt. Top each oyster with ⅓ oz/10 g of the cilantro-poblano butter. Bake in a 425°/220°C oven until heated through, 4 to 6 minutes.

3. Top each oyster with ⅓ oz/10 g of the salsa and serve warm.

TUNA CARPACCIO

Makes 50 portions (2½ ounces/70 grams tuna and 1½ ounces/45 grams salad each)

Bigeye or yellowfin tuna loins, trimmed	7 lb 13 oz	3.5 kg
CROUTONS		
Vegetable oil, as needed for frying	5 pt	2.4 l
White bread, crusts removed, brunoise	3 lb 12 oz	1.7 kg
Salt	As needed	As needed
Ground black pepper	As needed	As needed
SALAD		
Frisée, hearts only	1 lb 4 oz	570 g
Arugula, stemmed	1 lb 4 oz	570 g
Endive	1 lb 4 oz	570 g
Celery leaves	2½ oz	70 g
Red radishes, medium, julienne	30 each	30 each
Fennel fronds	1 lb 4 oz	570 g
Extra-virgin olive oil	1¼ cups	300 ml
Lemon juice	5 fl oz	150 ml
Salt	As needed	As needed
Ground black pepper	As needed	As needed
GARNISH		
Salsa Cruda (see opposite page)	2 qt	1.9 l
Picholine olives	150 each	150 each

1. Refrigerate the tuna to firm it for easier slicing. With a very sharp knife, cut the tuna into slices, 2½ oz/70 g each. Place each slice of tuna between 2 pieces of plastic wrap and pound it paper thin to the same diameter as the plate used for service, being careful not to tear through the tuna.

2. To prepare the croutons, heat the vegetable oil in a sauté pan over medium-high to high heat. Add the bread and pan fry until golden brown. Remove and drain on paper towels. Season with salt and pepper.

3. To prepare the salad, combine the frisée, arugula, endive, celery leaves, radishes, and fennel fronds. Dress lightly with the olive oil and lemon juice. Taste and season with salt and pepper.

4. To assemble each serving, remove the top piece of plastic from a portion of tuna. Turn the tuna over onto the plate, placing it in the center of the plate, and remove the remaining plastic wrap. Place 3 tbsp/45 ml of the salsa on the tuna and spread evenly. Sprinkle about 2 tsp/10 ml of the croutons over the salsa and place a very small amount of salad in the middle. Place 3 olives per plate around the tuna. Garnish with salt and pepper and a drizzle of the remaining lemon juice and olive oil. Serve immediately.

SALSA CRUDA

Makes 2 quarts (1.9 liters)

Extra-virgin olive oil	3 pt 7 fl oz	1.62 l
Red onions, brunoise	11¼ oz	320 g
Capers, nonpareils, salted, rinsed	1 lb 4 oz	570 g
Celery hearts, thinly sliced	12½ oz	355 g
Picholine olives, pitted, roughly chopped	10 oz	285 g
Garlic cloves, minced	10 each	10 each
Jalapeños, brunoise	3 each	3 each
Parsley, chiffonade	10 oz	285 g
Lemon zest, blanched, minced	¾ oz	20 g
Salt	As needed	As needed
Ground black pepper	As needed	As needed

Combine the oil, onions, capers, celery, olives, garlic, jalapenos, parsley, and lemon zest. Taste and season with salt and pepper.

CARPACCIO OF SALMON

Makes 50 portions

Salmon fillets	7 lb 8 oz	3.4 kg
White mushrooms, thinly sliced	3 lb 2 oz	1.4 kg
Cracked black pepper as needed	2½ oz	70 g
Extra-virgin olive oil as needed	20 fl oz	590 ml
Green Mayonnaise (page 390)	6¼ pt	2.95 l

1. Slice the salmon crosswise or at an angle into very thin pieces. For each serving, arrange about 2¼ oz/68 g salmon on a chilled plate, and cover with plastic wrap.

2. Using a spoon, spread out the salmon to the edge of the plate in a thin, even layer. Hold the plated salmon under refrigeration until ready to serve. Remove the plastic wrap just before serving.

3. Garnish each plate with 1 oz/30 g of the mushrooms and sprinkle with the pepper and oil.

4. Serve with 2 oz/60 g of the green mayonnaise on the side.

Tapenade

Makes 8 pounds (3.6 kilograms) or 100 portions (about 1¼ ounces/35 grams each)

Green olives, pitted	3 lb 2 oz	1.4 kg
Black olives, pitted	3 lb 2 oz	1.4 kg
Capers, drained, rinsed	1 lb 14 oz	850 g
Garlic cloves, minced	20 each	20 each
Lemon juice	7½ fl oz	220 ml
Extra-virgin olive oil	20 fl oz	590 ml
Oregano, chopped	1 oz	30 g
Basil, chopped	1 oz	30 g
Ground black pepper	As needed	As needed

1. In a food processor, combine the olives, capers, and garlic. Blend, incorporating the lemon juice and oil slowly, until the mixture is chunky and easy to spread. Do not overmix.

2. Transfer the tapenade to a bowl. Add the oregano and basil and stir to combine. Taste and season with pepper as needed.

3. The tapenade is ready to serve now, or it may be held under refrigeration up to 3 days for later service. Serve with sliced bread or crostini.

MARINATED OLIVES

Makes 50 portions (1 ounce/30 grams each)

Mixed olives (Manzanilla, Gordal, Niçoise, Kalamata, Atalanta, Picholine, Amfissa, Nafplion)	3 lb	1.4 kg
Oregano, preferably Italian or Greek	3 tbsp	45 ml
Rosemary needles	2 tbsp	30 ml
Thyme, picked	1 tbsp	15 ml
Marjoram, picked	1 tbsp	15 ml
Red pepper flakes	1 tsp	5 ml
Lemon, zest only, grated	1 each	1 each
Orange, zest only, grated	1 each	1 each
Extra-virgin olive oil	½ cup	120 ml

1. Spread the olives on paper towels and blot dry to remove most of the brine.

2. In a stainless-steel mixing bowl, combine the olives, oregano, rosemary, thyme, marjoram, red pepper, and citrus zest.

3. Sprinkle with the oil to moisten.

4. Marinate in a covered container at room temperature for up to 8 hours. Stir occasionally to flavor the olives evenly. The olives may be held under refrigeration up to 6 days for later service. Allow the olives to come to room temperature before service.

Warm Risotto Balls with Mozzarella, Harissa, and Red Pepper Coulis

Makes 150 risotto balls, or 50 portions

Extra-virgin olive oil	½ cup	120 ml
Onions, fine dice	8 oz	225 g
Garlic, minced	½ oz	15 g
Arborio rice	2 lb	900 g
Chicken Stock (page 83)	3 qt	2.8 l
Mozzarella, shredded	1 lb	450 g
Kosher salt	1 tbsp	15 ml
Cracked black pepper	1 tbsp	15 ml
Panko bread crumbs	2 lb	900 g
Olive oil for frying	As needed	As needed
Harissa (see opposite page)	½ cup	120 ml
Red Pepper Coulis (see opposite page)	4½ pt	2.2 l

1. Heat the oil in a deep pot over medium-high heat. Add the onions and garlic and sweat, stirring occasionally, until the onions are softened and translucent, 6 to 8 minutes.

2. Add the rice and mix thoroughly with the oil. Cook, stirring constantly, until the mixture gives off a toasted aroma, about 1 minute.

3. Add one-third of the stock to the rice and cook, stirring constantly, until the rice has absorbed the stock, 6 to 7 minutes. Repeat, adding the remaining stock in two more portions, allowing each to be absorbed before adding the next. Cook the risotto until the rice is just tender and most of the liquid is absorbed; the total cooking time is about 20 minutes. The rice should be creamy.

4. Fold in the cheese and then taste and season with salt and pepper. Pour into hotel pans and spread into an even layer. Chill the risotto completely under refrigeration.

5. Form the mixture into 1-oz/30-g balls. Roll each ball in the panko bread crumbs, coating evenly. Reserve on parchment paper–lined sheet pans under refrigeration up to 4 hours before frying.

6. At the time of service, heat the oil to 375°F/190°C in a deep fryer. Deep fry the risotto balls in the oil until golden and crisp, about 3 minutes. Blot the risotto balls on paper towels.

7. Serve immediately with the harissa and red pepper coulis.

HARISSA

Makes 2½ quarts (2.4 liters)

Dried habaneros	16 each	16 each
Red chiles, fresh, seeded, stemmed	4 lb	1.8 kg
Sun-dried tomatoes	1 lb	450 g
Garlic, crushed in salt	1½ oz	45 g
Turmeric	1½ oz	45 g
Ground coriander	2 tsp	10 ml
Ground cumin	2 tsp	10 ml
Caraway seeds	2 tsp	10 ml
Lemon juice	2 tsp	10 ml
Olive oil	¼ cup	60 ml

1. Toast the habaneros in a dry sauté pan over medium heat until the skin darkens and a small amount of smoke rises, about 15 seconds per side. Transfer the chiles to a bowl and add enough warm water to cover them. When they are soft and hydrated, about 20 minutes, drain and remove the stems and seeds.

2. Place the habaneros, red chiles, sun-dried tomatoes, garlic, turmeric, coriander, cumin, and caraway seeds in a blender and blend until smooth and homogeneous.

3. Add the lemon juice and oil. The harissa is ready to serve now, or it may be held under refrigeration up to 7 days for later service.

RED PEPPER COULIS

Makes 2 quarts (1.9 liters)

Olive oil	¼ cup	60 ml
Shallots, minced	1 oz	30 g
Red peppers, peeled, seeded, chopped	3 lb 8 oz	1.3 kg
Kosher salt, plus additional as needed	2 tbsp	30 ml
Ground black pepper, plus additional as needed	2 tsp	10 ml
Dry white wine	½ cup	120 ml
Chicken Stock (page 83)	1 cup	240 ml
Heavy cream (optional)	2 to 3 fl oz	60 to 90 ml

1. Heat the oil in a rondeau over medium heat. Add the shallots and sweat until they are tender, about 2 minutes. Add the peppers and continue to sweat until they are very tender, about 12 minutes. Season with salt and pepper.

Continued

2. Add the wine to deglaze the pan and simmer until the wine has nearly cooked away, about 6 minutes. Add the stock and simmer until the liquid is reduced by half, about 5 minutes.

3. Purée the sauce in a food processor or blender until very smooth. Add the cream, if using, to the puréed sauce. Taste the coulis and adjust seasoning with salt and pepper.

4. The coulis is ready to serve now, or it may be rapidly cooled and held under refrigeration for up to 3 days for later service.

Warm Risotto Balls with Mozzarella (page 406)

Beef Saté with Peanut Sauce

Makes 100 skewers, or 50 portions (2 skewers and ¾ fluid ounce/20 milliliters sauce)

PEANUT SAUCE		
Peanut oil	2½ fl oz	75 ml
Garlic, minced	½ oz	15 g
Shallots, minced	2½ oz	70 g
Thai chile paste	5 tsp	25 ml
Lime zest, minced	2½ tsp	13 ml
Curry powder	1¼ tsp	6 ml
Lemongrass, minced	2 tbsp	30 ml
Coconut milk	15 fl oz	450 ml
Tamarind pulp	2½ tsp	13 ml
Fish sauce (nuoc mam)	2½ fl oz	75 ml
Palm sugar	2½ oz	70 g
Lime juice	2 tbsp	30 ml
Peanuts, roasted and cooled, ground into a paste	15 oz	425 g
Salt	As needed	As needed
Ground black pepper	As needed	As needed
MARINATED BEEF		
Lemongrass, minced	2 tbsp	30 ml
Ginger, minced	5 tsp	25 ml
Garlic, minced	5 tsp	25 ml
Thai chile paste	2½ tsp	13 ml
Curry powder	5 tsp	25 ml
Palm sugar	2½ oz	70 g
Fish sauce (nuoc mam)	5 fl oz	150 ml
Flank steak, cut into strips 1 by 4 by ⅛ inches/ 25 by 100 by 3 mm	6¼ lb	2.4 kg

1. To prepare the peanut sauce, heat the oil in a sauté pan over medium-high heat. Add the garlic, shallots, chile paste, lime zest, curry powder, and lemongrass. Stir fry until aromatic, about 2 minutes.

2. Add the coconut milk, tamarind, fish sauce, palm sugar, lime juice, and peanut paste. Simmer the sauce until flavorful, about 20 minutes. Taste and season with salt and pepper. Cool the sauce to room temperature. If prepared in advance, the sauce may be held under refrigeration for up to 2 days.

Continued

3. To prepare the marinated beef, combine the lemongrass, ginger, garlic, chile paste, curry powder, palm sugar, and fish sauce. Add the beef, tossing to coat the beef evenly, cover, and marinate under refrigeration for 1 hour.

4. Soak skewers in cold water for 30 minutes. Thread 1 piece of beef onto a skewer, continuing until all the beef has been skewered. Allow any excess marinade to drain from the beef before grilling; blot if necessary. Grill the beef over high heat until hot, about 30 seconds to 1 minute per side.

5. Serve immediately with the peanut sauce for dipping.

Beef Saté with Peanut Sauce (page 409)

GRILLED PORK TENDERLOIN SKEWERS WITH GINGERED BARBECUE SAUCE

Makes 100 skewers, or 50 portions (2 skewers and 1 fluid ounce/30 milliliters sauce)

Onions, minced	3 lb	1.4 kg
Garlic, minced	2 oz	60 g
Thyme, picked	1½ oz	40 g
Salt	3 tbsp	45 ml
Ground black pepper	1 tbsp	15 ml
Molasses	1½ pt	720 ml
White wine	2½ pt	1.2 l
Soy sauce	1½ cups	360 ml
Olive oil	1½ cups	360 ml
Pork tenderloin, trimmed, cut into strips 1 by 5 by ⅛ inches/25 by 130 by 3 mm	12 lb 8 oz	5.65 kg
Gingered Barbecue Sauce (page 412)	3 pt	1.4 l

1. Combine the onions, garlic, thyme, salt, pepper, molasses, wine, soy sauce, and oil. Purée in a blender until smooth. Pour over the pork strips and marinate under refrigeration for at least 1 and up to 12 hours.

2. Soak skewers in cold water for 30 minutes. Thread 1 piece of pork onto a skewer, continuing until all the pork has been skewered. Allow any excess marinade to drain from the pork before grilling; blot if necessary. Grill the pork over medium-high heat until cooked through, 4 to 5 minutes per side. Let rest for 5 to 6 minutes before serving.

3. Serve with the barbecue sauce for dipping.

GINGERED BARBECUE SAUCE

Makes 3½ quarts (3.3 liters)

Vegetable oil	1 cup	240 ml
Onions, minced	3 lb	1.3 kg
Ginger, grated	4 oz	115 g
Garlic, minced	3 oz	85 g
Tomatoes, peeled, seeded, chopped	12 lb	5.4 kg
Sugar	3 oz	85 g
Ground cloves	1 tsp	5 ml
Salt	2 tbsp	30 ml
Ground black pepper	1 tsp	5 ml
Soy sauce	¼ cup	60 ml

1. Heat the oil in a rondeau or sauce pot over medium-high heat. Add the onions and sauté until they are golden and slightly caramelized, 10 to 15 minutes.

2. Add the ginger and garlic and continue to cook, stirring constantly, until aromatic, about 2 minutes.

3. Add the tomatoes, sugar, cloves, salt, pepper, and soy sauce and bring to a simmer. Simmer until the sauce is thick and shiny, about 10 minutes.

4. The sauce is ready to serve now, or it may be rapidly cooled and held under refrigeration for up to 5 days for later service.

GLOSSARY

ACID: A substance that tests lower than 7 on the pH scale. Acids have a sour or sharp flavor. Acidity occurs naturally in many foods, including citrus juice, vinegar, wine, and sour milk products. Acids also act as tenderizers in marinades, helping to break down connective tissues and cell walls.

ADULTERATED FOOD: Food that has been contaminated to the point that it is considered unfit for human consumption.

AEROBIC BACTERIA: Bacteria that require the presence of oxygen to function.

À LA CARTE: A menu in which the patron makes individual selections from various menu categories; each item is priced separately.

ALBUMIN: The egg white. Makes up about 70 percent of the egg and contains most of the protein in the egg.

AL DENTE: Literally, "to the tooth"; refers to an item, such as pasta or vegetables, cooked until it is tender but still firm, not soft.

ALKALI: A substance that tests at higher than 7 on the pH scale. Alkalis are sometimes described as having a slightly soapy flavor and can be used to balance acids. Olives and baking soda are some of the few alkaline foods.

ALL'ONDA: Description of doneness for risotto and similar porridges; indicates that risotto flows in a wave-like manner when served.

ALLUMETTE: Vegetables, usually potatoes, cut into pieces the size and shape of matchsticks, ⅛ inch by ⅛ inch by 1 to 2 inches/3 mm by 3 mm by 3 to 5 cm. Also called *julienne*.

AMINO ACIDS: The building blocks of proteins. Of the twenty amino acids in the human diet, nine are called "essential" because they cannot be produced by the body and must be supplied through a person's diet.

AMUSE-GUEULE: French for "tidbit"; a small portion (one or two bites) of something exotic, unusual, or otherwise special that is served when the guests in a restaurant are seated. The amuse is not listed on a menu and is included in the price of an entrée. Also knowns as *chef's tasting*.

ANAEROBIC BACTERIA: Bacteria that do not require oxygen to function.

ANTIOXIDANTS: Naturally occurring substances that retard the breakdown of tissues in the presence of oxygen. May be added to food during processing or may occur naturally. Help to prevent food from becoming rancid or discolored due to oxidation.

ANTIPASTO: Literally, "before the meal." Typically, a platter of hot or cold hors d'oeuvre that includes meats, olives, cheeses, and vegetables.

APÉRITIF: A light alcoholic beverage consumed before the meal to stimulate the appetite.

APPAREIL: A prepared mixture of ingredients used alone or in another preparation.

APPETIZER: Light food served before a meal or as the first course of a meal. May be hot or cold, plated or served as finger food.

AQUACULTURE: The farm raising of fish or shellfish in natural or controlled marine tanks or ponds.

ARBORIO: A high-starch, short-grain rice traditionally used in the preparation of risotto.

AROMATICS: Ingredients, such as herbs, spices, vegetables, citrus fruits, wines, and vinegars, used to enhance the flavor and fragrance of food.

ARROWROOT: A powdered starch made from the root of a tropical plant of the same name. Used primarily as a thickener. Remains clear when cooked.

ASPIC: A clear jelly made from stock (or occasionally fruit or vegetable juices) thickened with gelatin. Used to coat foods, or cubed and used as a garnish.

AS-PURCHASED WEIGHT (APW): The weight of an item as received from the supplier before trimming or other preparation [as opposed to edible-portion weight (EPW)].

BACTERIA: Microscopic organisms. Some have beneficial properties; others can cause food-borne illnesses when contaminated foods are ingested.

BAIN-MARIE: The French term for a water bath used to cook foods gently by surrounding the cooking vessel with simmering water. Also, a set of cylindrical nesting pots used to hold foods in a water bath or with a single, long handle used as a double boiler. Also, steam table inserts.

BAKE: To cook food by surrounding it with dry heat in a closed environment, as in an oven.

BARBECUE: To cook food by grilling it over a wood or charcoal fire. Usually some sort of marinade or sauce is brushed on the item during cooking. Also, meat that is cooked in this way.

BATCH COOKING: A cooking technique in which appropriately sized batches of food are prepared several times throughout a service period so that a fresh supply of cooked items is always available.

BATON/BATONNET: Items cut into pieces somewhat larger than allumette or julienne, ¼ inch by ¼ inch by 1 to 2 inches/6 mm by 6 mm by 3 to 5 cm. French for "stick" or "small stick."

BLANCH: To cook an item briefly in boiling water or hot fat before finishing or storing it. Blanching preserves the color, lessens strong flavors, and helps remove the peels of some fruits and vegetables.

BLEND: A mixture of two or more flavors combined to achieve a particular flavor or quality. Also, to mix two or more ingredients together until combined.

BOIL: To cook an item by immersing it in liquid at or above the boiling point (212°F/100°C).

BOUQUET GARNI: A small bundle of herbs tied with string. It is used to flavor stocks, braises, and other preparations. Usually contains bay leaf, parsley, thyme, and possibly other aromatics wrapped in leek leaves.

BRAISE: To cook a main item, usually meat, by searing it in fat, then simmering it at a low temperature in a small amount of stock or another liquid (usually halfway up the main item) in a covered vessel for a long time. The cooking liquid is then reduced and used as the base of a sauce.

BRAN: The outer layer of a cereal grain and the part highest in fiber.

BRAZIER/BRASIER: A pan, designed specifically for braising, that usually has two handles and a tight-fitting lid. It is often round but may be square or rectangular. Also called a *rondeau*.

BRINE: A solution of salt, water, and seasonings, used to preserve or moisten foods.

BROIL: To cook by means of a radiant heat source placed above the food.

BROILER: The piece of equipment used to broil foods.

BROTH: A flavorful, aromatic liquid made by simmering water or stock with meat, vegetables, and/or spices and herbs.

BROWN SAUCE: A sauce made from a brown stock and aromatics and thickened by roux, a pure starch slurry, and/or a reduction; includes espagnole sauce, demi-glace, jus de veau lié, and pan sauces.

BROWN STOCK: An amber liquid produced by simmering browned bones and meat (usually veal or beef) with vegetables and aromatics (including caramelized mirepoix and tomato purée).

BRUISE: To partially crush a food item in order to release its flavor.

BRUNOISE: Dice cut of ⅛-inch/3-mm cubes. For a brunoise cut, items are first cut in julienne, then cut crosswise. For a fine brunoise, ¹⁄₁₆-inch/2-mm cubes, cut items first in fine julienne.

BUTTERFLY: To cut an item (usually meat or seafood) and open out the edges like a book or the wings of a butterfly.

BUTTERMILK: A dairy beverage with a slightly sour flavor similar to that of yogurt. Traditionally buttermilk was the liquid byproduct of butter churning; today it is usually made by culturing skim milk.

CALORIE: A unit used to measure food energy. It is the amount of energy needed to raise the temperature of 1 kilogram of water by 1°C.

CANAPÉ: An hors d'oeuvre consisting of a small piece of bread or toast, often cut in a decorative shape, garnished with a savory spread or topping.

CARAMELIZATION: The process of browning sugar in the presence of heat. The caramelization of sugar occurs between 320° and 360°F/160° and 182°C.

CARBOHYDRATE: One of the basic nutrients used by the body as a source of energy. Types include simple (sugars) and complex (starches and fibers).

CARBON DIOXIDE: A colorless, tasteless, edible gas obtained through fermentation or from the combination of soda and acid, which acts to leaven baked goods.

CARRY-OVER COOKING: Heat retained in cooked foods that allows them to continue cooking even after removal from the cooking medium. It is especially important in roasted foods.

CARTOUCHE: a paper lid with a vent, used to cover foods as they steam or shallow poach.

CELLULOSE: A complex carbohydrate; the main structural component of plant cells.

CEPHALOPOD: Marine creatures whose tentacles and arms are attached directly to their heads, such as squid and octopus.

CHIFFONADE: Leafy vegetables or herbs cut into fine shreds; often used as a garnish.

CHILE: The fruit of certain types of capsicum peppers (not related to black pepper), used fresh or dry as a seasoning. Chiles come in many types (e.g., jalapeño, serrano, and poblano) and in varying degrees of spiciness.

CHILI: A stewed dish flavored with chili powder, meat, and beans (optional).

CHILI POWDER: Dried chiles that have been ground or crushed, often with other ground spices and herbs added.

CHINE: Backbone, or a cut of meat that includes the backbone. Also, to separate the backbone and ribs to facilitate carving.

CHINOIS: A conical sieve used for straining foods through a fine wire mesh.

CHOLESTEROL: A substance found exclusively in animal products such as meat, eggs, and cheese (dietary cholesterol) or in the blood (serum cholesterol).

CHOP: To cut into pieces of roughly the same size. Also, a small cut of meat including part of the rib.

CHOWDER: A thick soup that may be made from a variety of ingredients but usually contains potatoes.

CIGUATERA TOXIN: A toxin found in certain fish that is harmless to the fish but causes illness in humans when eaten. The poisoning is caused by the fish's diet and is not eradicated by cooking or freezing.

CLARIFICATION: The process of removing solid impurities from a liquid (such as butter or stock). Also, a mixture of ground meat, egg whites, mirepoix, tomato purée, herbs, and spices used to clarify broth for consommé.

COAGULATION: The curdling or clumping of proteins, usually due to the application of heat or acid.

COARSE CHOP: A type of preparation in which food is cut into pieces of roughly the same size. Used for items such as mirepoix, where appearance is not important.

COCOA: The pods of the cacao tree, processed to remove the cocoa butter and ground into powder. Used as a flavoring.

COLLAGEN: A fibrous protein found in the connective tissue of animals, used to make glue and gelatin. Breaks down into gelatin when cooked in a moist environment for an extended period of time.

COMBINATION METHOD: A cooking method that involves the application of both dry and moist heat to the main item (e.g., meats seared in fat then simmered in a sauce for braising or stewing).

COMPLETE PROTEIN: A food source that provides all of the essential amino acids in the correct ratio so that they can be used in the body for protein synthesis. May require more than one ingredient (such as beans and rice together).

COMPLEX CARBOHYDRATE: A large molecule made up of long chains of sugar molecules. In food, these molecules are found in starches and fiber.

COMPOSED SALAD: A salad in which the items are carefully arranged on a plate, rather than tossed together.

CONCASSER: To pound or chop coarsely. *Concassé* usually refers to tomatoes that have been peeled, seeded, and chopped.

CONDIMENT: An aromatic mixture, such as pickles, chutney, and some sauces and relishes, that accompanies food. Usually kept on the table throughout service.

CONDUCTION: A method of heat transfer in which heat is transmitted through another substance. In cooking, the transmission of heat to food through a pot or pan, oven racks, or grill rods.

CONSOMMÉ: Broth that has been clarified using a mixture of ground meat, egg whites, and other ingredients that trap impurities, resulting in a perfectly clear broth.

CONVECTION: A method of heat transfer in which heat is transmitted through the circulation of air or water.

CONVECTION OVEN: An oven that employs convection currents by forcing hot air through fans so it circulates around food, cooking it quickly and evenly.

CONVERTED RICE: Rice that has been pressure steamed and dried before milling to remove surface starch and retain nutrients. Also called *parboiled rice.*

CORNSTARCH: A fine, white powder milled from dried corn; used primarily as a thickener for sauce and occasionally as an ingredient in batters.

COTTAGE CHEESE: A fresh cheese made from the drained curd of soured cow's milk.

COULIS: A thick purée of vegetables or fruit, served hot or cold. Traditionally refers to the thickened juices of cooked meat, fish, or shellfish purée or certain thick soups.

COURT BOUILLON: Literally, "short broth." An aromatic vegetable broth that usually includes an acidic ingredient, such as wine or vinegar; most commonly used for poaching fish.

COUSCOUS: Pellets of semolina or cracked wheat usually cooked by steaming, traditionally in a couscoussière. Also, the stew with which this grain is traditionally served.

COUSCOUSSIÈRE: A set of nesting pots, similar to a steamer, used to cook couscous.

CROSS CONTAMINATION: The transference of disease-causing elements from one source to another through physical contact.

CRUSTACEAN: A class of hard-shelled arthropods with elongated bodies, primarily aquatic, which includes edible species such as lobster, crab, shrimp, and crayfish.

CUISSON: Shallow-poaching liquid, including stock, fumet, or other liquid, which may be reduced and used as a base for the poached item's sauce.

CURRY: A mixture of spices, used primarily in Indian cuisine. May include turmeric, coriander, cumin, cayenne or other chiles, cardamom, cinnamon, cloves, fennel, fenugreek, ginger, and garlic. Also, a stew-like dish seasoned with curry.

DAILY VALUES (DV): Standard nutritional values developed by the U.S. Food and Drug Administration for use on food labels.

DANGER ZONE: The temperature range from 40° to 140°F/4° to 60°C; the most favorable condition for rapid growth of many pathogens.

DEBEARD: To remove the shaggy, inedible fibers from a mussel. These fibers anchor the mussel to its mooring.

DECK OVEN: An oven in which the heat source is located underneath the deck or floor of the oven and the food is placed directly on the deck instead of on a rack.

DEEP FRY: To cook food by immersion in hot fat. Deep-fried foods are often coated with bread crumbs or batter before being cooked.

DEEP POACH: To cook food gently in enough simmering liquid to completely submerge the food.

DEGLAZE/DÉGLACER: To use a liquid, such as wine, water, or stock, to dissolve food particles and/or caramelized drippings left in a pan after roasting or sautéing. The resulting mix then becomes the base for the accompanying sauce.

DEGREASE/DÉGRAISSER: To skim the fat off the surface of a liquid, such as a stock or sauce.

DEMI-GLACE: Literally, "half-glaze." A mixture of equal proportions of brown stock and brown sauce that has been reduced by half. One of the grand sauces.

DÉPOUILLAGE: To skim the impurities from the surface of a cooking liquid, such as a stock or sauce. This action is simplified by placing the pot off center on the burner (convection simmer) and skimming impurities as they collect at one side of the pot.

DICE: To cut ingredients into evenly sized small cubes. The standard sizes are ¼ inch/6 mm for small, ½ inch/13 mm for medium, and ¾ inch/19 mm for large.

DIE: The plate in a meat grinder through which foods pass just before a blade cuts them. The size of the die's opening determines the fineness of the grind.

DIRECT HEAT: A method of heat transfer in which heat waves radiate from a source (e.g., an open burner or grill) and travel directly to the item being heated with no conductor between heat source and food. Examples are grilling, broiling, and toasting. Also called *radiant heat.*

DREDGE: To coat food with a dry ingredient such as flour or bread crumbs prior to frying or sautéing.

DRESSED: Prepared for cooking. A dressed fish is gutted and scaled, and its head, tail, and fins are removed (also called *pan-dressed*). Dressed poultry is plucked, gutted, singed, trimmed, and trussed. Also, coated with dressing, as in a salad.

DRY SAUTÉ: To sauté without fat, usually using a nonstick pan.

DURUM: A very hard wheat typically milled into semolina, which is primarily used in the making of pasta.

DUST: To distribute a film of flour, sugar, cocoa powder, or other such ingredients on pans or work surfaces, or on finished products as a garnish.

DUTCH OVEN: A kettle, usually of cast iron, used for stewing and braising on the stovetop or in the oven.

DUTCH PROCESS: A method for treating cocoa powder with an alkali to reduce its acidity.

DUXELLES: An appareil of finely chopped mushrooms and shallots sautéed gently in butter; used as a stuffing or garnish, or as a flavoring in soups and sauces.

EDIBLE-PORTION WEIGHT(EPW): The weight of an item after trimming and preparation [as opposed to the as-purchased weight (APW)].

EGG WASH: A mixture of beaten eggs (whole eggs, yolks, or whites) and a liquid, usually milk or water, used to coat baked goods to give them a sheen.

ÉMINCÉ: A cut for meats, fish and poultry that produces fine shreds or small thin strips.

EMULSION: A mixture of two or more liquids, one of which is a fat or oil and the other of which is water based, so that tiny globules of one are suspended in the other. This may involve the use of stabilizers, such as egg or mustard. Emulsions may be temporary, permanent, or semipermanent.

ENDOSPERM: The largest portion of the inside of the seed of a flowering plant, such as wheat; composed primarily of starch and protein. This is the portion used primarily in milled grain products.

ESSENCE: A concentrated flavoring extracted from an item, usually by infusion or distillation. Includes items such as vanilla and other extracts, concentrated stocks, and fumets.

ESTOUFFADE: A French stew with wine-moistened pieces of meat. Also, a type of rich brown stock based on pork knuckle and veal and beef bones that is often used in braises.

ETHYLENE GAS: A gas emitted by various fruits and vegetables; ethylene gas speeds ripening, maturing, and eventually rotting.

ÉTOUFFÉE: Literally, "smothered." Refers to food cooked by a method similar to braising, except that items are cooked with little or no added liquid in a pan with a tight-fitting lid. (Also called *étuver, à l'étuvée.*) Also, a Cajun dish made with a dark roux, crayfish, vegetables, and seasonings over a bed of white rice.

EVAPORATED MILK: Unsweetened canned milk from which 60 percent of the water has been removed before canning. It is often used in custards and to create a creamy texture in food.

FACULTATIVE BACTERIA: Bacteria that can survive both with and without oxygen.

FIBER/DIETARY FIBER: The structural component of plants that is necessary to the human diet and is indigestible. Also called *roughage.*

FILÉ POWDER: A thickener made from ground dried sassafras leaves; used primarily in gumbos.

FINES HERBES: A mixture of herbs, usually parsley, chervil, tarragon, and chives, that lose their flavor quickly. It is generally added to the dish just prior to serving.

FIRST IN, FIRST OUT (FIFO): A fundamental storage principle based on stock rotation. Products are stored and used so that the oldest product is always used first.

FISH POACHER: A long, narrow pot with straight sides and possibly a perforated rack; used for poaching whole fish.

FIVE-SPICE POWDER: A mixture of equal parts ground cinnamon, cloves, fennel seeds, star anise, and Szechwan peppercorns.

FLATFISH: A type of fish characterized by a flat body and eyes on one side of its head (e.g., sole, plaice, flounder, and halibut).

FLATTOP: A thick plate of cast iron or steel set over the heat source on a range; diffuses heat, making it a more even heat source than an open burner.

FOLD: To gently combine ingredients (especially foams) so as not to release trapped air bubbles. Also, to gently mix together two items, usually a light, airy mixture with a denser mixture. Also, the method of turning, rolling, and layering dough over on itself to produce a flaky texture.

FOND: The French term for "stock." Also, the pan drippings remaining after sautéing or roasting food, which are often deglazed and used as a base for sauces.

FOOD-BORNE ILLNESS: An illness in humans caused by the consumption of an adulterated food product. For an official determination that an outbreak of food-borne illness has occurred, two or more people must have become ill after eating the same food, and the outbreak must have been confirmed by health officials.

FOOD MILL: A strainer with a crank-operated, curved blade. It is used to purée soft foods while straining.

FOOD PROCESSOR: A machine with interchangeable blades and disks and a removable bowl and lid separate from the motor housing. It can be used for a variety of tasks, including chopping, grinding, puréeing, emulsifying, kneading, slicing, shredding, and cutting into julienne.

FORK-TENDER: A degree of doneness in braised foods and vegetables; fork-tender foods are easily pierced or cut by a fork, or should slide readily from a fork when lifted.

FREE-RANGE: Refers to livestock that is raised unconfined.

FRENCHING: The process of cutting and scraping meat from rib bones before cooking.

FRUCTOSE: A simple sugar found in fruits. Fructose is the sweetest simple sugar.

FUMET: A type of stock in which the main flavoring ingredient is allowed to cook in a covered pot with wine and aromatics. Fish fumet is the most common type.

GARNISH: An edible decoration or accompaniment to a dish or item.

GASTRIQUE: A combination of sweet and sour ingredients used as the flavoring for a sauce; the sugar is allowed to caramelize and is then dissolved in an acidic liquid such as orange juice.

GAZPACHO: A cold soup made from vegetables, typically tomatoes, cucumbers, peppers, and onions.

GELATIN: A protein-based substance found in animal bones and connective tissue. When dissolved in hot liquid and then cooled, it can be used as a thickener and stabilizer.

GELATINIZATION: A phase in the process of thickening a liquid with starch in which the starch molecules swell to form a network that traps water molecules.

GERM: The portion of the seed of flowering plants, such as wheat, that sprouts to form a new plant; the embryo of the new plant.

GLACE: Reduced stock. Also, ice cream.

GLUCOSE: A simple sugar found in honey, some fruits, and many vegetables. It has about half the sweetness of table sugar and is the preferred source of energy for the human body.

GLUTEN: A protein that develops when the gliadin and glutenin present in wheat flour are moistened and mixed, forming elastic strands that build structure and aid in leavening.

GRIDDLE: A heavy metal cooking surface, which may be either fitted with handles, built into a stove, or heated by its own gas or electric element. Cooking is done directly on the griddle.

GRILL: To cook foods using a radiant heat source placed below the food. Also, the piece of equipment on which grilling is done. Grills may be fueled by gas, electricity, charcoal, or wood.

GRILL PAN: A skillet with ridges that is used on the stovetop to simulate grilling.

GRISWOLD: A pot, similar to a rondeau, made of cast iron; may have a single short handle rather than the usual loop handles.

GUMBO: A Creole soup/stew thickened with filé powder or okra and a dark roux, and flavored with a variety of meats and fishes.

HAZARD ANALYSIS CRITICAL CONTROL POINT (HACCP): A monitoring system used to track foods from the time that they are received until the time that they are served to consumers, to ensure that the foods are free from contamination. Standards and controls are established for time and temperature, as well as for safe handling practices.

HOMINY: Corn that has been milled or treated with a lye solution to remove the bran and germ. Ground hominy is known as *grits*.

HOMOGENIZATION: A process used to prevent the milk fat from separating out of milk products. The liquid is forced through an ultrafine mesh at high pressure, which breaks up fat globules, dispersing them evenly throughout the liquid.

HORS D'OEUVRE: Literally, "outside the work." An appetizer.

HOTEL PAN: A rectangular metal pan in any of a number of standard sizes, with a lip that allows it to rest in a storage shelf or steam table.

HYDROGENATION: The process in which hydrogen atoms are added to an unsaturated fat molecule, making it partially or completely saturated and solid at room temperature.

HYDROPONICS: A technique that involves growing vegetables in nutrient-enriched water rather than in soil.

HYGIENE: Conditions and practices followed to maintain health, including sanitation and personal cleanliness.

INDUCTION BURNER: A type of heating unit that relies on magnetic attraction between the cooktop and metals in the pot to generate the heat that cooks foods in the pan. Reaction time is significantly faster than with traditional burners.

INFECTION: Contamination by a disease-causing agent, such as bacteria.

INFUSION: Steeping an aromatic or other item in liquid to extract its flavor. Also, the liquid resulting from this process.

INSTANT-READ THERMOMETER: A thermometer used to measure the internal temperature of foods. The stem is inserted in the food, producing an instant temperature reading.

INTOXICATION: Poisoning. A state of being tainted with toxins, particularly those produced by microorganisms that have infected food.

JULIENNE: Vegetables, potatoes, or other items cut into thin strips, ⅛ inch by ⅛ inch by 1 to 2 inches/3 mm by 3 mm by 3 to 5 cm is standard. Fine julienne is 1/16 inch by 1/16 inch by 1 to 2 inches/2 mm by 2 mm by 3 to 5 cm.

JUS: Juice. Refers to fruit and vegetable juices as well as juices from meats. Jus de viande is meat gravy. Meat served au jus is served with its own juice or jus lié.

JUS LIÉ: Meat juice thickened lightly with arrowroot or cornstarch.

KASHA: Buckwheat groats that have been hulled, crushed, and roasted; usually prepared by boiling.

KOSHER: Prepared in accordance with Jewish dietary laws. Also, to salt and soak meat to render it fit for consumption by observant Jews.

KOSHER SALT: Pure, refined salt used for pickling because it does not contain magnesium carbonate and thus does not cloud brine solutions. It is also used to kosher items. Also called *coarse salt* or *pickling salt*.

LACTOSE: The simple sugar found in milk. This disaccharide is the least sweet of the natural sugars.

LEGUME: The seeds of certain pod plants, including beans and peas, which are eaten for their earthy flavors and high nutritional value. Also, the French word for "vegetable."

LIAISON: A mixture of egg yolks and cream used to thicken and enrich sauces. Also loosely applied to any appareil used as a thickener.

LIQUEUR: A spirit flavored with fruit, spices, nuts, herbs, and/or seeds and usually sweetened. It often has a high alcohol content, a viscous body, and a slightly sticky feel. Also called a *cordial*.

LOW-FAT MILK: Milk containing less than 2 percent fat.

LOZENGE CUT: A knife cut in which foods are cut into small diamond shapes about 1/8 inch/2 mm thick with the sides of each piece about 1/2 inch/13 mm long.

MAILLARD REACTION: A complex browning reaction that results in the particular flavor and color of foods that do not contain much sugar, including roasted meats. The reaction, which involves carbohydrates and amino acids, is named after the French scientist who first discovered it. There are low-temperature and high-temperature Maillard reactions; the high-temperature reaction starts at 310°F/154°C.

MANDOLINE: A slicing device of stainless steel with carbon-steel blades. The blades may be adjusted to cut items into various shapes and thicknesses.

MARBLING: The intramuscular fat found in meat that makes it tender and juicy.

MARINADE: An appareil used before cooking to flavor and moisten foods; may be liquid or dry. Liquid marinades are usually based on an acidic ingredient, such as wine or vinegar; dry marinades are usually salt based.

MARK ON A GRILL: To turn a food (without flipping it over) 90 degrees after it has been on the grill for several seconds to create the cross-hatching associated with grilled foods.

MEDALLION: A small, round scallop of meat.

MERINGUE: Egg whites beaten with sugar until they stiffen. Types include regular or common, Italian, and Swiss.

MESOPHILIC: A term used to describe bacteria that thrive in temperatures between 60° and 100°F/16° and 38°C.

METABOLISM: The sum of chemical processes in living cells by which energy is provided and new material is assimilated.

MILLET: A small, round, glutenless grain that may be boiled or ground into flour.

MILLING: The process by which grain is separated into germ/husk, bran, and endosperm and ground into flour or meal.

MINCE: To chop into very small pieces.

MINERAL: An inorganic element that is an essential component of the diet. Provides no energy and is therefore considered a noncaloric nutrient. The body cannot produce minerals; they must be obtained from the diet.

MINESTRONE: A hearty vegetable soup that typically includes dried beans and pasta.

MINUTE, À LA: Literally, "at the minute." A restaurant production approach in which dishes are not prepared until an order arrives in the kitchen.

MIREPOIX: A combination of chopped aromatic vegetables—usually two parts onion, one part carrot, and one part celery—used to flavor stocks, soups, braises, and stews.

MISE EN PLACE: Literally, "put in place." The preparation and assembly of ingredients, pans, utensils, and plates or serving pieces needed for a particular dish or service period.

MOLASSES: The dark brown, sweet syrup that is a by-product of sugarcane and sugar beet refining. Molasses is available as light (the least cooked but sweetest), dark, and blackstrap (the most cooked and most bitter).

MOLLUSK: Any of a number of invertebrate animals with soft, unsegmented bodies usually enclosed in a hard shell; mollusks include gastropods (univalves), bivalves, and cephalopods. Examples include clams, oysters, snails, octopus, and squid.

MONOSODIUM GLUTAMATE (MSG): A flavor enhancer derived from glutamic acid, without a distinct flavor of its own; used primarily in Chinese and processed foods. It may cause allergic reactions in some people.

MONOUNSATURATED FAT: A fat with one available bonding site not filled with a hydrogen atom. It is helpful in lowering the LDL cholesterol level (the bad cholesterol). Food sources include avocados, olives, and nuts.

NAPPÉ: To coat with sauce. Also, the consistency of a sauce that will coat the back of a spoon.

NOISETTE: A hazelnut, or hazelnut colored. Also, a small portion of meat cut from the rib. Pommes noisette are tournéed potatoes browned in butter. Beurre noisette is browned butter.

NONBONY FISH: Fish whose skeletons are made of cartilage rather than hard bone (e.g., shark and skate). Also called *cartilaginous fish*.

NUTRIENT: A basic component of food used by the body for growth, repair, restoration, and energy. Includes carbohydrates, fats, proteins, water, vitamins, and minerals.

NUTRITION: The process by which an organism takes in and uses food.

OBLIQUE CUT: A knife cut used primarily with long, cylindrical vegetables such as carrots. The item is cut on a diagonal, rolled 180 degrees, then cut on the same diagonal, producing a piece with two angled edges. Also called *roll cut*.

OIGNON BRÛLÉ: Literally, "burnt onion." A peeled, halved onion seared on a flattop or in a skillet and used to enhance the color of stock and consommé.

OIGNON PIQUÉ: Literally, "pricked onion." A whole, peeled onion to which a bay leaf is attached, using a clove as a tack. It is used to flavor béchamel sauce and some soups.

OMEGA-3 FATTY ACIDS: Polyunsaturated fatty acids that may reduce the risk of heart disease and tumor growth, stimulate the immune system, and lower blood pressure; they occur in fatty fish, dark green leafy vegetables, and certain nuts and oils.

OMELET: Beaten eggs that are cooked in butter in a specialized pan or skillet and then rolled or folded into an oval. Omelets may be filled with a variety of ingredients before or after rolling.

ORGANIC LEAVENER: Yeast. A living organism acting to produce carbon dioxide gas, which will cause a batter or dough to rise through the fermentation process.

ORGAN MEAT: Meat from an organ, rather than the muscle tissue, of an animal. Includes kidneys, heart, liver, sweetbreads, and the like.

PAELLA: A dish of rice cooked with onion, tomato, garlic, vegetables, and various meats, including chicken, chorizo, shellfish, and possibly game. A paella pan is a specialized pan for cooking paella; it is wide and shallow and usually has two loop handles.

PAILLARD: A scallop of meat pounded until thin. It is usually grilled or sautéed.

PALETTE KNIFE: A small, long, narrow metal spatula with a rounded tip. May be tapered or straight, offset or flat.

PAN BROILING: A cooking method similar to dry sautéing that simulates broiling by cooking an item in a hot pan with little or no fat.

PAN FRYING: A cooking method used for tender items that are typically coated with a batter or breading and then cooked in enough hot oil to cover the item by one-third to one-half; sauces to accompany pan-fried foods are typically made separately and do not incorporate the drippings.

PAN STEAMING: A method of cooking foods in a very small amount of liquid in a covered pan over direct heat.

PAPILLOTE, EN: Refers to a moist-heat cooking method similar to steaming, in which items are enclosed in parchment paper and cooked in the oven.

PARCHMENT PAPER: Heat-resistant paper used in cooking for such preparations as lining baking pans, cooking items en papillote, and covering items during the process of shallow poaching.

PARCOOK: To partially cook an item before storing or finishing.

PARISIENNE SCOOP: A small tool used for scooping balls out of vegetables or fruits and for portioning truffle ganache and other such preparations. Also called a *melon baller.*

PASTEURIZATION: A process in which some foods are heated to kill microorganisms that could contaminate them.

PASTRY BAG: A bag—usually made of plastic, canvas, or nylon—that can be fitted with plain or decorative tips and used to pipe out icings and puréed foods.

PATHOGEN: A disease-causing microorganism.

PAYSANNE CUT: A knife cut in which ingredients are cut into flat, square pieces about ⅛ inch/2 mm thick with the sides of each piece about ½ inch/13 mm long.

PEEL: A paddle used to transfer shaped doughs to a hearth or deck oven. Also, to remove the skin from a food item.

PESTO: A thick, puréed mixture of an herb, traditionally basil, and oil. Used as a sauce for pasta and other foods, and as a garnish for soup. Pesto may also contain grated cheese, nuts or seeds, and other seasonings.

pH SCALE: A scale with values from 0 to 14 representing degree of acidity. A measurement of 7 is neutral, 0 is most acidic, and 14 is most alkaline. Chemically, pH measures the concentration of hydrogen ions.

PHYLLO/FILO: Pastry made with very thin sheets of a flour and water dough layered with butter and/or bread or cake crumbs; similar to strudel.

PHYSICAL LEAVENING: The leavening that occurs when steam is trapped in a dough through the introduction of air (as opposed to a chemical leavening), expanding and causing the cake or bread to rise.

PHYTOCHEMICALS: Naturally occurring compounds in plant foods that have antioxidant and disease-fighting properties.

PILAF: A technique for cooking grains in which the grain is sautéed briefly in butter, then simmered in stock or water with various seasonings until the liquid is absorbed. Also called *pilau, pilaw, pullao, pilav.*

PINCÉ: Refers to an item caramelized by sautéing; usually refers to a tomato product.

PLUCHES: Whole herb leaves connected to a small bit of stem; often used as a garnish. Also called *sprigs.*

POACH: To cook gently in simmering liquid that is 160° to 185°F/71° to 85°C.

POLENTA: Cornmeal mush cooked in simmering liquid until the grains soften and the liquid is absorbed. Polenta can be eaten hot or cold, firm or soft.

POLYUNSATURATED FAT: A fat molecule with more than one available bonding site not filled with a hydrogen atom. Food sources include corn, cottonseed, safflower, soy, and sunflower oils.

PORT: A fortified dessert wine. Vintage port is high-quality unblended wine aged in the bottle for at least twelve years. Ruby port may be blended and is aged in wood for a short time. White port is made with white grapes.

POT-AU-FEU: A classic French boiled dinner that typically includes poultry and beef, along with various root vegetables. The broth is often served as a first course, followed by the meats and vegetables.

PRAWN: A crustacean that closely resembles shrimp; often used as a general term for large shrimp.

PRESENTATION SIDE: The side of a piece of meat, poultry, or fish that will be served facing up.

PRESSURE STEAMER: A machine that cooks food using steam produced by heating water under pressure in a sealed compartment, allowing it to reach temperatures higher than boiling (212°F/100°C). The food is placed in a sealed chamber that cannot be opened until the pressure has been released and the steam properly vented from the chamber.

PROTEIN: One of the basic nutrients needed by the body to maintain life, supply energy, build and repair tissues, form enzymes and hormones, and perform other essential functions. Protein can be obtained from animal and vegetable sources.

PULSE: The edible seed of a leguminous plant, such as a bean, lentil, or pea. Often referred to simply as a legume.

PURÉE: To process food by mashing, straining, or chopping it very finely in order to make it a smooth paste. Also, a product produced using this technique.

RAFT: A mixture of ingredients used to clarify consommé. The term refers to the fact that the ingredients rise to the surface and form a floating mass.

RAGOÛT: A stew of meat and/or vegetables.

RAMEKIN/RAMEQUIN: A small, ovenproof dish, usually ceramic.

REDUCE: To decrease the volume of a liquid by simmering or boiling. This technique is used to provide a thicker consistency and/or concentrated flavors.

REDUCTION: The product that results when a liquid is reduced.

REFRESH: To plunge an item into, or run it under, cold water after blanching to prevent further cooking. Also called *shock*.

RISOTTO: Rice that is sautéed briefly in butter with onions and possibly other aromatics, then combined with stock, which is added in several additions and stirred constantly, producing a creamy texture with grains that are still al dente.

ROAST: To cook food by surrounding it with dry heat in an oven or by means of radiant heat on a spit over a fire.

ROE: Fish or shellfish eggs.

RONDEAU: A shallow, wide, straight-sided pot with two loop handles; often used for braising.

RONDELLE: A knife cut that produces round or oval flat pieces; used on cylindrical vegetables or items trimmed into cylinders before cutting.

ROUND FISH: A type of fish characterized by a rounded body and eyes on opposite sides of its head.

ROUX: An appareil containing equal parts of flour and fat (usually butter); used to thicken liquids. Roux is cooked to varying degrees (white, blond, or brown), depending on its intended use. The darker the roux, the less thickening power it has but the fuller the taste.

SACHET D'ÉPICES: Literally, "bag of spices." Aromatic ingredients, encased in cheesecloth, that are used to flavor stocks and other liquids. A standard sachet contains parsley stems, cracked black peppercorns, dried thyme, and a bay leaf.

SANITATION: The maintenance of a clean food-preparation environment by healthy food workers in order to prevent food-borne illnesses and food contamination.

SANITIZE: To kill pathogenic organisms by chemicals and/or moist heat.

SATURATED FAT: A fat molecule whose available bonding sites are entirely filled with hydrogen atoms. Saturated fats tend to be solid at room temperature and are primarily of animal origin, though coconut oil, palm oil, and cocoa butter are vegetable sources of saturated fat. Animal sources include butter, meat, cheese, and eggs.

SAUCE: A liquid accompaniment to food; used to enhance the flavor of the food.

SAUTÉ: To cook quickly in a small amount of fat in a pan on the stovetop.

SAUTEUSE: A shallow skillet with sloping sides and a single, long handle; used for sautéing. Referred to generically as a sauté pan.

SAUTOIR: A shallow skillet with straight sides and a single, long handle; used for sautéing. Referred to generically as a sauté pan.

SAVORY: Not sweet. Also, a course served after dessert and before port in traditional British meals. Also, a family of herbs (including summer and winter savory) that tastes like a cross between thyme and mint.

SCALD: To heat a liquid, usually milk or cream, to just below the boiling point.

SCALE: To measure ingredients by weighing, or to divide dough or batter into portions by weight. Also, to remove the scales from fish.

SCALER: A tool used to remove scales from fish by pushing a curved blade along the side of a fish, against the direction in which the scales lie flat.

SCALLOP: A bivalve whose adductor muscle (the muscle that keeps its shells closed) and roe are eaten. Also, a small, boneless piece of meat or fish of uniform thickness. Also, a side dish where an item is layered with cream or sauce and topped with bread crumbs prior to baking.

SCORE: To cut the surface of an item at regular intervals to allow it to cook evenly, allow excess fat to drain, help the food absorb marinades, or provide a decoration.

SEAR: To brown the surface of food in fat over high heat before finishing by another method (e.g., braising or roasting) in order to add flavor.

SEA SALT: Salt produced by evaporating seawater. Available refined or unrefined, crystallized or ground. Also called *sel gris* (French for "gray salt").

SEASON: To give foods a particular flavor by adding ingredients such as salt, pepper, herbs, spices, and/or condiments. Also, to build up a protective coating on the interior of a pan.

SEMOLINA: The coarsely milled hard durum wheat endosperm used for gnocchi, some pasta, and couscous. Semolina has a high gluten content.

SHALLOW POACH: To cook gently in a shallow pan of simmering liquid. The liquid is often reduced and used as the base of a sauce.

SHEET PAN: A flat baking pan, often with a rolled lip, used to cook foods in the oven.

SHELF LIFE: The amount of time in storage that a product can maintain its quality.

SHELLFISH: Various types of marine life consumed as food, including crustaceans and mollusks such as univalves, bivalves, and cephalopods.

SHERRY: A fortified Spanish wine varying in color and sweetness.

SIEVE: A container made of a perforated material, such as wire mesh; used to drain, rice, or purée foods.

SILVERSKIN: The tough connective tissue that surrounds certain muscles. This protein does not dissolve when cooked and must be removed prior to cooking.

SIMMER: To maintain the temperature of a liquid at a point just below boiling. Also, to cook in simmering liquid. The temperature range for simmering is 185° to 200°F/85° to 93°C.

SIMPLE CARBOHYDRATE: Any of a number of small carbohydrate molecules (mono- and disaccharides), including glucose, fructose, lactose, maltose, and sucrose.

SKIM: To remove impurities from the surface of a liquid, such as stock or soup, during cooking.

SKIM MILK: Milk from which all but 0.5 percent of the milk fat has been removed.

SLURRY: A starch such as arrowroot, cornstarch, or potato starch dispersed in cold liquid to prevent it from forming lumps when added to hot liquid as a thickener.

SMOKE POINT: The temperature at which a fat begins to break (and smoke) when heated.

SMOKE ROASTING: A method for roasting foods in which items are placed on a rack in a pan containing wood chips that smolder, emitting smoke, when the pan is placed on the stovetop or in the oven.

SMOKING: Any of several methods for preserving and flavoring foods by exposing them to smoke. Methods include cold smoking (in which smoked items are not fully cooked), hot smoking (in which the items are cooked), and smoke roasting.

SMOTHER: To cook in a covered pan with little liquid over low heat. The main item is often completely covered by another food item or sauce while it braises.

SODIUM: An alkaline metal element necessary in small quantities for human nutrition; one of the components of most salts used in cooking.

SORBET: A frozen dessert made with fruit juice or another flavoring, a sweetener (usually sugar), and beaten egg whites, which prevent the formation of large ice crystals.

SOUFFLÉ: Literally, "puffed." A preparation made with a sauce base (usually béchamel for savory soufflés, pastry cream for sweet ones), whipped egg whites, and flavorings. The egg whites cause the soufflé to puff during cooking.

SPÄTZLE: A soft noodle or small dumpling made by dropping bits of a prepared batter into simmering liquid.

SPICE: An aromatic vegetable substance from numerous plant parts; usually dried and used as seasoning.

SPIDER: A long-handled skimmer used to remove items from hot liquid or fat and to skim the surface of liquids.

SPIT ROAST: To roast an item on a large skewer or spit over, or in front of, an open flame or other radiant heat source.

STANDARD BREADING PROCEDURE: The assembly-line procedure in which items are dredged in flour, dipped in beaten egg, then coated with crumbs before being pan fried or deep fried.

STAPHYLOCOCCUS AUREUS: A type of facultative bacteria that can cause food-borne illness. It is particularly dangerous because it produces toxins that cannot be destroyed by heat. Staph intoxication is most often caused by transfer of the bacteria from infected food handlers.

STEAMER: A set of stacked pots with perforations in the bottom of each pot. They fit over a larger pot that is filled with boiling or simmering water. Also, a perforated insert made of metal or bamboo that can be used in a pot to steam foods.

STEAMING: A cooking method in which items are cooked in a vapor bath created by boiling water or other liquids.

STEAM-JACKETED KETTLE: A kettle with double-layered walls, between which steam circulates, providing even heat for cooking stocks, soups, and sauces. These kettles may be insulated, spigoted, and/or tilting. The last are also called *trunnion kettles.*

STEEL: A tool used to hone knife blades. It is usually made of steel but may be ceramic, glass, or made of diamond-impregnated metal.

STEEP: To allow an ingredient to sit in warm or hot liquid to extract flavor or impurities, or to soften the item.

STEW: To cook a main item using a method nearly identical to braising but generally involving smaller pieces of meat and hence a shorter cooking time. Stewed items may also be blanched, rather than seared, to give the finished product a pale color. Also, a dish prepared by using the stewing method.

STIR FRY: To cook foods in a wok over very high heat, keeping them in constant motion as they cook and using little fat. Most often associated with Asian cooking..

STOCK: A flavorful liquid prepared by simmering meat bones, poultry bones, or seafood bones, and/or vegetables in water with aromatics until their flavor is extracted. It is used as a base for soups, sauces, and other preparations.

STOCKPOT: A large, straight-sided pot that is taller than it is wide; used for making stocks and soups. Some have spigots. Also called a *marmite.*

STONE-GROUND: A term used to describe meal or flour milled between grindstones. Because the germ of the wheat is not separated, this method of grinding retains more nutrients than other methods.

STRAIN: To pass a liquid through a sieve or screen to remove particles.

SUPRÊME: The breast fillet and wing of chicken or other poultry.Also, segments of citrus with connective membranes and seeds removed. Suprême sauce is chicken velouté enriched with cream.

SWEAT: To cook an item, usually vegetables, in a covered pan in a small amount of fat until it softens and releases moisture but does not brown.

TABLE SALT: Refined, granulated salt. May be fortified with iodine and treated with magnesium carbonate to prevent clumping.

TABLE WINE: Still red, white, or rosé wine containing between 7 and 14 percent alcohol. This type of wine is suitable to serve with a meal.

TEMPER: To heat gently and gradually. May refer to the process of incorporating hot liquid into a liaison to gradually raise its temperature. May also refer to the proper method for melting chocolate.

THERMOPHILIC: Heat loving. A term used to describe bacteria that thrive within the temperature range from 110° to 171°F/43° to 77°C.

THICKENER: An ingredient used to give additional body to liquids. Arrowroot, cornstarch, gelatin, roux, and beurre manié are examples of thickeners.

TILT SKILLET: A large, relatively shallow pot mounted into a frame that permits one side to be raised in order to empty the contents easily; used for braising, stewing, and occasionally steaming.

TOMATO SAUCE: A sauce prepared by simmering tomatoes in a liquid (water or broth) with aromatics. One of the grand sauces.

TOURNER: To cut items, usually vegetables, into barrel, olive, or football shapes. Tournéed foods should have five or seven sides or faces, and blunt ends.

TOXIN: A naturally occurring poison, particularly one produced by the metabolic activity of living organisms, such as bacteria.

TRANCHE: A slice or cut of meat, fish, or poultry, cut on the diagonal in order to increase the surface area of the cut.

TRICHINELLA SPIRALIS: A spiral-shaped parasitic worm that invades the intestines and muscle tissue. Transmitted primarily through infected pork that has not been cooked sufficiently.

TRUSS: To tie up meat or poultry with string before cooking it in order to give it a compact shape for more even cooking and better appearance.

TUBER: The fleshy root, stem, or rhizome of a plant, which is able to grow into a new plant. Some, such as potatoes, are eaten as vegetables.

TUILE: Literally, "tile." A thin, waferlike cookie (or food cut to resemble this cookie). Tuiles are frequently shaped while warm and still pliable by pressing them into molds or draping them over rolling pins or dowels.

U

UMAMI: Describes a savory, meaty taste; often associated with monosodium glutamate (MSG) and mushrooms.

UNIVALVE: A single-shelled, single-muscle mollusk, such as abalone or sea urchin.

UNSATURATED FAT: A fat molecule with at least one available bonding site not filled with a hydrogen atom. Unsaturated fats may be monounsaturated or polyunsaturated. They tend to be liquid at room temperature and are primarily of vegetable origin.

V

VEGETABLE SOUP: A broth- or water-based soup made primarily with vegetables; may include meats, legumes, and noodles and may be clear or thick.

VEGETARIAN: An individual who has adopted a specific diet (or lifestyle) that reduces or eliminates animal products. Vegans eat no foods derived in any way from animals. Lacto-ovo vegetarians include dairy products and eggs in their diet. Ovo vegetarians include eggs in their diet.

VELOUTÉ: A sauce of white stock (chicken, veal, or seafood) thickened with white roux. One of the grand sauces. Also, a cream soup (usually puréed) made with a velouté sauce base and flavorings, which is usually finished with a liaison.

VENISON: Meat from large game animals in the deer family; often refers specifically to deer meat.

VIRUS: A type of pathogenic microorganism that can be transmitted in food. Viruses cause such illnesses as measles, chicken pox, infectious hepatitis, and colds.

VITAMINS: Any of various nutritionally essential organic substances that do not provide energy but usually act as regulators in metabolic processes and help maintain health.

W

WASABI: Root of an Asian plant similar to horseradish. It becomes bright green when mixed with water and is used as a condiment in Japanese cooking.

WHIP/WHISK: To beat an item, such as cream or egg whites, to incorporate air. Also, a special tool for whipping, made of looped wire attached to a handle.

WHITE MIREPOIX: Mirepoix that does not include carrots and may include chopped mushrooms or mushroom trimmings and parsnips. It is used for pale or white sauces and stocks.

WHITE STOCK: A light-colored stock made with bones that have not been browned.

WHOLE GRAIN: An unmilled or unprocessed grain.

WHOLE WHEAT FLOUR: Flour milled from the whole grain, including the bran, germ, and endosperm. Graham flour is a whole wheat flour named after Sylvester Graham, a nineteenth-century American dietary reformer.

WOK: A round-bottomed pan, usually made of rolled steel, that is used for nearly all cooking methods in Chinese cuisine. Its shape allows for even heat distribution and easy tossing of ingredients.

Y

YAM: A large tuber that grows in tropical and subtropical climates; it has starchy, pale yellow flesh. The name *yam* is also used for the (botanically unrelated) sweet potato.

YEAST: A microscopic fungus whose metabolic processes are responsible for fermentation. It is used for leavening bread and in the making of cheese, beer, and wine.

YOGURT: Milk cultured with bacteria to give it a slightly thick consistency and sour flavor.

Z

ZEST: The thin, brightly colored outer part of citrus rind. It contains volatile oils, making it ideal for use as a flavoring.

NUTRITIONAL ANALYSIS TABLE

RECIPE	CALS	PROT (G)	CARB (G)	FIBER (G)	SUGAR (G)	FAT (G)	SAT (G)	MONO (G)	POLY (G)	TFA (G)	CHOL (MG)	SOD (MG)
Brown Veal Stock	33	2.4	0.5	0.1	0.3	0.3	0.8	1.1	0.3	0.0	9.3	175.0
Chicken Stock	34	3.1	0.2	0.0	0.1	0.1	0.6	0.9	0.5	0.0	9.4	9.8
Fish Stock	39	4.9	1.0	0.0	0.2	0.2	0.4	0.0	0.0	0.0	0.0	0.0
Fish Fumet	64	4.0	1.2	0.0	3.5	3.5	0.3	0.0	0.0	0.0	0.0	2.4
Vegetable Stock	34	0.9	8.0	1.7	0.2	0.2	0.0	0.0	0.1	0.0	0.0	37.4
Court Bouillon	50	1.3	11.6	3.0	4.4	4.4	0.1	0.0	0.1	0.0	0.0	189.9
Espagnole Sauce	80	1.5	4.9	0.5	0.6	6.2	2.8	2.0	1.0	0.1	12.8	281.9
Demi-Glace	80	1.5	4.9	0.5	0.6	6.2	2.8	2.0	1.0	0.1	12.8	281.9
Jus de Veau Lié	104	5.7	2.4	0.3	0.5	8.0	2.2	3.7	1.7	0.0	22.6	304.5
Jus de Volaille Lié	104	5.7	2.4	0.3	0.5	8.0	2.2	3.7	1.7	0.0	22.6	304.5
Chicken Velouté	31	1.4	2.7	0.4	1.2	1.6	0.8	0.2	0.0	0.0	2.7	554.5
Béchamel Sauce	43	1.8	3.0	0.1	2.6	2.7	1.2	0.8	0.4	0.1	5.4	409.4
Roasted Butternut Squash Soup	80	2.8	12.4	2.5	3.3	2.5	1.2	0.8	0.2	0.1	8.1	332.2
Sweet Onion and Fennel Soup	191	2.5	11.8	3.4	4.6	15.4	5.4	8.4	1.0	0.2	25.4	311.7
Cream of Asparagus Soup	161	3.2	7.6	2.8	3.0	14.2	7.0	4.5	1.9	0.3	39.4	164.3
Corn Chowder	169	4.5	18.7	1.5	3.7	9.2	4.4	3.2	0.7	0.2	21.4	245.6
Cheddar Cheese Soup	349	14.7	8.7	0.4	0.4	28.1	17.1	7.9	1.2	0.3	88.2	858.5
New England–Style Clam Chowder	153	7.9	5.0	0.1	0.3	11.3	6.2	3.4	0.7	0.3	47.6	219.0
Purée of Split Pea Soup	201	12.3	27.7	0.4	3.2	4.7	1.1	2.1	1.2	0.0	7.0	342.8
Gazpacho Andaluz (Andalusian Gazpacho)	107	1.0	4.5	1.3	2.7	9.8	1.4	7.4	1.0	0.0	0.0	108.2
Vegetable Soup Emilia-Romagna-Style (Minestrone alla Emiliana)	195	4.5	27.7	3.1	2.2	8.0	2.3	4.5	0.7	0.0	6.9	148.3
Lobster Bisque	154	12.4	9.5	1.3	1.4	7.1	3.3	2.5	0.4	0.1	53.5	422.4
Chicken and Shrimp Gumbo	183	15.2	14.5	0.9	3.2	6.6	2.1	2.9	1.1	0.0	51.8	473.7
Roasted Red Pepper Gazpacho	82	2.2	13.9	1.6	4.4	2.4	0.4	1.5	0.4	0.0	0.0	336.5
Venetian Bean and Potato Soup	199	4.4	28.7	3.0	2.2	8.0	2.5	4.4	0.6	0.0	7.1	147.9
Tomato Sauce	24	0.7	3.9	0.8	2.1	1.1	0.1	0.6	0.2	0.0	0.0	76.5
Tomato Coulis	33	0.8	2.8	0.3	1.3	1.4	0.2	1.0	0.2	0.0	0.7	155.3
Marsala Sauce	81	0.7	9.8	1.0	4.8	1.5	0.2	1.2	0.2	0.0	0.0	265.4
Salsa Verde	40	0.7	1.4	0.5	0.2	3.7	0.5	2.7	2.7	0.4	0.6	368.0
Salsa Fresca	35	0.8	3.4	1.2	1.6	2.3	0.3	1.4	0.5	0.0	0.0	176.0
Roasted Tomato Salsa	27	0.7	5.9	0.9	2.9	0.3	0.0	0.0	0.0	0.0	0.0	391.0
Spiced Sweet-Sour Blackberry Ketchup	30	0.2	7.0	0.7	6.2	0.3	0.2	0.1	0.1	0.0	0.6	26.6
Poblano Chile Dressing	111	0.8	2.8	1.0	0.4	10.9	1.0	5.7	3.0	0.0	5.1	157.7
Zesty Chipotle and Bacon Ranch Dip	97	1.2	1.1	0.1	0.3	9.8	2.1	4.8	2.1	0.1	9.5	271.8
Romesco Sauce	102	1.6	3.0	1.3	0.6	9.8	1.0	7.2	1.2	0.0	0.0	120.4

RECIPE	CALS	PROT (G)	CARB (G)	FIBER (G)	SUGAR (G)	FAT (G)	SAT (G)	MONO (G)	POLY (G)	TFA (G)	CHOL (MG)	SOD (MG)
Latin Citrus Marinade (Mojo)	21	0.4	4.8	0.6	2.6	0.2	0.0	0.0	0.0	0.0	0.0	349.9
Arugula Pesto	116	3.6	1.6	0.6	0.3	10.7	3.5	5.2	1.9	0.1	10.3	238.5
Seasoning Mix For Spit-Roasted Meats and Poultry (3 g)	2.8	0.1	0.5	0.3	0.0	0.1	0.0	0.1	0.1	0.0	0.0	860.9
Barbecue Spice Mix (3 g)	8.1	0.3	1.5	0.6	0.4	0.3	0.0	0.0	0.1	0.0	0.0	270.7
Chili Powder (3 g)	14	0.5	2.1	1.2	1.1	0.8	0.5	0.0	0.0	0.0	0.0	4.6
Maître d'Hôtel Butter	165	0.5	1.1	0.3	0.6	18.1	11.4	4.7	0.7	0.5	47.8	90.1
Hard-Cooked Eggs	155	12.6	1.1	0.0	1.1	10.6	3.3	4.1	1.4	0.0	424.0	124.0
Poached Eggs	147	12.5	0.8	0.0	0.8	9.9	3.1	3.8	1.4	0.0	422.0	294.0
Poached Eggs with Smoked Salmon	329	14.0	34.8	1.6	2.4	14.8	6.7	4.7	1.2	0.0	301.5	492.9
Poached Eggs Farmer-Style	314	17.7	27.2	1.7	2.1	14.4	6.6	4.7	1.3	0.1	244.0	999.6
Poached Eggs on Hash	285	8.9	4.3	0.1	1.1	25.9	12.7	9.0	1.8	0.3	125.6	500.9
Fried Eggs (Sunny-Side Up, Basted, or Over)	185	12.5	0.8	0.0	0.8	14.1	4.0	5.8	2.5	0.0	420.4	187.7
Huevos Rancheros	426	16.4	30.5	9.3	1.5	28.8	11.3	10.9	2.6	0.2	250.1	470.3
"Spit in the Eye" with Turkey Hash	339	25.3	24.7	2.7	5.0	16.6	6.0	5.1	2.5	0.1	264.3	1034.1
Farmer-Style Omelette	381	23.0	8.5	0.8	2.4	27.7	8.9	11.4	3.4	0.0	653.8	735.1
Oven-Roasted Potato and Spinach Frittata	315	18.5	16.3	2.4	3.9	18.9	6.5	6.9	1.8	0.0	420.7	613.5
Sausage and Roasted Vegetable Frittata	354	21.3	8.2	0.8	3.6	25.8	8.0	10.9	3.9	0.0	444.7	726.2
Ranchero Egg and Avocado Casserole	300	14.6	26.5	6.6	1.0	16.6	4.6	6.8	2.9	0.0	281.3	558.6
Mushroom, Tomato, and Egg Wrap	311	1.4	7.1	1.3	3.8	31.0	3.5	22.7	4.2	0.0	0.0	413.2
Warm Goat Cheese Custard	473	13.6	11.4	0.5	7.8	42.3	25.3	12.3	2.0	0.8	318.6	933.0
Quiche Lorraine	285	8.9	4.3	0.1	1.1	25.9	12.7	9.0	1.8	0.3	125.6	500.9
Bananas Foster French Toast	614	12.2	100.9	6.0	76.7	19.2	9.6	6.2	1.6	0.0	243.0	329.4
Sunrise Smoothie	166	0.2	1.8	0.1	0.8	17.7	2.5	13.6	1.6	0.0	0.0	145.0
Red Wine Vinaigrette	84	0.2	0.8	0.2	0.4	9.0	1.3	6.9	0.8	0.0	0.0	113.0
Balsamic Vinaigrette	84	0.2	0.8	0.2	0.4	9.0	1.3	6.9	0.8	0.0	0.0	113.0
Herb and Truffle Vinaigrette	84	0.2	0.8	0.2	0.4	9.0	1.3	6.9	0.8	0.0	0.0	113.0
Almond-Fig Vinaigrette	152	0.7	3.5	0.6	1.9	15.2	1.7	11.1	2.03	0.0	0.0	202.26
Chipotle-Sherry Vinaigrette	166	0.2	1.8	0.1	0.8	17.7	2.5	13.6	1.6	0.0	0.0	145.0
Fire-Roasted Tomato Vinaigrette	101	0.1	0.1	0.1	0.0	11.1	1.6	8.6	1.0	0.0	0.0	0.5
Extra-Virgin Caesar Dressing	111	0.8	0.9	0.0	0.1	11.6	1.8	8.6	1.0	0.0	2.4	364.0
Aïoli	105	0.3	0.5	0.1	0.0	11.7	1.5	6.6	3.3	0.0	14.7	188.1
Baby Spinach, Avocado, and Grapefruit Salad	104	2.7	16.0	7.0	6.4	4.6	0.7	3.0	0.6	0.0	0.0	587.5
Wilted Spinach Salad with Warm Bacon Vinaigrette	100	2.7	14.8	7.0	6.4	4.6	0.7	3.0	0.6	0.0	0.0	587.5
Mushrooms, Beets, and Baby Greens with Robiola Cheese and Walnuts	102	1.4	9.9	1.1	6.7	6.4	0.8	4.0	1.3	0.0	0.3	210.0
Warm Bavarian Potato Salad	96	0.9	4.9	0.8	1.4	8.6	0.9	3.6	3.6	0.0	0.0	613.0

RECIPE	CALS	PROT (G)	CARB (G)	FIBER (G)	SUGAR (G)	FAT (G)	SAT (G)	MONO (G)	POLY (G)	TFA (G)	CHOL (MG)	SOD (MG)
Borlotti Bean, Onion, and Celery Heart Salad	180	7.2	23.1	4.8	0.6	6.9	1.0	5.0	0.8	0.0	0.0	209.0
Warm Bavarian Potato Salad												
Roasted Pepper Salad	102	1.4	9.9	1.1	6.7	6.4	0.8	4.0	1.3	0.0	0.3	210.0
Scallop and Shrimp Salad	97	8.0	3.3	0.5	1.2	5.6	0.7	3.9	0.6	0.0	9.6	273.8
Fajita Cobb Salad	588	31.4	39.1	8.3	2.0	30.8	10.7	11.6	2.4	0.0	173.9	871.8
Shrimp Escabèche	107	6.9	3.4	0.8	1.0	7.4	1.1	54	0.8	0.0	57.6	150.5
Curried Shrimp with Pasta	483	40.0	46.0	2.5	6.0	28.0	4.0	88.0	1.2	0.0	48.1	1369.0
Lobster Tortellini in Coconut-Curry Broth	394	32.0	44.6	2.2	2.5	7.2	3.8	2.0	0.6	0.2	101.7	502.7
Fresh Vegetable Kebobs with Orzo and Tomato Relish	442	17.6	29.8	6.2	13.0	28.7	10.2	10.6	1.8	0.0	40.5	469.5
Vegetable Panini with Tomato Chutney and Aïoli	295	8.6	40.6	8.6	8.6	13.4	2.0	5.8	4.8	0.0	13.0	890.7
Grilled or Broiled Chicken Breasts with Sun-Dried Tomato and Oregano Butter	406	34.7	1.0	0.1	0.2	29.0	14.0	8.8	4.0	0.6	145.5	378.8
Grilled or Broiled Paillards of Chicken with Tarragon Butter	406	34.7	1.0	0.1	0.2	29.0	14.0	8.8	4.0	0.6	145.5	378.8
Grilled or Broiled Chicken Breast with Honey-Marsala Sauce	284	31.8	12.8	0.8	2.0	10.4	3.0	4.3	2.2	0.0	83.1	759.9
Grilled or Broiled Pork Chops with Sherry Vinegar Sauce	406	34.7	1.0	0.1	0.2	29.0	14.0	8.8	4.0	0.6	145.5	378.8
Barbecued Steak with Herb Crust	386	25.5	7.5	0.5	2.1	27.6	11.3	10.7	2.6	0.2	80.2	591.8
Grilled Portobello with Barley Pilaf and Steamed Spinach	358	10.3	38.7	8.0	4.9	18.3	2.8	12.9	2.1	0.0	3.7	474.3
Roast Turkey with Pan Gravy and Chestnut Stuffing	402	56.0	23.0	0.3	0.2	8.5	1.4	3.1	3.1	0.1	131.5	685.0
Roast Chicken with Pan Gravy	625	68.2	7.1	0.8	1.2	34.0	9.5	13.3	7.4	0.0	216.7	411.1
Tri-Tip Beefsteak with Dark Onion Sauce	438	36.8	15.0	1.5	9.1	23.8	6.7	14.1	1.5	0.0	110.6	596.6
Pork Roast with Jus Lié	314	33.5	5.3	0.9	1.3	16.6	6.2	7.3	1.5	0.0	96.8	850.6
Lacquer-Roasted Pork Ribs (Kao Paigu)	434	16.5	32.0	1.0	22.4	26.3	8.8	10.4	2.4	0.0	76.4	1362.5
Pan-Roasted Duck with Potato Gratin, Spicy Greens, and Coriander Sauce	524	41.9	8.9	1.0	3.7	35.8	18.2	9.1	1.9	0.5	202.5	1016.6
Pan-Roasted Center Cut Pork with Marinated Peppers	586	54.9	3.6	0.6	2.0	37.4	11.9	18.5	3.3	0.0	180.1	514.7
Sautéed Chicken with Fines Herbes Sauce	338	53.3	8.4	0.3	0.2	8.5	1.4	3.1	3.1	0.1	131.5	685.0
Chicken Provençal	470	46.0	11.6	0.4	1.2	23.0	6.7	8.3	4.2	0.1	233.3	843.6
Portobello Stuffed with Corn and Roasted Tomatoes	488	39.6	2.0	0.6	0.7	38.7	13.5	16.6	4.1	0.0	133.5	754.2
Salmon Steak with Herb Crust and White Beans	469	39.4	7.7	0.8	0.9	30.3	13.3	7.4	4.8	0.2	148.0	241.1
Salmon Fillet with Smoked Salmon and Horseradish Crust	274	42.3	6.6	0.4	0.4	7.4	1.2	2.8	2.5	0.0	108.8	563.7
Beef Tournedos Provençal	530	35.1	9.4	0.6	0.7	38.1	13.4	16.4	3.9	0.0	114.9	734.5

RECIPE	CALS	PROT (G)	CARB (G)	FIBER (G)	SUGAR (G)	FAT (G)	SAT (G)	MONO (G)	POLY (G)	TFA (G)	CHOL (MG)	SOD (MG)
Veal Scaloppine Marsala	519	59.8	11.3	0.4	1.2	22.2	6.7	8.0	3.9	0.1	206.8	629.6
Swiss-Style Shredded Veal	877	11.8	8.4	1.2	5.5	89.9	15.1	41.1	28.9	0.0	34.0	790.1
Marinated Sea Bass Fillet	164	26.2	0.2	0.0	0.0	5.6	1.1	2.8	1.3	0.0	58.1	98.2
Ancho-Crusted Salmon with Yellow Mole	398	25.2	11.0	0.4	3.3	27.3	9.8	8.3	6.1	0.1	87.9	418.6
Buttermilk Fried Chicken	794	34.4	27.6	7.0	17.5	64.7	53.2	5.7	1.5	0.0	74.9	1316.1
Fried Fish Cakes	154	22.1	3.1	0.4	0.7	5.3	1.4	2.4	0.7	0.0	85.6	285.0
Corned Beef Hash	337	17.9	13.8	2.2	2.7	23.0	7.6	10.7	1.3	0.0	94.5	1274.7
Boston Scrod with Cream, Capers, and Tomatoes	258	22.4	3.7	0.4	0.7	16.6	10.1	4.4	0.9	0.5	100.5	497.8
Pescado à la Veracruzana	206	7.5	14.3	1.2	5.7	14.1	1.5	10.1	2.2	0.0	7.2	1358.1
Pork in Green Curry Sauce	435	18.9	15.1	3.8	9.6	35.4	29.2	3.1	0.8	0.0	41.1	721.0
Grilled Squash Jambalaya	258	22.4	3.7	0.4	0.7	16.6	10.1	4.4	0.9	0.5	100.5	497.8
Chicken Mole Poblano	514	35.6	26.9	4.9	13.2	30.4	6.7	15.3	5.7	0.2	89.0	1503.4
Braised Beef Short Ribs with Polenta and Roasted Cremini	528	24.3	19.8	2.0	4.5	37.2	15.2	16.4	1.7	0.0	77.8	420.9
Braised Veal Shanks with Braising Greens, Polenta, and Gremolata	438	36.8	15.0	1.5	9.1	23.8	6.7	14.1	1.5	0.0	110.6	596.6
Osso Buco Milanese	561	16.7	70.8	3.8	4.7	23.7	3.8	15.2	2.6	0.0	10.8	1013.3
Pasta Primavera with Pesto Cream	435	18.9	15.1	3.8	9.6	35.4	29.2	3.1	0.8	0.0	41.1	721.0
Fresh Egg Pasta	240	7.9	38.1	1.3	0.3	5.7	1.2	3.2	0.8	0.0	92.6	182.0
Mushrooms and Artichokes with Black Pepper Pasta	258	22.4	3.7	0.4	0.7	16.6	10.1	4.4	0.9	0.5	100.5	497.8
Orecchiette with Italian Sausage, Broccoli Rabe, and Parmesan Cheese	732	27.3	71.7	4.2	7.9	38.0	9.4	22.7	3.6	0.0	34.5	742.7
Paella Valenciana	503	32.5	46.2	2.8	6.3	20.1	4.8	9.7	3.5	0.0	91.0	966.9
Cioppino	359	46.3	26.7	4.2	2.3	7.1	0.6	1.5	0.9	0.0	163.6	1547.2
Duck Confit	914	49.8	0.3	0.1	0.0	77.6	26.7	34.5	10.0	0.0	271.0	3497.9
Pecan Carrots	49	0.8	9.6	1.9	5.9	1.2	0.1	0.6	0.4	0.0	0.0	134.4
Green Beans with Walnuts	127	3.3	6.3	2.6	2.6	9.8	2.7	2.5	3.8	0.1	10.0	111.6
Grilled Shiitake with Soy-Sesame Glaze	185	5.3	14.5	4.6	2.8	13.5	2.0	5.1	5.3	0.0	0.0	420.5
Oven-Roasted Tomatoes	96	1.2	10.1	2.3	5.3	5.7	1.9	2.8	0.7	0.0	5.7	322.8
Marinated Roasted Peppers	133	2.3	11.4	3.4	5.0	9.0	1.3	6.6	0.9	0.0	0.3	311.1
Roasted Carrots	98	1.2	10.3	2.4	5.5	5.8	1.9	2.9	0.8	0.0	5.8	330.0
Marinated Grilled Vegetables Provencal	100	1.3	6.9	1.4	3.3	8.1	1.1	6.0	0.9	0.0	0.0	127.4
Broccoli Rabe with Garlic and Peppers	107	5.3	7.4	0.1	1.8	6.8	1.0	5.2	0.6	0.0	0.1	468.3
Whipped Potatoes	138	3.2	9.1	4.3	2.0	9.1	1.2	6.5	0.8	0.0	0.0	285.0
Ratatouille	218	5.2	37.0	3.1	2.9	6.2	3.8	1.8	0.3	0.2	12.7	300.0
Braising Greens	87	5.3	8.2	3.6	1.5	4.5	1.1	2.5	0.5	0.0	6.7	730.0
Creamed Mushrooms	167	4.7	23.7	1.6	1.2	5.3	2.5	1.9	0.5	0.0	9.1	316.3
Baked Potatoes with Deep-Fried Onions	383	7.3	32.8	2.0	5.4	25.8	15.9	7.0	1.1	0.8	83.1	294.1

RECIPE	CALS	PROT (G)	CARB (G)	FIBER (G)	SUGAR (G)	FAT (G)	SAT (G)	MONO (G)	POLY (G)	TFA (G)	CHOL (MG)	SOD (MG)
Roasted Tuscan-Style Potatoes	217	4.7	33.0	2.4	1.2	8.1	3.4	2.6	1.5	0.1	36.7	250.4
Potatoes au Gratin (Gratin Dauphinoise)	163	3.1	13.9	0.9	2.3	10.9	6.8	3.0	0.5	0.3	35.2	124.8
Zucchini Provençal	78	1.2	5.0	1.1	2.1	6.4	0.9	4.8	0.6	0.0	0.0	338.2
Gnocchi Piedmontese	226	7.8	29.2	1.5	3.2	8.4	3.8	2.4	1.1	0.1	114.4	530.1
Macaire Potatoes	157	9.2	26.6	6.6	1.9	1.6	0.2	0.4	0.6	0.0	0.0	174.0
Potato and Parsnip Purée	147	2.0	13.8	1.6	1.2	9.5	5.9	2.6	0.4	0.3	29.8	738.9
Celery Root Mashed Potatoes	232	4.1	21.7	2.2	2.2	14.7	9.1	4.0	0.7	0.4	46.9	250.0
Boiled White Beans	53	3.2	9.5	3.6	0.1	0.4	0.1	0.1	0.2	0.0	0.0	93.0
Black Beans with Peppers and Chorizo	203	4.9	35.8	0.8	1.7	4.0	0.6	1.8	1.4	0.0	2.5	354.8
Southwest White Bean Stew	241	6.6	38.4	0.9	2.5	6.4	3.4	2.0	0.5	0.1	16.5	756.3
Vegetarian Refried Beans	173	10.0	31.3	10.2	1.5	1.4	0.2	0.3	0.5	0.0	0.0	686.2
Young Green Beans and Leeks	66	1.0	6.6	1.7	2.4	4.1	0.6	3.0	0.4	0.0	0.0	520.8
Basic Boiled Rice	101	3.3	19.4	0.5	1.3	0.2	1.7	1.0	0.2	0.1	8.3	382.2
Rice Pilaf	122	3.3	19.4	0.5	1.3	0.2	1.7	1.0	0.2	0.1	8.3	382.2
Risotto	203	4.9	35.8	0.8	1.7	4.0	0.6	1.8	1.4	0.0	2.5	354.8
Lobster Risotto	169	15.0	17.2	0.4	1.1	4.0	1.7	1.3	0.3	0.1	49.8	585.5
Basic Polenta	206	6.9	31.0	1.6	0.6	6.0	3.4	1.7	0.4	0.1	51.4	145.4
Pan-Fried Polenta with Parmesan and Rosemary	194	7.0	17.0	1.8	1.6	11.2	4.2	5.3	1.2	0.1	17.0	646.9
Toasted Quinoa and Sweet Pepper Pilaf	87	3.1	14.3	1.6	0.8	2.3	0.2	0.8	0.9	0.0	0.0	223.4
Bread Dumplings	226	7.8	29.2	1.5	3.2	8.4	3.8	2.4	1.1	0.1	114.4	530.1
Spätzle	232	7.4	27.0	1.0	0.8	10.2	5.4	2.9	0.8	0.2	129.5	130.8
Baked Acorn Squash with Hazelnut-Maple Glaze	296	3.5	39.0	8.0	18.8	16.2	6.3	8.1	1.4	0.0	24.5	467.0
Orzo and Pecan Sauté	151	2.0	16.0	1.6	1.2	9.5	5.9	2.6	0.4	0.3	29.8	738.9
Savory Bread Pudding with Roasted Garlic and Asiago	351	7.9	32.1	0.7	22.6	18.0	9.5	5.5	1.4	0.4	283.8	280.4
Focaccia	168	5.1	29.7	1.1	0.1	2.9	0.4	1.7	0.5	0.0	0.0	74.7
Ciabatta	137	4.7	27.5	1.0	0.1	0.6	0.1	0.1	0.3	0.0	0.0	69.3
Buttermilk Biscuits	194	4.5	24.2	0.7	3.1	8.7	5.1	2.3	0.5	0.2	59.4	194.8
Ham and Cheese Scones	401	15.3	40.0	1.0	7.8	19.8	11.5	6.0	1.1	0.4	82.1	511.5
Profiteroles	305	8.5	22.1	0.7	15.3	20.5	10.2	6.9	1.7	0.4	215.1	125.8
Cherry–Chocolate Chunk Cookies	352	4.5	50.2	2.7	29.8	16.1	9.6	4.7	0.7	0.3	48.2	297.7
Mudslide Cookies	247	3.9	33.4	1.4	21.2	13.1	6.2	3.0	1.8	0.1	43.5	47.7
Macerated Strawberries on Lemon Pound Cake	394	6.9	45.2	0.5	22.1	20.9	12.0	5.8	1.2	0.5	189.6	252.3
Flourless Dark Chocolate Cake with Frangelico Whipped Cream	443	6.1	28.4	2.8	23.7	36.8	17.8	10.8	1.7	0.5	134.0	36.4
English Trifle	55	0.5	10.4	0.2	7.42	1.4	0.8	0.4	0.1	0.0	9.9	19.4
Basic Pie Dough (3-2-1)	229	3.0	20.8	0.7	0.1	15.0	9.4	3.8	0.7	0.4	39.0	222.5

RECIPE	CALS	PROT (G)	CARB (G)	FIBER (G)	SUGAR (G)	FAT (G)	SAT (G)	MONO (G)	POLY (G)	TFA (G)	CHOL (MG)	SOD (MG)
Berry Cobbler	102	0.9	17.6	1.8	8.3	3.4	1.4	0.0	0.1	0.0	2.3	46.8
Fruit Crisp	313	2.9	52.4	7.3	24.7	10.1	4.4	0.2	0.4	0.0	6.8	149.7
Bread and Butter Pudding	351	7.9	32.1	0.7	22.6	18.0	9.5	5.5	1.4	0.4	283.8	280.4
Bread and Butter Pudding with Macadamia Nuts and White Chocolate	376	10.7	40.9	1.2	22.2	16.4	8.2	5.1	1.4	0.3	249.9	331.2
Simple Syrup	57	0.0	14.7	0.0	14.7	0.0	0.0	0.0	0.0	0.0	0.0	0.3
Dried Cherry Sauce	19	0.1	3.3	0.2	2.4	0.0	0.0	0.0	0.0	0.0	0.0	0.7
Hard Ganache	240	1.9	23.4	2.1	19.8	18.0	10.8	5.7	0.6	0.2	26.1	11.2
Whole-Bean Vanilla Sauce	71	1.3	5.4	0.0	5.0	5.1	2.8	1.6	0.4	0.1	71.4	9.8
Pastry Cream	61	1.7	7.1	0.0	5.5	2.8	1.5	0.8	0.2	0.1	40.0	19.5
Diplomat Cream	228	3.8	14.0	0.0	10.3	17.7	10.5	5.1	0.8	0.5	120.1	49.0
Chocolate Mousse	313	5.7	20.7	2.0	16.0	26.9	14.5	4.4	0.8	0.4	147.5	44.6
Crème Brûlée	499	2.0	46.6	0.0	43.8	35.2	21.9	10.2	1.3	1.1	130.4	152.6
Crème Caramel	222	6.0	36.9	0.0	36.7	5.9	2.5	2.0	0.7	0.1	166.6	63.1
Frozen Grand Marnier Soufflé	264	5.9	13.7	0.0	12.1	20.3	11.1	6.6	1.4	0.4	308.4	49.4
Grand Marnier Soufflé with Whole-Bean Vanilla Sauce	374	12.1	39.3	0.0	13.6	17.2	9.4	3.1	0.8	0.2	206.5	98.7
Tangerine Soup with Pineapple Sorbet	82	0.9	20.2	1.3	15.8	0.3	0.0	0.0	0.1	0.0	0.0	35.0
Gorgonzola and Pear Sandwich	90	2.8	13.2	1.6	3.9	3.4	1.9	0.6	0.3	0.0	8.9	366.3
Roasted Pepper and Goat Cheese Canapés	68	1.6	1.3	0.2	0.4	6.5	2.0	3.7	0.5	0.0	5.4	86.8
Crostini With Oven-Roasted Tomatoes	109	1.2	6.4	1.4	3.7	9.2	1.3	6.9	0.9	0.0	0.0	442.1
Chesapeake-Style Crab Cakes	217	10.6	10.2	1.8	1.2	13.9	2.0	1.6	1.1	0.0	57.3	589.3
Lobster Salad with Beets, Mangos, Avocados, and Orange Oil	153	21.5	4.7	0.6	0.6	4.9	0.7	3.2	0.5	0.0	107.7	563.5
Gravlax	213	14.5	25.5	0.7	21.9	5.9	0.9	2.6	1.9	0.0	37.4	3893.5
Lobster Soft Tacos	647	24.0	68.7	2.7	4.5	32.0	13.5	7.1	1.2	0.0	90.8	1605.0
Adobo Chicken Quesadilla with Roasted Tomato Salsa	442	28.6	12.0	2.5	3.9	30.8	10.8	13.0	2.8	0.0	182.6	766.0
Tequila-Roasted Oysters with Salsa Cruda	139	9.0	11.0	0.2	0.8	2.7	0.8	0.3	1.0	0.0	42.0	409.0
Tuna Carpaccio	827	20.3	23.8	3.2	2.4	73.7	9.8	44.8	17.3	0.0	25.9	1719.4
Carpaccio of Salmon	519	10.6	2.8	0.5	0.9	53.3	6.8	26.3	18.4	0.0	73.7	338.6
Tapenade	64	0.3	2.4	0.4	0.1	6.2	0.5	3.6	0.6	0.0	0.0	360.6
Marinated Olives	83	0.3	2.4	0.2	0.0	7.8	0.7	5.4	1.6	0.0	0.0	452.7
Warm Risotto Balls with Mozzarella, Harissa, and Red Pepper Coulis	168	6.1	24.2	0.9	0.5	4.8	1.6	2.4	0.3	0.0	17.3	331.6
Beef Saté with Peanut Sauce	172	12.4	6.7	1.3	2.9	10.9	3.8	4.2	2.0	0.0	15.9	994.1
Grilled Pork Tenderloin Skewers with Gingered Barbecue Sauce	172	12.4	6.7	1.3	2.7	11.0	3.8	4.2	2.0	0.0	15.9	994.0

Culinary Quality Assurance Process (CQAP)

CULINARY QUALITY ASSURANCE GUIDELINES

This process is an evaluation tool used by those charged wih training of line culinarians to improve the delivery of consistently prepared, high-quality foods.

Determine Process Paramaters

One or two menu items are selected by the chef on duty to be prepared by the appropriate line culinarian. The line culinarian must adhere strictly to the recipe manual specifications.

To ensure recpe accuracy, all items should be scaled and wieghed according tot he instructions.

All food is to be cooked ans served as described in the recipe formula; use plating diagrams and or photographic instructions accordingly.

During the evaluation and tasting processes

- Check for appropriate flavor profile and clean flavors.

- Make sure product tastes fresh and food is neither over- nor undercooked.

- Make sure all the elements in the menu item have the correct texture: soft, firm, fresh, crispy, or crunchy.

- Check that meats, poultry, and fish are cooked to the proper doneness and temperatures.

- Check that foods are served a the correct temperature. Cold prepartions should be served on clean and cold plates/containers. Hot items are to be served on clean and hot plates/containers.

- Make sure holding times bewteen productin and evaluation are as short as possible.

An evaluation form, such as the one shown on page 428, should be filled out by more than one person, if possible. The results should be tallied and averaged to determine average scores. Items with a minimum average score of 3.4 (or less) require further modification and or training before either retesting or serving to guests.

QUALITY ASSURANCE EVALUATION FORM

	Score	Note	Scoring Guidelines (use whole numbers only)
RECIPE/FORMULA (The food is prepared using the appropriate technique as stated in the recipe.)			**1** Not up to standard. Reproduce item again. Not to be served to guests.
APPEARANCE/FRESHNESS (Presentation looks fresh and follows formula specification, diagram, or photo.)			**2** Below standard. Not to be served to guests. Adjust according to suggestions and/or provide additional coaching.
TASTE/AROMA/FLAVOR (Food smells and tastes great with an appropriate flavor profile.)			**3** Executed within range of acceptability. May be served to guests after appropriate adjustments and/or additional coaching.
TEXTURE (Food has correct texture: e.g., crispy if fried, smooth if puréed.)			**4** Executed within range of acceptability. Appropriate to serve to guests. May consider minor adjustments or coaching to improve quality.
TEMPERATURE (Food served at the appropriate temperature: hot foods hot and cold foods cold.)			**5** Perfectly executed. Appropriate to serve to guests. No further modifications or coaching required.

Date	Item Prepared		Prepared by:	
			Prepared by:	
		Servable Y / N		Average score:

INDEX